Four Passions:
Conversations with Myself

by
Wallace Peters

Strategic Book Publishing and Rights Co.

Strategic Book Publishing and Rights Co.
12620 FM 1960, Suite A4-507
Houston TX 77065
www.sbpra.com

ISBN: 978-1-61897-095-4

www.wallacepeters.com

Synopsis

Like most creatures, we enter this world alone, open our eyes and look around. From his earliest childhood, Wallace Peters was fascinated by nature. Tropical medicine opens a broad highway into the complex relationship between man and his environment. This is the road Wallace pursued most of his working life. Starting alone in 1948, and later accompanied by his wife Ruth, he practiced medicine in many lands and studied how to combat the parasites and vectors that sicken and kill millions of people.

After thirteen years Wallace returned to Europe. There he worked in the laboratory and academia, holding Chairs first in the Liverpool and then the London Schools of Tropical Medicine for over forty years.

As Ruth and he approached middle age, the tempo of their lives inevitably changed; they were faced with the tensions of their mid-life crises. In 2007, at the age of only seventy-eight, Ruth died of cancer. The author was left to grieve and to find a new way of life.

Here Wallace presents a potpourri of personal insights into his peripatetic career in tropical medicine, of the challenges he and Ruth overcame and of the remolding of his life after Ruth's departure, once more alone.

Ruth, who would have understood.

Front cover based on original embroidery design by Ruth Peters entitled "*Round Mask*" (2001).

Table of Contents

Acknowledgements

Over a period of eighty-five years, the number of people whose lives crossed mine seems almost infinite; but among them are many who left a mark in the deep recesses of my memory. Whether that mark reflects a happy, a sad, or an emotionally indifferent occasion is irrelevant, I am indebted to them all. In the following pages you will encounter many of these individuals. Whether our acquaintance was brief or lifelong, each helped form me for better or worse. That is not for me to judge.

While writing this book I showed snippets to a few close friends and relatives. I especially thank my sister Ronnie, whose life in many ways has paralleled my own, for jogging my memory from time to time. Quiller Barrett, Sylvia Coury, Cecily Coales, Laurien Laufman, Tricia Gibson, Howard Engers, Harriet Muller, Anne Heslop and Sonia Shah gave me invaluable guidance and moral support along the road. Above all, I am deeply indebted to my friends Joyce and David Grigsby. They critically read whatever pages I burdened them with over many months without complaint and responded unflinchingly with their frank comments. Moreover, they were pillars of strength ever after I lost my late wife Ruth, the one individual whose opinions and criticisms I would have valued over and above those of anybody else. Special thanks go to my editor, Vern Westgate for his expert assistance and friendly advice, as well as to numerous staff members of the WL Literary Agency, and Strategic Book Publishing and Rights Co.

To my surprise my scribblings became an autobiography.

PART I

"A good conversationist is one who listens"
Peters, 2009

CHAPTER 1

An Overview

Alone and restless one cool winter dawn in my mid eighties, I was woken by a disturbing dream. A stanza from *The Hollow Men* by T.S. Eliot came into my mind; "This is the way the world ends. Not with a bang but a whimper."

The totality of my existence assembled itself and ran through my mind like a concerto. The first movement opened gently, presenting a theme that the orchestra would pursue with variations in the succeeding movements. These were slowly filled with a larger orchestral grouping that presented wildly contrasting motifs, tempos, and textures—each markedly distinctive and mostly transient, yet bound by a consistent, underlying harmony.

The pace quickened, with the addition of new instruments with their interplay, their individual voices, harmonies, and discords. From time to time the composition was dominated by a particular soloist or group of players, each contributing their variations to the basic themes. The tones fluctuated, sometimes peacefully, in other passages full of discord. At moments, the music of life was joyful, at others sad. Some passages showed humor, others tranquility, the whole orchestra at times unexpectedly reflecting tragedy.

Strangely, the musicians seemed to exert their own dominance on the patterns of the composition, defying the baton of the struggling conductor. Still the concerto retained its integrity, in the penultimate phrases of the closing movement resolving into a tranquil summation of the whole piece, finally fading out with incomplete phrases that seemed to quietly seek, yet not find, the concluding notes.

In the morning I decided that, whether Eliot would like it or not, I would go out, "Not with a whimper, but a bang—and not yet!"

Thirty-five years into our marriage, when we were just beginning to know each other, my wife Ruth used to ask me accusingly, "Why do you always say I?" I pointed out repeatedly how hard it is to conduct a conversation without this personal pronoun escaping one's lips. Frequently I try to adopt the artifices of using *you, we, them, our,* and other personal pronouns instead of *I* or *me,* both in conversation and subsequently in writing. However, this approach never really achieves anything and, as often as not, I become *I.*

My life was dominated by four passions to which I immediately confess; one personal and three scientific. These are;

Passion 1—*Ruth*

Passion 2—*Malaria*

Passion 3—*The many faces of Leishmaniasis*

Passion 4—*Entomology*

For those not familiar with the science, I have included in the following pages a brief explanation of some of the technical terms that I am obliged to utilize, as well as the nature of the scientific environment into which I was gradually absorbed.

When Ruth died of cancer in late 2007 and after fifty-three years of marriage this story began to write itself.

The following account inevitably describes previously unrecorded episodes of medical history. However, in this personal story of two people, the really important parts are very uneven in depth, tempo, and style. I make no apologies. This is not fiction but the autobiography of two people written as truthfully as memory and a few old notes that survive permit.

Ruth is no longer here to join in telling the story. I am left holding a series of *Conversations With Myself.* I am being as honest as I can be in telling, "The truth, the whole truth (as far as I recall it), and nothing but the truth," like it or not.

Following the Second World War, many bright young men and women flocked to join medical research, a new land of scientific promise. It offered routes and funds with which they could participate in exciting research projects and earn shiny PhDs. However, few wanted to spend their lives up to their eyes in mud in uncomfortable tropical countries, frequently in primitive terrain and living conditions. Yet it is at the grassroots level that the fundamental causes of many diseases lie. To this day they sicken and kill millions of people. I am one of the few surviving physician-biologists who had the passion to pursue these killers from the jungle to modern research laboratories. I studied the natural history of old and new diseases, searched for new ways to fight them, especially with novel drugs, and taught generations of young doctors and scientists how to deploy these innovations to their best advantage.

The life that Ruth and I shared acquired a new dimension in my 60s. I was obliged to retire from my university post in London with the parallel need to slow down my teaching, travel, and research. We were both restless individuals and had some difficulty in adjusting to a more sedentary existence, as do many in mid-life. We encountered each other as never before, not just the world's problems. In this situation we were not unique. I started to face the novel, sometimes mundane, and frequently traumatic problems posed by living together at a progressively slower rate. I had to review what one must face and come to terms with—growing older and often infirm.

From time to time it is essential to sit back, look, reflect, and listen to one's own thoughts and those of others. An enigmatic Swiss proverb says; "When one shuts one eye, one does not hear everything."

Since childhood I felt an urge to write, probably because I was lonely and found it hard to converse. From about the age of ten I jotted down odd, intimate thoughts. My bed was an old-fashioned one with a hollow brass frame. I could unscrew the knobs from the tops of the upright pillars to expose the hollow interiors. I concealed my secret notes there. One day my parents decided I needed a new bed and sold the old one when I was absent. I wonder if anybody ever found the papers and what they made of them. In later years, mainly when I was traveling on my own, I wrote many notes in small black diaries. Some were simply to remind me of movements and meetings, others of events and moods. Once I embraced the computer age, I would occasionally jot down more intimate comments. I have included some in the following pages.

A few years ago I destroyed the books for no good reason that I recall. However, I did keep all my old passports, the first from 1947. Today the entries trigger my memory. That year, as a newly fledged doctor, I undertook my first overseas visit by boat to France and then hitchhiked to Switzerland. It seems incredible to think that this was sixty-two years and seven passports ago.

The story of my working life falls neatly into sixteen periods covered in Chapters 4 to 19 and spanning over half a century. Certain patterns and passions run through these and my later life covered in Chapters 20 to 25. The Contents list serves as a skeleton on which to hang the flesh of the following account.

Without a shadow of a doubt, but only since her passing do I realize that my strongest and lasting passion was for my wife Ruth. Our marriage took Ruth abruptly away from Europe to spend the next decade traveling far and wide. Within a fortnight of marrying this stranger she had to exchange the carefree life of a young Swiss woman, at home in her beautiful country with its superlative skiing and many friends, for life in a simple tent set high on a barren, wind-swept plateau at the side of the Rapti River in the impoverished Nepalese Terai. Ruth's deep love of literature and music could not flower until our return to Europe in the 1960s. She read extensively, W.G. Sebald, V.S. Naipaul, and Proust being among her favorite authors. Ruth loved modern and classical music, especially the works of Mahler and modern French composers.

Ruth had many practical talents. Over and above these Ruth's greatest qualities were her deep sensitivity and love for her fellow beings, human and animal, her modest and generous-hearted nature, her loyalty, and her subtle sense of humor. The gold and blue crest of the Bernese root of the Scheidegger family bears the symbolic images of shared fields of golden grain. Ruth always shared the good things in her life with those close to her. For more than fifty years, she devoted her life selflessly to supporting me in my career. She was a shy woman at heart, but that heart was big and I loved her for it.

My next two passions must seem incomprehensible but, as I recount later, they dominated much of our lives. The last, entomology, was half work and half pleasure. Since early childhood, I was fascinated by the plant and animal life around me and my attention was especially focused on insects. Like Jean Henri Fabre, I would happily lie on the ground watching the creatures that crawled around in our small, urban garden. In the tropics where many such animals possess venomous bites or stings, I have to be more cautious. All my life I have retained my interest in insects, harmless ones and others that spread diseases. Much of this is reflected in the following pages.

Now that really is enough. I must listen for a change.

Chapter 2

Growing Up 1924–1939

In spite of my modern but elderly parents' acquaintance with the latest advice of Marie Stopes, I arrived on All Fools' Day 1924 like a bad joke, nine years after my next youngest sibling. Unlike more organized people, the lives of my parents and my own were punctuated more by accident or capricious judgments than by rational design. For example, an irritating smut from the chimneystack of a ship destined for the United States entered my then-bachelor father's eye when he was queuing for a medical examination while waiting to emigrate. The ship's doctor incorrectly diagnosed trachoma and sent him back ashore.

My father settled in London and married twice. His first wife died young from cancer of the liver leaving him with two small daughters. After a decent interval, he married again in 1913. I knew little about his first wife or her family except that they were among the founders of the new movement of Liberal Judaism, which radicalized his thinking and, in due course, mine. Henry's second wife Fanny bore him a daughter and, nine years later, a son. Thus by accident, I was born a British citizen, not American.

Our home, a square, grey-walled corner house, faced a large church in Finsbury Park, a once fashionable part of north London. There were a small fishpond and a large fountain in the garden, the first occupied by goldfish that froze under the ice each winter. We were owned by a huge brown dog named Prince, which I adored. In retrospect, he was probably a Pomeranian. In addition, we sheltered an old, very scruffy tramp we called Old Bill. He slept in a shed next to the back garden gate. He was a kindly old fellow whom we fed and clothed as necessary, and who kept me entertained as I grew with stories of his exploits. I think he was a veteran of the First World War. The house was only 100 yards or so from Finsbury Park itself where I was aired in my pram from which I would perversely expel my teddy bear as often as I could.

Fanny was a professional violinist and music teacher of modest talent, but the playing of any musical instrument was, unfortunately, a quality that I never acquired in spite of her efforts. However, I did inherit her deep love of music. Thus the family consisted of parents, eldest half-sister Sophie Alice (who became 'Pete'), middle half-sister Maisie, and sister Vera. During her army service in WW II Vera evolved into Veronica, then Ronnie. Nine years separated Sophie Alice and Ronnie, then a further nine between Ronnie and me. As the youngest of the family I was initially very spoiled and fattened up but, in later years, shunned as too young to be of any interest except as a sort of batman to my sisters.

The genes in my paternal family line we would now recognize as ones possessed of long telomeres. My grandfather was reputed to have lived to 100 and his mother 101, but they lived at a time when birth records in Poland were not a reliable source of one's personal history, especially among the often-despised Jewish families in small towns such as Sieradz or Lódz. However, Henry was recorded in an official document as having been born in that country in September 1879. A more accessible record lists his death in his 103rd year in London in January 1982. A number of Henry's brothers and his sister attained old age and an American nephew is an intellectually active ninety-seven. My sprightly sister Ronnie boasts of ninety-four. At eighty-five, I am one of the younger members of the Peters' clan.

The 1920s and 30s were the years of the zeppelins. I have still a vivid memory of being awakened on a warm summer's night to see through my bedroom window that huge dirigible, possibly the ill-fated R-101, floating serenely across the sky. How the world has changed since then! Now on many evenings if the sky is clear and I open my eyes around midnight I see the international space station (ISS) shining like an unblinking white beacon through my bedroom window. It has become a friend in my new loneliness and an icon of our global community. I try to visualize those incredibly brave but fortunate individuals, the elite of global travelers, who live in a small container 350 kilometers above us, with infinity beyond, circling our earth at nearly 28,000 kilometers every hour. There, in that distant white spot, they can devote their waking hours to esoteric research that we hope will one day be of unimaginable benefit to the inhabitants of our earth—but no malaria, no leishmaniasis, and no insects.

Through good fortune I was able to contribute in minuscule measure to knowledge and to the welfare of humanity. What follows is a brief account of treasured experiences I was privileged to enjoy and a few achievements. These were not just mine, but often accomplished with many friends and colleagues. Above all, I received infinite, selfless support for over fifty years from Ruth, a unique woman. None of us is a paragon of virtue; I hope I am honest enough to admit in these pages that I am no exception.

I went to a local council infant school where I learned to write using slates and chalk. On Empire Day we brought something to represent the large expanse of red that existed at that time on the world map. Most of us brought tinned fruit! Thus, my very first years were highly influential in developing my interests in natural history, geography, and humanity. Another zeppelin passed when I was in school and I recall the whole class being ushered into the playground to witness this extraordinary sight.

One year, my father Henry who rarely drank alcohol, decided to try to make wine. He exhibited an innate talent for scientific inventiveness, which, together with his genes for longevity, he must have passed on to me. Unfortunately, his endeavors were frustrated when all the bottles that he carefully nurtured in our cellar overheated and exploded. Thus ended my first science lesson. My introduction to medicine occurred when I acquired diphtheria and was isolated in my bedroom with a blanket soaked in antiseptic shielding the door. I followed this by being admitted to a hospital to have my tonsils removed. I have a vivid recollection of being transported on a stretcher through long corridors to the operating room. My main recollection after that is of receiving abundant supplies of ice cream to satisfy my hunger in spite of a very sore throat. I found that situation easy to bear. If this was medical treatment, I was all for it. Many years later I excelled in pharmacology and received an honorary Doctorate from the University of Paris at the Sorbonne. I wonder if it all stemmed from my tonsillectomy.

The financial slump of the 1930s hit my parents as hard as many others. They were obliged to downsize their home and open up a shop in order to supplement their income. We moved to the relatively new suburb of Hendon where we occupied a house with a long garden that was separated from the Underground railway line by a fence. A nephew of my father and his family, with two sons of about my age, lived a few hundred yards further along the road. On the other side of the railway line, reached by a footbridge, was Hendon Park. My sister Maisie, partly to achieve her independence, married a young man who was a bully and whom I detested. They lived a short walk away from us in a flat. In 1933, Maisie, of whom I was very fond, was killed in a car accident through the careless driving of her husband. It was a devastating blow to us all as she was the gentlest and kindest of all the family.

As I grew up I became more and more fascinated by the abundant plant and animal life around me. At about the age of eleven, when I was old enough to wander further afield, I spent as much time as possible roaming the wilds of Hampstead Heath or fishing for insects, newts, and stickleback fish with a small net and jam jar in the ponds of the heath or nearby Whetstone. The ponds there also contained an abundance of water insects, my introduction to entomology.

Our home was a short bus ride from the old Hendon airport where air displays were held once a year. One summer I received permission to go there on my own. On display was an autogyro, a quite spectacular monstrosity with about four layers of vanes to raise it from the ground. There were also a number of tiny machines, aptly called 'flying fleas' that just accommodated a pilot in a tiny, open cockpit. I would have liked nothing better than to have a ride in either type of aircraft.

The bus to the airport continued northwards towards Barnet, possibly as far as St. Albans, which was my destination on more than one memorable occasion in the future. In those days I attended a primary school situated a short bus ride south of Hendon. My main memory of that establishment is a set of steel gates guarding the lift, as I managed to catch my fingers in the damned thing and badly damaged them, fortunately only temporarily.

As I entered my teenage years it was necessary to find a secondary school to continue my education, but my parents could not afford the fees for any in our locality. In 1935 they located a well-reputed school not too far away in Muswell Hill, but for me to attend there we had to move and then apply for a scholarship. My enterprising parents achieved both objectives. By then my eldest sister was married so Ronnie, my parents and I, together with our old black cat, moved to a house on a steep hill in the appropriately named suburb of Muswell Hill. It was a fun house for me, as each house was on a different level because of the steepness of the road and had a cellar. I soon discovered that there were holes in the cellar walls through which one could pass along much of the length of the street unobserved by the inhabitants of the houses. I was enrolled in an excellent secondary school, Tollington Boy's School, a good half hour's walk from home. During this prewar period, Franco was decimating the Spanish population and Hitler started to exterminate the German Jews. I recall one boy who came to England, presumably with a Kindertransport group. He came to Tollington where he was initially very isolated as he spoke no English. However, students and staff rallied round him and he soon became a competent and productive pupil.

In several ways our Muswell Hill period was not the happiest. Ronnie bought a young dog, something she always wanted, but shortly after it escaped into the neighboring main road and was run over. Then one of my school friends who lived near the same part of that road, developed poliomyelitis and died after a short spell in a respirator.

My parents' business by then was located in Highgate, quite a distance from home. So they employed domestic help to manage the house and look after me. On their return home late in the evenings, our old black cat infallibly greeted them after walking several hundred meters up the road, by sitting on a garden wall where he waited for them.

One evening I stayed out late to watch a firework display in the grounds of Alexandra Palace, which was a few kilometers by foot from the house. I returned home later than I should have and was met by a couple of police cars, their occupants, and my distraught parents. Our domestic had shut herself in the bathroom and locked the door. They feared that something terrible had happened and that I might be involved. One can imagine the relief when I walked in the front door. The police broke into the bathroom through a back window and discovered the body of the poor woman submerged in the bath with a half-empty whisky bottle by her side. The relief at my resurrection was so great that I did not receive the scolding my late return home merited.

However, I was still a lonely boy. In retrospect, I realize now that the great age difference between my father and me, and the need for my parents to leave me to my own devices because they had to mind the shop, compounded to create a barrier between us. This deprived me of much of the normal formative interaction between father and son. If anything, I was spoiled by both parents in the material aspects of growing up. Not only did I lack the intellectual relationship that I craved from them, but the age difference was also a barrier from my much older sisters. I did develop friendships with a few young relatives and other children of my age group, but I see now that I knew very little of my parents and they of me. I had no knowledge of Henry's views on such matters as religion or politics apart from the obvious assumption that both he and my mother wished to steer me along a conventional religious upbringing. I had no idea of how they viewed the higher life.

I do recall that by my early teens Henry had moved from a traditional, albeit loose adherence to Jewish orthodoxy to Liberal Judaism. I had no idea why and never enquired. All I knew was that I no longer had to cover my head on the rare occasions that I attended the synagogue and that, as a bonus, much of the service was in English, not in Hebrew of which I had little knowledge and even less interest. I only recently discovered what a rebel my father was. He was a strong supporter of the Liberals and all they stood for including building a strong interfaith relationship with Christianity and other world religions. Perhaps my unusual parent-son relationship explains why I had selective amnesia for Henry's funeral until now. A very warm and touching eulogy was given by somebody who I believed was unknown to me. I now know that he was a rabbi related to us by marriage. He later became one of the Chief Rabbis of the Liberal Jewish Synagogue. (See Chapter 16, entry for January 13, 1982.)

Swimming was the sole sport in which I indulged. I was a junior member of our local swimming club, which was about three kilometers from our house. In warm weather, I often started the day by walking there to await the opening of the gate at 7:00 a.m. I would have a good swim, mainly under water which I enjoyed, and then walk back home in time for breakfast followed by a long walk to school. However, I had few friends.

My parents were not free to take me on holiday in those hard days so I was dispatched to children's' vacation homes. Broadstairs was a seaside home that I enjoyed because I could spend time wandering the beaches and rock pools, swimming, and helping the local sand artist collect pennies thrown to him from walkers on the cliff top. Another vacation home that I recall with affection was in the country somewhere; I believe it was in Kent. I helped gather the harvest on local farms and, on good nights, I slept on a rustic bed under the trees in the open air. When we awoke in the early mornings, the loud cooing of pigeons was an enormous pleasure and I learned to recognize the songs of numerous other wild birds. On one occasion, I saw a Camberwell Beauty trapped inside the French window of a room in the house. This was the first and last time I saw this rare butterfly in England. Many years later I saw another Camberwell Beauty specimen while walking with Ruth and our dogs near our home in Basle, Switzerland; another on the wall of a restaurant in Toronto, Canada; and two in the Tessin area of Switzerland where we were on vacation.

One day, perhaps due to my solitary nature, I decided that my future lay elsewhere and that I would leave home and go to sea. It was not clear in my young mind what I would do when I arrived there, but that did not deter me. My parents gave me a little pocket money that I supplemented by buying comic magazines and lending them out to school fellows for a penny or two. Thus I was in possession of a small cache of coins with which I felt I could achieve my aim. The precise sequence of events now evades me, but somehow I managed to take a series of buses that landed me in St. Albans, a city unknown to me at that time. It was a mild summer evening when I found my way there. I had had nothing to eat since leaving home without baggage. I was only motivated by an infantile notion that, if I traveled far enough northwards and then turned right, I would eventually reach the sea, and perhaps find a job on a ship. It is clear now that neither geography nor real life were my strong subjects. Today such behavior is recognized as a *crie de coeur*; a subconscious call for attention and love from parents and siblings who were simply too preoccupied with their own lives to recognize the needs of a small, lonely boy.

As night approached, I decided I needed somewhere to sleep and found a park bench on which somebody had left some newspapers. Probably influenced by Charlie Chaplin's tramp, I lay down and covered myself with the papers to prepare for the night. I do not know how long I lay there on that bench before I felt a hand gently tugging on my arm. I opened my eyes to find an elderly, dirty tramp looking down at me. He asked me in a kind voice what I was doing there. I told him quite simply that I was leaving home and making my way to the sea. He sat down and chatted with me for a while, discussing the hazards of heading into the unknown unprepared. Then he said goodbye and quietly disappeared. Shortly after, I was again aroused, this time by a policeman whom the tramp had alerted. I was gently taken along to a local police station where I was interrogated. My anxious parents were duly located and notified of their missing son's presence there. The police provided me with sandwiches and tea for which I was very grateful as I was quite hungry. Then they took me for a tour of the cells as a warning of where I might end up one day if I did not mend my ways. Before too long my relieved parents arrived, driven by one of our relations who owned a car, and we went home. Once more I escaped a severe chastisement for my adventure, but the whole affair created a new relationship between my family and me. For the first time, they recognized me as an individual with emotional needs. From then on, we began at last to understand each other.

As a Jewish boy I was undergoing religious instruction aimed at making me a good candidate for my Bar Mitzvah. However, I had an inherent dislike of religion of any sort. I was obliged to tolerate the requisite periods of instruction and ultimate ceremonials. But, as rapidly as I could, I discarded what I considered to be outside my nature. Yet I never considered myself to be an atheist. I only had to stand out of doors and observe the night sky to totally accept that, what most people accepted as the be-all and end-all of a mystic God was something far and above that concept. I yearned to learn more about the greater meaning of nature and to become, in some form or other, a scientist.

For starters, I busied myself constructing a cat's-whisker wireless. This was a wondrous piece of apparatus with which, through earphones and by dint of fiddling with the positioning of the wire whisker, I could receive the sound that accompanied the very first television broadcasts from the Alexandra Palace studios, which were almost within line-of-sight of the house. The construction of an apparatus to receive the vision was well beyond my capabilities, but I did have the thrill of watching the broadcast of the 1935 Royal Jubilee of George V on a primitive Baird television, with its whirling screen. It was the proud possession of one of my uncles who owned a radio and electrical business. I remember joining a shop full of his friends and neighbors to witness this spectacular event on the grainy, green screen. Before long I graduated to the construction of a real, but Heath Robinsonish radio, with second-hand tubes, transformers, and other components that I acquired from a local dealer. It is a mystery that I never electrocuted myself on this dangerous piece of equipment run, as domestic equipment was in those days, on a direct current mains supply.

The era of the 1930s was momentous on the national and international levels. Even as young as I was, these events did not leave me untouched. The world economy was in meltdown. This in turn led to massive social disorder in many western countries and the USA. Rumors reached the world that a rabid new Fuhrer named Adolf Hitler had taken over Germany. Among other social upheavals, he was planning a mass extermination of several political, ethnic, and religious groups, including communists and Jews. Spain was in turmoil with the ultra right General Franco, a crony of the fascist Hitler and Hitler's friend the Italian Mussolini, fighting a bloody civil war against the supporters of the political left.

Young or not, I was horrified by these events. My sympathies rapidly turned towards the USSR and the help that the communists were providing to keep Hitler in check and to fight Franco. Many young people joined the British Communist Party and the International Brigade. I heard of several who were seriously wounded or lost their lives in Spain. I tried to learn more about politics, but the dull nature of books on that subject blocked any serious advance I made along that line.

Shortly before the outbreak of WW II we were visited by my American cousin, Harold (Hal), the son of Henry's sister who migrated to Chicago at the turn of the century. (As I noted above, he now is in his ninety-seventh year.) Hal was a brilliant young man, a polymath, handsome, and athletic. He excelled in art, music, and surgery. My sisters adored him.

Supported by a generous Traveling Fellowship, he came to London for postgraduate studies at St. Marks Hospital where his surgical mentor was W.B. Gabriel. He was renowned as 'The Arseangel Gabriel' for his pioneering work on rectal surgery, in which Hal would later become an authority in his own right. (By coincidence, sixty years later I worked in a laboratory literally next door to St. Marks Hospital, but at its new site in Northwick Park in north London). At the time of Hal's visit, I was submerged in electronics and natural history in my small bedroom. I had a small terrarium in which I kept a number of African green tree frogs and a large common frog. The tree frogs, beautiful as they were, sang themselves out of a home during the mating season. Their incessant and extremely loud croaking, so disturbed us and neighboring house-holds that they had to be swapped for something less obtrusive.

During my cousin's visit the remaining frog managed to swallow a fishhook that was baited with a mealworm for a reason I no longer recall. I could not remove the object without seriously harming the poor beast, so Hal came to the rescue. I had a small bottle of chloroform that I used for killing insects. With me serving as anesthetist and Hal as the surgeon, we opened the frog's stomach, removed the hook, and sewed the patient up again.

He (or she) survived the ordeal and made a perfect recovery. The experience stimulated in me the first thought of becoming a doctor and my cousin did his best to encourage this ambition. He even suggested that I should join him and his family in Chicago where he was well placed to start me off on a medical career when the time came. As much as I appreciated his offer, I did not accept it for two basic reasons. First, I was frankly jealous of his many and diverse talents. Second, I was too proud to accept his help thinking, probably without reason, that to do so would place me under a massive obligation for the remainder of my days. I was then, and remain so ever since, very independent. I wanted to be my own man, an aim in which I succeeded, up to a point.

As I recall during this period I developed a new interest, stamp collecting. From various sources, I began to accumulate a motley collection of foreign stamps from which I learned more geography than I ever did from school lessons. In fact, geography with its many dry facts was one of my least favorite subjects as a youngster. This hobby did not survive long. A few years later, I disposed of my small collection to buy books that interested me more. Near the time I retired I once again took up philately as a hobby. In the interim I passed through various exotic countries and had a small number of their current issues for future reference. Eventually this became the basis of a serious collection focused on British stamps and those depicting natural history. I was obliged to dispose of all of these many years later when it became necessary for Ruth and me to exchange our house for a relatively small apartment in a retirement village. However, more of that later.

Chapter 3

Later School and
Student Years 1939–1947

In 1939 WWII erupted and the pupils of Tollington were evacuated to the small village of Buckden near Huntingdon. It was my final year before I was due to take my General School exam. After that I had to return to London and find a place in another school if I were to continue my education to the Higher School level. When I see old photographs of children with school caps and boxes round their necks, containing what were probably rather useless gas masks, I see myself among them. My contemporaries and I arrived by train, to be met by kindly ladies and elderly men. They sorted us out and allocated us, usually in ones and twos, to local residents who agreed to provide billets for evacuees. Another boy and I were allocated to a couple whose name, I believe, was Cowling. They had two grown daughters already living away from home, one of them a schoolteacher.

Our new home was a simple one. It had an outdoor toilet that was emptied daily by a man with a horse and cart. The bath was the portable zinc variety and the two of us took turns using it once a week. Our school activities were based in an ancient baronial house called Buckden Towers, which had extensive wild gardens containing ponds and other areas rich in wild life. In the twelfth century it was constructed as a fortified manor house for the Bishops of Lincoln and was then known as Buckden Palace. Social life among the good citizens of Buckden was reminiscent of *Just William* and one could recognize many of the characters depicted in Rachel Crompton's books. That whole corner of Huntingdonshire was a haven of wild life in those days. A couple of our younger schoolteachers and several of the older ones accompanied us to Buckden where they were also billeted with their families if they had children of appropriate age. The headmaster, who I recall was single, managed to get himself lodged in the best local hostelry! The transfer to the country gave us a fortuitous, unprecedented opportunity of knowing our teachers on a level that was not possible under normal circumstances.

I remember two in particular; an older man who we called Ernie Allen taught English and History, and a younger man named Huxley who we referred to, not surprisingly, as 'Bugs' Huxley. Both men had a great talent, which they may never have had the opportunity to exercise but for the war, to know their pupils and bring out the best in them. Up to then, history was a subject that bored me intensely with dates and names of events and people from centuries ago. From day one, Ernie Allen taught us history from the beginning of the twentieth century. He brought history alive to many of us for the first time. Ernie also recognized that the English language held a special fascination for me. He encouraged me considerably in my studies of grammar, composition, and literature for which I am ever grateful. He was also a very perceptive man and father who recognized, at one moment in Buckden, that I could have entered a false route in my life. He responded like a father and the moment passed forever. I have not forgotten his kindness.

Bugs Huxley saw the deep interest that I and a close school friend, whose name evades me, shared for natural history. Instead of obliging us to follow his lessons, he gave us free rein to follow our own interests, which we did with great enthusiasm. My friend was very knowledgeable about birds and their lives and possessed a good pair of binoculars. I was becoming something of a homemade expert on insects. We wandered the gardens and surrounding countryside of Buckden Towers together. He brought my attention to the birds that had usually flown before I could focus his binoculars on them. I would point to a flying insect far away and tell him exactly which species it was before he could see it, so we roamed together on an equal level. From Buckden it was possible to cycle eastwards to Wicken Fen, at the edge of the fen country where the Swallowtail butterfly still maintained a perilous hold on its breeding sites. This beautiful insect was, and remains, a protected species, but a collector was permitted to take two or three live specimens for breeding. An attempt was also being made to reestablish the Large Copper butterfly that became extinct at Wicken fen in England some years before. I collected some larvae of the Swallowtail and maintained them in homemade containers back in the house where they fed avidly on carrot leaves, pupated, and ultimately hatched.

I carefully preserved the pupal cases and adults, mounting the latter in a glass-covered insect box for the next sixty years when, along with a large collection of other English and European butterflies, I presented them to the North Herts Museum. I also found a dead pupa of the Large Copper that I kept in the box. My naturalist friend, an excellent nature artist, presented me with a superb pen and ink drawing of one of my Swallowtail butterflies. Unfortunately, that drawing disappeared in the intervening years.

The Buckden area was also rich in reptile life with crested newts, frogs, and toads abounding in the local ponds. The river Ouse crossed our main road about a kilometer away and was notorious for flooding in the winter, which it did while we were there. One day I cycled down to have a look and discovered a remarkable sight. The picket fence lining the road was bright with masses of hibernating ladybirds of several species that had lodged themselves in the cracks of the posts. It was rather like seeing trees in California covered with hibernating Monarch butterflies. In this case, the posts were covered with small, red and black insects, a sight that has remained in my mind's eye. Unfortunately, in those days I did not possess a camera, not even a box Brownie, to immortalize the picture.

Another of my loves in that last preliminary school year was French. I do not recall who our teacher was. He had the good sense not to stuff our minds with grammar but encouraged us to read popular books of fiction such as Maurice Leblanc's *The Adventures of Arsène Lupin* and to read aloud. This subject and biology served me well when the final examinations arrived.

Early in the oral exam, my examiner asked me if I had any hobbies and I told him about my interest in natural history. I feared I may have opened a black pit for myself since I knew none of the French words for the various creatures with which I was familiar. However, my obvious enthusiasm for the subject struck a chord in him. He responded by asking me to tell him about my activities without worrying about the technical translations which I did with enthusiasm. We proceeded in this way throughout the oral exam and the outcome was that I received a good Pass for French in my Matriculation as well as Passes in English, English Literature, Elementary Mathematics, and Biology. After this I returned home to London.

The period from 1939 to 1940, the year of the phony war, proved to be one of mixed fortunes for everybody. My enterprising parents discovered that scholarships were available for entry to Haberdashers Boys' School, at that time situated in Cricklewood. However, they were limited to people living within a defined area around the school. They took the great leap of selling their business in Highgate and the house in Muswell Hill. With the proceeds of these sales they acquired a first floor flat over shops along the main road running through West Hampstead. Then they applied for and were granted a scholarship for me to attend Haberdashers, which was a fairly short cycle ride away. I spent the next two years in that renowned school studying for my Higher School certificate. By then I was aiming at entering medical school so I concentrated on science subjects that were appropriate for a medical education. Meanwhile WW II raged around us.

We were not unscathed. The Blitzkrieg was in full swing and bombs fell around us every night, but mercifully they missed us. Then one day, my mother's nerves failed her. My father and I decided to take her to stay a few nights in the country to give her a chance to rest. On our first night there we received a phone call to tell us that the block of flats we lived in was hit by incendiary bombs. Our home was not burned, but destroyed by water poured on it by the fire brigade to extinguish the inferno. Henry and I returned home the next morning to view the damage and to find out what had happened to our home and to our black cat that we left behind to be fed by a neighbor in our absence. We found the poor animal sitting disconsolately on top of some furniture, unharmed, but wondering what had happened. Under the dire circumstances of that day and time, we had no hope of finding an alternative home for her and had to face the unhappy choice of calling in the RSPCA. It was a very sad day for us all.

Since it was obvious that we would not be able to return to the flat, we tried to organize the removal of our surviving and salvageable property into storage, pending our finding a new place in which to live. Meanwhile we were sheltered by one of my mother's widowed sisters whose house was not too far away. She generously offered us its use while she stayed in a temporary home in the country. Months passed before our flat could be emptied. By this time most of our possessions perished from the effects of the water in which they remained, partly submerged and thoroughly saturated. Eventually we found a flat on a road in Maida Vale. We were very fortunate not to lose that in the continuing blitz, since another block of flats 200 meters away was demolished one night by a V2 bomb. Amazingly, I did not even hear the detonation. The only damage to our flat was that the French window of my bedroom that faced the explosion was blown open by the blast!

At around this time I became strongly politicized thanks, firstly, to the Spanish civil war and subsequently the war with Germany. At Haberdashers I joined the Air Training Corps in the hope of training as a pilot with the RAF. To my regret, I was rejected for that role as not being sufficiently fit. Instead, I started to train in the ATC as a navigator. This was the time for me to decide which direction to take for my future career. Perhaps partly influenced by the pre-war visit of my American cousin Hal, I decided to study medicine. Under other circumstances I would have opted for a degree in Biology. However, realizing that this would take second place, I applied for entry to a number of medical schools and was eventually accepted by both University College and St. Bartholomews. To go to either I would need a scholarship, which I was fortunate to obtain. I decided to accept the offer from Barts where an old school friend, Max Skoblo, was already accepted.

During the years in Maida Vale I received more than a formal education. I also began to learn of the more subtle side of human nature. I fell in love, as I understood that term, with a delightful young girl who lived in a nearby flat. Helen's father was a chemical engineer and he generously taught me much of that subject that was valuable to my school studies in science. Visits to his home also gave me a good opportunity to see his daughter. Soon our relationship grew to a more intimate, but still naive phase. We reached the stage of exchanging confidential and emotional letters, but little more. Helen's mother, who for some reason took a dislike to me, intercepted one of my missives and henceforth forbade her daughter from seeing me. Sadly, but perhaps wisely, I had no choice but to submit to her wishes. I sometimes wonder what the years brought to Helen.

I also met a young female biology student, Rosemary, with whom I almost entered the next phase of my sexual education. However, I was beaten to the post by a young, intellectually endowed ex-German refugee student whom she later married. In time he became a Cambridge don. I had to wait a few more years to lose my virginity thanks to a red-haired war widow, which was an interesting experience, but one of which I will write no more.

As a parting gesture to my old school in which I was by then a sub-prefect, I became an air raid warden, both in the school and around our home in Maida Vale. Early one morning one of my schoolfellows and I had the unforgettable experience of finding a cache of plans for the design of a new type of aircraft. It transpired that these must have been stolen from the nearby Handley Page factory, probably copied, and then dumped in a corner of one of the outbuildings on the school grounds. After reporting our find to the police, we were interrogated by government security officers but, not surprisingly, heard no more about the event. It was perhaps just as well that our interrogators were unaware of my political affiliations!

Once we settled back in London with the war still raging around us, I paid more interest to politics. By then, we were allied with the USSR and support for communism was extensive. A number of my contemporaries joined the Communist Party. Not one to do things by halves, I did likewise. I frankly cannot recall that I made any useful contributions to that organization, but was a card-carrying member in 1942 when I became a medical student. When my school studies were completed and just before I joined Barts, I learned that the study of medicine was a 'reserved occupation.' That meant that once accepted for that role, I would not be accepted into the armed services. However, that did not diminish my political ideals. Therefore, I entered university as a youthful, but highly immature communist, totally unaware of the network of genuine would be revolutionaries who were already ensconced in the city of Cambridge. I found little time for political activities there and gradually drifted away from the communists. Unlike a few now infamous academics, I was not recruited by any of the notorious Russian agents who were based in that university. Clearly I was not considered to be promising spy material. However, my transient political affiliation did reflect on the course of my subsequent career as I mention below.

Not surprisingly, university life in Cambridge at that time was very serious. It lacked many of the life-enriching social activities that most students had previously enjoyed in that and other university environments. In place of a social life, we devoted ourselves steadfastly to our studies and gave our spare time to service in various civil defense or similar projects. However, all was not lost.

A subject that particularly interested me was embryology. Associated with that were the physiological changes in the female associated with the development of eggs and the embryo. Apart from the good fortune of our having the subject taught by a leading authority in these fields, I got to know some female students who were willing to collaborate with me by providing samples of various cells from intimate parts of their anatomy. That enabled me to study the physiological changes that they underwent during the menstrual cycle. I have to say that this was as intimate as I became with these particular changes in the female of our species, but this did not preclude me from learning something about other aspects of the opposite sex. My Cambridge days were well ahead of the swinging sixties, but human nature does not change all that much. The female population was a great center of attraction for young, lusty males, and not just students. Many servicemen were posted in the area and were glad to make new friends. I was able to extend my inherent interest in natural history into the rich area of human nature and behavior and did so with enthusiasm.

Another opportunity to study human nature arose during one vacation, when I volunteered to assist in the medical department attached to a large munitions factory near Speke, which lies just outside Liverpool. (I returned to Liverpool twenty-four years later and lived in a suburb not far from Speke.) The war was still raging and there was every chance that the Speke factory would receive the attention of the Luftwaffe as the Liverpool docks had earlier. While this fortunately did not happen, we suffered explosions of our own making. The sheds design was such that, should an explosion occur, the walls would remain solid while the roof was liable to be blown away and prevent the blast from spreading to neighboring sheds. One shed was devoted to the preparation of mercury fulminate and another to the hand filling of detonators with lead azide, both highly sensitive explosives. I visited the first shed and was horrified to see a young woman standing, patting a small sack of a grayish powder that was removed from a container of water and suspended from a hook to dry. A couple of days later we received a message that there was an explosion in one of the sheds. The same young woman was brought into the surgery minus several fingers. She was rapidly transferred for surgery to the main hospital in Liverpool. A couple of weeks later I was astounded to encounter her back at her job. At that moment I realized how resilient a human being can be in the face of serious trauma.

My preclinical days in Cambridge were followed by clinical studies in several centers. First was in Hill End Hospital, an old fashioned and grim mental hospital that was taken over by Barts during the war to accommodate repatriated servicemen with medical or surgical needs, especially those requiring plastic surgery, as well as civilian patients. Thus I returned to St. Albans, the scene of a prior adventure, but in a more mature role. We received patients with a wide range of medical problems of great interest. Some of the soldiers admitted to Hill End were suffering from tropical diseases.

It was there that I received my first practical experience of the diagnosis of such conditions as malaria. A small drop of blood smeared thinly on a glass slide, stained in shades of pink and mauve, on a microscope—and I was hooked for life. The blood belonged to a soldier in Hill End hospital in St. Albans. He was admitted for treatment of malarial fever he acquired somewhere in the tropics in 1944. As a student there I spent spare time in the pathology lab. It was love at first sight; me and malaria parasites. I remained faithful to them all my life in a paradoxical way—I did my best to kill them and the mosquitoes that transmit them!

That is a slight exaggeration because there exists not just one kind of malaria parasite, but possibly hundreds. Beyond the five that make humans ill, I became and remain fascinated by those that infect other mammals, reptiles, amphibians, birds, and other living creatures. Later in these memoirs I recount how some colleagues and I discovered a previously unknown malaria parasite in orangutans. However, we certainly do not want to eliminate either that parasite or its host. Malaria parasites, especially one justifiably known as the 'malignant tertian' parasite, or to give it its scientific name, *Plasmodium falciparum*, infect over 500 million people and kill between two and three million of them every year. These are the ones I wanted to kill.

My second exposure to malaria was also at Hill End. Prior to and during WW II, a lethal, sexually transmitted condition known as neurosyphilis was relatively common and often incurable. Prior to the discovery of penicillin, it was accepted practice to deliberately infect sufferers from neurosyphilis with the less dangerous type of human malaria, the benign tertian type caused by a parasite called *Plasmodium vivax*. Fortunately for such patients, the chronic bouts of fever that this parasite produced in them killed the microorganisms that cause syphilis, but not the human sufferer who could later be cured with one or other antimalarial drug and sometimes a combination of both.

These drugs, quinine (then believed to be the oldest known anti-malarial) and pamaquine (a 1920s German derivative of quinine) were both toxic and caused very unpleasant side effects. The ideal way to infect such patients was to use them to provide lunch for mosquitoes that had received a blood meal about a week earlier on another patient who already was infected with *Plasmodium vivax*. During that interval, the parasites undergo a cycle of development in the insects' stomachs, from which they invade their salivary glands. At the next meal, these infective stages, called sporozoites, are injected into the new patient in whom they multiply first in the liver and then the red blood cells. These they destroy and, in so doing, cause fever. The new offspring then make their way into other red cells. It requires forty-eight hours for this cycle to be completed. Each time, it is accompanied by a bout of fever. The malignant parasite, *Plasmodium falciparum*, also needs forty-eight hours to complete this cycle. However, the infection that results is much heavier and more dangerous so it was not normally used to treat neurosyphilis. On the other hand, in infection with the benign parasite, some organisms remain behind in the liver in which they mature after intervals of months or even a year or more. They produce relapses of fever later, well after the patient thinks he is cured.

This process was carried out mainly at the Horton Hospital in south London, a center at which research on malaria and its treatment with new drugs were conducted before the war. Two on the technical staff were responsible for much of the laboratory work involved. This included the maintenance of colonies of *Anopheles* mosquitoes with which to transmit the various species of malaria parasites from man to man. One day these two, Miss (Maid) Marion and P.G. Shute, arrived at Hill End bearing small containers of infected mosquitoes that were placed on the arms of one of my patients. The hungry insects fed on his blood through the gauze cover of the containers. Twelve days later and every alternate evening thereafter my patient had a high fever that neither he nor the spirochaetes causing his neurosyphilis, appreciated. I was able to make and study the parasites in smears of his blood to my heart's content until his malaria was eliminated with the drugs. He was then given therapy to end the malaria infection, but not before I had the great experience of studying the parasites on thin films of his blood, carefully prepared at frequent intervals and stained with Giemsa stain according to the instructions of Shute in his classic handbook.

There is a postscript to this story. Some weeks later a resident of an area not far from Hill End, developed a PUO, a fever of unknown origin. It was eventually diagnosed by an astute laboratory technician as vivax malaria. I leave it to the imagination as to how this individual was infected in an otherwise totally malaria-free part of England. Remember also that there were locations where species of *Anopheles*, capable of transmitting malaria under appropriate climatic conditions were breeding, and a number of servicemen were returning from overseas with chronic, but unrecognized and potentially infective malaria infections. Indeed, minor epidemics of malaria had been and would continue to be recognized in other areas. For example, this occurred in parts of California during the wars in Korea and Vietnam. The coincidence with the visit of Marion and Shute in our case, however, seems to be rather overwhelming.

Apropos of penicillin, a Professor of Medicine at Barts during that period, Ronald Christie, was one of the first to conduct clinical studies with that remarkable substance. It was the first radically new drug with which to treat a wide range of otherwise lethal bacterial infections. It was incredibly active. For example, as few as 250 units cured even life-threatening streptococcal septicemia. It was in such short supply that we would collect the patients' urine in which it was excreted so it could be chemically extracted and recycled. However, the use of such a low dose permitted the selection of mutant bacteria that proved to have the ability to survive this drug. Before long, doses were given in mega units; the first serious example of antimicrobial drug resistance and a major problem that persists to this day with many types of bacterial and parasitic infections. This included malaria, which was to become one of my major interests.

For most of the next sixty years I devoted much time exploring how to stop malaria from being transmitted and seeking novel drugs for its prevention and treatment. The following pages describe the circumstances of my search, how my career evolved around this primary theme, and where we stand on malaria today. In a nutshell, much has been done but relatively little has been achieved to date. This holds true even though we are forever on the brink of massive breakthroughs by exploiting the latest technological advances aided by the abrupt appearance of vast sums of money with which to carry out this task.

("The more it changes, the more it's the same thing.")

However, malaria was not the only health problem to a resolution of which I wanted to contribute.

D-day followed shortly after this episode. I recall walking outside the ward at Hill End early one morning to find the sky as far as one could see in every direction covered with large aircraft, many of them towing gliders and all heading south. On the previous day we suspected that something dramatic was impending as we were directed to free as many beds as possible as rapidly as possible for an unspecified but imminent event. D-day it was and, before long, casualties began to arrive and the plastic surgery unit was filled to overflowing.

Subsequently I returned to our home base of Barts adjacent to the old Smithfield market. There I gained practical training in obstetrics and gynecology in a prestigious department directed by Professor Wilfred Shaw, and held under the firm thumb of a diminutive, but phenomenal ward Sister whose name unfortunately evades me.

To gain experience, one of our tasks was to go out to assist the local midwives in the delivery of babies to mothers in their homes in surrounding areas of the city, and what a fantastic experience that was. We took turns going out on the district and, as a remarkable proportion of births seemed to take place in the middle of the night, it was rare that we were able to benefit from more than the occasional full night's sleep in our accommodation in the hospital precincts. In fact, at times I was so exhausted that I only had to sit down in a comfortable chair before I fell asleep. Nevertheless, I found this part of my training to be fascinating. I learned how to cope with both routine and difficult labor under less than ideal conditions, how to react with mothers undergoing the ordeal of childbirth, and to share with the family the joy of delivering a new life into the world.

It also taught me something of the practical hazards of cycling to homes in unknown streets in the small hours of the morning, bearing two large stainless-steel drums containing sterile dressings and instruments strung over my shoulder with a rope. On one such occasion, I realized I was being shadowed silently by a car. This turned out to be a police car, which stopped in front of me.

A uniformed officer stepped out and challenged me, "And where do you think you are going?"

"I'm a student from Barts and I'm going to help deliver a baby. Can you tell me where (such and such) a road is please?"

"Ah, that's no problem. Follow us."

He and his driver led me to my destination and dropped me at the front door just as the midwife was arriving. The lucky woman was in her car. It was lucky as this turned out not to be a 'BBA' (born before arrival). I was able to add the new baby, after several long hours of patient waiting, to my list of successful deliveries. In future years my obstetric experience was to prove of inestimable value when I worked in remote tropical areas.

In due course I sat my final examinations and, hedging my bets, I took both those of the Royal College of Physicians and Royal College of Surgeons as well as those of London University. To my disgust, I failed that of the second college, but gained the London Bachelor of Medicine and Bachelor of Surgery (MB.BS.) degree, with Honors in Applied Pharmacology and Therapeutics, and Obstetrics and Gynecology on my first attempt. Thus I was able to apply for inclusion on the Medical Register to which I was added in April 1947. I became a full fledged and very ignorant doctor just after my twenty-third birthday.

From sheer cussedness, I re-sat the final for the MRCS twice and passed it in 1948, to add MRCS, London, and LRCP, England to my qualifications.

Chapter 4

First Experiences in Europe 1947–1948

"Make me chaste and continent, but not just yet," Saint Augustine.

Finally qualifying as a doctor seemed to be the right occasion to make my first venture across the Channel. In May I obtained a Swiss visa and the grand sum of £27 in Traveler's Checks and cash before taking the train to Newhaven and then the ferry to Dieppe. I recall hitchhiking across northern France, which still showed many signs of the war. I have strangely little recollection of this grand venture, although my passport tells me that I crossed the border from France to Switzerland and arrived at Basle on May 20th. However, I do vividly remember the devastation in Alsace and the stark contrast this made to the cleanly washed streets of Basle. I also recall my first meal there, a gigantic Wiener schnitzel, twice as much as I could eat and the largest I had ever seen. I never imagined that, over a decade later in 1961, I would be married to a young Swiss woman and return to Basle where we would spend the next five years. I believe that on that first visit to Switzerland I continued on to Geneva to see my sister Ronnie. By then, she was working with the Interim Commission of the World Health Organization as an Administrative Assistant to Dr. Brock Chisholm, a Canadian psychiatrist. She continued to work with him when he became the first Director-General of WHO in 1948.

After graduation, I applied for a house job at Barts with my sights set on a surgical unit. Barts, in those days was, and probably remains, a highly conservative organization with a long tradition of an old boy network among the senior staff. In spite of my academic achievements, I was not offered a house job in any surgical or other unit. I had gained the highest level in my final MB.BS. In fact I achieved the second place in the whole of London University that year, as well as one or two of Barts' own internal awards. I then applied for the post of Casualty House Surgeon at Tilbury Hospital where the assistant head of Bart's Department of Gynecology was a consultant. In his letter of congratulation on my MB. BS. the Dean of Barts wrote; "I should very much like to congratulate you, both from myself and on behalf of the College, in doing so well in the Final M.B. I am very glad about your double distinctions and I hope this will prove a prelude to a very successful career."

A little later in a letter of recommendation for the post at Tilbury he wrote; "It is a very great surprise to me that he has not immediately obtained a House Appointment at the Hospital associated with his own Medical School. The fact that he has not done so is not due to any defect in his own character but to one of those unfortunate chances by which, presumably, he was not well known to the Heads of any of the Units whose House Appointments were vacant."

"....not well known...." my eye! I suspect that the old boy network included some contacts with MI5, the Security Service. In any case, my non-conformist attitude to Bart's tradition was well known. For example, I wrote a letter for publication in the *Barts Journal* that strongly criticized the total refusal of the authorities to admit women students. One of their excuses was that new toilet facilities would have to be built to accommodate them. Years after I graduated this policy was overturned, not only at Barts, but also in most of the other great medical schools in London.

Thus, in the summer of 1947, I moved to the hospital at the side of Tilbury docks where I worked for nearly a year, gaining excellent practical experience in general and trauma surgery under the tutelage of an Australian surgeon and his British assistant. I also gained interesting insights into the life of Tilbury dockers and of the initial workings of the National Health Service (NHS) that was just inaugurated.

The advent of the NHS was greeted by many ordinary citizens as an occasion to demand as their right, any and every medication, bandage, and other medical items that they could think of. I remember some coming to the hospital, or sending their children with a note, to demand such things as a packet of aspirins and an elastic bandage. The quality of hospital administrator also left much to be desired. For example, in Tilbury we suffered from a small, round, pompous little man who considered that his job included telling everybody, including the medical staff, exactly what they should or should not do, when, where, how, and for how long. To put it politely, he was a pain. As far as possible, we all did our best to ignore him, much to his fury.

My view of many of the hard-working, hard-done-by dockers also took a large turn. It went from viewing them as the salt of the proletariat earth to a bunch of scheming rogues who would sooner steal something out of a packing case than give you the time of day. I remember one individual was brought in by ambulance after falling off the ferry from Gravesend to Tilbury in a drunken state and being ignominiously fished out. He lay in his soaking clothes, dripping large pools of Thames water on to the surgery floor. As we started to unclothe him, a wide variety of small objects that he had pilfered from various ship's cargoes fell out of his pockets!

Other more somber occasions come to mind including the time I was called out to see somebody sitting in the passenger seat of a lorry. The driver had seen him by the side of the road looking unwell. He stopped to give him a lift, but was so concerned when he arrived at the door of the outpatient department that he forgot to turn off his engine. I went out to see the man, only to find him bouncing up and down with the motion of the lorry, but stone dead.

In May 1948, I enjoyed a long and eventful vacation in France. I had reached the mature age of twenty-four and all my life was ahead of me. I bought the huge sum of £35 in Traveler's Checks and once more took the train and ferry to Dieppe, then continued to Paris. In those early postwar days, many young people were taking their first opportunity to visit mainland Europe. In a park close to the Musée Rodin, the authorities had set up a site for 'camping en pleine aire' where I stayed for a self-conducted, mainly pedestrian and metro sightseeing tour of the city. I encountered many congenial youngsters of my age, many of them students, including a pretty American girl. In talking with her one day, we discovered that she was the best friend of my cousin Hal's first wife; the latter a poet whom I was shortly to meet on an unanticipated visit to Chicago. Could there have been a more remarkable coincidence?

In fact there could be, and there were others in my life that I will touch on later.

I also befriended a very genial Dutch girl who would cause me some embarrassment when, six years later, she arrived on my doorstep in London with a husband in tow. At that moment I was out and she stopped simply to say "hello." However, she encountered my newly married wife, Ruth! It was many years before I could live down that episode or even mention the word "Dutch" without raising hackles. It was unnecessary I hasten to add.

From Paris I hitchhiked south, carrying a small tent in a rucksack, and stopping in various youth hostels en route. It was my first experience in the south of France, the Midi. I was enchanted by Avignon with its historical town and famous bridge. Moreover, the local dialect, 'l'accent du Midi', was music to my ears, especially the leisurely pace at which most locals spoke. It was a marked contrast to the rapidity of speech and frequent use of argot of many Parisians.

From Avignon I traveled via Arles and other romantic towns to the Côte d'Azur.

After exploring Nice with its avenues of orange trees lit up after dusk by large numbers of fireflies, I crossed over to the enchanting little Île Ste Marguerite which was the site of what was one of the most attractive youth hostels in the country. The silence of the warm, soft-aired evenings was broken by the song of nightingales and the shrill rasping of numerous cicadas. Congenial company was abundant. I encountered a friendly young Parisienne with whom I later cycled to the village of La Sainte Marie de la Mer, just west of the Camargue where we arrived just in time to witness the annual, colorful, Fête des Gitanes. I had a drink with a Scottish fellow resident in the bar of Castle Village one evening sixty years later and he mentioned that he crossed France on a tandem bicycle with a friend and stayed on the same island a couple of years after I did. He was equally enchanted and amazed to meet, after all these years, somebody else who had been there.

The south of France was a paradise for a naturalist in other directions too. The slopes of the Alpes Maritimes abounded with butterflies, among which fritillaries of numerous species could be seen. Scorpions were found in more sandy soil and there was prolific plant and bird life. I added a considerable number of species of butterfly to my growing European collection, as I never traveled far in those days without a folding net and a container in which to store specimens. This involved killing them by nipping the thorax, then placing each insect in a small, improvised paper triangle on which I wrote the details of date, place of capture, and other notes for future labeling once they were relaxed and set for identification and storage in my collection. Over the years I acquired a considerable collection, from not only Europe, but also the various tropical countries in which I later lived or visited. The first of these was the West African country of the Gold Coast which became Ghana soon after.

Chapter 5

The Royal Army Medical Corps
and West Africa 1948–1949

By the time I completed my medical training, WW II ended with the disastrous nuclear bombing of Japan. In the autumn of 1948, not long after I completed my first postgraduate training as a Casualty Officer in Tilbury and my holiday in France, I received orders to report for military service. Having been found unfit for training as a pilot because of defective physique and eyesight as a student, I was enlisted in the Royal Army Medical Corps. With a contingent of contemporaries, I was posted for induction and basic training to Aldershot under the command of a notoriously fierce commanding officer curiously named, Colonel Officer. His task was to turn us into officers and gentlemen as well as army doctors. The experience was both interesting and of lasting value because it offered an excellent opportunity to obtain firsthand knowledge of medicine in the tropics.

As a clinical student, I had encountered a number of service personnel who were repatriated from tropical countries suffering from a variety of infections such as amoebic dysentery and malaria. I spent as much time as I could in the laboratory of Hill End hospital in St. Albans. It was being used by my parent hospital as a wartime overflow center where service personnel were sent for the treatment of such conditions or for plastic surgery. I already had a strong taste for anything relating to natural history and the study of tropical diseases fitted squarely into my sights.

As we completed basic training, the moment arrived to receive our postings. We had no choice in this procedure and I was sent to a post in Vienna. A fellow recruit was posted to the Gold Coast. Vienna was to me a glamorous city in which to spend the next year or two, but my colleague was bitterly disappointed. He wished to go somewhere in Europe so he could fulfill his hopes of marrying the young lady to whom he was engaged. West Africa was hardly the best place for him to work so his plans were in clear jeopardy. We discussed our mutual situations and decided to appeal to the Commanding Officer to trade postings. To our surprise and delight, our appeal was granted. I did not know at the time that Africa was the last place in the world to which most of my colleagues wished to be sent.

He was posted to Vienna where he and his fiancée married. I went to Accra on the Gold Coast, a country of ill repute as far as health was concerned. I was thrown into the deep end of both general medicine and tropical diseases. It proved to be the start of my lifetime career as a tropical physician, entomologist, and medical researcher.

After a long flight with BOAC via Kano I arrived in the capital, Accra, where the 34th Military Hospital of the Royal West Africa Frontier Force was sited. Accra was and remains an interesting city in many ways. In those days Pidgin English was widely spoken and the local dialect was intriguing. It contained such picturesque expressions as that for the word 'God' who was defined as 'One big fella Elder Demster foreman, he walk long top.' The delightful term for a fisherwoman on the quayside was 'Fatmama.'

Local soldiers included men from the north to the south of the country and some from neighboring Francophone countries. Each group had their own language such as Hausa from the north and

Twee from some coastal areas of the Gold Coast. A batman named Gabriel Mossi, a delightful and cheerful young man, was appointed to me so all my minor domestic affairs were taken care of. He came from Ouagadougou, in a Francophone country now named Burkina Faso beyond the northern boundary of the Gold Coast. It was not far from Bobodioulasso where I was to visit over ten years later.

The names of many towns in that part of Africa are poetic to my ear. Until then, I thought that Tombouctou was an imaginary place in the neighboring country of Mali to the south to which you dispatched people you did not like. Although I never had the opportunity to visit it, I did go many years later to Ouagadougou which was not far away by African standards—about 600 kilometers.

One of my main roles was to ensure that the expatriate army personnel in my care took precautions against acquiring malaria and treating them if they fell sick. Most of the indigenous troops were infected before or shortly after birth and had gradually acquired some level of immunity to the disease—if they survived their early years of life. Within my first few months I learned that not even our best antimalarial drugs were always effective.

The strange working hours of our military duties, a very early start in the mornings, finish routine work by midday, and a long lunch followed by a siesta suited me admirably. I occupied much of my siesta time, when I had not consumed too many gin and bitters before lunch, by searching the surrounding countryside where I found many species of butterflies that were totally unknown to me at the time. As I had plenty of leisure hours, later in the day I would occupy myself with setting the insects and mounting them in mahogany cork-lined boxes that I had made especially for the purpose by a local carpenter. I also collected other insects that were unwise enough to come my way. These included many spectacular moths and beetles that were attracted to the light at night. This also brought in numerous colorful geckoes that hung upside down on the ceiling and gazed down at me or fell into my supper. We were also visited by scorpions and other arthropods, so it was prudent to hold shoes upside down and give them a good tap before putting them on in case they were selected by one of these animals for a nap. Snakes were also frequent visitors. For my part, all visitors were welcome. When I finally returned to England, I donated a number of snakes to the Wellcome Museum in Euston Road, a wonderful center where postgraduate students in London were taken as part of their training in tropical medicine.

Accra was blessed with superb beaches for swimming with smooth sand and comfortably strong surf. However it could be exceptionally powerful on occasion. One day I plunged into a high wave and came face to face with a large fish. We were both surprised. Then the wave flung me down violently and I hit the sand with a huge thump that knocked the breath out of me. I managed to struggle out but feared I had broken ribs. Luckily I had not, but from then on I was more cautious how I surfed and made sure that there were other people within view.

I had good reason to do so. The airport was a transit point for passenger flights of Pan American World Airways traveling from New York to South Africa. The aircrews would change over and stay there for a couple of days between tours of duty. They usually took the opportunity of going to the beach. In August 1948, a young pilot had the gross misfortune to trip over a small sandbar, fall on his head, and fracture his neck. He became totally paralyzed as a result. Rather than keep him in the government hospital, the airline decided to fly him back to New York where he could receive expert attention; probably better than was available in Accra. The problem was; what medical staff was available to accompany him on the long journey?

An appeal was made to the military command and I was asked to take on the role of accompanying doctor. The patient would be taken aboard a Pan Am flight to New York and several of the female flight attendants, who were trained nurses, would assist me.

Inexperienced as I was in managing such cases, I could only agree.

The local US Ambassador ensured that my passport was appropriately endorsed, I was provided with a medical kit that included morphine, and off we went with the patient's neck suitably immobilized for the long journey. We occupied the space of half a dozen seats at the front of the cabin where we had ready access to the crew facilities and caused minimum disturbance to the other passengers. Our journey included stops in Dakar and Newfoundland, before we finally arrived in New York and were met by the pilot's family and an ambulance. Throughout the flight he was remarkably brave and uncomplaining and his general condition appeared to be reasonable under the circumstances. I later learned that shortly after being reunited with his wife and being admitted to hospital, the poor fellow died. It was ironic that this young man with the world before him had survived combat as a fighter pilot during WW II only to die as the result of a simple fall. He retained the strength of will to rejoin his young wife and then his body gave up. I was very saddened.

There was no return flight scheduled to Accra for a few days so I arranged to fly on to Chicago to visit my cousin Hal. On this memorable occasion, he once more tried to persuade me to work with him in the US and I once more declined with thanks. I did not pay another visit to the US for sixteen years.

From Accra I was posted to Takoradi, the port town west of Accra, where I was in charge of the medical center. I had to rely on the local government hospital with excellent government doctors and nurses for inpatient care of my patients. The hospital had an X-ray department with an excellent radiographer. From him I realized that my lack of specialized training and my use of an X-ray machine to which I was unwisely given access during my first hospital appointment, might have exposed me to a dangerous level of radiation. During many years of marriage, my wife and I never had offspring. Due to the relative lack of knowledge of the causes of infertility and its treatment in our early years, we never solved this problem and regrettably remained childless.

My stay in Takoradi was both medically and entomologically interesting. I had the excellent company of a congenial colleague, Bob McMinn, a conscript RAF doctor stationed in Takoradi. Bob later became Professor of Anatomy in the University of London. There in 1973, he and his chief assistant at the Royal College of Surgeons produced a revolutionary, photographic *Colour Atlas of Human Anatomy* that sold 1.5 million copies worldwide in six editions by 2008. A third member of our company was the army padre, a young, jolly Scot and good drinking companion. My faithful, French-speaking batman, Gabriel Mossi, was allowed to accompany me to Takoradi much to my delight. As I needed independent transport there, I was allocated an army dispatch rider's motorbike but I had never driven one and found it hard to even hold it upright. I was put into the hands of a tough RAOC sergeant to receive instruction. Having a good sense of priorities, he started by telling me how to throw myself off backwards when meeting oncoming traffic at a good speed. Fortunately, I never did have to take advantage of this advice. My sturdy motorbike served me well.

On one occasion, I had the interesting experience of taking the OC of our unit from the officer's bar and his evening drinks to pacify a group of soldiers from a northern tribe who were about to attack soldiers from the coast who, they claimed, were abusing their wives. As we arrived, they were about to storm the local police station. With strong words from the OC, and threats about my own supernatural powers as a doctor, we were able to forestall what could have ended up as a serious riot. Useful or lethal, I did not feel that a motorbike was the optimal transport for me and I finally managed to have a four-by-four truck allocated for my personal use. I had to learn to drive that as well as I had never driven a car before. It was an old-fashioned vehicle with a crash gearbox. Learning to master it was valuable for learning to drive other, more modern machines later on.

I do not recall receiving an official driving permit from the army, but it was assumed that I possessed one. When I returned to England they accepted that my army experience qualified me for a driving license. I kept it renewed thereafter. It was not until my wife and I went to live in Switzerland several years later, that I ever took an official driving test. In the meantime, I taught her to drive while we lived in Papua New Guinea where we were both given local driving licenses. We each had to take a test when we returned from Switzerland to live in England in 1966. In advance of that, we both took the precaution of taking a few lessons from the British School of Motoring before we took our tests. I was relieved when we passed.

I was not many months in Takoradi when the army decided they needed somebody to command the 37th Military Hospital in Freetown, Sierra Leone and oversee the health of the army personnel stationed in The Gambia. Again, I landed in a job that proved very interesting both from the medical and natural history viewpoints.

In those days, Freetown was just as Graham Greene described it in his classic story, *The Heart Of The Matter*. On social occasions one could recognize a number of the old-timers on whom Greene had based some of his characters. Moreover, the hotel in the town in which he lived while working on his book remained virtually unchanged. When I paid a return visit to that town in 1960, I swore that I not only slept in the same hotel room, but was accompanied by the descendants of the same cockroaches that he had enjoyed. As another strange coincidence, thirty years later my wife and I moved to a village adjoining Greene's home town of Berkhamsted where we lived for twenty-eight years.

Freetown is reputed to have one of the heaviest rainfalls in Africa and it was a rare night that was not disturbed by the incessant beating of rain on the corrugated iron roof of my house in the hospital grounds. The level of humidity, as well as the temperature, was high all year round. Every morning it was necessary to clean off the mold that appeared overnight on one's shoes, as well as shaking them upside down to dislodge any scorpions or other noxious visitors that arrived overnight. This climate accompanied a superabundance of plant life, which included a lush area of rain forest that covered the large hill behind Hill Station where the hospital was situated.

I learned that the forest was an excellent butterfly site when an old African collector arrived on my doorstep one day to sell me some. This was too good an opportunity to miss. I promptly befriended the man and arranged for him to be my guide and mentor to sample the butterfly fauna on the hill. He taught me a number of invaluable tricks for trapping these insects of which there was a very large variety of species and my collection grew rapidly. We drove my Land Rover to the edge of the forest, then walked into its depths along footpaths that he knew like the back of his hand until the day when I felt that I knew them by heart. I learned to make a large folding trap that could be hoisted into a tree. Once it was loaded with suitable bait, it attracted large numbers of such butterflies as the swift-flying, beautiful *Charaxes* that were extremely difficult to net. He showed me how to make bait from rotting fruit or, best of all, the dung of predators such as leopards that roamed in the forest. I would return home in the evenings to pin and set as many of my catch as I could. I stored the rest in triangles made from old newspaper. I mentioned earlier that this is an excellent way to keep them undamaged and dry for future handling.

One day my hunter was not free to join me. I decided that I was sufficiently familiar with the forest paths to make a sortie there alone. The rest of the story takes the form of an obituary to a retired engineer, Owen Williams, whose father, Sir Owen Williams, was responsible for the construction of the famous 'Spaghetti Junction' on the M1 motorway. We first met Owen when we moved to the Hertfordshire village of Little Gaddesden in 1979, another of life's coincidences that I mentioned earlier. I wrote the following for the local Parish News on July 21, 1996.

"We all grieve deeply the sad passing of a good friend, Owen Williams but I, in particular, have a special reason to do so. In 1948 when I was a young army doctor in Sierra Leone, I spent much of my spare time hunting exotic butterflies on a large forested hill behind Freetown. After my first visits when a local African collector had guided me, I felt sufficiently confident to climb the hill on my own. In the excitement of the chase I mistook the path and suddenly realized that I was lost in the thick rain forest. The notion of having to pass the night in the forest, protected only by a large butterfly net, was somewhat daunting, as it was known to be a haunt of leopards and other interesting wild life. Following what I thought was a sound principle, I decided to head upwards in the mistaken notion that I would be able to orientate myself from the hill's summit. Eventually I arrived, only to find that the trees were far too dense for me to see anything in the distance. Uncertain what to do next, I wandered about on the summit until, to my amazement and relief, I suddenly encountered a large water tank with a pipe leading down the hill. After following the pipe for what seemed miles, I arrived at a small encampment on the coast that proved, in fact, to be diametrically opposite the place where I had parked my vehicle at the foot of the hill to start my walk. I was safe. In conversation nearly fifty years later with Owen, he happened to mention that he was stationed at one time in Sierra Leone and, as one does, we swapped experiences about that fascinating country. I told him then how I had been lost in the forest and that my life was quite probably saved by coming across a reservoir at the top of the hill and following the pipeline down to the coast. Owen's eyes lit up and he smiled his unforgettable and ready smile. 'Funny thing, Pete,' he said, 'You know, I built that reservoir.' "

Besides butterflies, there was an abundance of other insect life in and around Freetown. Every night, large numbers of exotic moths, beetles, and other fascinating creatures flew into my house attracted by the lights. Naturally I collected and preserved a good sample of them, which I later presented to the Natural History Museum in London. First, I needed to transport my growing collection and that story will follow.

In addition, there was a variety of small, wild mammals in the area and it was not long before I acquired a beautiful, sleek, civet kitten that I nourished initially with the aid of a pipette. This little animal rapidly bonded with me as its surrogate mother and we were almost inseparable. It lived freely in the house and used to wake me in the mornings by climbing inside my mosquito net, demanding its breakfast. It was great company and very clean by nature. Unfortunately the time would come when I would have to part with it and this would be, I recognized, a traumatic moment. I was spared this, however, by the fact that my kitten grew into a young female. Before long she was attracting male company and began to spend time away from home. The duration of her absences gradually increased and, to my relief, one day she failed to return. I hope she mated up with a feral partner. Being the temporary owner of young wild animals, while always a very agreeable and rewarding situation, is also associated with the day when you have to separate from them. Later on you will read of other such occasions in my life.

As the administrator and CO of the hospital, I was obliged to leave most of the day-to-day clinical work to my medical and nursing staff. Of the few events that remain in my mind, two bear a direct relation to malaria, a topic that would occupy much of my career in later life, and one to my interest in obstetrics and gynecology.

In the late 1940s two antimalarial drugs were widely used; proguanil (Paludrine) for prophylaxis and mepacrine for treatment. Both were very effective, especially against the potentially lethal, 'malignant tertian' parasite, *Plasmodium falciparum*. Any non-African soldier who developed infection with it was immediately suspected of not having taken his prophylactic as instructed; i.e., a tablet of proguanil every day. It was usually possible to identify an occasion when the individual failed to take his tablet. I recall the case of a fellow officer who I knew had overindulged at one mess dinner to the extent that it was highly likely that he forgot to take his medicine the next morning. Years later, we realized that the duration of action of proguanil in the human body was so short, that omitting a single day's dose could result in a breakthrough of infection. Worse still, we recognized that such an action could be responsible for the emergence of parasites that were resistant to proguanil.

The second event relating to drugs was the night when I was called out to see one of the medical orderlies who appeared to be completely maniacal. He was a very large and normally gentle man from the north of the Gold Coast. However, at that moment he was marching up and down the ward in which he was supposed to be in charge, alternately shouting and singing, to the horror of the patients who hid in their beds in fear and trembling. It was obviously necessary to remove him in a way that would cause the least disruption to all concerned and ultimately we called in the military police. An even larger sergeant of police from the same tribe arrived and spoke quietly to the orderly in his own language. They laughed together like old friends, but somewhat more loudly, they kept on laughing and chatting all the way into an ambulance, and from there into a prison cell where he was kept for the night. The next morning when I went to visit him, he was completely normal. Further investigation revealed that he had developed a fever, perhaps malaria, which he decided to treat himself as he had ready access to the drugs cupboard. He had taken a large dose of mepacrine that he knew we used to treat malaria in our patients. What he did not know nor did I realize until then, was that a side effect of mepacrine overdose could be acute mania. Once he had excreted enough of the substance, his mental state returned to normal.

My obstetric memory relates not to a soldier but to one of the army nursing staff, an Irish girl whom I will call Mary. She was a young, single, rather plain, devout, and prudish Catholic. One day some of her colleagues came to see me as they were becoming worried about Mary's health and asked if I would see her. As the girl had not reported being unwell I needed her to submit herself for an examination. A few days later, she reported that she had fallen and slightly injured herself. With the connivance of the hospital matron, a wise woman-of-the-world of considerable experience, we arranged for an examination for Mary. To everybody's surprise, I found that she was in an advanced stage of pregnancy. Ultimately, it transpired that she was genuinely unaware either of her condition or, allegedly, how it occurred; rather surprising in a trained nurse!

We tracked her condition to one of the officers based in Freetown. The Brigadier Commander of the local unit hauled him over the coals and the girl herself, now known widely as the 'Virgin Mary', was shipped home. The incident taught me another lesson in human nature.

From Freetown, I made an inspection tour of the troops in The Gambia to the West of Sierra Leone. To reach there I had to cross the river to the airport on the west of town, then fly in a peculiar old plane that had two engines and a square body. This leaked badly as we flew through ever-present torrents of rain. Luckily, I brought an umbrella with me. We were so wet that I sat in the plane with my umbrella up until we arrived at Bathurst. It was the first and last time I ever needed an umbrella inside an airplane. In those days, the small country of Gambia had an unenviable reputation as a hotbed of disease. Many expatriates knew it as 'The arsehole of the Empire' and Bathurst, the capital, was said to be 100 miles up that organ.

Malaria and malnutrition were major problems there and the Colonial Office had requested that the Medical Research Council establish a research team to look into these. During my visit, I called on the team headed by the late John Waterlow to discuss their work. He later became the Professor of Nutrition at the LSHTM. I was so inspired by what I saw and heard that on my return to Freetown, I conducted a nutritional survey of our African troops. I discovered that the standard army diet they received had many suffering from a shortage of certain vitamins. This was remedied and I accumulated data that I later used to prepare my first medical paper that was published in the *Journal of the RAMC* while I was working at the London School for the DTM&H during 1950.

Before returning to Freetown from Bathurst, I seized the opportunity to pay a quick visit to what was the French colony of Senegal at that time. I borrowed a Land Rover from the army. In retrospect it was unwise as I drove alone down a very rough track through the rain forest, heading for I was not quite sure where out of sheer curiosity. I think I expected to meet somebody like Claude Rains as a customs officer, cigarette in mouth, drinking a glass of wine in the local bistro, while waiting to examine my passport. Fortunately, I took that with me. After a few miles of bumping along this very isolated road, I spotted a post stuck at the side with a small wooden notice board nailed to it. On one face was painted a crude Union Jack, and on the other side the French tricolor below which was written just legibly, the order "Ici on conduit à droite". Continuing a couple of kilometers, I came across a small native village with one slightly larger grass thatch roofed construction and a sign on the wall declaring it to be the 'Poste de Douanes'. I attracted the attention of a lounging villager who beckoned me to enter the house where I found myself encountering an unkempt European, in what appeared to be a sort of uniform shirt and shorts, glass at his elbow and cigarette, a Gitane by the smell of it, lodged between nicotine-stained fingers.

We greeted each other in French, much to his relief, and he summoned a youngish African woman to offer me a glass of wine, which was very welcome. I must have been the first foreigner to enter his realm from The Gambia in months and the poor man was delighted to have somebody to chat with. It was a lonely post and I wondered what misdemeanor he had committed to be assigned to this outpost of French empire. Eventually it was time for me to thank him for his hospitality and beat a retreat, but I wanted to ensure that I had proof of my visit before departing. We jointly searched his office and the building next door that appeared to be a sort of primitive post office, where we finally discovered two rubber stamps and a nearly dry inkpad. My passport was stamped with an illegible round stamp, plus a clearly readable one that told me I was in a village with the romantic name of Diouloulou. My host kindly endorsed these in partly readable handwriting "Vu l'entrée en Casamances ce jour .... 20-8-49. Le Chef de Poste. ....." It was tempting to address him as Monsieur Rains, but I do not think he would have appreciated the allusion. I arrived back in Bathurst unscathed and prepared for my flight back to Sierra Leone.

Finally, the time came for me to return to England. In some mysterious fashion, and with the connivance of Bob McMinn, I received permission to fly back from West Africa in a Lancaster bomber of the RAF, which was flying via Nairobi, the Suez canal, and Aden to an RAF base in the south of England. This was a great opportunity as it enabled me to take all the boxes of insects that I had collected during my tour of duty with my normal personal goods. A problem was that it was very cold in the plane and I wanted to spend much of the trans-African journey lying on my belly in the bomb bay from where I had a superb view of the terrain below. Nearing Nairobi, I moved up, wearing a fleece-flying jacket lent to me by one of the crew, and sat in the co-pilot's seat. It was approaching dawn when I saw the peak of a very high mountain, probably Kilimanjaro. The plane was on autopilot and it seemed to me that the pilot was asleep. We came closer and closer to the mountain until I could resist temptation no more and tugged the pilot's arm. He woke with a start, immediately disengaged the autopilot, and changed direction a fraction to port. We made an uneventful landing in Nairobi, but I still wonder what might have happened had I not awakened the pilot?

When we reached our destination, we had to pass through HM Customs so I hauled my large package of insect boxes onto the customs table for inspection. The customs officer accepted my word on the nature of the delicate contents. I was just about to remove the package from the table when a young WAAF, who had joined the flight in Aden, swung her bulging kitbag up onto the table and knocked my package to the floor. The customs officer and I looked on in dismay thinking that my collection must have been damaged by the stupid girl's carelessness. I could only pick everything up and pray, but the officer upended the girl's kitbag and tipped its contents out all over the table. It was a minor revenge, but appropriate. When my boxes reached home and I opened them, I found a remarkably small proportion of the collection was seriously damaged and some of those could be mended.

Chapter 6

Interlude in England 1950

In March 1950, I was officially released from the RAMC with the rank of Honorary Captain, and given early leave so I could commence the course to study for the Diploma of Tropical Medicine and Hygiene (DTM&H) at the London School of Hygiene and Tropical Medicine in Euston. That did not turn out to be the end of my military service. Thirty-six years later, I was appointed by the Ministry of Defense to the War Office as their Honorary Consultant in Malaria. I was told I held the equivalent civilian rank of a Brigadier, a post I filled until my retirement three years later.

Our home was only a couple of miles from Hampstead Heath so I frequently walked to that remarkable stretch of relatively unspoiled countryside that lies within north London. The heath was, and as far as I know, remains a wild life haven. At the time I was an active member of the Amateur Entomological Society where I met and befriended John Hillaby, a journalist who lived close to me. John, also a keen and well-informed nature lover, became well known for writing a series of books about his walks across England. He had a remarkable knowledge of Hampstead Heath and shared this with me freely.

Sometimes I wonder how I managed to squeeze in so many

activities during that year. My old passport records show that, on my birthday, I purchased the enormous sum of £5 worth of Traveler's Checks in preparation for another visit to France. Unfortunately, my passport only tells me that I entered Dieppe on April 6th, presumably from the cross channel ferry, and left Dieppe again on the 22nd of that month. Surprisingly, I have no recollection of that visit whatsoever. I must have started the DTM&H course just after my return.

At this time I was still living with my parents in their apartment in Maida Vale, which was a convenient distance from the London School and from the Natural History Museum in South Kensington. I returned from Africa with a large collection of butterflies. I presented many to the museum where Graham Howarth was curator of lepidoptera (butterflies and moths). He had helped me identify numerous specimens. That year I applied to become a Fellow of the Royal Entomological Society of London (RES) that had a magnificent library in Queen's Gate, just across the road from the museum. Although I had access to the necessary books there and in the library of the RES, it was apparent that no single book listed all the known species of butterflies from Africa. Therefore, I decided that, with guidance of members of the museum staff and the librarians of the two institutes, I would write my own 'Checklist'.

I'm not sure how I managed to study for the DTM&H, produce the manuscript of the book, take a spring holiday in France, and spend months working as a backup doctor for a general practitioner in south London all in one year. I persuaded an entomologist friend, Eric Classey, to undertake the publication of *A Provisional Checklist of the Butterflies of the Ethiopian Region,* a first book for both of us. It was published in a slim, limited edition in early 1952. Eric went on to become an eminent specialist vendor and publisher of books on natural history.

Spurred on by the knowledge I acquired at the LSHTM, much of which informed me of the mistakes I had made as a totally ignorant young doctor on the African West Coast, and a strong desire to return to work in the tropics, I looked actively for a new job. Through contacts with the senior staff at the School, I was approached by the Director of a well-known malaria research center at Amani, in what was then called Tanganyika Territory. As I reflect on my interview with this eminent scientist, I remember feeling that I did not want to spend the rest of my career working on malaria, a single disease. Little did I know that that was almost precisely what I would eventually do. However, I did not know that the Colonial Office, that would be my employer, followed a strict screening procedure of candidates for their service.

I did not receive any feedback from that organization for some time. However, in the interim, I was somewhat amused to learn from our apartment block caretaker, that he was quizzed about me by a man in a dark suit. He asked about my personal background, acquaintances and possible political affiliations about which, our caretaker knew little and cared less. I eventually received a polite response from the Colonial Office declining my application. I guessed that the reason was that, somewhere in the files of a government security office, they found a record of my transitory student association with the Communist Party.

That left me still looking for an overseas job. Fortunately, a new project was being established by a different government organization. The Colonial Development Corporation (CDC) was starting a major program in the highlands of Tanganyika, based in a small, very remote town called Njombe. They required a trained, experienced medical officer to care for their large expatriate and local staff; who better than me? I was employed and set off the following summer for Dar-es-Salaam, the capital of Tanganyika,

In the autumn of 1950, I passed the exams for the DTM&H. As mentioned earlier, I took a post as a backup doctor with a GP, Dr. Hoogstraal. I earned a modest living while awaiting news of a new overseas job. Our principal was an Anglo-Indian whose wife was a nursing sister when he was still working in India. They returned after the war to England where he settled down to establish a good local practice under the NHS. By chance, his senior backup doctor turned out to be a very agreeable young Indian who was a fellow student of mine at Barts. My brief experience as an assistant in general medicine was both interesting and invaluable in future years. There were times when I would need all the skills I acquired to cope with conditions I faced in tough situations, sometimes hundreds of miles from other medical facilities. Within a few months I reverted to being a general practitioner in a malaria-free highland area of Tanganyika for a couple of years.

In those days, it was normal for a GP in England to be called out to see patients at night. I remember one particular extremely foggy night when I received an urgent call to see a woman living in a gypsy encampment in a field a few miles from our house where I was lodging with Dr. and Mrs. Hoogstraal. It was very difficult to see where I was driving and even harder to locate the site of the travelers' camp, but I eventually found it. I do not remember what ailment the patient had, but have a vivid memory of the remarkable comfort and cleanliness of that family's caravan and the warm welcome that I received there. It completely changed my previously biased view of gypsy life.

My experience in general practice also gave me an opportunity to put into effect some of the applied pharmacology and therapeutics lessons I absorbed as a student. That was one of the subjects that I found most interesting; the other was obstetrics and gynecology. I earned the Barts Brackenbury Prize for my preclinical results in that subject. My undergraduate days had coincided with several major advances in the field, the introduction of sulphonamides, the discovery of penicillin, clinical trials with that miracle drug in which I was involved, and the development of novel, synthetic hormones. I must have been among the earliest to deploy estrogen for the treatment of menopause in general practice, and it worked wonders for a number of our previously long-suffering patients.

Chapter 7

Tanganyika and Wattles 1951–1953

The entries in one of my old passports remind me that I first arrived in Dar-es-Salaam, the capital city of Tanganyika on July 4, 1951. (It was later renamed Tanzania.) From there I flew to Iringa in the Southern Highlands on August fifteenth. For the past five years, Tanganyika had been the center of a massive and ill-conceived scheme by the Overseas Food Corporation. This newly formed department of the British Government grew groundnuts on a massive scale on 100,000 acres in a little developed part of the south-west. The intent was to promote the development of that region and provide a badly needed source of vegetable oil at home. Large numbers of people were recruited and sent out to set up and run the program. It rapidly failed for a number of practical reasons; mainly a poor understanding by all concerned of the potential problems involved in mass tropical agriculture. When the scheme closed down in January 1951, it had produced a paltry 2,000 tons of groundnuts at a cost of £49 million. The groundnut scheme fiasco left a number of expatriates looking for alternative work. Luckily for some of them, the Colonial Development Corporation planned to establish large plantations of the green wattle tree at about that time. The bark of this tree is a rich source of tannin for industrial use.

Unlike the low-lying parts of Tanganyika where the general disease pattern was little different from that which I had encountered in West Africa, the highlands above about 2,000 meters were relatively healthy for native and expatriate populations alike, with an equitable daytime climate and very cold nights at times. However, a major problem for the locals was malnutrition. The main food staple was maize from which a porridge called posho was prepared. Protein was relatively scarce and green vegetables, although abundant, were not consumed as they should have been. In years when drought or maize pests were a problem, hunger affected many people. Some sugar cane was grown and fermented into a potent local brew called pombi. They consumed this in abundance when somebody died and this could provoke further trouble. On one occasion we were notified that many people were dying in some villages not far from the district headquarters. Investigation revealed that numbers of friends and relatives were so overcome by pombi at the wake that followed each death, that they failed to get home and developed pneumonia by spending the night lying unprotected in the cold outdoors. This sustained a cycle of deaths as a wake was held for each person who died.

Njombe, the center of the Tanganyika Wattle Estates, was the site of the district headquarters of Ubena. The place was too large to be called a village and too small to justify a town name. It was situated at an altitude of about 2000 meters in the Southern Highlands, about midway between the towns of Iringa and Mbeya. The unpaved road from Iringa to Njombe ran through beautiful game country that lay at about 1200 meters, then climbed rapidly up an escarpment to Mufindi, the site of a tea plantation, then continued higher to Njombe. The entrance to Njombe was marked by a small but spectacular waterfall. Unfortunately, it was the breeding site for myriad vicious biting flies known as blackflies or *Simulium*. These are the vectors of parasitic worms called *Onchocerca volvulus* that embed in subcutaneous nodules in the human body. Inside the nodules, the male and female worms produce larvae that migrate through the body and cause damage to the eye. In many parts of Africa and Latin America the infection causes blindness. Fortunately, that was not the case in Njombe, but the heavy fly population made any approach to the falls very difficult.

A genial but firm forester who previously worked on timber estates in Burma directed the estates. He and his family were my neighbors and we became good friends. Nearby was the estate's clubhouse where the senior employees met in the evening. Most of these young men were expatriate Englishmen, but some had moved south from Kenya where they had lived. Some were born on farms belonging to white settlers. Life in Kenya had become very hazardous due to the rise of the Mau Mau rebellion. Such farms were attacked frequently and their inhabitants, both white and black, injured or killed. Fortunately the movement never spread to Tanganyika where there was little in the way of farmland taken over by expatriates and the tribal structure was entirely different. The house I was allocated was new and I had an extensive area of garden on the slope behind the house. With the help of a local gardener, I organized the planting of a large number of trees and flowers but, unfortunately, did not remain in Njombe long enough to see the garden mature. At least I hoped to leave it as a heritage for the future.

The country surrounding Njombe had long been divested of its original forest and had evolved into rolling hills and dales of grassland, interspersed with small, interconnecting valleys that contained relicts of the original montane forest. My studies of the rich insect fauna of the valleys later helped to reveal how, in the course of evolution of this part of the East African highlands, its original links with the massive rain forests of Central Africa and the Congo could still be traced. The wattle project entailed planting thousands of these trees, to replace the grassland slopes. The climate was delightful; warm and brilliantly sunny by day and comfortably cool by night. It bore a close resemblance to the Scottish highlands. A comforting log fire was a welcome feature in most people's dwellings. Njombe was the only center of trade between Iringa and Mbeya. Each town was well over 200 kilometers away. They had a number of stores owned by expatriate Indians, most of who had originally migrated to Tanganyika to take up government jobs. A British District Officer and one assistant officer, Brian Eadie, headed the local administrative center.

The only medical service provided was a small center composed of half a dozen mud and wattle huts with corrugated iron roofs. A very competent African medical assistant who trained at the famous Makerere Medical School in Uganda ran it. Patients with complicated conditions were sent by road to the hospitals in Iringa or Mbeya; no mean journey as I discovered. The wattle scheme had no medical facilities of its own, but my reasonably large house was situated on the fringe of the town and my kitchen served, on more than one occasion, as an operating theatre. About forty kilometers east of Njombe at a higher altitude was another agricultural development that cultivated pyrethrum flowers and sweet-scented geraniums. The first was used to produce pyrethrum as an insecticide and the latter produced geranium oil. In the center of this area was a Catholic convent, staffed by delightful and very down-to-earth nuns. It was there that expatriate British wives and Asians went to have their babies. I used to drive out there and deliver the infants, a skill for which my student experience and interest served me well.

Moreover, my training as a casualty officer in Tilbury also proved invaluable, as a number of serious incidents occurred during my stay in Njombe. Among many African patients treated in the Njombe center, I recall especially two. One was a woman with obstructed labor that eventually was terminated by a rather unorthodox but lifesaving technique for the mother, of delivery of a dead infant. The second was a man from a village far from Njombe where it was reported that he had murdered his wife in a dispute then, in a fit of remorse, tried to kill himself. First he attempted to emasculate himself, but with a very blunt knife. He followed that up by trying to cut his throat with the same knife, but only succeeded in making some deep but non-lethal gashes. At that point he was overcome by other villagers and brought in to Njombe in the back of an old pickup truck. By the time my African assistant and I saw him, he was in a sad but not life-threatening state and in urgent need of surgery. By good luck, another Ugandan medical assistant was visiting his colleague. I decided that the patient had to be taken to my kitchen to be attended to. We boiled the appropriate instruments on my kitchen stove, laid the man on my table, and the visitor served as my anesthetist using a drip bottle of chloroform and a rag for the purpose. The operation went well and the patient's wounds healed rapidly, but I was dismayed to realize a few days later that his eyes were going yellow. He was suffering from the toxic effects of the chloroform on his liver, a well-known hazard, but I had no other option. The end of this saga was sad and ironic. The man made a complete recovery from his jaundice and was tried for murder by a district court. He was sentenced to hang. In spite of my plea to the court for mitigation, the sentence was carried out.

Another memorable patient was an English wife who I recognized had a ruptured ectopic pregnancy, a serious condition that could lead to her death without surgery. On this occasion, it was clear that my facilities in Njombe were totally inadequate. There was a short airstrip the other side of Njombe at that time which could only be used by a small, single-engine plane. I requested the District Officer to call up a plane to fly my patient to a hospital in Iringa or Mbeya, but he was unable to persuade any pilot to accept this task as there was only room in these planes for one passenger. (There is now an unpaved airport with a 2,000-meter runway at Njombe).

The decision was made to drive the unfortunate woman to hospital. I accompanied her while her husband drove down the long, rough road. With great good fortune and skilful driving, we reached the hospital where she was immediately transfused and taken to the operating theatre. To everybody's immense relief, she made a rapid recovery.

Soon after this incident, I received news that an African driver had overturned his tractor and suffered a severe crushing injury of one leg when he was trapped under the machine. This was also a life-threatening situation for which my facilities were quite inadequate. Again, we had to drive the poor man, well sedated, to a distant hospital where, I am glad to say, he made a full recovery after receiving excellent surgical care.

My next and most nerve-racking case was a young English plantation supervisor whose vehicle overturned on a bad road. In this case, I was called out to see him on the spot since his colleagues had fortunately recognized that he must have damaged his spine. My examination showed that he had indeed broken his neck and was totally paralyzed. Luckily as an ex-RAF fighter pilot, he was a very fit young man. After improvising splints to immobilize him as well as possible, we drove him in the back of a truck to Njombe where a decision had to be made what to do next. There was no question of transferring him by air since, even if an air ambulance or helicopter was available, which they were not in those days, it was unlikely that they could land on our airstrip. We decided that the long drive down the mountain to Mbeya hospital was the only possible course of action. We set off at dusk with Brian the ADO driving while my assistant and I cared for the patient. We had arranged for him, carefully splinted, to ride on the floor of the covered pickup truck.

The road to Mbeya was bumpy and our patient, in spite of his paralysis, was in a lot of pain, but our only option was to continue slowly and carefully along the mountain road. At about 2:00 a.m. to our utter amazement, we saw the bright lights of another vehicle coming up the road towards us. As we came close, both vehicles stopped. We could not believe our eyes; the car facing us was a large, very new Rolls Royce! The driver was an engineer from Rolls Royce who was flown to Tanganyika especially to repair the luxury car that was recently bought by a wealthy farmer. Having completed this job in Dar-es-Salaam, he was returning it to its owner. We soon parted and continued on our way to Mbeya, where a skilled surgical team awaited our arrival. Happily, my patient made excellent progress and eventually recovered most of his mobility, as I learned some time later.

Although forensic medicine was not my favorite subject as a medical student, some aspects were of distinct interest. For example, an estimate could be made of the time that a corpse exposed to the elements in the ground had been there by identifying the species of flies and their maggots that had invaded it. This nugget of knowledge, combined with my inherent interest in entomology served me well. One day, a badly decomposed body was delivered to my doorstep by the police. They asked me to perform a postmortem on it to determine the cause and approximate time of death. The malodorous remains were surrounded by large and small flies emerging from pupae in the body. I caught some of these and identified them as species that are late invaders of decaying flesh. That fact and others that emerged when I performed the disagreeable task of dissection of the cadaver, together with data on the recent weather of the locality where he died, indicated that the man had been dead for at least two weeks and that his uvula was removed. The latter observation suggested that this might have been a ritual killing as the victim had resided in a remote mountain village where witchcraft was not uncommon. I was glad to hand over a report of what I had found and leave it to the judicial authorities to sort out the rest of the case.

Aside from that incident, most of my adventures in entomology in Tanganyika were an enriching continuation of the studies on butterflies and biting flies such as *Simulium*, horseflies, and mosquitoes in which I had indulged in West Africa. I constructed a new portable butterfly trap of the type I used in Sierra Leone. It could be suspended in a tree and baited with rotting fruit or carnivore dung. With these tools and accompanied by my Sealyham terrier, 'Shortie',

I wandered far and wide. I accumulated a representative collection, which included a number of new species from this region, a part of the country that up to then had been little studied. In particular, I was able to provide new evidence for the former pattern in which many species of invertebrate fauna was distributed from West Africa all the way across to East Africa.

The Njombe area was over flown every year by a huge migration of white butterflies. I attempted to keep notes of the numbers passing by; no mean task as the insects were so abundant. After a time, I sent my accumulated records to an entomologist who specialized in insect migration at the Rothamsted Research Institute in Harpenden near St. Albans where the data were integrated into a major reference bank. I also arranged to send a number of swallowtail butterflies back to Liverpool where an amateur entomologist, Cyril Clarke, bred them in large insectaries to use in his pioneering genetic research. In another of my life's coincidences, Cyril became Professor of Medical Genetics in Liverpool University where he carried out seminal research on heritable blood disorders of man. In particular, he researched the genetics of the 'rhesus factor' that caused many fetal deaths. He later became a Fellow of the Royal Society and received a knighthood for his outstanding studies. The nature of the coincidence was that, in 1966, I became Professor of Parasitology in the Liverpool School of Tropical Medicine, which was almost next door to Cyril's department, and one of my first junior lecturers was a defector from his staff.

Tanganyika held another major interest for me in that the main lingua franca was Kiswahili, a rich and logically constructed language. I learned as much as I could in the short time I lived there. Kiswahili contains numerous words absorbed from the languages of its former colonists; English, German, and Arabic. However, it has a distinctive grammatical structure of its own. Moreover, each tribal area had its own variation, such as Kibena in the Ubena district where Njombe is situated. My houseboy was from a neighboring district where they spoke Kiwewe. It was a little like parts of Switzerland where, as my wife later informed me, in addition to Schweizerdeutsch, a variant of the German tongue, each canton had at least one dialect of its own. It was essential for me to speak some Kiswahili in order to converse with my patients. As I enjoyed learning languages, I managed to reach a sufficient level of fluency to pass the first level of the government service examination. Had I stayed longer in Njombe I would have also gained a working knowledge of Kibena since I was taking lessons in that dialect from the District Officer's chief clerk who was the son of a local chief.

One day in the Njombe clinic, I had the misfortune to treat an unfortunate villager who had an excruciating toothache from a badly rotted molar. Although I had dental forceps in the clinic's scanty equipment cupboard, I had no suitable general anesthetic to use. Even if I had access to one with which to give a local anesthetic, as a medical student I was never taught how to administer it. My choice would have been to send the poor man to see a dentist if there was one in Iringa or Mbeya, but he pleaded with me to remove the ailing tooth. With some assistance I finally succeeded in removing the tooth, but was so sorry for my patient that I immediately made my mind up to go to the dental center in Dar-es-Salaam as soon as I could to receive instruction in the use of local dental anesthesia. A few days later, I drove the considerable distance to the capital where I attached myself to the senior dentist for a week. After that, I felt sufficiently proficient to return to Njombe without living in fear of having to repeat my, or any patient's experience, in the future.

About halfway home, I encountered a gang of road maintenance workers who were digging up the tough gravel surface of what passed for a major highway in those days, in order to resurface it. After waiting some time until they made way for me, I tried unsuccessfully to restart my engine, only to realize after a while that I had no petrol. My petrol tank was penetrated by a lump of rock sticking out of the partly dug up road and all my petrol drained out of the tank while I waited. I was at least fifty kilometers from the nearest petrol station. After discussing the problem with the gang's foreman, I learned that a couple of kilometers ahead of me was a large, Greek-owned sisal plantation. I negotiated with the road gang to have my car hauled there to seek help. To my relief, the plantation manager was a young English expatriate who immediately welcomed me in, offered me hospitality, and instructed his transport manager to repair the hole in my petrol tank so I could continue on my way the following day.

Although I was well versed in entomology, my knowledge of birds was poor. I could recognize most game birds since small parties of my colleagues from the plantation would descend the escarpment to the game country below on weekends to hunt wildfowl as well as the occasional small deer for the pot. This was a great opportunity to see other wild game such as giraffes, but for the most part. the fauna was limited to various species of deer and multitudes of exotic birds. In the course of conversation over a cool beer, I learned that my host was a keen and expert amateur ornithologist and taxidermist. He had a large collection of excellently prepared and labeled birds from many parts of Tanganyika. We were immediately on common ground and formed a friendship that lasted through my remaining stay in Tanganyika. It was an invaluable learning experience for both of us. Unfortunately, I lost touch with him when I left the country and crossed back to West Africa. As much as I enjoyed working in Njombe, I felt the need to seek a more challenging position and was interested in obtaining a position somewhere or other with WHO. At the end of 1952, I resigned from CDC with regrets on both sides.

The Tanganyika Wattle Estates eventually became a limited company, which has evolved into a valuable source of renewable energy. By 2005, it was contributing over 2,000 kilowatts of hydropower to some 4,500 inhabitants of the region through a 120-kilometer mini-grid. Sometime after my departure a government hospital, built partly to my amateur specifications, was constructed at Njombe. Over the years this grew to become a District Hospital.

In August 2008, a new labor ward and renovated postnatal ward were dedicated there, courtesy of the US Aid for International Development program. By then a separate hospital was also built for the Wattle Estates.

"From little beginnings..."

PART II

Chapter 8

Introduction To Ruth and
the World Health Organization 1953

My sister Ronnie had been a staff member of WHO in Geneva for some years. At this time, she was an Administrative Assistant to the Eastern Mediterranean Regional Director, Sir Aly Tewfik Shousha, Pasha, in Cairo. She mentioned my situation to a colleague of hers, Leonard Bruce-Chwatt, who was responsible for malaria control programs in WHO. His director was a quiet spoken, very distinguished Italian malariologist, Professor Emilio J. Pampana. I departed from Njombe in early 1953 and flew via London to Geneva where I do not recall even seeking employment. I was offered a post as Medical Entomologist with a WHO project to eradicate malaria from Liberia. This idiosyncratic West African country was governed by the descendants of freed American slaves since 1822. It was to prove a move that totally changed the direction of my life and that happened partly by accident.

On my journey from London to Geneva, I encountered a young woman and we got into conversation. As we left the airport she was met by a friend to whom she kindly introduced me. I have no recollection of my travel companion's name, but her friend's name was Ruth. We all had a drink together and I learned that Ruth had recently returned from working in England as an au pair with a doctor and his family. Before long, she moved to Geneva where she was employed with the Swiss branch of an American pharmaceutical company as a translator of technical documents between German, French, and English. One of her sisters lived in Geneva and was married to a Swiss-French man who was a senior employee in the air traffic control center at Cointrin, the Geneva airport. It was a weekend, we both were free, and I was delighted when Ruth accepted my invitation to join me for an evening meal. We enjoyed a relaxed evening together and agreed to meet again.

It was not until 1990, nearly fifty years later that I chanced to obtain from a Swiss Lexicon a deeper knowledge of Ruth's family background, which could not have been more different from my own. Her family name, Scheidegger, is familiar in Switzerland. As early as 1317, Chunradus de Scheidegga lived in the Canton of Bern. The original branch of this family extended over much of the Canton including the town of Sumiswald where many of Ruth's ancestors lived. Jakob Scheidegger, an artist, lived there from 1777 to 1858. Theodor, born in 1850, was also an artist and Samuel, born four decades later, was renowned as an author of books of history and of historical fiction. Many Scheideggers were farmers or politicians. Ruth's father, Ernst, a resident of Sumiswald, moved to Herisau, a small center in the northeastern Swiss German Canton of Appenzell, where he married Ruth's mother, Maria Gertrud Frehner. Ruth, their youngest, was born there on September 4, 1929 at 1:15 a.m. Her mother tongue was Schweizerdeutsch. She received her primary school education in Herisau and her secondary education in the nearby cathedral town of St. Gallen with its world famous library. Ernst instilled in her a deep love of nature. The Scheidegger talent for creative art and literature did not mature early in Ruth. Perhaps she was too busy skiing! However, her gift for languages emerged early. Much later Ruth's remarkable talent for creative art embroidery matured as you will read in Chapters 21 and 22.

The following Monday I paid my first of many visits to the headquarters of WHO which was situated in the Palais des Nations, the old headquarters of the League of Nations set in Ariana Park on the outskirts of Geneva. Pampana was one of a group of malariologists responsible for the elimination of malaria from the Italian Pontine marshes, a groundbreaking pre-war endeavor in the days before the introduction of the new generation of insecticides beginning with DDT. Malaria control in Italy was pioneered by a dedicated group of young malariologists. A number of them later helped found the original staff of the WHO malaria section. Outsiders knew them as the 'Malaria mafia' and among them was a man of early middle age named Luigi Mara. He was employed in former times as a malariologist in Italian Somalia and later in Ethiopia and Libya I believe. He was a flamboyant character with dark hair and a pointed black beard. He lived in Geneva with his petite but domineering wife, their young son, and a Somali servant.

Pampana, then Director of the Malaria Section of WHO, was looking for staff to accompany Mara and heard about me, probably through Leonard. To this day I am not quite sure why I was offered work as a medical entomologist by WHO as my knowledge of entomology was entirely gained through practical experience and the DTM&H course in London in 1950. Nevertheless, I became a medical entomologist and was offered a posting on the new project to be headed by Mara in Liberia. I accepted with alacrity.

It proved to be an invaluable assignment. In that intensely endemic country I learned much about the powers and limitations of modern insecticides to kill the mosquito vectors of malaria and about medical and general entomology. My eyes were also opened to the toxic hazards of insecticides to man as well as of the remarkable ability of these compounds to select mutants of mosquitoes, flies, and other insects resistant to their action. Moreover, although it was outside my assignment, I learned of the delicate balance between malaria infection and increasing immunity with age in the

African to which I allude later, as well as the efficacy or otherwise of our limited range of antimalarial drugs.

During the brief period in Geneva being indoctrinated into the workings of WHO, I had plenty of time to inspect the splendid building that it occupied. The main conference hall was especially imposing, a very tall chamber with extravagantly painted wall panels and ceiling, and a long series of glass-walled rooms on one side for a battery of interpreters. The gardens of Ariana Park were beautifully laid out, enjoyed a broad view of Lake Geneva and its waterspout, the landmark Jette d'Eau, and were embellished with sculptures, including one large, bronze, mesh-like world globe. Beyond the lake is the splendid vista of the French Alps. The Palais hosted a number of major international conferences including one in 1954 that marked the end of the French Indochina War.

Delegates for the international peace conference who met in Geneva when I was in the Palais, probably being debriefed after my Liberian tour, included such powerful figures as the USSR's Foreign Secretary, Andrei Gromyko. Security in those days was taken lightly relative to the world situation a decade or so later. So I was able to join a small crowd lining the door through which the delegates passed directly from their limousines into the Palais. A small number of uniformed Swiss police stood guard and, no doubt, a few plain-clothes secret service personnel. However, nobody challenged my presence or my right to take photographs of the delegates as they passed by within arm's length. One of my subjects was Gromyko and another the main Vietnamese delegate.

Years later in the mid-1970's I encountered another major political figure, the American Secretary of State Henry Kissinger. He was attending a conference in the Tanzanian capital, Dar es Salaam when I was staying in the adjacent hotel. I crossed the street to buy something from the lobby store in the hotel next door and arrived within minutes of Kissinger. He was surrounded by a phalanx of American and a few Tanzanian secret service bodyguards, mini radio-speakers in ears and microphones on lapels. I stood quietly in the lobby wearing a gaudy floral shirt and long khaki slacks. I think I was mistaken by the guards as one of them as nobody challenged me. However, all I saw of the fairly short Kissinger was his head as he was wafted hastily from the main entrance into the elevator into which he disappeared, squeezed in with his entourage. On leaving the hotel lobby, I was about to be challenged by a Tanzanian plain clothes security man, but I smiled at him, greeted him in Swahili, and went slowly and empty-handed on my way. Driving out of town later, I spotted the large Air Force One sitting on the airport tarmac.

The mid-1950s were the heady days of 'Malaria Eradication.' This global program was devised by Pampana and a panel of world experts on the basis of two novelties. The first was an ingenious mathematical formula that showed how, by shortening the life expectancy of vector mosquitoes, it should be possible to eliminate malaria. The second was the magical concoction of the potent, long-lasting insecticide DDT, to attack the insects, plus the relatively new antimalarial drug chloroquine to kill existing parasites in the human population. In hindsight, this was a dream program.

Later in my career, I came to know several of the savants including the Venezuelan malariologist Arnaldo Gabaldon and the epidemiologist George Macdonald of the LSHTM, who did the arithmetic. Other major figures who created the dream were Fred Soper of the Rockefeller Foundation. He masterminded the elimination of the most dangerous of the African malaria vectors, *Anopheles gambiae* from Brazil. This insect was accidentally introduced to the New World by a ship from West Africa in 1931. A further expert was Paul Russell, another eminent American malariologist from the Rockefeller. Macdonald's papers on the mathematical analysis of the factors governing the transmission of malaria were seminal in forming the strategy for the elimination of malaria that was accepted as the new global policy by the World Health Assembly in 1955, hence the Liberian project to which I was to be attached.

Many years later I told a journalist, "I set off for Africa like a knight in shining armor, to eradicate malaria with a bucket of DDT in one hand and a bottle of chloroquine in the other. About fifteen years later I returned and found that nothing had changed."

To my amusement, several years later I attended a lecture at the Royal College of Physicians in London where a senior Nigerian colleague, Adeotumbo Lucas, a major figure in WHO, gave a prestigious lecture on the control of malaria which he concluded with virtually the same words—but unattributed. In 1969, the policy of malaria eradication was officially put to rest. One fundamental reason for its downfall was the failure to include the human factor in Macdonald's equation.

I was due to travel to Monrovia, Liberia in March that year. This gave me the opportunity to see more of my new friend, Ruth, with whom I already felt a close affinity. We conversed in a mixture of English and French, which was very generous of her as her knowledge of my language, was far better than mine of French in which she was totally fluent. I knew nothing of the German-speaking part of Switzerland, apart from a brief visit I made to Basle some years before and I certainly had no knowledge of German. So Ruth offered to show me something of her home canton and to meet her family. They were most hospitable and, with Ruth's help as an interpreter, we found an instant rapport. Close to their hometown, Herisau, is a beautiful mountain area dominated by the Säntis mountain; the other side faces Lichtenstein and southern Austria. It is a beautiful area in which to walk and there is an abundance of wild fungi in the woods. On one occasion we found an enormous boletus, at least half a meter across but too old to be edible. Back in Geneva I met a number of Ruth's friends including a Bernese sculptor, Pierre (Pitch) Siebold. He had a house and workshop near Versoix, a few kilometers east of Geneva. He specialized in modeling with forged iron from which he produced astounding and original sculptures, some of which adorn major buildings in Switzerland.

Pitch was and remains a very modest man. For that reason, his work has had little recognition outside Switzerland.

With reluctance, I took leave of Ruth and we promised to keep in touch by letter while I was absent. We kept our word over the following year and a half.

Chapter 9

Liberian Adventures 1953–1954

Late March 1953 found me in Monrovia where I registered with the British Embassy; a useful precaution in that unsettled country. Mara, his family, and family retainer named Ali whom he had enlisted years before in the Arabian gulf, arrived at about the same time, along with an English public health inspector named George Wilson who was responsible for spraying operations, and an American administrator named Hayden Walling and his French wife. In Monrovia, we became acquainted with the staff of the American Public Health Service who were based there, including a very genial African-American epidemiologist also named George. I mention him in particular since, in later years he twice figured in my remarkable coincidences. We were introduced to the Director of Public Health and Sanitation, a small American-trained doctor by the name of Joseph Togba and other government doctors of whom two in particular remain in my mind, both German.

One was a Dr. Schnitzer who was an Assistant Director of Health. The other was Herman Knüttgen who subsequently became a Professor of Tropical Medicine in the University of Tübingen. Schnitzer later had the unenviable task of investigating the source of smallpox cases that were reported up country. His enquiries pointed to the victims having been in a part of the rain forest that showed no villages on the maps. He headed a small expedition, supported by soldiers and police, which located an illicit diamond mine in the middle of nowhere, from which they eventually had to be rescued by helicopter. Herman was assigned as government physician to work with us in Kpain, a village in the interior of Liberia where we established the headquarters of what became a joint program to eradicate both malaria and yaws. Yaws is a devastating, non-venereal spirochaetal disease, akin to syphilis. The director of the yaws program was a memorable Portuguese Professor of Medicine by the name of Fernando da Cruz Ferreira. He was a huge, jovial individual who, in his early life, was a wrestler and he looked every bit the part although he was a very kind and gentle person with whom I became good friends. However, he was not above putting his strength to good use.

We often worked side-by-side during our fieldwork in the isolated villages around Kpain. On one memorable occasion we arrived at a remote village after marching some miles along rain forest paths and the village chief had failed to assemble the inhabitants. Liberia at that time was, and probably remains, a lawless country with relatively little respect for life, but great respect for tribal hierarchy. There were several occasions when my personal freedom was threatened. As usual, we had sent a message ahead to the villages we intended to visit via the 'talking drums.' This usually ensured that the villagers would be awaiting our arrival. The drums were an excellent means of communication in the roadless rain forest terrain in the absence of such sophisticated gadgetry as radio.

After telling the village chief, through our interpreter, precisely what he thought of him, Fernando stooped down, picked the chief up by his ankles with one large hand, upended him and shook him gently, to the enormous hilarity of the onlookers. He told him that the next time he informed the man that the show was coming to town he expected its inhabitants to turn up! Faced with the delicacy of his position, both physically and as regards his reputation, the unfortunate victim could do little but to join in the mirth and assure us that such a mishap would not happen again, which it did not. I have little doubt what would have happened to me had I attempted to employ the same tactic.

Luigi Mara was a man built of a different cloth from Fernando. Arrogant in what I can only call an Italian style, he was reluctant to do anything that would cause him discomfort. That included making field surveys.

My task was to investigate the role of the local mosquito population in the transmission of malaria, which was intense in that area. I had a small team of Liberians to whom I taught the techniques of collecting, identifying, and dissecting mosquitoes. This was essential to determine the role the various species played in transmitting malaria and also lymphatic filariasis, which was also common in that area. This severe worm infection, like malaria, is transmitted by mosquitoes. It causes massive and disabling swelling of legs, scrotum, and other parts of the human body.

With my interest in mosquito taxonomy, I made a thorough collection of the local mosquito fauna in all its stages. We established fixed larval collection sites as well as those for adult insects. I knew perfectly well which species were most likely to be present in which sites. For several days running I noticed that the wrong species were becoming dominant in larval collections from a number of the more remote sites. It was obvious that the collectors were cheating by collecting all their specimens from a very few sites nearer to home so that they could then relax for the rest of the day.

I called them into my lab and charged them with this, which they totally denied. The next day I received a warning that I was likely to be thrown out of the country without delay because I was subjecting the miscreants to racial abuse and they had complained to the local authorities. It was only through the intervention of a more senior Liberian member of our technical staff who had political influence that this complaint was dismissed and the complainants were summarily sacked.

Liberia was a dangerous country in which to raise political hackles. Numerous stories circulated about individuals who were indiscreet in their criticism of various politicians, usually those of President Tubman's party. Their bodies were subsequently recovered, floating gently in the surf close to Monrovia. On one occasion I was driving back from Monrovia when I encountered a solitary man walking ahead of me. I recognized him as one of our more senior technicians who had not appeared at work for some time. It transpired that he too was the victim of a false charge of criticizing a local politician and he had found himself close to joining the band of the many political victims who never returned.

In spite of these problems most of the Liberians were hard working, hard playing individuals with somewhat liberal sexual mores. Our local village chief could not understand why I would turn down the offer of a nubile young village maiden as a companion and was convinced that there was something wrong with my manhood. My Portuguese colleague, in keeping with his national tradition, took another view of the offer and acquired a good local reputation. Social life took several forms in the hinterland. From time to time a prominent government administrator would visit. On one such occasion, we on the WHO program were invited to attend a gathering in the remote district headquarters of Gbanga, which was to be honored by a visit from President Tubman himself. In due course, we arrived after a long, hot, and dusty drive and were invited into a meeting room to quench our thirsts. The room was being prepared for the formal evening meal and a number of Liberians in shirtsleeves were standing around, or preparing the table. Being a sociable individual, I walked up and greeted some of them, including a smallish man with glasses and dark trousers with whom I chatted casually for a few minutes before going to the room allocated to me for the night to wash and change. Towards the end of a sumptuous and well-lubricated dinner, our team were invited to go to the head table to be introduced to the President. He turned out to be the individual I had chatted with earlier, but neither of us acknowledged that we had already met. After the dinner, a band imported from Monrovia struck up some enjoyable African dance music and we were invited to participate. I was joined by a delightful and attractive, rather fair-skinned girl, who informed me that she was the District Commissioner's secretary. Warning lights flashed before my eyes and I made a rapid decision to be extra discreet.

Discretion was generally a valuable attribute in Liberia. On one occasion, I was due to make surveys in villages that came within the domain of a tribal chief whom I had never met. It was suggested that I start by paying him a visit. This I did, accompanied by a case of good whisky that he happily accepted. Returning the courtesy, he invited me to dine with him and offered me the best his cook could produce, goat stew. It was a delicious meal, but so hotly spiced that I found myself obliged to consume it carefully, each spoonful separated by a large gulp of water. Even then, I ended the night with the most acute gastritis I have ever had and thought I would develop a perforated gastric ulcer! Another memorable meal was offered by the chief of a small village I visited. It tasted excellent, but the skin of the 'fish' was rather on the tough side. I noticed that my Liberian assistant was scraping away the skin on his helping. After examining it, he told me that he had never seen a fish quite like this and we soon realized that it was an unidentifiable species of snake. Frequently we were offered coconut milk to drink. This was excellent as long as we were able to drink it straight from the nut, but risky if it was extracted some time earlier, as this usually meant that it was well fermented and quite lethal.

In the north of the Liberian hinterland and the neighboring area of Sierra Leone, most of the population belong to the Mende tribe. The social culture among males is based around a widely distributed, secret organization known as the Poro Society. The local leaders were usually the village blacksmiths. During their long initiation period, young males converse in a secret language and employ secret passwords. The Poro symbols were the now familiar tribal masks, often decorated with fur and feathers, and painted sometimes with vivid colors. These masks were worn on ceremonial occasions during which individual society members carried a token of membership in the form of a small carving known as a Janus hand piece, a double headed figurine about ten centimeters high. On entering a village and meeting the village chief, I was sometimes greeted with a peculiar handshake that I imagine is much like those used by Freemasons in other countries. However, being associated neither with the latter nor any local branch of the Poro Society; I was unable to respond appropriately. These traditions were well known to an American medical missionary, George Way Harley, whose hospital was in Ganta, not far from Kpain. George was an expert anthropologist as well as doctor and an honorary member of the Poro Society about which he wrote widely in scientific journals. Over the years, he and his botanist wife Winifred, accumulated an important collection of masks and other artifacts produced in the region and they contributed numerous articles on the subject to the Peabody Museum.

The government officially took a dim view of the activities of the Poro Society. The members were not always in favor with the local government administration. On one occasion I had the good fortune to be present when police raided a village and arrested a number of society members. In so doing, they uncovered a rich cache of such items as Janus hand pieces that they informed me they would destroy. With the aid of a little softening-up gift, I was able to persuade the police not to destroy these precious artifacts, but to pass them to me on the understanding that I would take them with me when I left the country. I did this and eventually presented them to the British Museum to be incorporated into their anthropological collections.

Surveying in the more distant villages involved long walks along narrow jungle paths, which fascinated me as they were usually excellent sites for insects and I could collect en route. Often we were obliged to pass the night in a village hut. Early one evening I heard a group of locals approaching, playing odd tunes on pipes and drums. Very quickly my hosts bundled me into a hut, locked me in, and closed shutters on the windows. One man explained to me that I must not look out until the people had passed by as the 'country devil' was coming through the village. Since he stayed by my side to ensure that I did not cheat and take a peep outside, I was unable to see exactly what was happening, but I later learned that the 'country devil' was a masked man on his way to participate in a ritual in the next village.

One particularly bright moonlight night, I was awakened in the small hours by drumming and chanting. This time I was more fortunate. I got off my bunk and walked outside, to be greeted by the sight of a stilt dancer, resting on the roof of the hut opposite. On this occasion I was not incarcerated in my hut so I enjoyed the remarkable sight of the masked dancer performing his act in the center of the village, surrounded by singing and applauding villagers. It was an unforgettable occasion. Unfortunately I rarely used a camera in those days.

Back at headquarters in Kpain my time was spent in the laboratory where we found that as many as 5 percent of all the local *Anopheles gambiae* female mosquitoes were infected with malaria. The implication of this was that each individual in the village risked receiving somewhere in the order of forty infected mosquito bites a year. It was little wonder that there was such a high mortality rate among the local infants and children. Those who survived, however did so because they gradually built up a high level of immunity to the parasites that affected them less and less year-by-year.

The objective of our malaria project was to reduce the size of the local vector mosquito population by spraying the inside walls of all dwellings with a long-lasting insecticide. To this end, we were comparing three sectors, each treated with one of three compounds; DDT, benzene hexachloride (BHC), or the newest and most potent of these organochlorides, Dieldrin.

Anybody with fever and a blood film that contained malaria parasites received an appropriate dose of chloroquine. This sounded like a simple formula and it was, based on the principle that if carried out over a sufficiently large area for a long enough time, perhaps a year or two, malaria transmission could be stopped and, in time, the disease eradicated. For many reasons this proved to be a pipe dream. To this day malaria in West Africa remains one of the populations' major health challenges.

One of the first problems that arose, was that the extensive use of these insecticides resulted in the selection of insecticide resistant mutations in the local vector mosquitoes. Not only were mosquitoes affected but also the local species of houseflies. For example, in Kpain where Dieldrin was being used, these flies had always been present, but they were not especially conspicuous. Suddenly we faced huge populations of the insects that made life a total misery for man and animal. I collected some and tested their response to Dieldrin, using a modification of the test we used for mosquitoes. They showed an astronomical level of resistance. When I reported this to malaria headquarters in Geneva, my observations were treated with skepticism.

However, my report reached the eyes of an American entomologist who worked in another section that specifically studied the broader subject of insecticide resistance. Years later, in an international meeting in London, I was gratified to hear that my report on Dieldrin resistance in houseflies was the first from the field. Studies based on my observations revealed that such resistance in flies was paradoxically associated with a massive increase in their longevity. In the jargon of the day, we were producing 'super' flies.

In my spare time I studied and collected other insects, especially butterflies, in that little known corner of the West African rain forest.

Several species of so-called birdwing butterflies were known to occur in such terrain, but were very rare and extremely difficult to capture. They normally live high in the forest canopy, well out of reach of even a long-handled net. In the late nineteenth century one of Walter Rothschild's hunters succeeded in catching some that were later held in the famous collection in Tring. One day I encountered a Danish entomologist who was spending time in the north of Liberia and the adjoining ex-French colonies and we spent a short time collecting together. He had the good fortune to find a birdwing and I was able to photograph it sitting, half stunned, on his hand. Sometime later I was walking down a forest path near our base in Kpain, when I spotted another of these large insects that came down to drink from a puddle in the middle of the path just ahead of me. With bated breath, I very carefully stalked the spectacular insect. With a sharp thrust of my net, I captured it. At that moment I realized that, in concentrating on the hunt, I had walked across a column of massive driver ants, which immediately dispersed in all directions including up my legs. Suddenly I realized that I was being bitten unmercifully. I fled the scene until I was clear of the swarming ants and then stripped off all my clothes, all the while taking extreme care not to release my captive swallowtail from the net. I finally managed to free my body and clothes from the vicious insects and turn my attention to killing and securing my captive. It was the first and last such swallowtail that I ever saw in Africa. Years later, I lived on the other side of the world in Papua New Guinea where other huge birdwing butterflies appeared daily to feed on the flowers in my garden without the hazard of driver ants.

Among the major problems we encountered in our malaria project was the need to inform the local population about the nature of malaria and the reasons we were intruding into their homes with our spraying. Health education was clearly called for. In that neck of the woods, malaria may have been the most serious killing disease, but it was only one of a host of conditions caused by parasites and bacteria. Yaws, which was hyperendemic, was the subject of our partner control project. Tsetse flies that carry lethal sleeping sickness were abundant in some localities, especially around rivers, and this disease was not uncommon. Filariasis and other tissue-dwelling worms, as well as just about everything that could inject parasites into the intestines were abundant, leprosy was a major problem, and skin infections of all kinds were a serious hazard.

One day, out of the blue, a van loaded with a cinema screen and projector arrived with health education films complete with operator. The population of Kpain and the surrounding area were invited to an open-air film show that was attended by large numbers of men, women, and children none of whom had ever seen a film before, much less one that talked, sang, and danced. They saw a film of the life cycle of malaria, with commentary translated by a local interpreter. They were enormously impressed by the sight of a greatly magnified mosquito on the screen, and amazed by the idea that it could bite you and give you fever; but the sight did not move them much.

As one elder commented to our interpreter, "This is very interesting, but we don't have anything as big as that where we live!"

Later on in the evening a general interest film was shown to widen their appreciation of the world beyond theirs. I believe it was about the Middle East, and included some shots of people at prayer in a mosque. For some reason, the crowd found this hilarious, but this nearly had disastrous consequences. When the show concluded and the villagers dispersed, there was a minor uproar in one corner of the compound. Mara's servant, little Ali, an ardent Muslim, was so shocked by the total lack of reverence shown by the audience for his fellow Muslims that he went temporarily berserk. He had to be restrained by Mara and several others, to prevent him harming himself and those around him. Poor Ali spoke no English and only a minimum of Italian, while none of us spoke Arabic. As a consequence, he lived a solitary existence. He was exported by Mara, first from his homeland and then from Geneva. Mara and his wife were about the only people who could converse with him at all. Fortunately there were a number of converts to Islam in the north of Liberia. A call went out requesting a local Imam, who could speak Arabic, to come posthaste to Kpain to calm down the unfortunate Ali. The outcome was that Ali was repatriated as rapidly as possible. However, we never learned where he ended up from his boss. So much for health education.

Unfortunately neither Mara nor his sharp-tongued wife endeared themselves to the other WHO staff in Kpain nor to the Liberian authorities. The Ali episode was probably a major factor that led to his withdrawal from the malaria project.

I was put in charge until a replacement was sent out. Though I was officially the medical entomologist of the team, it also fell on me to continue the medical survey work that was falling behind schedule. I did this with great interest, sending detailed periodical reports back to Geneva until my successor, Dr Sam Avery Jones, came out to take over. Unfortunately I did not keep personal copies of my reports as they were the first to reveal the epidemiological status of malaria in that remote corner of West Africa. I was not permitted to send any material for publication since WHO policy is that nothing will be published until a project reaches its completion.

Over a decade later, I was passing through WHO headquarters when I was requested to call on the current director of the malaria unit. After exchanging greetings, he asked if I could tell him something of the malaria situation in the Kpain area when the program began there. I was surprised by this request and pointed out that I retained my personal files from that time, but was not permitted to publish the findings. I reminded him that all our work was reported back to Geneva. To my astonishment, he said nobody was able to locate any of those reports in the files, so they were in the dark about the start of the whole campaign!

I found this extraordinary. My successor was an experienced and competent malariologist who I was sure would have filed his reports at HQ. He was succeeded by another Italian, a young and respected malariologist, who also had a good reputation. However, I suspect he hinted that if anything was wrong with the project at the start, the fault should be laid at my feet, and not at those of his compatriot.

Another disturbing problem in Liberia, was the extent of primary rain forest destruction. It was not to exploit its magnificent timbers, teak, ebony, and mahogany, but simply to clear small patches of land as temporary gardens to plant rice and other crops. I remember almost weeping at the sight of huge, probably century-old mahogany trees, felled and left to rot in the middle of a miserable, deserted patch of garden. The occupants would exhaust the soil, then move on to clear another patch of forest and plant a bit more rice. This destroyed magnificent trees and decimated the wild animals that lived in them. Chimpanzees and monkeys were killed indiscriminately for food and baby chimps were no exception.

One day, somebody brought me such a victim, a young female chimp with a broken arm. She was terrified, half- starved, and screamed at the approach of a human. We pacified the poor creature, splinted her arm and fed her. Then the problems of where to keep her and what to do with her arose. The best temporary solution was to fit her with a nappy and keep her on the verandah of my house that was enclosed by mosquito netting. We did that and she rapidly bonded with me to such an extent that it grew difficult to free myself from her embrace when, for example, it was time to bed her down for the night. However, with time and patience she settled down, her fracture healed, and I needed to find a more practical home for her.

Fortunately I learned of a young American couple who lived near Monrovia. They took in orphaned chimps. I transported our youngster to them where she joined other infants in the Americans' well-managed colony. I believe these young animals were eventually placed in various zoos. It was not possible for them to adapt for release into the wild in Liberia.

Many years later, I encountered a center where orphaned baby orangutans were cared for and eventually released back into the Borneo jungle.

I have said little of the yaws project that was made possible with the introduction of oily depot preparations of penicillin. A single large injection could cure, or at least reduce the severity, of a high proportion of cases. In the 1950s yaws was estimated to affect about 600,000 of the 1.5 million Liberian population. The population has since grown to about 3.75 million.

Fernando and my teams often worked side by side in the villages. This proved both practical and instructive on my part. He and his colleague, Hank Sterenberg, found clinical signs of the disease in over half of the 20,000 villagers they examined, but additional serological evidence boosted their estimate to an overall prevalence in the region of 70 percent.

One problem we discovered was that a number of villagers were receiving injections for a variety of illnesses from local quacks that allegedly were penicillin. We investigated and found that discarded depot-penicillin bottles were collected and recycled after refilling, probably with unsterile water, and then sold as medicine to an unsuspecting population. From that day on, a large hammer was part of our equipment. We ensured that every empty bottle was thoroughly destroyed. Sometime later, during the rainy season when travel was only practical on foot, we were visited by a senior observer sent out by UNICEF to report on our joint program. At the time we had postponed a round of treatment as some of the roads were impassable for our Jeeps. He was a kindly old retired American banker who simply could not understand how we could let such a minor problem disturb our schedule. So much for visiting firemen.

Once Sam was well installed, I decided I needed a change, so I wrote to the Regional Director of WHO in Brazzaville and tendered my resignation. In due course this was accepted and I made plans to return to Europe. Nearly thirty years later, I was attending a meeting

at the Karolinska Institute in Stockholm where a number of enthusiastic young Swedish doctors told me about their recent field surveys
in the north of Liberia a few kilometers from Kpain. They were
excited by the high levels of malaria and other diseases there and
were planning what action they could persuade their colleagues and
government to take to remedy the situation. As I listened to them, I
realized that nothing had changed since the start of the WHO
eradication campaign. So much for DDT plus chloroquine.

My journey back to Europe was not simple. I had to fly from
Monrovia to Dakar and then to Chad to wait for an Air France flight
to Paris. From Paris I could connect to Geneva. All went well until I
reached Chad where I was told that the next connection was a few
days off. I stayed in a local hotel and spent interesting days visiting
the city and nights wondering at the origin of strange rustling sounds
that disturbed my sleep. On the second night I discovered that the
noise I heard was made by gigantic tropical cockroaches nibbling
my hair. They marked another landmark in my knowledge of
tropical entomology.

As you would expect, I took my Liberian butterfly collection
along. This included many small blue specimens; a special interest
group to a Parisian entomologist named Henri Stempffer. On arrival
in Paris, I contacted him as we had corresponded earlier. I received an
immediate invitation to spend the night with him and his wife in
their apartment. I was delighted to accept. I was able to make his
acquaintance at a personal level and I could benefit from his
examination of my blues collection. He later wrote and told me that
there were several new species among my specimens. The next day I
caught a flight to Geneva and persuaded the crew to announce my
pending arrival to Robbie, Ruth's brother-in-law. He was in charge
of the Geneva control tower, so he could let her know I was on my
way back. One can hardly imagine being able to do such a thing in
this day and age. It was an unbelievably happy return.

Without losing any time I proposed to Ruth and she accepted, somewhat to my surprise. In Liberia I had gained weight without realizing it. I soon realized I looked quite revolting, especially set against Ruth's slender figure. My aging parents were on holiday in Lugano, so we took a train there so I could introduce Ruth to them. Then we visited Ruth's parents in Herisau in the north of Switzerland.

From there on, events followed in rapid succession. I returned to the Palais des Nations which was still the headquarters of WHO. I believe that the Malaria Division had a bad conscience over the Mara affair. They asked if I would accept another posting; this time as medical entomologist in a new malaria project being established in the Nepalese Terai. The idea appealed to us both so I accepted the offer. The following day we sought a jewelry shop in the town to buy our wedding rings. Feeling slightly embarrassed since neither of us had done this before, we told the jeweler's female assistant what we wanted.

Across the busy shop she shouted across to the proprietor who was ensconced behind his worktable, "Alfred, les alliances!"

He emerged with a tray full of simple gold rings from which we made our selection. From there we took a tram to the other side of Geneva to the Civil Registry Office so we could post notice of our wish to have a civil wedding as soon as possible. A notice equivalent to the marriage banns that are publicized in England was duly posted outside the office and, in the ensuing two weeks, nobody claimed to be the spouse of either of us.

We were duly married there by the Registrar on September 18th 1954, in the presence of Ruth's sister Marianne, with her husband Robbie, and small daughter Eliane, as our witnesses. The 'Livret de famille' was duly handed over to me as the 'chef de famille', a Swiss custom that I found rather consoling, but that Ruth viewed with a certain mistrust! Ours was the 1,029th entry in the Geneva register of marriages for 1954, a vintage year for us.

A passerby took the first and only group wedding picture when we all went for a walk in the sun in the Jardins des Anglais park in the center of Geneva. Robbie drove us over the French border to a restaurant for our wedding lunch, before we returned to Ruth's top floor apartment near the main station, an apartment that we called 'Old Smoky' because it overlooked roofs filled with chimney pots of varied and strange shapes that somehow seemed picturesque. Then we left to spend a short time in London before departing for Delhi, the Southeast Asian regional headquarters of WHO.

While in London we managed to complete the necessary formalities by which Ruth became a British citizen while retaining her Swiss nationality. One of my unforgettable memories during our brief stay there, was an evening spent listening enraptured to Humphrey Lyttleton, in his Oxford Street club. Ruth was a great lover of good jazz, more than me at that time, although over the coming years she also instilled me with her enthusiasm, and such performers as those of the Quintet of the Hot Club of France and the Dave Brubeck quartet delighted us both. Ruth was an extremely modest young woman, and I did not yet know how broad her musical tastes and other intellectual talents were. It was many years later, when we were once more settled in Europe, that we came to share the joy of classical music at concerts in the various cities where we lived and where she was able to develop her exceptional artistic ability.

One of Ruth's favorite composers was Gustav Mahler. Some of his wonderful and moving music was played for her over fifty years later at her memorial service.

At the beginning of October, two weeks after our wedding, we flew to India where we hoped to find time to enjoy a brief, working honeymoon, before moving on to Kathmandu.

Chapter 10

With Ruth to Nepal 1954–1955

Neither of us had been to India before and Ruth had never ventured beyond Europe. Delhi in comparison was another world, not just another continent. How Ruth had the courage to accept my madcap decision to relocate her there after two weeks of marriage astonishes me to this day. She was both unbelievably trusting and very adventurous. Our backgrounds, our life experiences, and our religions were totally different, yet there was an indefinable affinity between us that even the worst of our future long life together could never dispel. We both had rough edges to our characters that would take years to smooth down. The conditions we were to encounter, in the Himalayan Kingdom of Nepal with such majestic mountains as Everest and K2 and far beyond, were not always conducive to that process.

In reality we knew very little of each other, either physically or emotionally. Our temperaments differed as greatly as our likes, dislikes, and intellectual abilities. In a few days we began seriously to learn a bit of each other's vices and virtues. In Delhi we were introduced to the WHO staff who oversaw malaria control operations in the Southeast Asian Regional Office. The Director, Dr. Mani, was a very capable Indian who was a Colonel in the pre-independence Indian Medical Service. Working with him and responsible for Nepal was a kind elderly Ceylonese doctor named Chellapah who was trained in England. During our induction period in Delhi we had sufficient spare time to sightsee in New and Old Delhi. In Old Delhi we bought a couple of ex-Army folding wooden camp beds and sleeping bags in anticipation our field work in Nepal.

(You will read later of my sister Ronnie. In 1956, she was rescued from Egypt and posted to the Delhi office.)

Of particular interest was our visit to the Taj Mahal in Agra. It was a short train ride east of Delhi. We arrived late in the afternoon and by the time we settled into a local hotel, night fell. A few hours later we had the thrilling opportunity to see the Taj for the first time in broad moonlight. It was an unforgettable sight and a wonderful way to help celebrate our honeymoon. Our return visit the next day let us see more of the Taj and the surrounding complex of magnificent Mogul dynasty buildings, but that was also when our previously unrecognized rough edges began to appear.

For some years I was an increasingly keen photographer, but Ruth had other interests. Before long she began to show resentment at the time I spent taking pictures. As it turned out, she had no need to feel that way. In time, with her box Brownie, she took a number of excellent black and white photographs while I squandered reels of Kodachrome in my sophisticated camera. Nevertheless, our introductory visit to the Far East was revealing and mostly enjoyable. We both learned of the pleasures and hazards of Indian food in a number of excellent traditional restaurants in Old Delhi. Notable among them was the Moti Mahal where we were introduced to tandoori chicken cooked in decades-old, traditional deep ovens.

Back in Delhi from Agra we met Colonel Jaswant Singh, the Director of the Malaria Institute of India, and his staff. They were continuing a long tradition of research that dated back almost to the days when Ronald Ross first demonstrated that malaria was transmitted by anopheline mosquitoes. Some of the pioneering studies on malaria parasites and the use of new drugs for the treatment of this devastating disease were carried out by Jaswant Singh and his colleagues. By the early 1950s, they were deeply involved in the early stages of the WHO-inspired Malaria Eradication campaign which I had already worked on in Liberia. I was fortunate in forming close bonds with a number of scientists at the institute. Two of their laboratory technicians were seconded to work with the team that we were to set up in Nepal, along with a young Nepalese who was trained at the institute.

In 1963 the institute was enlarged and renamed the National Institute for Communicable Diseases to reflect its expanded area of studies.

At WHO in Delhi we met a Bihari doctor, N.K. Mukherji, who worked for some years with the Indian Ministry of Health on malaria control. Mukherji was an example of an individual who enjoyed the role of administrator and the petty power that accompanied that position. Based on his experience in this role he was appointed as the Chief of Mission for the WHO team in Nepal. It was anticipated that he would be an ideal man to establish a close liaison with the Nepalese Ministry of Health. He would serve as the medical malariologist and I as the medical entomologist; and never the twain would meet!.

It was clear from our first meetings in Delhi that working with Mukherji would not be easy. It soon transpired that he was one of many ex-employees of the former British Raj who deeply disliked the English. He had acquired most of his administrative skill from the expatriates, but together with that, he inherited many old civil service bad features. It was not a very promising start as we soon discovered once we reached Kathmandu.

The overall disease pattern in Nepal was totally different from that which I experienced in Africa, except in the East African highlands. Over most of the country the majority of ill health was due to poor nutrition, respiratory infections, bacterial and parasitic infestations of the gut, and various skin diseases. Horrendous fly populations due to poor sanitation were responsible for many of the problems. As in many mountainous countries, goiter due to an iodine deficiency was prevalent. In the river valleys of the Terai south of the foothills that separated Nepal from India, malaria, visceral leishmaniasis, and virus diseases such as Japanese encephalitis were prevalent. Malaria control was a priority and the objective of our WHO mission. It was a major obstacle to agricultural development in that fertile and potentially productive region. Government medical services were limited and focused mainly in the Kathmandu valley. Farther east in Dharan, a British army hospital as well as a major recruiting and training center for Gurkha soldiers was built in 1953.

After a couple of weeks, pre-monsoon weather became extremely uncomfortable. We flew with Air India to Patna that was furnace-like, and from there, in a very rickety old Douglas Dakota DC3, north across the lower hills and rivers of northern India into Kathmandu. The interior of the plane itself was a change for us. A row of seats faced inwards along each side of the main cabin with baggage stowed down the center. Most passengers were simple local people, Indian and a few Nepalese. If my memory serves me right there were a few small animals. The Indian pilot invited us to stand behind him in the cockpit as we flew over the last range of hills and started the descent into Kathmandu. From that excellent viewpoint I had my first unforgettable view of the snow-peaked Himalaya range directly ahead. Ruth who was not a keen air passenger declined the invitation to join the pilot. She would far rather have traveled from India by road but none existed at that time. As we soon learned, the first motor road was then being constructed by engineers from the Indian army; of whom more later. Over the next few months we developed a considerable admiration for the old DC3s and the Air India crews who flew them. On one occasion we heard that one of these planes on the same route as the one we took ran into a problem that necessitated making a forced landing on a dried-up river bed well south of the capital. Through great fortune and skill, the pilot landed without striking any major obstacles or significantly damaging the plane. The passengers were offloaded and guided on foot by local residents to a nearby village. From there they and their belongings were transferred to the nearest motor road.

Air India was then faced with the question of whether their DC3 could be salvaged. A team of engineers dispatched from Delhi, examined the plane and concluded that the aircraft was virtually unharmed and safe to fly. The question then was how it could take off from the riverbed. They eventually decided to bring in a large gang of laborers to clear the riverbed of rocks and other obstacles and to render it as smooth as possible. Several days later, the workers pulled the plane to one end of the cleared area and turned to face the prevailing wind. A new Air India pilot and co-pilot got into the plane, revved the engines to full throttle with the brakes on, and to everybody's relief succeeded in getting the empty DC3 airborne and on its way over the hills into Kathmandu.

On another occasion, the Indian army engineers decided that the task of constructing the new road would be facilitated if they worked on it from both the south and the north using heavy machinery including a large mechanical roller. This worked relatively well from the south since the beginning of the southern sector was reached from India by a road of sorts. However, getting a road roller to the northern sector required that it was first taken to the Kathmandu valley. This would be impossible using only human labor. Air India came to the rescue again. Another DC3 was flown to a small airstrip just south of Hetaura where a road roller awaited. Army engineers dismantled the main roller, which weighed several tons, and ingeniously improvised ramps and pulleys that succeeded in maneuvering it into the interior of the DC3 from which everything else was removed.

With great aplomb, the pilot and co-pilot ran the sturdy engines at full throttle moving the plane forward. We stood well clear of the airstrip anxiously and watched the plane creep upwards inch by inch. A few feet from the end of the short runway, its nose lifted just enough for it to clear the trees. To everybody's disbelief and relief, the DC3 continued to rise. In about thirty minutes, it reached Kathmandu airport where it landed safely. If anybody deserved medals for skill and courage they were the crewmembers of Air India.

At the conclusion of our safe flight, we were greeted at the airport by courteous Nepalese from the Ministry of Health and driven in old cars to the government rest house, a very basic, small building in the center of town. Mukherji and his wife preceded us and, befitting his superior position, took over the best accommodation available. They left, no doubt with great pleasure, a rather wretched ground floor room to my new bride and me.

One of our first obligations was to make ourselves known to the British Embassy where we were welcomed by Ambassador Christopher Summerhayes, later to become Sir Christopher. The previous year, he was the first to convey the news of Hillary and Tenzing's conquest of Everest to the outside world. He and his wife were typically formal, old-fashioned diplomats who kindly invited us to dine with them and briefed us on a number of the facts of life, social and political, that we would encounter.

Having become a British subject only a few weeks earlier, Ruth needed to acquire a British passport. Mr. Price, the embassy's Vice-Consul, could provide this, but first he had to find one together with the appropriate official stamps. He issued what we believe was one of the first such passports ever delivered by the Kathmandu Embassy. It was issued on November 9, 1954.

Settling down in the local guesthouse was an interesting experience. In the absence of decent restaurants, we were provided a Nepalese cook and houseboy. The cook was a grizzled old-timer with a basic understanding of English. The houseboy was a cheerful youngster who we named 'Bubi', a Swiss-German term of endearment for a young boy. Our cook knew how to make two main courses, 'chikeni stew' and 'brownie stew'. The latter was made of buffalo meat since the cow is a sacred animal in Hindu countries. His method of chopping fruit and vegetables, as Ruth discovered to her horror one day, was to hold his razor-sharp curved-blade kukri between his feet and chop. I remember her coming one day into the sitting room of the house that we later shared with other Swiss residents and announce that we should not be too surprised to find bits of toenails or fingers in the dinner.

Nepal in the early 1950s was still almost a closed country. Apart from a very small group of missionaries, the few outsiders living there, apart from Indians, mostly worked for various United Nations agencies or one of the unilateral aid agency teams from Switzerland and the United States. This proved to be fortunate for us since, shortly after we arrived in Kathmandu, we came to know the Swiss group. They were by chance all Swiss-Germans who occupied a small house, known locally as a 'palace', in the south of Kathmandu. They generously invited us to stay with them. From there we regularly commuted by foot over two mountain roads to my working base in the Terai.

Kathmandu was a treasure house of Hindu and Buddhist culture to which our hosts introduced us. They had a very ancient, open-topped old Morris car, which was a great help in getting about, in spite of the fact that gear shifting was accomplished by inserting a large steel knitting needle into the steering column. The original gear lever had long since vanished. It usually worked.

Although the country was not yet open to tourism it did host the occasional mountaineering team. When we lived there two hotels, both converted minor palaces, catered to expatriates. The Royal Hotel was largest and was run by a colorful Russian emigré named Boris Lissanevitch. The Snowview was the other and had an Indian manager. The smaller hotel was favored by the mountaineers including Raymond Lambert, a Swiss, and Hillary in the spring of 1952, the same Hillary, who with Sherpa Tenzing Norgay, were the first conquerors of Everest in May 1953. But more of that later.

In the spring of 1950, Switzerland established its mission to Nepal. One of the first to take up residence there was a geologist named Toni Hagen. He conducted some of the first detailed geographical surveys of the country. Hagen established his base in a minor palace on the outskirts of Kathmandu and was joined there in 1952 by a Swiss dairy expert working for the UN Food and Agricultural Organization. His name was Ernst Siegenthaler who brought his wife and young son. Ernst and two assistants, Werner Schultess and Hans Mülli, initiated the cheese making industry in Nepal using the milk of hybrids between yaks and cattle called 'chauris.' Like yaks, the hybrids tolerated the temperature extremes in the foothills of the Himalayas, but they produced milk that was superior for cheese making. From their simple beginning in a single small shed came two factories that are capable of producing over 14,000 kilograms of cheese per year.

We saw little of Toni, who spent most of his time in the field. However, during his infrequent and short stays in the Swiss house, we learned a great deal about Nepal and the Nepalese. Toni subsequently wrote a number of classical books on Nepalese geology and expanded his interests to humanitarian matters, including the plight of Tibetan refugees who were flooding over the Himalayas from Lhasa into Kathmandu. He took up a post with the High Commissioner for Refugees for the UN and pioneered the settlement of some 2,000 Tibetans in Switzerland. In the early 1980s, he established the Toni Hagen Foundation Switzerland to further his desire to reinforce aid to Nepal and the Tibetans. He died in 2003 at the age of eighty-five just as he was about to depart for a last visit to Nepal.

Very few foreigners visited Nepal in the 1950s, but one of them was my sister Ronnie who flew to Kathmandu from Delhi in 1957. Somehow, Werner Schultess heard of her arrival and invited her to dinner in the house that Ruth and I shared with him and our other Swiss friends a couple of years before. In 1999 nearly half a million tourists visited Nepal. By 2008, over twenty-six million travelers from over 190 countries planned to visit the country where tourism became the biggest single industry

When we arrived the administrative center of Nepal was a very large palace known as the Singha Durbar. It was reputed by the populace to have 400 rooms but in the view of us outsiders, only one lavatory. Hygiene was not a major consideration of many Nepalese in those days and this was reflected in interesting ways. Nepalese men wore a very long shirt hanging down over their baggy trousers and it was a common sight to see somebody squatting at the side of the road with no apparent objective. In the market it was sometimes easier to see flies on the food than the food. It was no surprise that intestinal diseases, such as amoebic dysentery, were rife among population and visitors alike. Our mission was to eliminate malaria transmission in the potentially fertile flood plain area that bordered the Rapti River south of Kathmandu. I was anxious to spend as little time as possible in the city in order to establish a field laboratory and accommodations for my technicians and ourselves with a minimum of delay.

My team leader had other ideas. He was determined not to budge from Kathmandu until the Ministry of Health provided him all the equipment he insisted he needed. This was over and above that already sent out for him by WHO and included accommodation for him and his wife that he considered befitting of an international specialist of his eminence. In other words, he had no great desire to do anything and was not pleased when I took it into my own hands to move Ruth and my small team down to the Rapti Valley.

Our first move there from Kathmandu was on foot accompanied by a Sherpa, Bubi, and a small train of Newari porters carrying our worldly goods that consisted of about a dozen small wooden boxes. For some inexplicable reason, we did not provide ourselves with appropriate footwear, possibly because during my previous experience of fieldwork in Africa, the order of the day was simple, rubber-soled athletic shoes. The harsh ground and sharp rocks of the footpaths we encountered soon filled our shoes with holes, but it was not easy to find replacements. A short time after our first foray we were back in Kathmandu for a short period and were invited to attend a high-powered conference in the great meeting hall of the Singhar Durbar. I still remember our embarrassment at wearing our hole-filled athletic shoes, but somehow I doubt if anybody was looking at us and certainly not at our feet.

In 1954 communications between India and Kathmandu were very limited. There was a small airstrip about forty kilometers south of Kathmandu, which I referred to above. It was also possible to take a tiny, single-track train from Raxaul, the northernmost town of India, into Nepal as far as Birganj but no further. From there on one could drive a four-wheel drive vehicle over an alternately very dusty or flooded unpaved road as far as Bhimphedi that is located at the northern end of the Rapti River. On one occasion when we were living in Hetaura, we realized we were running out of cash but still had some US dollar Traveler's Checks. Rather than walking back to change them in Kathmandu, it seemed logical that we could travel to Raxaul where an Indian bank would carry out the transaction for us. We decided to make the long combined journey by car and rail to that small town. We arrived black with dust only to be told that the manager of the tiny bank there could not help us as he had no authorization to carry out such an unusual transaction. We went back on the train to Birganj where, by great good fortune, we found a small American mission station. Unsightly as we were, we were warmly welcomed, offered a shower, food, and shelter for the night and an offer to change Traveler's Checks for us, all of which we gratefully accepted. The train ride itself was picturesque, but it was hazardous to lean out of our window to see the view as many of our fellow passengers further upwind had the habit of expectorating vehemently out of their windows to clear the dust from their throats.

At Bhimpedi the road ran out and it was walk or horseback from there to Kathmandu. Although neither of us had horseback experience, one time we borrowed two horses from somebody in Kathmandu to make the journey southward back to our field station. Never again. On a very narrow mountainous section of the road, we encountered a small herd of buffalo being driven in the opposite direction by their young guardians who were walking between the animals and the edge of the path that overlooked a very steep and long fall. The horses, with us still miraculously on their backs, and the buffalos stared at each other for a few moments before the latter decided to run past us, fortunately on the outer side of the path. The young men held on to the leaders by ropes and, to this day, I swear they were swung outwards and suspended momentarily over the abyss like Mickey Mouse in a Disney cartoon, before landing on solid ground as the buffalos passed behind us.

We concluded our journey on foot and never again ventured on horseback. Where the road passed through the forest were large patches of wild rhododendrons that made a magnificent show during the rainy season. They were also home to hoards of starving leeches that latched onto any passing object, usually our legs from which they were hard to dislodge. On one occasion, we walked back to Kathmandu to spend some time in the Swiss house, when Ruth discovered that she had left some essential item of hers back in Bhimphedi.

In an enthusiastic display of marital affection I told her, "Never mind. Tomorrow I will walk back with Bubi and get it for you."

Each leg of the walk was at least twenty kilometers. So I walked about sixty kilometers in two days, arriving back in the Swiss house exultant but exhausted. For Bubi this was nothing, but my untrained leg muscles were so stiff that I nearly hit the roof when Ruth, just for fun, pushed her finger into one of my thighs. If ever there was a proof of love, I felt that was it.

The few vehicles, including the Rolls Royce owned by King Mahendra, that were seen miraculously driving in a small area around Kathmandu, were all literally carried intact by large gangs of porters up and over the saddle-backed range of hills that pass from Bhimphedi into the Kathmandu valley, about twenty-five kilometers further north. Nepalese mechanics were extremely competent in their ability to dismantle an old vehicle and reassemble it using the most ancient spare parts imaginable. The results of their efforts served mainly as taxis or small pickup vans driven in the confines of the valley. Many cars had virtually no brakes. We once hired a taxi to bring us from the northern terminal of the footpath from Bhimphedi down the steep road into the valley to save us the last few miles of the walk. We learned that the procedure for slowing or stopping this strange hybrid vehicle was to remove a rubber tube that led from a can of petrol between the driver's legs into the engine's carburetor. To restart, he would replace the tube in the can. We decided it was safer to walk the rest of the way, tired as we were. By good fortune we encountered a Land Rover being driven by Indian soldiers and, to our great relief, they stopped and drove us the rest of the way. Their vehicles were also carried to Kathmandu some time before.

To remedy the situation and to permit India better access from Nepal over a mountain pass into Tibet, the Indian government agreed with that of Nepal to construct a motor road, not just from India to Kathmandu, but beyond it as far as the frontier. One of the army bases on the way from India was at a village called Hetaura through which the existing road passed before reaching Bhimphedi. I was offered a room by the authorities in the Dahramsala, government rest house, in Hetaura. But one glance at this derelict structure that was used mainly to shelter animals was all I needed to decline the offer. Fortunately we had met some of the Indian army engineer officers while in the village, and the Sikh major in charge generously and readily offered to let us stay in their tented accommodations. They provided us with several army tents, one for my technicians, one for Ruth and me, one for use as our private toilet, and one to be adapted as a laboratory. To gain working height for the laboratory we had it erected over a deep hole in the ground. In the center of the hole we placed two stout poles so that we could place our lab table, chairs, and other furniture sufficiently far from the tent roof so we could walk about comfortably inside. Ruth and I were made honorary members of the officers' mess where we took our meals and drank our fill with our new colleagues. They were very genial company. When we had free time we would accompany some of them in an army Land Rover and on foot on local forays along jungle paths beside the river to hunt birds and small game for the pot. We were protected from the cold nights by good army rum.

Living in a tent situated on an exposed ridge above the river was an interesting experience since the area was shared with a number of larger animals, such as leopards. One night we were disturbed by shuffling noises. The next morning I spotted leopard tracks just outside our tent. A few months later we moved up river to Bhimphedi where I rented a small house from a local minor notable who had moved back to Kathmandu. It was a pleasant but rather spooky building. It was immediately below the foot of the path leading into Kathmandu and was convenient when we needed to commute back to town. It was a cool spot aptly named 'Chisapani gahri' or cold water center.

Before we left Kathmandu somebody loaned me an old army revolver and two Gurkha curved knives, one for each of us. The latter were potentially lethal weapons that required skill to unsheathe without taking one's fingers off. The revolver was less dangerous. The roof of our Bhimphedi house was frequented by rats and I thought it might discourage them if I shot one or two. My trial was futile since none of the cartridges I put in the revolver would fire. I decided to return the weapon and ammunition to its owner. A local forester based on the slopes around Bhimphedi kept an official eye on firewood collecting from the hillsides. The government was attempting to protect the local timber from indiscriminate destruction. Anybody wishing to cut wood had to obtain a pass from the forester. The pass was a dried leaf from the tree that he had marked in indelible black ink with an official stamp. The terraced hillsides above the river held a large, impoverished and under-nourished population. While the Rapti valley flood plains would have been a rich source of farmland, the hill dwellers had never succeeded in establishing farm settlements there since the incidence of malaria and other fevers was extremely high, and the level of immunity acquired by the hill dwellers was minimal. The object of our mission was to investigate the epidemiology of malaria and attempt to control it with the aid of DDT and antimalarial drugs.

In the 1950s the official relations between the Indian and Nepalese governments were tense, as were the internal politics of Nepal itself. However, the Nepalese had to depend on India for numerous functions such as the postal service. The limited amount of internal mail was handled by the Nepalese postal service and country stamps were issued for many years, but postal communication with the outside world passed through the Indian postal service that maintained a post office in Kathmandu. All our mail sent home bore Indian stamps. The mail we sent to Europe and incoming mail traveled through that office. We were amused when our local grape-vine one day told us the previous post of a new junior official appointed to the large Indian embassy in Kathmandu was Berlin. I believe that no more than a handful of Nepalis had the faintest knowledge of German, but several expatriates living there were Swiss-German and normally communicated in the German language between themselves in Nepal and in their letters to Europe.

A great deal of paranoia was in the air related to the Indo-Nepali relationship and in the rivalry between the main Nepalese political parties. In 1958 a writer by the name of Elizabeth Comber who was invited to Nepal at the time of the new King's coronation, published a popular book under the pseudonym of Han Suyin, titled *The Mountain Is Young*. She wrote a remarkably accurate account of life in Kathmandu shortly after we lived there, of the political infighting, the opening of Nepal to tourism and its consequences. She wrote of the terse relations between the few Christian missionaries and local inhabitants and between each other, the expatriate staff of the UN, and other national and international bodies, and a number of the Indian military staff then living in the country. The senior military man was a handsome Brigadier engineer, a very capable and likeable Madrasi who was responsible for the later stages of construction of the Nepal-Tibet highway. Ruth and I were asked by our Sikh host to vacate our tents in their Hetaura base temporarily in case, during one of his periodical visits, the Brigadier discovered we, as unofficial members of his army, lived there. I met him later and realized that, had he known, he would have been greatly amused.

The majority of Nepalis were either Hindu or Buddhist and the villages and small towns of the valleys were rich in Hindu architecture and artifacts. In the middle of the main Durbar Square was a massive, terrifying statue of the God Kali, and the streets were a hazard for all due to the numbers of sacred cows that meandered about. I was obliged to apply for a Nepali driving license, a curious requirement for a country with very few motor vehicles at the time. But I took a driving test and have the license to prove it. After half an hour with me driving about five miles per hour through the main streets of the city, my inspector agreed to pass me, but warned me that it would be very dangerous for all concerned if I persisted in driving so fast. The highlight of the Buddhist community, which rapidly increased its size by Tibetan flight into Nepal following the Chinese invasion of their country, was the huge stupa at Swayambunath. It was also known as the 'monkey temple' because of the large population of wild macaques that inhabited the area. The

Chini Lama, the representative of the Dalai Lama, lived near this temple. The Dalai Lama was moving between Lhasa and Delhi at that time, trying to gain support for his people from the outside world. We paid a courtesy visit to the Chini Lama who offered us a cup of chang, hot tea with rancid butter, a popular drink with the Tibetans. It was quite revolting and I managed to empty my cup surreptitiously into a large plant pot near my chair. My observant hosts quickly spotted my empty cup and refilled it, so I drank it in their full sight to save face and avoid a refill.

For expatriates living in or around Kathmandu and the few foreign visitors, the largest hotel and focus of social life was the Royal Hotel, a converted palace run by Boris, a colorful, larger than life White Russian whose life story was well told in the book *Tiger For Breakfast* by Michel Peissel in 1966. The hotel was frequented by a number of influential Nepalese including the young Third Prince, a good friend of Boris's second wife, an attractive young half-Danish girl named Inger. Because of the increasing tension that existed between the major political parties, a state of curfew existed in Kathmandu and it was unwise to move unescorted, or without a password, through the city after dark. On more than one occasion Ruth and I were glad to be driven back to the Swiss house by some of the prince's Gurkha retinue, with a piece of paper in my hand on which was written "Password" in large letters.

On another occasion, we were entertained by Nepali friends at Boris's enjoying the juices of a delicious curry that we were consuming on one hand with a glass of Boris's hooch in the other when a sudden hush fell over the company. A small procession of Nepali men entered the large room and walked quietly across to take their place opposite us. Gradually the conversation picked up again, but in a rather more subdued fashion. One of our hosts discreetly informed us that the newcomers included opposition party leaders who were at loggerheads with the ruling royalists at the time. Fortunately the political mayhem that followed commenced long after our departure from Nepal. At the time we were in the country nobody would have dreamed that a large part of the royal family would be assassinated one day by one of their own family, and that it would not be long before an entirely new system of government was established by the former Maoist rebels.

For Ruth and me Boris's hotel was a refuge to which we retreated from time to time for a bootleg drink and a meal. On one splendid occasion, it was a Christmas holiday complete with hot water in a bath. One of the hotel's attractions was a delightful pet red panda that was fondly called 'Panduli'. These rare animals are related to the giant pandas of China and are a threatened species that are becoming ever more so as agriculture develops in their home territories at the foot of the Himalayas. Ruth whose skill at sewing and embroidery knew no limits, created a magnificent blazer as my Christmas present from green beize that she managed to find in the market. When flattened out, it reminded me of a crumpled billiard tabletop but, on my back it was a triumph. For her I had the good fortune to meet a Tibetan refugee from whom I bought three very unusual, long ovoid stone beads made from agate. Years later we learned that these 'Dzi beads' are exceptionally rare, their origin is a mystery, and they are held in high regard by the Tibetans who attribute magical properties to them. Some of the beads have been dated back to around 2,000 BC. To this day, it is unknown how artists of old marked mark them with indelible designs. Modern craftsmen are unable to replicate them in modern imitations currently manufactured in the Far East.

About halfway through our stay in Nepal, we moved back into the Swiss house at Jawalakhel. This is a suburb of Kathmandu south of the Bagmati river on the northern bank where funeral pyres stood and unpleasant, meaty fumes often reached our noses on the wind. By then we had made friends with a congenial group of American aid workers. They set up headquarters in a plush palace in town and generously invited us from time to time for a hot bath and a meal.

The only other place we ever had a hot bath was at Boris's hotel when we went there to spend the Christmas holiday. The Americans told me that their government agreed with the Nepalese to post a man to help in malaria control operations in the Rapti valley, but his arrival was delayed until they could find him accommodations. They finally arranged to send a well-furnished mobile home from India. It was deposited at the foot of the escarpment where the army officers' mess and our tents were based. I remember going to see the locked vehicle. Even through the windows it made my mouth water as it would have made a superb home for Ruth and me.

We heard later that the malaria expert finally arrived, took one look at the luxurious mobile home and forcibly said, "If that is the best our government is able to provide, they will have to find another man for the job."

Within days he returned to the US. Shortly after we left Nepal, the US government built a splendid two-story house for their field staff in Hetaura on the very site where we had pitched our tents.

About thirteen years after I terminated my contract with WHO I paid a return visit to Nepal and flew over the route we had walked from Bhimphedi into Kathmandu by helicopter. It was astounding and gratifying to see that the entire Rapti valley was converted into lush farmland, well dotted with villages, and clearly highly productive with a wide variety of food crops. During my return visit a young American couple invited me to take tea with them in the house. I listened patiently while they poured their hearts out about the terrible life they led there. They could only have supplies flown in once a week from Kathmandu by helicopter. Nothing, but nothing could ever be accomplished in the way of reducing malaria in the Rapti valley and so on they went. I tried to explain quietly that since our time there, a succession of expatriates had spent their year or so on the job and each left with the impression, as indeed had I that little would ever be achieved. However, seeing the situation in 1954 and again at this late stage, I reassured them that the little each team had achieved added up to a considerable success in turning steaming empty jungle into a thriving, wealthy food basket for a significant proportion of the Nepalese population. I didn't go into details of the living conditions my new bride and I had tolerated in our tent that was situated a few yards from their splendid house. There was no mistaking the location as a solitary tree that flourished a few meters from our tent was now a tall, bare but proud relict of that tree.

In spite of all the difficulties we faced, my technicians and I succeeded in revealing much of the epidemiology of the area. That, in turn, laid the groundwork for the eventual control of malaria in the Terai, but not by our friend Mukherji. He finally was the master of his own fate. The Nepalese Ministry of Health became so frustrated with his constant niggling over his requirements and his failure to make a start on actual control operations, that they requested WHO headquarters in Delhi to replace him.

In sheer frustration I decided to resign from WHO, for the second time, because of the turmoil in our lives caused by working under the direction of our very incompetent project leader who did his best to block my contribution to the progress of the program. Worse still, he delighted in making life as difficult as he could for Ruth and me, even writing a scurrilous annual report about me back to Delhi. Fortunately it was a WHO rule that the subject of such a report had the obligation to scrutinize it prior to its dispatch and the right to add his own comments. I did that in no uncertain measure.

One evening in the 'palace' in Kathmandu we sat down to discuss what our next career move should be. My first step had been to resign from WHO. I would shortly be out of a job, short of funds, and we would be on our way back to Europe. I had written to an old friend and colleague from my days in Accra, Derek Eaton. I learned that he was in Canada working with a government program to develop health services for various Eskimo communities. Derek suggested that we might consider joining him there and we were seriously thinking about doing that. However, Canada did seem rather a contrast from the warmer climates to which we were adapted.

We pondered other possibilities while sitting in our little room in Kathmandu that constantly rained a dust composed of dehydrated droppings from the numerous pigeons that nested in the roof. Each morning we beat a tattoo on the ceiling with a broom handle to stop the noisy cooing that woke us up and received another shower. Reflecting on which part of the tropics might attract us to go to next, we looked for a world map, but the only one we found was a tiny one in the back of a small diary. We took a pin, closed our eyes and took turns in sticking the pin into the map to see where it would land. For the first few attempts it arrived either in the middle of an ocean or an unpromising corner of a cold continent.

Finally one of us struck gold, Australia! I recalled that Australia had something called a 'flying doctor service'. Apart from the obvious likelihood that it served remote outlying communities of that massive country, we knew nothing about it. However, it seemed to be a challenging prospect and I impulsively wrote a letter expressing an interest in the organization. I posted it to a government body in Canberra more in fun than expecting a response.

We promptly forgot about it and started to prepare for our return to Europe. We departed from Kathmandu on March 22, 1955 and headed back to the WHO Regional HQ in New Delhi, where two years later, my sister Ronnie worked with a senior assistant of the Regional Director, Dr. Mani. There we were mildly chastised by the Director for daring to oppose my project chief, Mukherji. Even though in the meantime, he was withdrawn from his post following protests from the Nepalese government. We got sympathy from the kindly Ceylonese Assistant Regional Director who asked me to withdraw my resignation from WHO so they could find me another field post. However, twice bitten forever shy. I certainly had no intention of exposing my young wife to another situation as frustrating as that she had faced in Nepal. So we flew back to London with a short break in Hong Kong for a few days' respite.

In retrospect, I realized recently that, for the first time, I did not make any serious inroads into the local butterfly population. When I reflect on the reasons for this I find three. I was very busy with my mosquito studies, experienced butterfly collectors had already hunted in the area where we lived and worked, and, probably the most important, I was no longer lonely. I would stay that way for the next half century, but I did not come back empty handed. I had a small bottle of alcohol in which two wingless flies, about the size of houseflies were preserved. I found them parasitizing a mongrel puppy that Ruth befriended during our brief stay in the Royal Hotel. The flies, to my disappointment, did not turn out to be a new species.

Chapter 11

Papua New Guinea, Ruth and Babar 1955–1961

My parents in London rented a flat for us in Maida Vale close to their home and opposite a block of flats in which my eldest sister, Pete, and her husband lived. While there, I received another invitation to join Derek and his new wife in Canada. He had divorced his first wife who I knew in Accra. Abandoning thoughts of returning to a hot climate and with no specific job in view, I persuaded Ruth that Canada offered us a future and promptly purchased two boat tickets to the New World. It was almost winter in England, which reminded us, that we needed something warm to wear in Canada. With little left in the bank, we went shopping for warm woollies and coats. About a week before we were due to depart, a letter came from the Australian embassy in London asking me to go there for an interview that I did. I expected a possible offer to work with the flying doctor service. I was surprised to receive an offer to go to New Guinea, the second biggest island in the World, to develop a program to control malaria.

I returned to the flat and gave Ruth the choice of going to cold Canada to look for a job or hot New Guinea where one awaited me. The following day I accepted the latter option, got a refund on our boat tickets, wrote an apologetic letter to Derek, and booked tickets for a flight to Switzerland to see Ruth's family before setting off again. Our travel to the Antipodes was to be via Sydney on the good ship Canberra. It was to depart a couple of days before Christmas 1955. We returned to London to spend our last weeks with my family, to dispose of our new, unused winter clothes, and to buy a few that were suitable to a month-long, first-class sea voyage to Australia. While in London awaiting our next move, we took a short-term rental on a small flat adjoining Hyde Park near Marble Arch. One day we went out and bought a boxer puppy. Why we did I no longer remember, except Ruth had always wanted a dog. (The small wild animal she acquired in Kathmandu could not be brought back to England, much as Ruth would have liked to keep it). In retrospect, I cannot imagine a more stupid thing to do, but it was done. It took most of my remaining scanty resources to have this monster vaccinated, certified, insured, packed, and shipped ready for sailing by Christmas. He had such huge floppy ears we called him Babar after the elephant. Meanwhile he was a source of amusement and embarrassment. When I took Babar for walks along the path in Hyde Park I was approached by numerous young 'ladies' to see if we needed company.

The day of departure arrived, Babar in the shipper's van and us by train, to be reunited on board the Canberra at Southampton en route for Australia. We sailed a couple of days before Christmas. We spent Christmas in our cabin as we crossed the Bay of Biscay on a stormy night. Heavy furniture slid from side to side across the first class lounge but few passengers were watching it. A magnificent Christmas buffet meal was set out by the chef and his staff. He and the officers were probably the only ones who appreciated it. It was not the happiest Christmas Ruth and I experienced. After a day or two people emerged in ones and twos from their cabins, all looking hungry but still a shade of green. From there on our journey was more of a luxury cruise rather than a forced migration.

At the time, my sister was still working in Egypt. The Canberra was due to berth at Alexandria before entering the Suez Canal, so Ronnie persuaded two of her Egyptian colleagues to give her a lift to meet us on the ship; the second time she met Ruth. In October 1956, Ronnie and other WHO staff had to flee Alexandria on an American battleship as refugees when Britain attacked the Suez Canal. New Year's eve of 1955–1956 saw us pass through the Canal in style, celebrating with all and sundry and flinging empty champagne glasses overboard with great gusto.

During the journey, when the weather was suitable, we were able to join Babar who was allowed to exercise in a dog pen on deck. He seemed to be enjoying the journey more than were we. Unfortunately, he was separated from us and transferred into the Australian quarantine center on our arrival in Sydney. He parted from us a small puppy, rejoined us in Port Moresby, Papua, several months later, a handsome, half-grown dog, with large floppy ears, and was as huge a delight for Ruth as ever.

After leaving the Canal we headed for Bombay for refueling. There was little to help us pass the time in the port so most passengers relaxed in the lounges and bars. Those who wished for a cool scotch and soda were told that no alcohol was allowed, even on board ship. In those days, the Indian authorities enforced a strict ban on alcohol. This presented no problem to our enterprising barman who served our refreshments in colorful teapots with matching cups and saucers. Dinner most evenings on the Canberra was formal, evening dress for the ladies and white evening suit for the men. This went against the grain for Ruth and me, but I had a tropical evening suit made before we left Geneva and Ruth bought an elegant green evening dress. It required all her ingenuity to make her dress look like several different ones by adding or subtracting various bits and pieces as the evenings passed. This was complicated in that everybody was allocated a place at a table for ten people on our second night aboard and we sat there each night for six weeks. A ship's officer at each table acted as host, so there was no escape. Our host, a young man, for some reason considered it his duty to peel grapes to present to the ladies at his table. By the end of the trip we wished never to see a grape again.

Most of the women seemed to have a different dress every evening, but we suspected that some of them adopted the same tactic as Ruth. On warm bright nights after dinner, it was a great pleasure to stand on deck and watch the vivid fluorescence on the water as the waves broke over the bow. During the day we were often accompanied by families of playful dolphins that must be one of the most endearing animals in the world, as well as by small shoals of flying fish leaping out of the sea.

After several days we reached Colombo in Sri Lanka, still called Ceylon at the time. We visited the city, our first opportunity to do some shopping. By then our funds were running very low as life on board was expensive. We knew that we needed enough reserve cash to clear final bills and tip various members of the staff before disembarking in Sydney, and we were to visit Adelaide and Fremantle en route. However, we were young and could not resist visiting jewelers where the local gems enchanted Ruth. At the risk of going bankrupt, we bought a small, beautiful ruby ring that was one of her favorites for the rest of her life. By early January 1956 when we reached Sydney we were almost penniless. Luckily, we were warmly welcomed by people from the Australian Department of Territories who had rented a flat overlooking the harbor. We were to spend the next month attending an indoctrination course for new employees before proceeding to Port Moresby in Papua. The next morning I took a tram and a ferry to our meeting place, the Australian School of Pacific Administration. I just had enough money to pay for the journey. Fortunately, one of the first actions my new employers thoughtfully took was to provide me with Australian currency.

When I returned to the flat I was surprised to find Ruth examining the mattresses of our beds. It was summer in Sydney and we had spent a very hot, uncomfortable, and restless first night there. In the morning we both found numerous insect bites acquired during the night. Ruth suspected mosquitoes were the culprits but my entomological eye soon saw that the flat was plagued with fleas. My first purchase in Australia, apart from tram and ferry tickets, was a large can of insecticide spray. We saturated the flat and solved the problem. Later we were told that large outbreaks of fleas were quite common in Sydney. Insect pests seemed to greet us whenever we took up a new residence in the Antipodes. In Port Moresby we were greeted by an army of cockroaches living under the mattresses of our beds.

In addition to attending the indoctrination course, which provided us with much useful and interesting information about the history and governance of Papua and New Guinea, then known as The Territory of Papua and New Guinea, we visited the prestigious Sydney School of Public Health and Tropical Medicine where we came to know an eminent malariologist, Robert Black.

Bob was one of a team established by Brigadier Sir Neil Hamilton Fairley, then Director of Medicine of the Australian Military Force in Cairns during WW II. They investigated the reasons why the new antimalarial prophylactic drug, mepacrine, did not seem to work properly in the north of New Guinea. The team was also performing clinical trials on army volunteers of a promising new compound called proguanil (Paludrine, see Chapter 5). It was just developed by Davey and other chemists at ICI, the pharmaceutical branch of the Imperial Chemical Industry near Manchester. By chance, much of the preliminary animal work with proguanil was done by another Australian, Brian Maegraith and his associates at the Liverpool School of Tropical Medicine; more later.

Bob played a prominent role in managing malaria in the allied troops who fought the invading Japanese forces in New Guinea. He later continued this work when Australian and American soldiers encountered chloroquine-resistant malaria during the Vietnam War. He was an unassuming, quiet-spoken man whose delightful wife, Nora, was the daughter of one of Australia's most famous artists,

Hans Heysen. Nora, who became one of Australia's most renowned painters, was Australia's first war artist. During her wartime assignments to Papua she met and married Bob. They were a generous and very hospitable couple and the first to introduce us to the culinary delights of Sydney. Bob was very knowledgeable about Australian wines and vineyards that in those days were still in an early stage of development. Fortunately for us, a considerable volume of wine was exported to New Guinea, strictly for the use of foreigners.

Nora painted a well-known portrait of Fairley who became the Wellcome Professor of Tropical Medicine at the London School of Hygiene and Tropical Medicine. It was Fairley who interviewed me in London for the post in Papua and reported to John Gunther, the director of Health Services and later the Deputy Administrator of TPNG.

In 1990, Gunther wrote of me in his historical account of the medical services, "I asked Sir Neil to interview him. Sir Neil advised me that he was good, that he wanted to continue to work in malaria and realized that if he walked out of a field program again he could expect no further similar employment. It was a risk, I took it."

In Sydney we met a young science graduate from Brisbane, Harry Standfast, his young wife Marion, and infant son. Harry became my right-hand man when I developed the Malaria Section of the Department of Public Health in The Territory of Papua and New Guinea. Our joint adventures started in Sydney when our wives set out on a shopping expedition in one of the main stores and we arranged to meet them later in the day at the main entrance. Unfortunately, there were two main entrances, one at each end of the building. I do not recall how we resolved that episode, but it was a good introductory exercise in improvisation and cooperation. At the beginning of 1956, we and the Standfast family moved from Sydney to Port Moresby, the capital of TPNG.

This name requires explanation. The islands composing New Guinea were taken over at various times by Germany, Holland,

England, and Australia. In 1884 the northeast quarter of the main island and those of the Bismarck Archipelago, including what are now called New Ireland, New Britain, and Bougainville were absorbed into the German Empire. Their main objective was exploiting the natural resources of copra, a source of much-needed coconut oil. The area was called Kaiser Wilhelmsland. In 1899 it was placed under the direct control of Germany and was thereafter known as German New Guinea. It was occupied in 1914 by Australian troops and in 1920 it was formally made an Australian protectorate by the League of Nations and named the Territory of New Guinea.

The southern portion of the main island was annexed by the Colony of Queensland in 1883 and declared a protectorate, British New Guinea, in 1888. This was renamed the Territory of Papua in 1905 to be administered by Australia. After the area was freed of the WW II Japanese invaders in 1945, the two areas were replaced by international agreement into a single administrative entity named The Territory of Papua and New Guinea, TPNG. This title was formally confirmed in 1949 and remained in effect until 1972 when the name was changed again to Papua New Guinea, PNG. When PNG received its independence in 1975, it was named The Independent State of Papua New Guinea.

The western half of the main island formed part of the extensive Dutch East Indies colonies. It was named Dutch, or Netherlands, New Guinea and remained so between 1898 and 1949. In 1949 the Dutch East Indies won independence and were renamed Indonesia. The Dutch retained control of western New Guinea until 1961. It was put under the control of the United Nations in 1963. In 1969, it was formally annexed to Indonesia.

The main island of New Guinea is very heterogeneous in both terrain and population. From the coasts up to an elevation of nearly 2,000 meters, the land is covered by some of the most extensive rain forests in the World, interspersed by networks of rivers. Some, such as the Sepik, are among the longest in the World. As the land rises the vegetation becomes more like that of temperate areas and similar to that of the East African highlands. The Bismarck Range is higher. This chain of mountains extends from East to West and rises to 4,509-meter Mount Wilhelm, which is perpetually snowcapped. Just above the fertile highland valleys the mountain slopes are covered in moss forest with its bizarre vegetation. The fertile highland valleys such as the Wahgi valley at about 1,600 meters have large indigenous populations who were only discovered in the early 1930s.

There was no site suitable to land even a small airplane. To prepare for this momentous event a foot patrol went out to organize some of the highlanders to gather for a large 'sing-sing' where hundreds of feet would stamp down a large area of vegetation and form a crude airstrip on which a plane could risk landing. When this dramatic event took place, the highlanders assumed that it was a huge bird and one or two of the more intrepid warriors, carrying spears, bows, and arrows cautiously approached the belly of the monster bird. They were curious if it was a male or a female. The descent of the pilot, a decidedly male Australian, reassured them that all was well. Mount Hagen, the largest town, stands at the western end of the Wahgi valley and was just a small district headquarters in the 1950s when I first visited. It is now the third largest city in PNG, with massive tourist and agricultural industries and main trunk roads connecting the highlands with the northern coastal cities of Lae and Madang.

At lower altitudes, the climate is typical of tropical rain forest terrain with high temperatures, humidity, and seasonal rainfall. The population of PNG is currently about 6.7 million and rising at a rate of over 3 percent annually. About 40 percent of the population inhabits highland areas. In addition to three lingua franca; English, Melanesian Pidgin (Tok Pisin), and Motu, there are 860 other languages. About half are related. Some are spoken by only a few hundred people but Enga, a highland language, is used by over 130,000. Missionaries, especially the Catholics, have converted about

96 percent of the population of PNG to Christianity and made extensive contributions to education and health services.

In the Sepik district, the heartland of indigenous art is best exemplified by the magnificent Haus Tambaran cult or spirit houses. We encountered an excellent, but not exclusive integration of traditional native with Christian custom. During the time we lived in Maprik the Catholic authorities constructed a magnificent church in the form of a Haus Tamberan from local materials. It was complete with brightly painted masks fixed to the upright inner supports. In other parts of TPNG there was less success in conversion rates of the local inhabitants who met the less open-minded Christian missionaries. Some took a hard line on local customs, going as far as to make some village communities burn down their cult houses and the magnificent ancestral carvings they contained. Maprik is where Ruth first encountered the rich indigenous art and mythology of the Papuans. This knowledge was later reflected in her imaginative embroidery.

In such varied terrain it is not surprising that almost the whole gamut of tropical diseases were rampant. In addition were those associated with life in the cooler highlands, such as respiratory infections. Of all the parasitic diseases present in the lowland areas and in certain years extending up to the highland valleys, malaria was the major problem. The general disease pattern included a high prevalence of yaws that closely resembled that which I had experienced in Africa. Moreover, TPNG had a few diseases not seen elsewhere including Pigbel, a form of intestinal infection acquired from eating partly cooked pigs, and the infamous and lethal condition known as kuru, which I address later.

Life in Port Moresby was fascinating in many ways. During our early days there we lived in a small house near the center, with glass shutters near the floor of outward-facing rooms. These were designed to increase ventilation in the absence of good fans or any form of air conditioning. For privacy at night we relied on heavy roll-up shutters made of woven palm strips. During the rainy season severe storms blew in the Coral Sea along the north shore where the town lay. During one particularly fierce storm, we awoke to see the heavy shutters blown horizontal against the ceiling by the fierce gale. The floor shutters disadvantage was that they did not provide privacy, even when closed. One night we were awakened by a loud scuffling under the house which stood on stilts nearly a meter off the ground. When I went out to explore, I found our Papuan houseboy grappling with another Papuan who he spotted crawling under the house. Moresby was not a safe town then and became progressively more dangerous as the years went by.

Since I traveled around TPNG extensively leaving Ruth alone, I borrowed an automatic pistol that I taught Ruth to shoot. On my return from one journey she told me that she was disturbed by noises the previous night and took the pistol out and cocked it. Fortunately, nothing happened so she put the weapon under her pillow. I recovered it the next day and found she had left it cocked. Had it gone off accidentally, it could have injured her or easily have sent a bullet through the flimsy wooden wall of our house and shot a neighbor! I returned the pistol to its original owner without delay. In 2004, Port Moresby was judged the most crime-ridden capital city of the world.

In the 1950s, the Department of Health recruited a number of doctors who emigrated to Australia as refugees from East European countries. Known as 'New Australians' they could not practice medicine in Australia but an arrangement was made so they could work as doctors in TPNG. After several years of satisfactory service they could be accepted for medical registration to practice back in Australia. That made some excellent doctors available to fill positions as general practitioners or specialists in many of the larger towns of TPNG. Some even manned smaller medical centers such as that in Maprik. We made friends with several during our stay in Moresby;

most were Hungarians. They helped make social life a remarkably cosmopolitan affair. Some of the Hungarian women also made life interesting for a number of the young, and not so young, Australian men. They were naturally exuberant, intelligent people with few inhibitions.

We also met a number of young Australian police officers who helped us obtain driving licenses that were also valid in Australia. Fortunately I bought a rather weatherworn, open-topped car to enable us to move around the local area and took advantage of a nearby deserted wartime airfield to teach Ruth how to drive. The car had old-fashioned crash gears that were excellent for teaching the basics of handling a car. Anything more modern would be very simple to handle in the future. We had all the room in the world to maneuver and there was nobody else with whom we could collide. The old bomb had the added advantage that its condition could not get much worse. It was parked outside our house when not in use. One morning I got in and found it crawling with termites that decided the stuffing in the seats made an excellent place for their new nest. Back to the insecticides! Although I held a British driving license for many years as well as my Nepalese one, Ruth never took a driving test, but our police friends assumed she had and gave her a TPNG license without hesitation. We did not disillusion them and Ruth never had a single accident in her life. I did—a single one in Basle of all places. That's where we went to live after we left TPNG.

I was allocated a small laboratory near the medical HQ and next to the old hospital. It was constructed on stilts and projected out over the sandy beach. Its floors were planks with large slits between them through which the beach or the sea could be seen. In those days I smoked quite heavily when using my microscope and the slits between the floorboards provided a very simple way to dispose of my cigarette ash and stubs. I also had an office in the HQ but avoided it as much as possible. Routine administration was something I always sought to avoid. The main town of Port Moresby was a small, bustling center of commerce with one bank and a cinema. *The King and I* was running at the time. Along the beach west of the town is Hanuabada, the largest village in Papua. To the east on the way to the big market village, Koki was Ela beach, an excellent swimming beach dotted with tall casuarina trees. Ruth, Babar, and I enjoyed the warm, gentle surf and the company of friends in our spare time. Swimming far from the shore was discouraged as swimmers were attacked by sharks. There was no protective reef such as exists beyond the beaches near Wewak on the north coast.

The sale and consumption of alcohol was strictly forbidden by the government for the indigenous population. This caused resentment among some of the more sophisticated of them. On one occasion we were working in Port Moresby and I heard that my senior technician, Muka Haroi, who was an excellent man, was put in jail for being drunk. It transpired that he and some of his colleagues in the medical department decided to 'borrow' some alcohol from the stores to enliven a party. Unfortunately, they helped themselves not to ethyl, but methyl alcohol. One member of the party was blinded, but fortunately not Muka. I decided not to make efforts to have his jail sentence dropped to make sure that, in the future, he would remember the difference between the two compounds. We used both routinely in the laboratory. Once TPNG gained independence, alcohol was sold to all and mayhem resulted, especially in the area of Port Moresby.

Providing health services was always a major priority of the Australian administration, which established an extensive network, ranging from simple village dispensaries to modern hospitals in the main towns. John Gunther, the Director of Public Health was the wartime malariologist for the Royal Australian Air Force. He realized that malaria control was a top priority, but was not convinced of the best way to set about achieving this aim. He needed to recruit somebody at his side who could establish a plan for TPNG.

In 1949, he decided that an immediate practical aim would be to drain the malarial swamps of the Wahgi valley in order to open that densely populated highland area for agricultural development. Unlike the situation at lower altitudes of TPNG where malaria transmission was perennial and often at a level paralleled in the most highly endemic areas of tropical Africa, highland malaria was seasonal and varied greatly from year to year. In the worst years, the estimate was that as many as one percent of many village populations perished. The task was handed to an expatriate English Health Inspector, Stan Christian. He developed an exceptional rapport with the highlanders. Gunther realized the need to educate both medical and administrative staff in TPNG on the overall problems of malaria and how to control it. He gave Christian the job of setting up and running a malaria control school to be based at Minj.

By 1956 when I arrived on the scene, the school at Minj was in full swing with an Australian doctor, Terry Spencer and his entomologist wife Margaret in support. Minj was the first place my colleague Harry Standfast and I visited. We immediately established a strong personal and professional rapport with Stan who was a rather dour, quiet bachelor about ten years older than we were. As far as I could judge, he was mainly self-taught in the field of malariology.

His friendship with the local villagers was reinforced as he trained a number of them, including a bright young local woman. They worked with him on quite sophisticated activities, including establishing entomological surveys and mosquito control. Stan spent the rest of his life in Minj. He became a sort of honorary brother to the highlanders who built him a house where he spent the rest of his days with his female assistant when he reached retirement age.

The Spencers, who had contributed to the medical side of the malaria surveys in the highlands, were later transferred to the D'Entrecastaux islands off the eastern tip of the New Guinea mainland. There they explored the problems of malaria control in an entirely different environment, within the framework of the national plan that I established during my initial year in TPNG.

One of the fascinating features of the highland populations was their variety of customs, which incorporated regular pig feasts, dances, wearing of brilliant traditional headdresses by the men, and inter-tribal village battles. You could equate the last with weekend football matches as we know them; except they used bows, arrows, and spears and frequently ended in loss of life. That was reason for a return match and the situation would spiral. On one occasion I accompanied an Australian patrol officer and his policemen to a very remote area near Tari where matters were getting out of hand. Their intent was to arrest the ringleaders, but we ended up beating a hasty retreat before we became embroiled ourselves. I have a shaky photograph to prove it. The exotic nature of the men's headgear and facial adornment was an everyday affair and not restricted to ceremonial occasions. It soon attracted international attention and probably contributed to eventually opening up the area to tourism.

Clearing areas such as the Mount Hagen end of the Wahgi valley led to massive agricultural and other development of this region. Mount Hagen is now the third most populated town in TPNG with international airport access.

However, it was different in our day. Over the next few years I made many visits to Minj. In due course, Stan and I published an analysis of the epidemiology and recommendations for control of highland malaria. Meanwhile we were both studying the general mosquito population of the Wahgi valley. With the help of Stan's staff and porters from the local village, I set out to climb into the moss forest above Minj to place light traps to capture mosquitoes and other insects. The traps were heavy and ran all night from twelve-volt car batteries, but such loads posed no problem for the porters. To my embarrassment, I found that I was totally incapable of climbing the steep clay-based footpaths that ascended the mountain and ended up having to be virtually passed from one man to the next until we reached a suitable collecting site. There we hung the traps in trees, attached them to the batteries, descended for the night; I mainly skidded down on my backside. When we made the ascent again the following morning, I was delighted to find that we had trapped a large assortment of insects. We later discovered we had trapped a number of previously unknown species.

Malaria at lower areas, especially the northern coastal regions of TPNG, was a very different story. One of my first expeditions was to the Fly River in the Western District of Papua. This region was relatively little known from the medical point of view, but known to be highly endemic for malaria. To travel there from Port Moresby it was necessary to sail in a small, flat-bottomed boat with a five-foot draft that was able to navigate the shallow stretches of the Fly River. One first had to journey across the Coral Sea to Daru. Ruth, Babar, our houseboy Jacob, and I set off in the vessel hoping for a tranquil crossing. The Coral Sea was notorious both for its fickle weather and as the site of an important WW II sea battle when the Japanese fleet was forced to abandon the takeover of Port Moresby. We left the harbor in the first week of November 1956. On our first evening, the wind increased dramatically. Our small ship was not a good one in which to travel across a smooth sea much less a rough one. There was one small cabin with a bunk on board where I bedded Ruth down for the night. Babar slept on the floor and I sat in a seat next to the bed holding Ruth so she would not roll out as the ship tilted from side to side. Neither Babar nor I were good sailors but I managed to save him from harm by keeping a foot on him. It was a most uncomfortable night. The arrival of dawn was a welcome relief. I went on deck and saw one of the crew perched on the top of the mast looking for land, totally unperturbed by the ship's motion. Suddenly he called out that land was ahead. The sea became calm again and we decided to make a brief landing. I soon realized the small, uninhabited, sandy island that we found was Bramble Cay, the northernmost extension of the Torres Straits and Australian territory.

As we approached shore, I was surprised to see another boat about the same size as ours moored on the far side of the island. We lowered the lifeboat and Babar and I were helped into it so that the poor well house-trained dog could relieve himself on the beach. Looking across the sand, I was stopped short by the sight of several very large turtles lying on their backs waving their legs in the air. Babar and I walked over to have a closer look. As we approached the unfortunate animals, two shots rang out and I saw jets of sand arise a couple of yards from our feet. Two men with rifles at the ready approached us across the sand. They were Australians who I classified as pirates, hunting turtles that were officially protected by the Australian government.

"'Oo the bloody 'ell are yer and what d'yer think y'er doin' with our turtles?" they demanded.

I tactfully explained exactly who we were, but declined from asking them the same question. I told them that I was a government official from TPNG and would report their attack on us when we reached Daru. They told me that we were trespassing because Bramble Cay was Australian and we had no right to be there! What could I say? We bundled Babar back into the lifeboat before they took it into their heads to shoot him as a token of their feelings. We boarded our ship and set off for Daru, the small town at the mouth of the Fly River.

We safely moored at the jetty and disembarked by climbing up a plank pointing upwards at a steep angle since the tide was low. Ruth and I made it to solid land with some assistance from the crew, but we still had to land Babar. With some pushing and shoving he was about halfway up when he lurched and fell into the sea between the ship's side and the jetty. It was a very precarious position for the dog who looked sadly up at us as he trod water. Without hesitating, Jacob jumped fully clothed into the water, grabbed Babar by his collar and swam to the end of the jetty with him. The land there descended to the water's edge and they got out onto dry land. It was an unforgettable moment.

By this time the news of our arrival had reached the District

Medical Officer, another 'New Australian' of Hungarian origin named George Harmos. He came down to greet us and take us to his house. We were warmly welcomed by his wife and his old mother who spoke very little English, but could converse with Ruth in a sort of German. It was obvious that they were delighted to have company. Without doubt, they were leading an extremely isolated existence in Daru.

I went with George to make my presence and mission known to the District Officer, to arrange for my journey up river, and to report our incident on Bramble Cay. He let me know there was nothing he could do other than pass the information back to Port Moresby. If anybody was in the wrong on our side it was me. I had landed without permission back on Australian territory—that little spit of sand.

The Harmos house only had two bedrooms and one was occupied by the old lady. In the absence of alternative accommodation that first night, we mutually agreed that Ruth and I would share the large bedroom occupied by the good doctor and his wife who had a very wide bed. They divided it in two by hanging a sheet from the ceiling to the bed. This provided room for all four of us for the night. Ruth and I were so tired from our journey that I think we could have slept on a bed of nails and could not contemplate returning to our ship soon. It only had one small bunk. The plan was that George and I, with some of our Papuan staff, would set off upriver the next day, leaving Ruth and Babar in the care of the Harmos ladies.

After our departure, they found more suitable sleeping accommodation for Ruth. They were pleased to have a guest from Europe. We did not realize that George and I would be carrying out our survey, which extended to the Kiunga area about 800 kilometers from Daru, for the next three weeks. It could not have been easy for Ruth to depend on the generosity of her hosts for so long, but she was a remarkably adaptable and imaginative woman. She never complained to me about being deserted so long then or later.

Our voyage up the Fly River and our surveys of the village populations and mosquitoes along the way led me to conclude that this area
of TPNG would not respond to the new method being introduced
for malaria control. After the expedition, I reported our conclusions;
that malaria was hyper endemic in the Western District. For a variety
of practical reasons it was not suitable to apply DDT in mass house
spraying. In that report I suggested that an antimalarial drug such as
primaquine could destroy the stages of the malaria parasites infective
to the mosquitoes. Injections could be given in a depot formulation,
especially to infants and young children who were the heaviest
carriers of such parasites. It could provide a major weapon in
interrupting the transmission of the disease in this area.

While no such drug was yet discovered in those days, I found that
a novel analog, tafenoquine, produced by American chemists about
forty years later, came close to this ideal. Unfortunately, clinical trials
to ensure that it is safe enough to use for mass chemoprophylaxis
have not been made to date.

The northern limit of my survey was the Kiunga region. It
stretched northwards to an area where, years later, the Ok Tedi
Mining company was established to extract gold ore from the upper
reaches of the Fly River that runs south from the slopes of the Star
Mountains. This large organization set up an excellent medical
center. It was joined in 1982 by a young Canadian of Dutch
extraction, Gerritt (Gerry) Schuurkamp. He worked as a medical
entomologist and parasitologist for the TPNG Department of Public
Health from 1978, long after my departure. From his base at Ok Tedi
he extended field and clinical studies on malaria well beyond the
point that we reached and confirmed our original findings.

Gerry who was a superb photographer, made contact with me in
1982. He produced a thesis for an MSc degree with the University of
Sydney. I was invited to serve as an external examiner. I was pleased
to do this and reported back that his MSc thesis was so good that it
would have satisfied me even if it were put forward for a PhD.

Ultimately Gerry assembled all his observations, which he presented as a thesis for a PhD with the newly formed University of Papua and New Guinea in 1992. I was delighted to receive a copy of this superb thesis that he kindly dedicated to me. It was, and remains, the finest thesis I have ever encountered. It was later published in book form, but Gerry persuaded the Ok Tedi authorities to publish a small, but equally well-illustrated, free booklet, *The Ok Tedi Liklik Piksa Buk*, as a token of appreciation for all the cooperation give by countless villagers of the Ok Tedi region in the development of the public health services in their area.

Travel along the Fly River was not all work as it opened up an endless vista of the most wonderful natural history. The presence of hoards of mosquitoes, as along the Sepik, (the headwaters of the two rivers were not far apart in the mountainous area north of Ok Tedi), meant that it was far more comfortable to obtain some air movement by sailing slowly along than by mooring. Crocodiles were abundant and often seen sunning themselves on the sandy shores. Sometimes at night we would leave the ship in the main stream and take a shallow, punt-like vessel with a small outboard motor to venture across the deep reed beds into the adjacent lagoons. There we some-times hunted crocodiles, using headlamps to spot them by the reflection from their eyes. If we saw a double reflection we knew the animal was facing us and could make a shrewd guess as to its size. If only one light spot was seen, it was not always possible to tell if it was a small crocodile whose two eyes appeared as one or a large beast whose side we were facing. In a large lagoon one night we saw a single large reflection and approached it quietly. Suddenly we almost bumped against it. The beast was huge. Our punt was five meters long—about the same size as the crocodile's body not counting its enormous head and tail. It was very fortunate that we had not shot at it. Had we wounded it, the chances are that it would have turned on us and knocked us, lock stock and barrel, into the water of the lagoon where we would probably perish.

We restarted the motor and beat a hasty retreat back to the ship. A short way further up the river we told of our encounter to the chief of a small village. He told us they knew there were huge crocodiles in the area and that villagers frequently lost their dogs during the night. It was fortunate that none of the people were taken. The chief took us to a section of beach where he unearthed the skull of an animal they killed months before. The skull alone was nearly a meter long.

On board ship the crew would carefully remove the skins from any crocodiles that were shot during the night. On one occasion I was intrigued to see a dead animal with large numbers of horseflies feeding on it. I always thought that these insects only fed on warm-blooded hosts. For some reason I failed to collect specimens for later identification, which I now regret. The crew retained the crocodile tails as they provided good meat for them, but discarded the remainder of the carcasses for their reptilian brothers and fish to consume. The skins were scraped clean and packed with salt for eventual dispatch to Brisbane where they were prepared for sale. I later retained two skins from animals I shot. They were professionally tanned and dyed a rich maroon color. After our return to Switzerland I had a superb pair of shoes and a handbag for Ruth made from them.

On moonlight evenings at dusk we sometimes saw large colonies of fruit bats leaving the tall trees lining the banks and filling the air on their nocturnal feeding expeditions. At dawn we would hear and see them reappear and the trees once more filled with their suspended bodies. They would continue to chatter away loudly, then gradually subside to sleep off their evening meals of insects and fruit. I made blood films from some of these animals that we later found were infected with a malaria-like parasite of the genus *Hepatocystis* that is known to infect such animals. Along many stretches of the riverbanks, trees were filled with fireflies, so that it looked as if we were sailing quietly along an avenue illuminated by millions of tiny, winking green lights, a sight never to be forgotten. Birds of many sorts were abundant, some fishing along the shore or diving for their food in the deeper parts of the river. On one occasion the crew spotted and shot a cassowary. This large, colorful bird has a very dangerous spine at the back of each foot and can give a lethal blow to an attacker. It was hauled aboard and dismembered as its meat was highly rated by the Papuans. George and I were too sorry to see it killed to join in the feast.

In the belly of the boat I set up a microscope that I used to examine the hundreds of blood smears we collected from the villagers during our surveys. We preserved mosquitoes for later identification by my colleague, Harry Standfast, after our return to Port Moresby. In retrospect, I regretted that I did not collect any butterflies. I was far too occupied with my survey work to contemplate sparing time to collect insects other than those that bit us.

After a successful prolonged journey we returned to Daru, having completed the first malaria survey ever made in the northern Fly region. With many expressions of gratitude to the Harmos family for their hospitality, Ruth, Babar, and I left for the return journey to Port Moresby.

After a day's sailing we reached the mouth of the Turama River where there was a Dutch mission and there we decided to seek lodging for the night. The ladies there were welcoming but only had a single bed free, so we agreed that Ruth would stay there and Babar and I would sleep aboard the boat. I was amused next day by Ruth's account of hearing from her hosts how they slept with a pillow between their legs in order to help keep cool in the intensely hot and humid night air. The pillow was known colloquially as a 'Dutch wife' that leaves something to the imagination. The following day we resumed our voyage back to Port Moresby with nothing more eventful than seeing, quite far out at sea, a very long and active snake.

It was not one of the highly colored species of sea snakes but a simple, olive grey color. We arrived at our destination at the end of the month.

I first met Brian Maegraith, who I mentioned earlier in this chapter, in 1957 when he visited TPNG and I accompanied him on a tour of the main island. One of our first ports of call was the highland town of Goroka where we were welcomed by a 'New Australian' of Lithuanian origin, the District Medical Officer, Vincent Zigas of kuru fame, and his wife.

In the late 1950s an epidemic was reported among the South Fore people who live in the Okapa District of the Eastern Highlands province of TPNG. The condition was characterized by headache, trembling, and irrational outbursts of laughter especially in women and to a lesser degree in children. It was invariably fatal. At the time, the Fore people followed a ritual type of cannibalism of the dead. The female kin would remove muscle and brain for food. Tasty morsels of brain and other organs were given to children and old people. In the years between 1957 and 1968 it was estimated that some 1,100 of the 8,000 population died of this neurological condition.

The lot of investigating its cause fell to Vin, a tall, handsome, dynamic young doctor who looked and spoke remarkably like the well-known American comedian, Danny Kaye. He was both charming and more than slightly hypomanic.

The exuberant Vin would barely let us sit down before he burst out, "My dear Professor, I have discovered a new disease in my area."

He proceeded to recount how people were dying of a mysterious form of brain disease that he hoped Brian would help him investigate. I was ready to take up his request, but for reasons best known to himself, Brian did not take Vin seriously. I think he jumped to the false conclusion that this effervescent young expatriate with the strange accent who stood before him waving his arms in a state of high excitement as he spoke, was slightly unhinged. I remember that Vin, his wife, Brian, and I were sitting round a table in the tiny

Goroka hotel drinking a cool beer. There was a table-tennis table next to us.

Brian said soothingly, "There, there Vin. That's all very interesting, but let's sit down, drink our beer and relax a bit."

After a while Brian said, "Vin, why don't we have a game?"

He promptly stood up and picked up a bat, followed reluctantly by Vin who proceeded to trounce Brian. By that time Vin had lost some of his enthusiasm for his story and Brian did not raise the subject again. So the Maegraith name was never associated with the history of kuru. The investigation resulted in a Nobel Prize won by Daniel Carleton Gajdusek in 1976.

The next morning Brian and I left for Wewak, the main town of the Sepik District. From there we flew inland to Maprik, which I adopted as the center of a pilot malaria control project. Nine years later, I found myself appointed to the Liverpool School of Tropical Medicine where Brian was the long-standing Dean and I replaced him in that position when he retired in 1975.

Gajdusek graduated in medicine from Harvard Medical School in 1946 and had many interests. Among them pediatrics and neurology were prominent. In 1954 he went to the Walter and Eliza Hall Institute in Melbourne. While he was there he heard rumors of a strange new disease that was killing many people in TPNG. He met Zigas shortly after Brian and I visited and was immediately stimulated by the account he received of kuru. With his intense interest and broad experience in degenerative neurological diseases, he recognized that the Fore people were suffering from an unidentified condition. He sought to obtain postmortem material to examine, i.e., a brain. As I understand the situation, other Australian neurologists were becoming interested and were somewhat upset by the idea that a foreigner, and an American at that, was intruding on what they felt was their territory. They took steps to ensure that Gajdusek would not be permitted to collect and export specimens before they had the opportunity to do so.

Gajdusek, a most determined and enterprising investigator, got around the dilemma by entering TPNG indirectly via Dutch New Guinea. He made his way to Goroka where he arranged with Zigas to collect and preserve a whole brain from a newly deceased Fore villager. He left the country by the same route and took the specimen back with him to the National Institutes of Health in Washington. A complete and thorough examination revealed the presence of a strange, spongiform change in the brain tissue of a kind never before known in humans. However, it bore a resemblance to a familiar sheep disease known as 'scrapie'. The cause of scrapie was unknown, but it was neither the effect of a known virus or bacterium, nor did it appear hereditary.

The subsequent study of this and other newly recognized conditions of man and animals by Gajdusek, Baruch, and others revealed the existence of abnormal proteins in the brains of sheep with scrapie. They were later named 'prions'. These have since been shown to be responsible for 'Bovine Spongiform Encephalopathy', or Mad Cow Disease in cattle. They also cause a previously unrecognized, lethal condition known now as 'New variant Creutzfeldt-Jakob disease' in people who consumed meat from infected beef. In 1997 an American scientist, Stanley Prusiner, was awarded a Nobel Prize for his revelation of the biochemistry and infective properties of prions.

To be at a social gathering with Vin and Gajdusek was quite an experience. Ruth and I joined them one evening in Port Moresby at an informal reception given by colleagues from the Department of Public Health. For the entire evening the conversation was dominated by the two who engaged in a rapid-fire dialogue that was very interesting to the rest of us, but very hard to follow. Conversing with one hypomaniac is difficult enough, but to be present when two of them get together is altogether another situation. I kept in touch with Gajdusek from time to time after he returned to Washington. He sent me a couple of volumes of the eighteen journals he wrote about his experiences studying child development and disease patterns among the Australian aboriginals and populations of New Guinea as well as some photographs of Fore villagers suffering from kuru.

This remarkable man took a number of orphan children, who he met during his field studies, back with him to be educated in Washington. His journals contained many revealing and sometimes shocking accounts of the sexual development of various aboriginal peoples he encountered. It is a tragedy that he was charged with child molestation in 1966. It was partly following an accusation by one of his adopted children and partly based on accounts in his journals. He was imprisoned for some months but finally released on probation.

A number of prominent scientists believed that there was a miscarriage of justice. I last met Gajdusek when he presented a lecture at the Royal College of Physicians in London while receiving an honorary degree there years later. He died in self-imposed exile during the winter of 2008 in Tromsø at the age of eighty-five.

The history of how malaria turned the tide of WW II and how its mastery by the allied forces prevented an Australia invasion by the Japanese forces has been recounted elsewhere. Suffice it to say that a major focus of the action was in the Wewak-Aitape area not far east of the northern border with Dutch New Guinea. Our colleagues, led by Dick Metselaar from the Dutch Royal Tropical Institute in Amsterdam, had established a pilot project to investigate the epidemiology of malaria on their side of the border near the then capital of Hollandia. They followed the same approach that I had already determined I would employ on our side of the border. It was based on a practical application of the magical, mathematical formula contrived by George Macdonald, the Professor of Public Health at the LSHTM. It correlated all the factors implicated in malaria transmission, rather like Einstein's formula, $E = mc^2$ that explains the equivalence of energy and matter.

The initial stage was to determine the various factors that dictated the level of endemicity such as human blood infection rates at different ages, mosquito vector species and their population densities, the number of potentially infective bites per year, vector biting sites, e.g., in houses or outdoors, and their breeding places. The next stage involved establishing pilot control areas in which we hoped to determine to what degree the transmission of malaria could be controlled by spraying long-lasting insecticides, such as DDT, inside the houses. As soon as we could Harry and I flew up to Wewak to assess the situation. We felt that a suitable base to establish a pilot project was Maprik. It was sixty kilometers southwest of Wewak by air and forty kilometers north of Marui on the Sepik River.

Maprik was a little village with an Assistant District Officer and a small hospital run by another 'New Australian' doctor, a Hungarian named Szymicek. He lived there with his wife Livia and two small daughters. Other expatriates included an old ex-gold miner named Bill Royal with his wife and an Australian who ran a small trading store. Even then, Maprik was renowned as a major center of Sepik art and was the site of a magnificent men's Haus Tambaran. Of importance to us was the presence of holoendemic malaria. In the early 1920s, alluvial gold was discovered near Morobe along the Bulolu and Watut rivers and a number of Australian prospectors braved the dangers there to pan for this precious metal.

Among them was young Bill who struck it rich and rapidly acquired a fortune. He returned to his hometown in Australia where he dissipated his riches equally rapidly. Bill was married to a very loyal nurse who returned to New Guinea with him to continue prospecting, but industry overtook him and he was never able to scrape more than a meager living by panning in gold-poor streams as far away as Maprik. The two remained there living a basic existence. They were still there when we set up our project.

We made our preliminary survey of the Wewak-Maprik area in April 1956 when we determined that malaria transmission was holoendemic, i.e., as intense as anything experienced in the most highly endemic parts of Africa. However, there were a number of important differences in both the species of parasite present and of the mosquito vectors. We also found that the blood of 8 percent of the population was infected with the parasitic worm, *Wuchereria bancrofti*, which can cause the disabling condition known as elephantiasis. The survey was enough to demonstrate that the area was suitable for a pilot malaria control study.

After concluding that Maprik was an excellent base site for the project, I had to negotiate with our Moresby HQ and the local authorities in Wewak to release funds for the Department of Works to erect housing for my staff, ourselves, and a small building to use as a laboratory.

Running a pilot project would take several years in the field. It was clear to me that I could only manage the job by living on site and not leaving it all to Harry, capable as he was. First, he was a biologist, not a doctor. Therefore, he could not be responsible for the medical side of the project. Second, no one else in the Department of Public Health had the requisite malariological training and experience to run Maprik.

Without making an issue of my intentions to John Gunther, and with Ruth's agreement, I arranged for us to take up residence in Maprik. From there I could return to Port Moresby when necessary and visit other parts of TPNG to explore the possibilities of setting up control projects elsewhere as part of a national program. In order to ensure that work on our Maprik base moved ahead as planned, I decided to move from Port Moresby to Wewak. Ruth, Babar, and I boarded a smallish Australian ship that sailed along the coast in a leisurely fashion past Milne Bay, Lae, and Madang to Wewak where we disembarked. It was an enjoyable trip during which we played innumerable games of Scrabble with a new set that we purchased in Sydney. I still have the set with its pieces. Ruth and I played many games during the last months of her life and she usually won.

We initially stayed at the Wewak hotel, which gave me the

opportunity of establishing good links with the local administration, and senior District Medical Officer, another Hungarian whose name escapes me, but who also lived in the hotel. A number of copra traders made their base in Wewak where they had ready access to coconut plantations on islands further north. There was a young, attractive Australian woman named Sue living in the hotel who was later featured on Australian television teaching a fitness program. Babar slept in the hotel outside our room door. In the middle of one night we woke up to a female scream. Sue was leaving my colleague's room and had tripped over Babar in the dark. I had no idea which of them was more shocked.

One of the pleasures of being in Wewak was to go to one of the nearby beaches that were totally isolated. Ruth, Babar, and I and sometimes our pilot friend Brian swam to our hearts' content within the safety of the coral reef. Wearing a simple facemask and snorkel, we moved along the coral and enjoyed its endless beauties and its inhabitants, gloriously colored fish and other marine creatures. It was unforgettable. Unfortunately in those days I did not possess a camera that took underwater photographs.

While living in Wewak I bought a second-hand Morris Minor that I felt would be useful when no official car was available. To reach our favorite beach we drove there. This involved negotiating a final roadless stretch that dropped steeply down to the beach. It was an excellent chance to try out our new purchase. We reached the isolated beach with little more than odd scraping over projecting stones and enjoyed a pleasant swim. Later that afternoon when we set off for the journey home. the engine started, gave a couple of sighs, and then cut out. It refused to start again. I got out to see what had happened. To my horror, I saw that a stone we scraped had punctured the oil tank. All our oil was in the sand. We were stuck a couple of miles from Wewak wearing only bathing clothes, but fortunately protected by Babar. By an exceptional stroke of good luck we heard another car approaching the beach. It was driven by an Australian who we did not know. He offered to drive all three of us back to Wewak where we could seek the aid of the owner of the small garage where we just bought our car. The next day he salvaged the unfortunate vehicle, took it back into his garage and informed us sadly that it needed a new engine. However, he had a new Morris Minor and offered to trade our car in at a good price if we would buy it. We had no option but to agree. He was no doubt happy in that outpost of empire to sell us two cars in two days. Once we moved into Maprik we had to sell the new car back to him as it was utterly useless away from the few paved coastal roads. However, we were still young and foolish.

Eventually, our accommodations and lab in Maprik were ready. We packed our equipment, personal goods, and Babar into the corrugated aluminum body of an old Junkers freight plane and headed inland to the old wartime airstrip at Hayfield, a few kilometers south of Maprik. We were met by Harry who went ahead with a Land Rover. There was a long, barely passable track from Wewak to Maprik that took a couple of days to negotiate. In part that is because it was often necessary to improvise a temporary bridge to cross some small creeks. For the final stretch, one traversed a fairly wide, but shallow river at a sort of ford. This required removing the starting belt and moving almost inch-by-inch using the starting motor alone. Once the engine was completely waterlogged, one had to summon as much manpower as possible and push.

In Maprik we were welcomed by the Assistant District Officer, Dr. Szymicek and his wife, and the owner of the tiny Maprik hotel. The main access to food, mail, and essential supplies was through the Maprik store. Supplies were usually delivered weekly by air to the tiny airstrip next to the store. There were often delays during the rainy season. Supplies of petrol and kerosene arrived via the Junkers at Hayfield as they were too heavy to be landed at Maprik.

One of Ruth's first activities in Maprik was to convert the area around our new house into an attractive garden with masses of colorful flowers, various fruit trees including bananas, papayas, and custard apples. She planted a sizeable vegetable garden and grew a wide variety of edibles, including adjacent rows of melons and cucumbers. These cross-fertilized and produced interesting, but rather tasteless fruits that we named 'melumbras'. We also organized the digging and cementing of a small swimming pool about four by three meters by one meter deep. This had to be filled with rainwater from the roof of the house but there was no shortage of that. The pool gave us and our neighbors hours of cool pleasure. It was occasionally visited by wild life such as small snakes and, on one memorable occasion, a brilliant small kingfisher. One hazard we had to lookout for when we gave a party was that none of our guests fell into the pool. While most of us tended to drink surprisingly good Australian wine or beer, it was the custom in Maprik to offer drinkers the bottle from which to help themselves. One evening a total stranger, who none of us had met, turned up and was welcomed like everybody else. He vanished before the party was over. When I noticed his absence, my first thought was to use a flashlight and look for him in the pool. He was not there. We found him lying underneath a Land Rover snoring blissfully in the cool night air. We never did find out who he was nor where he came from. He left the next morning for an unknown destination.

The best Wewak and Maprik connections were made by hiring a single-engine plane such as a Cessna or one of the old WW II Norseman radial engine planes still flown by pilots of Gibbe's Sepik Airways. To carry freight we could charter a twin-engine De Havilland Dragon Rapide, but that was the largest plane that could land safely on the small Maprik airstrip. To transport heavier freight, we had to organize a flight on the old Junkers. This plane could land at Maprik with luck, but taking off was risky so the pilots preferred to use Hayfield. However, this always necessitated sending somebody ahead by Land Rover to make sure that the ground was sufficiently firm for a plane to land if it had rained the previous night. The Catholic mission in Wewak owned three Cessnas flown by the American Bishop, Leo Arkfeld, or Brother Peter Ruiter. Ruth, who did not like to fly, said she preferred to go with the Bishop since that way she was supported by an extra pair of wings.

The Dragon Rapide was flown by the young Australian named Brian. We met him in Wewak and he was something of a daredevil, but a very skilled pilot. Our house in Maprik was built on top of a small escarpment overlooking the airstrip below and was bordered by tall sago palm trees spaced about twenty feet apart. One day I heard the familiar sound of the plane's approach. I was emerging from the lab when I was greeted by the sight of Ruth standing outside the house waving a broom in the air.

She was shouting, "The bloody fool! He'll kill himself."

Almost over our heads and flying on its side came the plane, shooting just above and between the palm trees before doing a ninety-degree twist to straighten out, then circling the area again before landing below us. Ruth gave him a severe ticking off, but we always retained an affection for the young man and we took him swimming when we found ourselves together back in Wewak.

Luckily the Dragon Rapide was a remarkably sturdy and forgiving machine. It had two propellers that could be started by swinging them by hand if the self-starter failed. You had to be very quick in your reactions to do that. On one occasion Brian had just taken off from the Wewak airfield when one prop fell off, fortunately not hitting any one on the ground. Brian managed to turn around and land again without much difficulty. Then he had to find his missing propeller.

Ruth did not like flying in that plane as its fuselage was con-structed of rather flimsy fabric that did not give her a sense of security. The old Norseman was flown by an equally old Australian veteran, a very tranquil person. I sat next to him on one occasion when we were looking for a tiny airstrip in a remote mountain village and he was quietly and competently darning a pair of socks. Unlike Brian, he was no daredevil.

He once said to me, "I don't want to be the best pilot, only the oldest."

We became good friends with a number of the Catholic missionaries and regularly invited them from Maprik in for a meal. Father Cruysberg, a delightful old Dutchman, had no problem about helping us out if our somewhat sporadic wine supply failed. He could always muster a bottle of altar wine to breach the gap. One year I was invited to attend a regional malaria conference in Bangkok shortly before Christmas. The journey there from Maprik was rather complicated. I had to fly to Wewak, then by Australian Airlines to Hollandia where I caught a KLM flight to Bangkok via a route that I forget. It was an interesting meeting and gave me the opportunity to shop for presents for Ruth. However, I was concerned about being unable to get back to Maprik in time for Christmas Day for which Ruth had arranged a lunch for a number of the local priests. The inevitable happened. My return flight via the Dutch island of Biak was delayed by bad weather and I returned to Hollandia too late to catch the connecting flight back to Wewak.

My colleague, Dick Meuwissen, who was with me at the conference, and his wife kindly invited me to stay with them until I could get another flight. But this meant missing Christmas completely. We managed to get into radio contact with Wewak to give Ruth the bad news. My predicament reached the ears of the Catholic mission and they said they would try to get me back to Wewak. Early in the morning that day I sat disconsolately with my friend and baggage on the deserted airfield outside Hollandia. Then we heard the sound of an aircraft approaching. Moments later, we saw a lone Cessna approaching. Peter Ruiter made an illegal flight from Wewak with no official permission to cross the border, but cross it he did. Without delay he loaded me on board and returned to Wewak. After a brief stop to refuel, he continued on to Maprik where I arrived just in time for Christmas lunch. We could not have had a better Christmas present; one for which my pilot sacrificed most of his long-anticipated Holy Day.

The task of Harry, our TPNG staff, and me was to select and map out three sectors around Maprik to make baseline surveys of malaria in the population and determine more accurately the species and infection rates of malaria in the local mosquitoes. We also had to investigate the social customs of the villagers and breeding and feeding sites of the vectors. This involved establishing sample sites that could be visited regularly over a period of several years and in all seasons. This is no mean feat in that intensely hot and humid climate as heavy seasonal rainfall regularly obliterated the few motor tracks. The three sectors each contained about 5,000 persons. To this we linked the spraying of all homes in one sector with DDT and a second sector with Dieldrin at three-month intervals. This was not easy since many of the houses, all constructed from local materials such as palm thatch and bamboo, were as much as eight or nine meters tall with a high front and a roof sloping down towards the back like a miniature Haus Tambaran. The third sector was unsprayed as a control to observe the effect of this intervention on the incidence and prevalence of malaria in the community. We were especially evaluating its impact in reducing malaria transmission to infants. The infant infection rate from birth to five years of age was the most sensitive indicator of the value of and method of control. Anybody from any sector who suffered a fever was examined either by a medical aid in the villages or at the Maprik hospital, where their blood was examined. If necessary they were treated with antimalarial drugs.

From our field surveys we learned that malaria was being caused by one, or simultaneously by several of three main parasites. *Plasmodium falciparum* the most dangerous killer parasite, *P. vivax* which commonly produces multiple relapses, or *P. malariae* a parasite that can cause kidney disease and last many years. Moreover, unlike in most heavily infected parts of the world, simultaneous infection with two or three species was almost the norm.

More recent observations, using molecular techniques that became available in the past two decades, have revealed the presence in that area of a very small number of infections with a fourth parasite that produces a vivax-like infection, *P. ovale.*

Collecting and examining blood and mosquito specimens involved an enormous amount of time and effort in both the field and the laboratory. Blood collection entailed gathering the entire populations of selected sample villages and preparing blood smears on microscope slides from each individual. Mosquito samples had to be collected at frequent intervals from sample houses, taken to the laboratory for identification, and then each individual female mosquito of the *Anopheles* species had to be dissected to see if its stomach or salivary glands contained malaria parasites. Today such studies are carried out far more rapidly using so-called DNA molecular probes to examine and identify parasite species in large batches of blood or mosquitoes, even in a relatively unsophisticated setting. However, three years passed before Watson and Crick revealed the structure of DNA that gave rise to the birth of molecular genetics. In the 1950s life in the laboratory was not simple.

Some villages could be reached by Land Rover over very basic, unsurfaced tracks, but others had to be visited by foot. As was the case in Liberia, we sometimes sent word ahead of our arrival by sending messages on the talking drums. We often heard the booming in the early evening from our house in Maprik. One day Ruth was with me when I was collecting blood specimens from about a hundred villagers in a distant village. The spot of blood from each individual was smeared on a glass microscope slide and the slides were returned to the Maprik laboratory where they were stained in large batches and examined under the microscope. The staining technique was simple once one was familiar with it and Ruth saw us carry it out many times. This day, wanting to help, she took it on herself to stain about half the slides for me, with the disastrous result that all the bloods floated off the slides. My poor wife was in tears and me too almost. There was nothing to be done except to give her a strong hug and a kiss and write off half of that day's work, as we certainly could not return to collect more blood from those villagers whose specimens we lost.

The noise of the drums was not the only nocturnal musical entertainment. At that time, computers of a manageable size had yet to be invented. I designed a punch card printed with details of blood examinations, mosquitoes, and other factors to help me to prepare analyses of our material from the field and laboratory. For example, data on numbers of malaria-positive blood films were extracted by the simple expedient of pushing a knitting needle through the desired, punched-out position on bunches of cards, and then the cards were counted. To facilitate the mathematical analysis of these data I acquired a Facit calculator. This machine was full of cogs and knobs into which numbers were fed. One cranked a handle backwards and forwards by hand, making a lot of noise, until it spewed out the answers. My enthusiasm for completing these analyses knew no bounds, so rather than go to sleep in an evening with an incomplete analysis, I would take the Facit to bed and crank the handle until I had my results. This lasted about two nights before Ruth understandably gave me my marching orders. It was she or the Facit. What choice did I have?

The spraying was carried out with hand-operated pumps containing the insecticide. It was sometimes necessary to transport the water needed for this operation in containers improvised from long, hollowed-out, thick bamboo stalks. Moreover, the workmen had to be protected so that they were not covered in the spray. Through the entire operation I am glad to say, we did not have one case of insecticide poisoning except for one misguided villager. He stole some DDT powder, thinking it was flour. He and his family survived.

What did not always survive however were some of the lizards that lived in the palm roofs and normally fed on insects. With their disappearance numerous palm-thatch-eating insects survived and thrived to the extent that many village houses were damaged. This was an especially serious matter when the building housed the valuable yams that were the main food crop of the region and the pride and joy of the population.

This understandably aroused the ire of the village elders in some cases and necessitated a change of tactics to overcome the problem, including the introduction of more solid structures for the storage houses. Nevertheless, the pilot project did yield encouraging results that I hoped would permit the extension of malaria control over parts of TPNG that shared a similar ecology and social pattern to that of the Sepik District.

Ruth, who took on the job of administrator for me, sometimes accompanied me on field surveys. She was especially interested in learning about the local cultures and arts. Many years later she enriched her very creative embroidery by incorporating some of what she learned in her themes. Part of Ruth's job was to order and control the project's supplies and pay the local staff. Strange as it sounds today, one official form of payment for laborers was old-fashioned stick tobacco that was greatly appreciated by both men and women. With it one had to supply old newspaper, as the custom was to roll the shredded tobacco in paper to produce cigarettes, each about twenty centimeters long.

In the highlands both tobacco and small cowrie shells were widely used as currency at that time, although the use of the former was severely frowned on by some of the more restrictive and narrow-minded Christian missionaries.

In addition to all this, Ruth took on virtually all the household chores with the aid of our houseboy, Boro, and one of the inmates of the local jail, who we called 'the calaboose.' He was responsible for providing firewood for the hot water and stove.

Ruth rapidly gained a wide reputation as the best hostess in that neck of the New Guinea woods. Apart from local visitors, we had a number from overseas. We had entomologists such as George Davidson, a specialist in insecticide resistance from the LSHTM, John Smart from the Natural History Museum in London who came to look for various biting flies, and Elmo Hardy of the Bernice Bishop Museum in Hawaii who studied tropical fruit flies. He brought with him, and left for my use, an ingenious trap to monitor the populations of these insects using a remarkably powerful synthetic pheromone bait that continued to work for several years after it was placed on a cotton pad inside the trap. I sent him specimens and data for a long time after he left.

We also played host to a Swiss visitor. I believe he was the owner of the company that makes Ruth's favorite mustard. When he learned this he was both surprised and pleased. After his return to Zurich, he sent us a large box of Thomy's mustard, a very welcome supplement to our diet.

As I intended that our pilot malaria control area would extend south from Maprik as far as the Sepik river, Ruth and I drove the Land Rover past Burui on several occasions. There was a small agricultural center in Marua, a distance of about forty kilometers. We did not intend to spend the night by the Sepik as it was notorious for being solid with particularly vicious *Aedes* mosquitoes. The villagers who lived along the riverbanks protected themselves by sleeping in large rolled-up rush mats. These contained a slow-burning smudge fire at one end and were tied up at the other. The whole family would sleep in such a shelter. It was jokingly said that it was not necessary to paddle a canoe on the river since a hoard of hungry mosquitoes would settle on it and fly it downstream so that they could enjoy a good feed on its passengers. In spite of this, several villages along the riverbanks had beautifully decorated Haus Tambarans and a number of excellent wood carvers still produced wonderfully colorful, traditional masks and other artifacts. Many of the carvings included stylized figures of crocodiles, pigs, and other animals that were abundant in the area.

On the way back we stopped overnight at Barui in the house of the agricultural officer and his wife. He was an Australian of German origin and she a rather prim and proper English teacher. It was remarkable to find them living an almost isolated existence in Burui since both were cultured individuals whom one would have expected to encounter in a far larger community, but they seemed to be happy in their unusual way of life. Their house was well protected from the ubiquitous mosquitoes, but we found our mosquito nets surrounded by them. In the middle of the night when I got out of bed to see how they were getting into the room, I discovered that the mosquito wire on the window had a small hole around which the hungry insects were queuing to get in.

About two years after we went to live in Maprik, we received the inevitable notice that John Gunther intended to pay us a visit. A new Director of Public Health, Roy Scragg, was appointed and Gunther, who was soon to become the Deputy Administrator of TPNG, had never seen the pilot project. He was astounded to see what a solid establishment we had built up in Maprik. He never envisaged that I would achieve this without his prior knowledge and approval. Rather than giving us the benefit of his valuable comments and possibly his advice, his reaction was to command me to return to the Port Moresby headquarters and hand over the pilot project to Harry. I would go back to live in Maprik, he warned me, over his dead body! And so it was. We reluctantly uprooted ourselves. Ruth, Babar, and I returned to Moresby.

In our absence the administration carried out a considerable amount of building work that included the construction of a new suburb on a hill to the north of the city. There they established a new modern hospital with a laboratory and several groups of bungalows for government employees. We were allocated one of these within easy reach of the hospital and a laboratory in that building. There was a shortage of experienced administrative staff in the old medical headquarters downtown. Ruth was quickly offered and accepted a post there.

Being based in HQ did not limit my ability to travel to outlying parts of TPNG that was essential to my work. Over the next couple of years I visited all the larger islands such as Manus in the Admiralty islands, New Britain, New Ireland, and Bougainville as well as Honiara in the British Solomon islands. Before launching on these journeys we decided it was time Ruth and I took some overdue leave and arranged a short visit to Australia. First we needed to find someone to look after Babar and a stray cat that he had adopted. Luckily we arranged for one of the Australian health inspectors and his family to occupy our house and take care of Babar and puss in our absence.

Harry and Marion's families lived in Brisbane, which was our initial port of call when we flew out of Port Moresby. There was a long delay in clearing Customs at Brisbane airport because one of our suitcases became soiled with oil on the journey and the customs officer suspected that we were trying to smuggle something illicit into the country. He insisted on keeping us to the last so that he could give we pommies a thorough going over. We were finally released. Having missed the airport bus, we had to take a taxi to our hotel in town. We found Brisbane to be a delightful city. Harry and Marion had arranged for us to meet their families who gave us a very warm welcome. Our intention was to buy a second-hand car and this was made simple for us as one of Harry's relatives was a car dealer. We bought a Holden, the Australian national car. It was in excellent condition and very reasonably priced. After a few days enjoying life in the big city we set off south down the coastal route via the Queensland Gold Coast, a fabulous resort area. The trunk road had excellent traveler hotels where we could overnight. Crossing the border from Queensland into the next state we went through a quarantine barrier to ensure that we were not carrying any fresh food, including fruit of any kind. The Australian authorities were very strict in controlling the movement of potential agricultural pathogens from state to state. Fortunately we were clean.

The first city we stopped at was Canberra, but we did not stay long as we were very keen to visit Melbourne and Sydney. It is strange that I have few memories of our stay in either city other than an incident when I skidded on the tramlines in Sydney and the Holden turned a half-circle in the middle of the road and left us facing the way we had come. Luckily I did not hit anyone. My main memory is of the drive we made up into the mountain area behind Brisbane on the return leg of our holiday journey. Mount Glorious, about 600 meters above sea level and only thirty kilometers from the city center, contains an interesting tropical rain forest that is less dense than that of TPNG and has some resemblance to a moss forest. We found the climate to be delightful the day we visited it and we saw that an attractive suburb was springing up along the road that approached the mountain from the city. Our brief glimpse of the area appealed to me so much that I thought I could happily have retired there, but Ruth found it far too isolated for her taste so I dropped the idea. We renewed contact with the Standfast family and were able to sell back the Holden before returning to Port Moresby.

There was still much work that I could do from HQ, including visit some of the smaller islands north of the New Guinea mainland to explore extending the control program. These visits gave the opportunity to study the mosquito fauna of different ecological areas where few were collected before. On most of the islands the population were Polynesians, rather than Melanesians. However, that made little difference in their response to malaria infection. Towards the end of 1959 I organized, with the WHO Regional Office for the Western Pacific, the First Inter-Territorial Conference for the South-West Pacific, in Port Moresby. Delegates from the three countries in which malaria control projects were under way and delegates from Australia and WHO attended. I was delighted to see my old friend

Bob Black among them. Another delegate was Patricia Marks, an entomologist from Queensland University. This was an invaluable encounter since, when we left TPNG, I arranged for her to transfer the bulk of my large mosquito collection to her department where I knew it would be studied in detail and carefully conserved. By the time of the conference I was allocated £142,000 for malaria control for the coming year or 5.8 percent of the total health budget for the whole Department of Public Health. I submitted a proposal to extend the TPNG program for fourteen years at a total cost of £2.3 million, a large sum in those days. Malaria eradication was still being proposed and supported by WHO, although it was not yet shown it could be achieved in highly endemic tropical places such as Africa and New Guinea.

During our conference, the idea was put forward for me to visit across Africa to look into the problems that many countries were encountering in meeting this objective and to see how those problems might relate to the efforts being made in the South-West Pacific. In May and June 1960, I received a special Fellowship from WHO for this purpose.

Once more I left Ruth and Babar alone in Port Moresby and went back to Africa. My first port of call was the headquarters of malaria control operations in the Centre Muraz in Bobo-Dioulasso, the second biggest city of what was then the Haute Volta Republic— now Burkina Faso. Five years of house spraying with DDT or Dieldrin and intermittent administration of the antimalarial drug pyrimethamine, had failed to make a significant impact on malaria transmission. Rather, it had created pyrimethamine resistance in the most dangerous malaria parasite, *Plasmodium falciparum*. Next, I visited a large control campaign based on Bernin Kebbi in the north of Nigeria. This was the first area where resistance of the main vector, *Anopheles gambiae*, to Dieldrin along with cross-resistance to a related organochlorine insecticide, benzene hexachloride was discovered in 1955. A change to DDT did not improve matters there and I saw several basic reasons why this was the case; not least observing that the insecticide spray did not reach the nooks and crannies of the roof and walls inside the dwellings where it was sprayed. Only in the South Cameroon region was insecticide spraying successful. However, this was not matched in North Cameroons by the time of my visit and everything went back to pre-campaign levels. On my way to East Africa I passed through Brazzaville just as the Belgians were fleeing the ex-Belgian Congo. It was in the process of becoming independent. There was near panic in the airport and round about. I was pleased to leave the area without encountering any untoward events.

My destination was the East African Institute of Malaria and Vector-Borne Diseases at Amani in Tanganyika, the country I worked in some years earlier. It was the institute I might have worked in had MI5 not decided that my views were too radical to risk admitting me to the Colonial Medical Service. In Amani I met Mick Gilles again, an old colleague from London and the son of the father of plastic surgery, Sir Harold Gilles. Mick and his associates took me into the field to see the excellent work being carried out on the Pare-Taveta scheme where Dieldrin was the main insecticide used for residual spraying. It was the only time that I have collected mosquitoes in the field at night while somebody stood guard over me with a shotgun in case a lion decided I would make a good meal.

However, in spite of the scheme's successes that included eliminating one of the two main vectors, *Anopheles funestus*, from the area, transmission still continued. This was partly due to the presence of large numbers of cattle that provided an alternative blood source for the remaining vectors that did not come into contact with insecticides. My final visit was to the island of Zanzibar off the east coast of Tanzania where the ecology was entirely different. Again my inspection revealed many simple, practical reasons why residual spraying could never be complete. Mass drug administration was added to the regimen on the neighboring island of Pemba, but that only made an important impact when given in schools under supervision.

My overall conclusion, put politely was, "The progress of malaria eradication in Africa has suffered considerably from a tendency to over-generalize. For example, it was assumed that the only important building material in native dwellings is mud. Also, that *A. gambiae* is essentially anthropophilic, endophagic, and endophilic, i.e., it mainly feeds on human blood indoors and rests indoors after feeding. And that Dieldrin remains effective for one year and DDT for six months, so spraying Dieldrin yearly and spraying DDT bi-annually for three years will interrupt transmission; that *P. falciparum* infections burn out in twelve to eighteen months; that most Africans sleep indoors; and many other generalizations."

This was not the conclusion WHO wanted me to draw. Eradication was the objective so eradication had to succeed. Any other view was heresy. I made a number of positive recommendations, but my conclusion was that, "It is premature to commence any new mass eradication campaigns in the less developed African territories where current economic and social conditions are too unstable to guarantee continuity of the means of realizing such campaigns. Furthermore no foolproof economical method has yet been found to completely interrupt transmission in the savannah countries."

For TPNG, they needed a major reorganization of the campaign to ensure total coverage of residual spraying before it was extended over the mainland. This was heresy indeed. I submitted my report to the TPNG administration and to WHO in July 1960. I believe it was quietly shelved. After that, I was *persona non grata* in Geneva for a number of years. When I reappeared, I wore different hats; first as a member of the WHO Expert Advisory Panel on Malaria from 1967, and second as Director of the WHO Collaborating Center on Antimalarials in the Liverpool School of Tropical Medicine from 1969. In 1969, WHO officially abandoned its policy of malaria eradication and the campaign was closed down, but I do not claim responsibility for that belated decision.

Overall, our pilot project was a great success as specifically reflected in the dramatic fall in the infant parasite rate from 72.4 to 7.9 percent per year at the end of three years of spraying. In addition, there was a parallel decrease in the size of the vector mosquito population in the sprayed sectors over the same period. A similar result was obtained by our colleagues in Dutch New Guinea and augured well for extending this method of control over a larger part of the malarious regions of TPNG. However, it was vital that the cycle of insecticide spraying was maintained regularly and the quality of insecticide should be as high as possible. The importance of this became evident a year after I left TPNG. My job as malariologist was taken over by an inexperienced 'New Australian' who decided to accept the lowest bid rather than the highest quality when new supplies of DDT were purchased. The infant parasite rate reverted to its original level within the first year. A similar problem occurred in a second pilot project that I organized in a less endemic area, Ferguson and Goodenough islands in the d'Entrecastaux group off the eastern coast of TPNG, under the supervision of Terry Spencer. His former experience in malaria control was in the Wahgi valley in the Eastern highlands where the malaria incidence was both much lower and seasonal. The results in the islands were similar in the first year to those in the Maprik project, but they faltered in the second year when administrative problems disrupted the normal spraying cycle.

The vicissitudes of life in TPNG and the isolation finally began to get the better of Ruth. I enjoyed my life and work and could happily have settled in Australia, but Ruth missed Europe and her Swiss homeland. We made another life-changing decision. We would return to Europe. When I told my Director Roy Scragg, that I wanted to leave before my contract officially terminated, he was not pleased nor was John Gunther. I had some difficulty with the TPNG authorities in obtaining my release from their service for the sake of Ruth's wellbeing so I got help from the Medical Defence Union in order to do so. In the end, Ruth went ahead of me, leaving Babar and me in the house in Port Moresby over the 1960 Christmas period. I will never forget the hours I spent in the Moresby main post office, trying to get a telephone call through to Ruth in Herisau to give her my Christmas wishes. Finally, much to my surprise, I received an answer. It was my dear old mother-in-law. Ruth was out having her hair done! In my primitive Swiss-German I chatted a few costly minutes with her and asked her to give my love and Christmas greetings to Ruth and the rest of the family, before the operator terminated the call. Happy Christmas and back I went to the empty house with Babar to drown my sorrows. In many ways I would regret leaving TPNG. The stay there was of considerable scientific and general professional interest. For Ruth, the experience was more stressful, albeit it educational and rewarding in extending her knowledge and understanding of an alien environment. In many ways, she had willingly tolerated a relatively lonely existence.

I was finally able to leave Port Moresby, but not before I managed to find a new home for our beloved Babar. There was no direct route by air or sea by which a dog could travel to Europe, nor could he be readmitted to Australia. The health authorities there unjustifiably feared rabies. It had never been recorded in TPNG or Australia but the authorities were afraid that the virus may have been taken to TPNG by Japanese police dogs during WW II. That did not happen. Because the only route for Babar to return to Europe was via Australia and the Australian authorities totally forbade the admission of a dog from TPNG, even through quarantine, I was desperate to find a place where Babar, a sturdy, fully-grown boxer, would be happy.

Eventually I was put in touch with somebody living in the highlands who was ready to give him a home. I had a large crate made and floored it with some of my warmer clothes with which he was familiar. We arranged for our young friend Brian to fly Babar to his new home, accompanied by his favorite toy, an old slipper of mine. He arrived safely, the only boxer in all of New Guinea. I heard much later that he established a large line of half-boxers in the vicinity of his new home.

Sadly, Brian died when his plane flew into a mountain in clouds a couple of years later. He was flying a modern, small passenger plane for Australian Airlines in the TPNG highlands when he encountered heavy mist and lost his way. Flying was the life he loved and for him it was an apt way to depart this world, but we were all grieved at his loss.

Regarding the outcome of our efforts to control malaria in TPNG, in 2006, forty-five years after my departure, 1.5 million cases of malaria and 3,000 deaths were recorded among a population of 6.2 million and 94 percent still live in areas of high endemicity. In short, for all our efforts, the situation there as in West Africa changed little. It is in total contrast to Nepal and a number of other less endemic tropical and subtropical countries. Now that more affluent individuals, funding organizations, and countries are pouring millions into the fight against malaria in the world's problem countries, we may begin to see major progress. However, my opinion is that the emphasis is on the word 'may'.

PART III

Chapter 12

Basle and Beyond 1961–1966

I arrived back in Herisau to be reunited with Ruth early in 1961 and set about looking for work. As I had acquired considerable experience using insecticides to control malaria I decided to approach someone in a major Swiss pharmaceutical company. I succeeded in making an appointment to visit the renowned Swiss chemist, Professor Paul Müller in the research laboratories of the Geigy Company. I was rather shy at encountering this eminent scientist. He had received the Nobel Prize in 1948 for his 1939 exposure of the potential value of dichlorodiphenyltrichlorethane (DDT), a simple organic chemical first synthesized in 1874. It kills insects over a long duration of time. This work was one of the major foundations of the malaria eradication program. He was a most welcoming host who expressed a genuine interest in my DDT field experience and concerns for its future. However, when I enquired whether the Geigy Company might have a position for a man of my experience and talents, I drew a blank.

DDT was also used as an insecticide for the mass protection of agricultural crops such as rice. Although this revolutionary compound saved millions of lives over coming years, because of a threat it posed to the ecosystem when deployed on a massive scale, it was discarded for a long time. Ironically it made a recent comeback for use as one of the components of the current WHO push 'Roll back malaria'. In later years, I came to know one of the company owners, the biologist Professor Rudolf Geigy. Unfortunately, I did not know him at that time.

Never easily discouraged and beginning to run low on funds, I approached other Swiss companies with the same query. Over the years, I forget how it happened that I was offered a position with the clinical research department of the CIBA pharmaceutical company in Basle, but I was and I accepted it with alacrity, even though I had little idea of what the work implied, nor knowledge of German.

Basle is a great Swiss city justifiably renowned for its culture and its industry. As a place to live, the contrast with the conditions I had inflicted on Ruth in our seven years of marriage was stark. She was back in her homeland, albeit a canton where an entirely different dialect of Schweizerdeutsche was spoken. She lived a much more civilized existence here. The CIBA offices, laboratories, and a factory were situated in the west part of Basle near the conjunction of Switzerland, France, and Germany.

We rented a small house on a road called 'Beim Letziturm' close to the River Rhine near an ancient Basle tower. It was a charming corner of town with ready access to CIBA by tram. Not far along the river to the east on the opposite bank sat the tower block of the major pharmaceutical company, Hoffmann-La Roche. I would develop important collaborative research with them twenty years later. I suspect one reason I received the post was that CIBA was investigating some promising new compounds to treat schistosomiasis, a tropical worm disease. I was aware of this, but I had not seen it since 1950 when I studied for the DTM&H in London.

In CIBA, I had the good fortune to work under the direction of a Swiss-German physician, Fritz Kradolfer, who was interested in tropical diseases, and with a Swiss-French doctor, Claude Lambert, who spent some years in the ex-Belgian Congo. My primary responsibility was to plan and organize clinical trials for compounds destined to combat completely non-tropical conditions of which I knew little. However, my training in statistics and epidemiology in London served me well in Basle. Some of the compounds being introduced into clinical trials were totally outside my experience. For example, anti-inflammatory drugs, compounds for the alleviation of spasticity in patients with neurological diseases, anabolic steroids, corticosteroids for the treatment of skin disorders, drugs to relieve hypertension, renal disease, and more. My main contribution to their development was the design of statistical tests for the evaluation of their action in the clinical trials. My job entailed travel to numerous medical centers, both inside and outside Europe. Some travel was to Brazil where, among other drugs, we studied the potential value of new compounds that Claude helped to develop to treat schistosomiasis and other worm infestations.

In Basle our many new acquaintances were, Swiss, German, French, Italian, Dutch, and English. My immediate supervisor was Gerry Bassil, a genial English doctor. We became lifelong friends with him and his family. Gerry died of cancer many years later in their home near Sydney. An Irish physician who had one child who had the gross misfortune to be one of the first thalidomide-damaged infants of the early 1960s joined us. Later on Jeffrey Fryer, his wife Mary, and their children came to Basle and have remained friends ever since. In addition to Fritz, whose specialty was infectious diseases, there were other outstanding research workers in CIBA. Professor Franz Gross, an aesthetic-looking German, was an authority on renal physiology and hypertension as was George Peters, another German scientist. Franz who had a touching respect for the British, used to invite Gerry and me to his house outside Basle for agreeable informal discussions accompanied by excellent wine. I believe he rarely shared evenings with his other associates. The overall Director of medical research in CIBA was a brilliant young doctor from an eminent Basle family, Hubert Bloch, who spent some years as a professor in an American university. He was a tall, boyish-looking, charming man with an equally charming family. They occupied a penthouse apartment not too far from our first home. They too, invited Ruth, me, and a select few of our colleagues for memorable and delightful soirées. He and his wife were great music lovers as well as competent performers and supporters of Basle musical society. Sadly, he died suddenly at a very young age shortly before we left Basle.

After a year or two we accumulated adequate funds (I was short of cash most of the time) to leave Beim Letziturm and rent a second-floor flat in a newly constructed apartment block in Riehen. This northernmost suburb of Basle adjoins the Black Forest area of Germany. The building was at the top of a hill, about a kilometer by foot from the main Number six tramline that ran into the center of Basle from the frontier. We enjoyed a magnificent view from our front balcony over part of Germany and Basle itself. From the back of the flat we were frequently entertained by a young accomplished flutist, practicing either her scales or entire pieces of classical music. She was a daughter of the Hoffmann family who were part owner-directors of the Hoffmann-La Roche Company and strong supporters of the arts.

The Bassils who were great dog lovers and had a Yorkshire terrier, imported puppies from England to keep the old dog and themselves happy. One day they phoned us to say their puppies had arrived and invited us to see them. It turned out that they received not two, but four youngsters. What were they to do with them all? This appeal for help was one that Ruth could not possibly refuse. We left their house the proud possessors of two of the most appealing, tiny animals one could imagine. We promptly named them Mike and Minnie as they looked barely bigger than a Mickey Mouse. They remained with us and were great company for the remainder of our stay in Basle. We eventually repatriated them in 1966 to England when we moved to Liverpool which, by chance, is where they originated. To this day, I strongly suspect that the Bassil's importing four puppies was not simply a mistake! The dogs survived the standard six month quarantine period in kennels outside Liverpool where we visited them almost every weekend. By the time they were released from quarantine we had moved to a house in a Liverpool suburb next to a small wood and they shared our lives in that house for the next twelve or more years.

Our five years in Basle were an enriching experience in many ways; I was opened to the Swiss way of life that was Ruth's birthright. Living there offered an excellent opportunity for Ruth and me to become familiar with Switzerland and the neighboring European countries. We had seen little of them in our marriage because of the peripatetic nature of my career. We visited Ruth's family members in Herisau, Bern, Zurich, and Geneva with great pleasure. Walking was a favorite pastime that we continued to pursue later in life. Herisau itself is close to the delightful countryside of the canton of Appenzell. A small railway runs from the town and terminates behind a mountain called the Säntis in the Alpstein range. This is a most picturesque area, as is the town of Appenzell with its colorful buildings, local traditional costumes, and folklore events. The canton is divided into two parts, inner and outer. Herisau is the urbanized 'Ausserhoden' and Appenzell is the farming area in the 'Innerrhoden.'

The whole canton is one of the most staunchly traditional in all of Switzerland. Only men were entitled to vote in cantonal elections until 1971 when the government passed legislation giving women the right to vote in federal elections. Until then it was tradition that the men would walk to whichever village was the site for the 'Landsgemeinde' where the voting was to take place. Each was supposed to carry a sword that he held aloft to indicate for which candidate he was voting. Another very colorful tradition in Appenzellerland is the 'Alpauffahrt,' the annual migration of the villagers' cattle from their winter quarters in the area around Urnäsch, to the alpine pastures of the Schwägalp at the onset of spring. All the farm animals, cattle, goats, and dogs are decorated with bells while the farmers and family members wear special costumes. I recall an occasion early one spring morning when Ruth and I spent a few days in a delightful village inn near Urnäsch and woke to the sound of bells as the farmers and animals walked by. We arose and witnessed the scene from the bedroom window. People from the village prepared food and drinks for the farmers as they passed their way and shared merry chatter as they paused to enjoy the refreshments.

As in much of Europe, spring is the season of carnival and Basle is famous in Switzerland for its 'Fasnacht' festivities. Many Baslers belong to local groups known as 'cliques' and spend much of their spare time during the winter preparing music, spoken commentaries called 'Schnitzelbänke', and costumes for their nocturnal procession the 'Morgastreich'. Each clique patronizes one of the restaurants that were originally formed by the tradesmen's guilds. There they prepare its program of sketches, mercilessly lampooning the local goings on and general scandals of the town. At four o'clock in the morning of the Monday following Ash Wednesday, the cliques set out through the streets and alleys of the old town. The processions of gaily-costumed clique members that wind through the streets are led by the musicians who play hideously, deliberately out-of-tune music, on a weird assortment of instruments, plus drums and flutes, known locally as 'Guggenmusik'. This great folklore occasion was one that Ruth and I greatly enjoyed a number of times.

Just north of our apartment in Riehen lies a narrow strip of woodland, a couple of hundred meters wide that juts into the neighboring corner of Germany. Known as the 'Eisener Hand', it was much sought after during WW II by refugees attempting to escape from Germany into Switzerland and was heavily guarded on both sides. Nevertheless, some unfortunate individuals succeeded in entering Switzerland only to leave it unintentionally a couple of hundred meters further on and returning to Germany. When we lived nearby, the barriers surrounding the Eisener Hand were gone. It was easy to stroll from one country to the other and back without formalities. However, this was not encouraged by either the German or the Swiss authorities. On one occasion Ruth, I, and our two Yorkshire terriers were making our way home from a walk there when a young Swiss border guard stepped out from behind a tree and challenged us. We had no identity papers of any sort with us. Fortunately a few words in Schweizerdeutsch with Ruth convinced him that we could not possibly be from anywhere other than Switzerland and we continued on our way home.

In the winter months, Ruth indulged in her old love; skiing. We took regular holidays in the Pontresina area of the Engadine where she started to do cross-country skiing, known as Langlauf. Although I had never skied in my life, I was determined to try and got myself fitted with appropriate clothing and a pair of the special skis used for this sport. I was not a great success. I ended up with bloody heels and a bruised backside. However, for Ruth, it was a delight. To make it up to me to some degree, we returned to the area one summer and enjoyed walking through the forest and valleys of the superb country around the Engadine and down to the lakes that stretch from St. Moritz to above the Swiss-Italian border to the west.

Many years later, we revisited all these areas passing the days in less arduous ways. Living in Basle gave us the opportunity to visit not only parts of Switzerland with which we were not acquainted, but also neighboring countries, France, Germany, and Italy. In the appropriate seasons, it was a pleasure to cross the French border into Alsace to indulge in delicious asparagus and the German border into the neighboring Black Forest where superb game was found in country restaurants. In the summer of 1965, we bought a new Peugeot 403 to collect from the Peugeot office in Paris, and then drive for a holiday to Spain, which neither had visited.

We had never driven this type of car so we arranged for a driver to take us from the center to the southern outskirts of Paris. From there

I drove to the Spanish frontier. In late afternoon it began to get dark so I switched on the headlights. No problem until I tried to dip them without success. In the end we were obliged to find a room for the night in the nearest hotel and set off again in the morning. The next morning, we reached the border and were infuriated when the Spanish customs officers refused to let us in because our new car was still running on an international triptych and not a national number plate. In disgust we turned around and headed east across France. We knew that Ruth's sister Marianne and her family were on holiday in Rimini, on the west coast of Italy, so we drove there to join them. By then the sun was beginning to set and we needed to find a room for the night. We were approaching Montpellier, so entered that town and found a vacant room in a small hotel. Little did I know that the university of that ancient town would one day be one of the most fruitful centers of academic research with which I would develop a close and lasting collaboration.

Overall, I felt that by starting to build a life in Basle, I was compensating Ruth to a minor degree for the many pleasures of life she was deprived of by marrying this strange foreigner. Whenever possible she accompanied me when I traveled outside Basle for my work. One advantage of my involvement in clinical trials was that it was necessary to visit centers where they were conducted in numerous places around the world.

This gave me an unprecedented opportunity to meet and converse with specialists in many different disciplines. Those who interested me the most were involved with treating diseases of the tropics and subtropics, such as malaria, my personal special love, worm infestations such as schistosomiasis, also known as bilharziasis or 'snail fever' after its 1851 discovery by the German parasitologist Theodor Bilharz, or disrespectfully as 'Bill Harris' by irreverent British soldiers in Africa, and unusual fungal infections. CIBA encouraged me to participate in periodic scientific meetings such as the International Congresses of Tropical Medicine and Malaria and International

Congresses of Parasitology, both held in a different country every four years, and the Annual Meetings of the American Society of Tropical Medicine and Hygiene. There were many other excellent meetings on pharmacology, therapeutics, and infectious diseases. These were invaluable occasions for making new acquaintances, keeping up to date on the latest developments in research, and to generally enrich my knowledge.

A rewarding feature of my way of life was that it provided the opportunity to form warm personal and scientifically fruitful relationships with likeminded colleagues around the world. I became aware of this when we returned to Europe in 1960 and I began attending national and international meetings of medical and parasitological societies. I found myself joining a remarkable camaraderie.

One notable associate was Robert (Bob) Killick-Kendrick. I first encountered Bob in the 1950s. He had recently returned from Nigeria where he was studying trypanosomiasis, a disease spread by tsetse flies, to take a post with Professor Cyril Garnham, then the Professor of Protozoology in the London School of Hygiene and Tropical Medicine. Bob's original role there was to assist his chief, together with Bill Bray, a young, brash, Australian, in studying the life cycle of malaria parasites, especially in rodents and monkeys. At that time Professor Alain Chabaud of the Muséum National d'Histoire Naturelle of Paris, together with a young assistant, Irène Landau, was also doing parallel research. In 1968 Jeff Bafort, a Belgian physician from the Institute of Tropical Medicine in Antwerp, joined me in Liverpool. From that institute Ignace Vincke in 1948 had discovered the first malaria parasite known to occur in rodents in African tree rats. It was a seminal moment in developing experimental models for malaria research. He named it *Plasmodium berghei*.

During the 1960s, Irène was working in London on temporary assignment to Garnham's department. That is where I first met this dynamic young woman. Like me, she had originally qualified in medicine but abandoned this to follow the life of a research parasitologist. She made frequent visits to West and Central Africa where she studied the protozoal parasites of wild animals, especially rodents. Bob, Irène, and I rapidly bonded as members of a strange group who became known as *plasmodiacs*. Much of my subsequent research on malaria and leishmaniasis was in association with these colleagues.

The first time I visited Latin America for CIBA was 1962. I made an extensive, ten-week tour to orientate myself on medical centers that were foci of research on tropical and parasitic diseases. From CIBA's point of view, the most important then was schistosomiasis. Some of the chemists and Claude Lambert had developed an entirely novel drug, first named niridazole and later, Ambilhar. This disease was highly endemic in Brazil, especially the impoverished northeast, and the compound was undergoing clinical trials there. It proved to be very active, but showed some toxic side effects. It was ousted shortly after by a quite different compound, praziquantel, that was developed by Bayer. It later not only proved to be very safe, but also effective against a wide spectrum of other helminth parasites, both of man and animals.

In 1964, CIBA organized an international symposium on schistosomiasis in the Institute of Tropical Medicine in Lisbon. The focus was to assess the progress being made in clinical evaluations of its new drug, niridazole. I had the unexpected pleasure of reuniting with my old colleague, Fernando Da Cruz Ferreira there. We worked together over a decade earlier in Liberia. When Ruth saw his impressive size, she realized that my story of his holding a village chief upside down with one hand and shaking him was not a fiction of my imagination.

These meetings were invaluable in bringing together experts on this topic who worked in centers around the world. A second meeting was organized in 1967 in Philadelphia. They were not the free holidays handed out by pharmaceutical companies that have been severely criticized in recent years, but invaluable forums for the presentation and discussion of new data and new ideas on recent scientific discoveries and developments.

With CIBA, I learned much about the world of pharmacological research, from bench to clinic. This gave me an entrée into many aspects of the tropical world and its diseases that were new to me. Regarding malaria, drug resistance was emerging as a major threat to managing one of the world's most ravaging diseases. The Vietnam War began in 1959 and by 1960 American troops being deployed there in great numbers were suffering increasingly from malignant malaria that longer responded to treatment with the best drug, chloroquine. I already had several years of practical field experience in malaria research, both as a physician and entomologist.

I was keen to get an opportunity to carry out laboratory research on antimalarial drugs. I managed to persuade Fritz to let me use a small laboratory and provide technical assistance to direct some of my energy into basic laboratory research on the problem of chemotherapy and especially to search for new drugs. I was allowed to employ two assistants, a young Basle science graduate, Peter Suter, and a very competent German technician, Herr Uschmann. Together we built what evolved into a highly productive program. To do this, we first set up an experimental model of malaria. At that time, it involved infecting white mice with *Plasmodium berghei*. This parasite of wild rodents was discovered, as I mentioned earlier, by Professor Ignace Vinckei of the Prince Leopold Institute of Tropical Medicine in Antwerp, in the Katanga highlands of the Belgian Congo in 1948. In later years, other species and strains of malaria that infected laboratory mice were discovered by Meier Yoeli of New York University, Alain Chabaud and Irène Landau from the Museum of Natural History in Paris, Bob Killick-Kendrick from the LSHTM, and Jeff Bafort from Antwerp.

There was an excellent scientific rapport and generosity between all these scientists and I gradually accumulated a collection of these parasites. My first objective was to develop a chloroquine-resistant parasite we could use to infect laboratory mice, as a model of the drug-resistant strains of the 'malignant tertian' parasite, *Plasmodium falciparum*, that infected man. In 1976, after many years, William Trager and his colleagues in New York succeeded in developing a method of growing this human parasite in continuous culture in the laboratory and opening a new avenue in the search for new drugs. Meanwhile, the choice of a model lay between an avian malaria parasite that infected day-old chicks, another that grew in ducks, or a parasite of macaque monkeys. These all had serious practical and theoretical disadvantages, even though the avian models were exploited prior to the discovery of *P. berghei*.

I now had two concurrent positions in CIBA; first in the clinical trials section and second in the research laboratory. The latter began a new, lifelong phase of my career. A few years later CIBA constructed a new tower block of twenty stories on the northern bank of the Rhine. I was allotted a splendid new laboratory on the fourth floor and an office on the fourteenth. From my laboratory window I had a superb view over the river, looking towards France to my right and the tower block of the Sandoz Company, the third of the four major pharmaceutical companies of Basle, on the south side of the river.

Basle is the home of the Swiss Institute of Tropical Medicine, the brainchild of the late Professor Rudolf Geigy, part owner of the fourth great Basle pharmaceutical company that amalgamated with CIBA just after my departure and became the CIBA-Geigy company. Over the course of time, the organization further metamorphed and emerged under the name of Novartis. Interestingly, in the 1990s, this company was the first to exploit the potential of novel antimalarial drug combinations (ACTs) for the prevention and treatment of multi-drug resistant falciparum malaria. This was along lines that I long advocated. It was finally adopted by WHO as an essential tool in managing malaria at a global level in 2001.

Geigy was a biologist who not only created the Institute for which he justifiably became the first Director, but donated a considerable sum to permit the famous Basle zoo to construct a new, ultramodern ape house. He was a modest and very likeable man. In his huge house situated between our home in Riehen and the center of Basle, Geigy and his wife were great hosts. I had the privilege of being invited to lecture to students attending courses at the institute, much like those provided in London, and was able to join the budding Swiss Society of Tropical Medicine. In time I was made an Honorary Member. Geigy's senior assistant, Thierry Freyvogel, succeeded him when he retired. He was also a biologist, and leader of a 'Fasnacht clique', whom I got to know well when he was studying the effects of high altitude on malaria in birds. He investigated this subject very appropriately in the building on top of the Säntis mountain, not far from Ruth's hometown. Over the years, the institute produced a number of eminent specialists in infectious diseases and parasitology. This included Willy Burgdorfer, the discoverer of the cause of tick-borne Lyme Disease, a spirochete later named *Borrelia burgdorferi*.

One eminent visitor to the Institute was Professor P.C.C. Garnham, the doyen of malaria parasitology who was one of my teachers at the LSHTM in 1950. I had the good fortune to persuade him to visit my laboratory where it was my pleasure to demonstrate some very unusual parasites to him. These had appeared in one of my strains of *P. berghei* in which I produced a high level of resistance to chloroquine and which I named the 'RC strain'. Garnham, who I later came to know as Cyril, failed to recognize it as a malaria parasite, but it most certainly was. Over the years it has contributed to the recognition of the vital role of hemoglobin, the red oxygen-carrying compound in red blood cells, in the way antimalarial drugs function, and how parasites become resistant to them. Yet, to this day, nobody has explained how our RC strain parasites survive in red blood cells without producing the black pigment that is a diagnostic feature of a malaria parasite, in all other cases. Fifteen years later, I succeeded Cyril when he retired from his Chair at the LSHTM.

I would like to be able to look back on my days in the CIBA

laboratory and claim that my efforts and those of my colleagues resulted in the development of one of today's wonder drugs. Unfortunately, life is not always like that in the pharmaceutical industry. Both in Basle, and later in Liverpool and London, my teams and I studied hundreds of novel compounds. A few nearly, but not quite, reached the clinical trials stage. However, we did make a number of significant contributions to the evolution of the few compounds we currently depend on to prevent or treat malaria. In particular, they include combinations of various derivatives of artemisinin, a compound found in a Chinese weed known popularly as 'Sweet wormwood', with synthetic compounds such as mefloquine. I was very involved in all of these.

To illustrate how long the odds are for a successful new compound emerging from drug screening, consider mefloquine. It was one of only a handful that survived in clinical trials out of well over 300,000 structures that entered the US Army antimalarial drug development program established towards the end of the Vietnam War. In the end, the ancient Chinese remedy proved most effective! More on that in Chapters 16 and 17.

While malaria was the main target of my research, South America is infamous for another group of very severe protozoal infections caused by parasites called *Leishmania*. As I noted in Chapter 1, the various species of these organisms are responsible for a range of skin diseases from simple, self-healing ulcers, to dreadfully disfiguring ones that can destroy an entire face. Other species produce kala-azar, an often fatal disease of organs such as the liver and spleen. Although, at the time this area received hardly any attention from pharmaceutical companies, the main exception being Burroughs Wellcome, the cases that later came to my attention were to trigger considerable interest in me. This is described in Chapters 15 and 16.

Much of Central and South America is plagued by a protozoan parasite, akin to the trypanosomes that cause 'sleeping sickness' in tropical Africa. My first introduction to this was in Chile where Professor Hugo Schenone showed me some of the ecological features of this condition called 'Chagas' disease' that is caused by infection with *Trypanosoma cruzi*. The parasites are spread by large biting bugs that infest houses and do life-threatening damage to the muscles of the heart and intestines. Its incidence is decreasing now following an international campaign to destroy the vectors. However, large numbers of people remain infected and a safe, curative drug still eludes us.

Thus, there was much for me to learn about some of the more exotic New World diseases. This is not to mention what one might call banal or everyday infections such as those in the gut and liver caused by *Entamoeba histolytica*, which has a near-global distribution. Students learning about these infections in such places as the London or Swiss schools of tropical medicine, for the most part were shown preserved specimens of tissues or body fluids containing immobile, usually stained organisms, on a microscope slide. However, in Brazil especially, I had the thrill of feasting my eyes on a veritable menagerie of such parasites in hospitals and medical aid-post laboratories. I called this 'parasitology on the hoof.' In parts of South America, some very severe fungal infections of skin, lungs, and other organs occur. There were few effective drugs so CIBA and other major pharmaceutical companies actively searched for novelties in this field. CIBA had developed a new drug that was being used to treat many cases of leprosy in Latin America. This compound called, rather unimaginatively, CIBA 1906 (thiambutosine) was a new type of antibacterial agent. Although clinical trials proved its efficacy against both leprosy and tuberculosis, it was soon superseded by safer more active drugs.

During that first Latin America visit, I was introduced to a number of physicians in Argentina by a Belgian representative of CIBA, Dr. Ruyfellaert, a local resident in Buenos Aires. It was a troubled country at the time. One morning as I was dressing for the day, I picked up the newspaper that was slipped under my door and read that there was an overnight revolution.

I phoned my colleague and said, "There go our appointments!"

"Not a bit of it," he replied. "We have one of those almost every day."

Sure enough, when we walked out into the street all was quiet. It was only when we took a taxi to our first destination that we noticed some fresh bullet holes in the wall of a government building near the main square. Parking space was at a premium in central Buenos Aires so the custom was to park cars bumper to bumper without applying the brakes. To cross the road on foot, one made a gap between two vehicles large enough to reach the road and then made a dash for it. To drive away, you got into your car, started it, and then made gentle back and forth motions until there was room to drive out. It was a case of living dangerously.

Revolutions were, and remain, common in other Latin American countries. In Colombia, I was being driven to the airport to catch a flight out and we were held up in a long traffic queue that was halted by police along the highway. In the rearview mirror we spotted a small convoy of black cars heading for the airport at full speed. As the convoy came up behind us, we saw from the number of dark-suited and clearly armed passengers, that some very senior government officials, maybe even the President, were also going our way. As the last car passed, my driver pulled out and joined the convoy. Luckily, we were in a black car with official number plates and were able to enjoy a rapid and otherwise uneventful ride to catch my plane. On another occasion in Venezuela, I visited an eminent malariologist, Professor Arnaldo Gabaldon who was the Minister for Health. As we were already acquainted, he invited me to his club for dinner and arranged for me to join him in his office en route. I was met by two large pistol-toting bodyguards who escorted me to his office and accompanied us both in the elevator and into his car when we left. I was not used to this sort of personal attention. The next day I was due to move on to my next port of call and that morning read in the local newspaper that an unkind individual had planted a bomb in the men's lavatory, adjacent to the bar of the hotel in which I was staying. I began to understand why there were so many armed police around my plane as I left. It was the beginning of an attempted revolt in the nearby city of Puerto Cabello.

I had the good fortune to return to Brazil on a number of occasions from Basle and later, from Liverpool. When I went to Rio de Janeiro in 1966, I had the opportunity to visit the doyen of tropical medicine in Brazil, Professor Rodrigues da Silva, in the company of my American friend, Paul Thompson. His team at the Parke Davis Company did outstanding research in developing long-acting anti-malarial drug combinations. Paul's efforts culminated in the production of an oily, injectable preparation named CI 564. A single intramuscular injection protected volunteers in American penitentiaries against repeated bites from malaria-infected mosquitoes for nearly a whole year. Da Silva used this to protect a group of paratroopers who were dropped into a dense Amazonian rain forest area where they were trying to flush out bandits. Although no significant side effects of the injection were reported in the prisoner volunteers, a high proportion of the Brazilian troops developed severe, deep abscesses in their buttocks where the injections were made and the men had to be evacuated from the jungle by helicopter back to the hospital in Rio. Paul was shocked by this news. He asked Da Silva if any of the same batch of CI 564 remained. Fortunately, Da Silva could produce one.

Paul took one look at it and said, "This was not made by us."

This very promising compound had already been pirated by a small company in São Paulo, a common practice in Brazil in those days. Fortunately, later experience with CI 564 in Brazil and elsewhere in the world was more positive. However, it was finally dropped as it failed to achieve its secondary target, namely the prevention of infection by malaria parasites that were already resistant to one or other of the two components of CI 564. This was learned in a trial conducted by my former assistant, Karl Rieckmann, in TPNG in 1967.

The 7th International Congress of Tropical Medicine and Parasitology was held in Rio de Janeiro in 1963. At the scientific level the meetings left me with a number of vivid memories. The first was that the growing problem of resistance to chloroquine in the malignant tertian malaria parasite, *Plasmodium falciparum*, dominated the proceedings. This situation provided an opportunity for me to call attention to some of my team's early observations on drug resistance in malaria parasites. In Basle we were beginning to achieve success in developing invaluable new experimental models in mice infected with *Plasmodium berghei*. A second memory was seeing Ignatius Vincke, the Belgian who first discovered this parasite in 1948, being presented with a medal by the congress organizers for his seminal work. We were gathered in a crowded meeting room in the hotel when the award was solemnly announced. Where was the recipient? I had been talking with him in the crowd only a few minutes before. There was mild consternation at the presentation table. Then suddenly Vincke's diminutive figure emerged on hands and knees from under the table that he had reached by squeezing through the audience, then crawling on the floor to reach the other side. As his smiling face emerged a great cheer went up and the medal was duly bestowed on the modest little man.

The following year, in Basle we succeeded in producing a strain of his parasite that had an extremely high level of resistance to chloroquine, which was the most potent compound used to treat malaria at the time. We reported this at the First International Congress of Parasitology in Rome in 1964. A year later, at a special colloquium on malaria held at the tropical institute in Antwerp, we presented details of the intimate structural changes that we found in these parasites by using electron microscopy. There again, I had the pleasure of meeting not only Vincke, but also the American medical parasitologist, Meier Yoeli, as well as Brian Maegraith whom I first met a few years earlier when he visited TPNG from Liverpool.

The Rome meeting was especially significant as it was there that Ruth and I befriended Herbert Gilles and his wife Mina. Herbert who worked for several years in Ibadan University in Nigeria and then at the research institute of the British Medical Research Council in The Gambia, returned to Liverpool where he became a Senior Lecturer in Brian's Department of Tropical Medicine in the Liverpool School of Tropical Medicine (LSTM). Herbert and Brian had a natural affinity since both were recipients of prestigious Rhodes Scholarships. From Basle I visited the Liverpool School to carry out joint experiments and discuss our work on malaria. I first made Herbert's acquaintance there. Shortly after the Rome meeting, Brian sent Herbert as an intermediary to sound out my reaction to possibly joining the LSTM.

The 1963 Rio congress was memorable on several counts, in addition to the professional ones. On my arrival in my hotel along the main road flanking Copacobana beach, a pageboy escorted me to my room, then switched on the television and sat on my bed to watch it. It transpired that our congress coincided with an international football match and Pele, Brazil's national hero was playing. I had little choice but to relax and watch the game with him.

Near the northern end of Copacobana the Hotel Gloria, a majestic white building, housed the congress. More than most of the proceedings of the congress, I recall the sight of the large ground floor bar-lounge where many of the world's most eminent tropical experts sat in the early evenings to cool off with beers or caipirinhas. Interspersed along the benches were the wenches, very seductive young ladies of all shades. They clearly took pity on the poor visitors, mostly male, who had obviously had a hard day giving or, even harder, listening to erudite lectures on horrific topics. The different reactions to the female company of the younger and older congress members had to be seen to be believed. Some of the latter, whom one might expect to maintain a discreet distance, were the first to strike up conversations with the local ladies—I name no names—while many of the younger members with whom I was acquainted, to my surprise were reticent about fraternizing with them—at least in public. Of course, it's possible that they expected their spouses to return and join the party at any moment after a day's relaxation on the beach.

My next visits to Brazil were in 1964 and 1966. In Rio in 1964 one of my hosts, a young Brazilian doctor named Carvalho Neto who worked with the local headquarters of CIBA, invited me to the sports stadium to see that great little man Pele play his last major game. Although he failed to score a goal, his teammates did their best to place the ball at his feet, but without success. Nevertheless, when the match ended, Pele removed his shirt and made several victory circuits of the pitch, to immense and terrifying applause from the huge number of spectators. We were in the middle of the first tier and were bombarded by firecrackers thrown down by the occupants of the tiers above us. The experience was far more hair-raising than anything I experienced in London during the blitz.

In 1966, I went to the prestigious Instituto Butantan adjacent to the campus of the University of São Paulo. The institute was founded in 1901 in the tradition of the famous Pasteur Institutes, by the pioneering physician, Vital Brazil. There I met Professor Fritz Köberle, an authority on the pathology of Chagas' disease that was very common among the rural population at that time. The absence of any safe and effective form of treatment left many people suffering from chronic damage to their hearts and intestines. It was said, with good reason, that at many local football matches one of the players would drop dead from acute heart failure. To this day there is still no safe remedy, but the numbers of new cases has been radically reduced by public health measures carried out on an international scale. It is based primarily on the use of insecticides to kill the 'kissing bugs' that spread the disease. The institute is internationally renowned not only for its collection of about 54,000 venomous snakes used in the production of antivenoms, but also for its development of vaccines against poisonous arthropods such as spiders, scorpions, bees, and wasps. A view of the pits in which many of the snakes are kept leaves a lasting impact, as do the staunch snake handlers, some of whom have survived repeated bites by the serpents they care for. Over 110 million doses of vaccines, including a number against bacterial and virus infections, and 300 thousand vials of hyper immune sera were produced at the Instituto Butantan in 2001.

I continued to visit Latin America for various reasons in the following years. The range of reasons has an historical overlap with the events I have described so far. Fortunately, one series of handwritten notes survived the now inexplicable and irrational decision I took years ago to destroy my whole collection of little black-covered diaries. In these I had maintained inconsistent notes on passing events and encounters during my overseas travels. In order to retain some historical continuity I have appended what remains to Chapter 15.

One day early in 1966 a letter reached us in Basle inviting me to apply for the post of the Walter Myers Professorship of Parasitology in the LSTM. The invitation was hard to refuse. We pondered over the situation at great length. I was only too aware that the city of Liverpool could hardly compare in any sense with the city of Basle. In 1966, it was a grimy, old-fashioned place with an economy largely developed around its famous port. It had a history of commercial exploitation of the tropical world and much of its wealth in Victorian times was built on the backs of slave labor in such centers as the sugar plantations of the West Indies. In this way it became one of the great cities in the British Isles. Culturally it ranged from the mainly working class 'scoucers' with their distinctive dialect and humor, the large population of Chinese, most of whose male ancestors had arrived as seamen, and the elite businessmen and industrialists who had built up the famous Liverpool docks and factories, such as that which produced Tate and Lyle's sugar. My introductions to Liverpool were, as mentioned earlier, as a volunteer in a munitions factory medical center at the end of WW II and as a visiting researcher to the LSTM from Basle.

As much as I could appreciate the numerous good points about Liverpool and its residents, as well as the LSTM, I found it hard to imagine how Ruth would accept such an abrupt and radical change of milieu after five years back in Basle. Admittedly, it was not like asking her to live in a tent in the Nepalese Terai again or in an isolated home in the relative wilds of TPNG. In the end, we decided that no harm would be done by applying for the post since there was no guarantee that I would be the only applicant, much less the successful one, so I applied. It was another rash decision that we made that could turn our lives around.

And it did. I went to Liverpool to face a stern selection committee led by the President of the Council of the LSTM, Brigadier Sir Philip John Denton Toosey of River Kwai fame. I returned to Basle as a Professor Elect and handed in my resignation to CIBA.

Chapter 13

In and Out of the Liverpool School of Tropical Medicine 1966–1979

In April 1966, after living in Basle for five years, I was accepted as a permanent resident. In September the same year, I returned my resident's card with thanks and we set off for Liverpool. We had some misgivings. Our journey with the two dogs in our Peuguot was relatively uneventful. We drove from Basle across France to Le Touquet airport on the French Channel coast from where we flew, lock, stock, dogs, and barrel to Lydd. With Mike and Minnie running happily on the shelf inside the rear window, we presented ourselves to the rather shocked officers of H.M. Customs. They hailed the driver of a waiting van into which our unfortunate pets were incarcerated for their ride into the animal quarantine station just outside Liverpool. We knew that we had to wait six months for the Yorkies to be delivered back to us, but we made up our minds to visit them every week, as we did.

Feeling very sad, we cleared the rest of our baggage, and set off towards the Lake District where I planned to spend the night. I felt it was wiser to introduce Ruth back to England gently, rather than deliver her straight to Merseyside. As I hoped, the weather and the countryside that greeted us were beautiful so that we could rest, then complete our journey to the northwest the next morning. With help from Herbert Gilles, we were fortunate in renting a bungalow near his home in Birkdale. This is a small center just south of Southport and is best known as the home of one of Britain's most renowned golf courses, the Royal Birkdale. It was just a walk away from where we were to live for the next year. Neither Ruth nor I were golfers but the course lay along a stretch of the Birkdale sands that are a natural beauty site and home to rare toads and other creatures. Birkdale lies north of Liverpool with easy access to the LSTM via the docks area. As soon as one left middleclass Birkdale, the neighborhoods became bleaker and bleaker. The town itself stands on the north bank of the Mersey River and is not very appealing. It is dirty and dusty, especially when strong winds blow up from the river.

Mike and Minnie survived the quarantine kennels and, shortly after their release, we moved to a house in the Liverpool suburb of Woolton where they shared our lives for the next twelve or more years. Once settled in Woolton, we began to discover an entirely other side of Liverpool; its rich cultural life. We realized that the town carried a special atmosphere that overrode all the grime, and even that has been completely transformed over the last two decades by the town being radically rebuilt as a City of Culture. Our arrival on the Mersey scene coincided with the birth of the '60s generation's phenomenon and the rise of its most famous offspring, that group of talented musicians who called themselves 'The Beatles'. This name greatly appealed to my entomological tastes, as did their music to us both once they and we became a little older.

Moreover, the city already boasted some excellent and historical buildings, museums, and art galleries as well as the top class Royal Philharmonic Orchestra among other interesting centers. Across the Mersey, or under it via the Mersey tunnel, lie Birkenhead and the Wirral. Each is endowed with cultural attractions, as well as access roads to Anglesea and North Wales. Liverpool is also well endowed with hospitals. In the center of the town stood a prominent road traffic sign "Liverpool Maternity Hospital—No accidents". Scouse humor did take a little getting used to as did the accent. The latter problem was two-sided as Ruth, who had a slight trace of Swiss accent when she spoke English, discovered one day when she was trying to locate a probation client in one of the seamier districts. She stopped to ask some children for directions and had to repeat her question several times.

Eventually one of the children turned to her in exasperation and asked, "Why cern't yer talk Scouse loik ers?"

(My apologies to Scousers if I've got their accent wrong.)

In spite of such minor problems, it was not long before we were accepted by a welcoming group of neighbors. Many of them were also in the medical fraternity and one was a dentist who lived opposite us in Woolton. My main memory of him was the occasion when, without asking permission, he got into the driver's seat of my car that was standing just outside the open garage door in our drive. Never having driven a car with automatic gear change, he started the engine and drove it full pelt into Ruth's car that was parked in the rear of the garage! Fortunately, it did not push her car through the rear garage wall. We were not very close friends after that incident. However, that was an exception. We developed a deep friendship with the other two neighbors that lasted until all but one of our four good friends died. By a strange coincidence, I encountered the surviving lady again over forty years later.

It was obvious from the start that I was going to have an exceptionally busy life in Liverpool and overseas for the unforeseeable future. I was concerned with how Ruth would adjust to yet another phase of our lives with long periods of separation caused by my peripatetic life style. We were fortunate in that we could enjoy the cultural life that Liverpool and its neighboring towns had to offer; music, art, some beautiful countryside, and ready access to London with all its attractions. Then there was the great social level support we received from newly made friends and some of my colleagues in the school and university. Ruth made big contributions to extracurricular activities by inviting students home, and participating in social activities of the school. Her warm, cosmopolitan character endeared her to many of my staff and other colleagues. Unlike the ambience of the LSHTM that we would encounter much later, the smaller size of the LSTM made the ambience warmer and more sociable, partly because most people lived within relatively easy access of each other.

After some time, she befriended a lady who worked with the Liverpool probation service. Ruth offered her help as a part-time volunteer with that organization. For the remainder of our stay in Liverpool, she devoted a significant part of her abundant energy to visiting long-term prisoners and their families. From time to time she drove across the country to Wakefield prison where one of her clients was a man serving a life sentence for murder. Whenever possible, she took the man's wife and children with her for a family visit. Sometimes she took the children out for a day's treat, such as the Chester zoo or the Welsh coast. On one of the latter outings she had the misfortune to lock her keys in the boot of her car. Even the RAC could not retrieve them since she was driving an American-made Chrysler and nobody seemed to have a master key. This was in the days before mobile phones were invented. I received a desperate call from a public phone box. Ruth was stranded along a beachside road somewhere in north Wales with which I was entirely unfamiliar, the children were hungry, thirsty, and restless. What could she do?

"Just describe as well as you can where you are, then try to pacify the kids and wait for me," I told her.

Fortunately, I had a spare key so I immediately dropped what I was doing and sped to the rescue. Luckily, I found them, sitting forlornly by Ruth's car at the side of the road, exactly where she said they would be. We fed and watered the children, then drove home in convoy to deliver them back to their mother. On another occasion she phoned me at the school to tell me that she was bringing another of her client's home. She was a youngish, half-Indian woman who was on probation for threatening to kill her husband. We knew that she was a strange person with a fiery temper and Ruth was seriously afraid that if she returned to her own home that night she might carry out her threat. Would I mind if she spent the night with us! What could I say? We did not have a spare bedroom, but did have a mattress that I set up on the sitting room floor. Ruth returned home with this rather scary woman in tow, and my job was trying to converse with her while Ruth prepared an evening meal. In due course we all retired for the night which passed uneventfully, to my enormous relief. The following morning, Ruth returned the good lady to her home, after briefing her probationer colleagues on the situation. We were fortunately relieved of the responsibility of protecting her husband any longer.

The University of Liverpool, a red brick university founded in 1881, is one of the largest in England with over 20,000 students. It has one of the leading departments of Medicine, allied to its School of Tropical Medicine. Among the University's eight Nobel Prize winners, four were associated with the Department of Medicine, including Sir Ronald Ross who first revealed the life cycle of the malaria parasite and became Professor of Medicine in the LSTM. The LSTM's senior staff are also members of the Department of Medicine and participate in many of the University's organizational activities. We rapidly became acquainted with colleagues in the medical and other faculties, including several who lived on our small road in Woolton. Another neighbor on the next street was Brian Epstein, the original and colorful manager of the Beatles, although we never did happen to meet him or his young performers.

Heading the Department of Medicine at the time of our arrival was Cyril Clarke, the geneticist to whom I had sent swallowtail butterflies from Tanganyika over ten years earlier. He and his wife invited us to visit their home in the Wirral where they had constructed several large greenhouses. In these they grew numbers of exotic plants on which they bred and crossbred colorful butterflies from Africa and other tropical countries as well as moths. The studies that Cyril conducted there linked well with his research on medical genetics. He first discovered the significance of the rhesus blood factor in humans as the cause of fatal haemolysis in newborn infants and how to prevent this. For this major advance, he was later made a Fellow of the Royal Society (FRS) and knighted. Cyril's senior lecturer and collaborator was a stolid Welshman, David Weatherall. He was a good friend of Herbert due to their shared interest in the genetic aspects of malaria. After serving as the Regius Professor of Medicine in Oxford from the year 2000, he received a knighthood as had his former mentor. Incidentally, this honor evaded the long-term Dean of the LSTM, Brian Maegraith. He would have liked nothing better, but in time, both he and Herbert were awarded a CMG for their services to tropical medicine among other honors.

This is not the place to write a history of the LSTM. That has been elegantly presented by more capable medical historians including Brian. The Liverpool School vied with the London School of Hygiene and Tropical Medicine for the distinction of being the first ever of such institutes. It was created with the support of wealthy Liverpool industrialists. It was officially opened in April 1899, just a whisker ahead of the London School. From the 1920s onwards, the LSTM was a leading center for research on drugs against parasitic protozoa, especially those causing malaria, sleeping sickness, and Chagas' disease. Prior to WW II, the school's Department of Chemotherapy was staffed by such notable scientists as Warrington Yorke who became the Walter Myers Professor of Parasitology in 1914 and Professor of Tropical Medicine in 1938, and Frank Hawking, father of Stephen Hawking. Yorke established fruitful relationships both with the Medical Research Council and pharmaceutical companies such as Imperial Chemical Industries, inventors of the antimalarial proguanil; May and Baker, inventors of sulphonamides; and Burroughs Wellcome, developers of pyrimethamine.

A prime interest of these investigators and their associates was the study of mechanisms of action and drug resistance in parasitic protozoa. They developed novel ways of growing some of the organisms in the test tube (*in vitro*), rather than only in animals or birds. They were particularly successful with African trypanosomes, but not with malaria. It was 1976 when Trager and Jensen in New York were able to grow malaria parasites *in vitro*. A Tropical Disease Center was founded during WW II to treat the many servicemen and women who were repatriated with tropical diseases. These individuals were some of the first to benefit from a number of the new drugs. This service was continued long after the war as a center for the clinical management of such patients and especially repatriated ex-prisoners from the Far East theater of war. Warrington Yorke died in 1943 and his place was taken by Maegraith the following year.

Then thirty-seven years old, Brian Gilmore Maegraith was a jovial, charismatic Australian who served in the tropics for several years during WW II. His interest lay especially in pathophysiology and pathology, particularly in relation to tropical diseases. He gradually took over the school's departments of Tropical Medicine, Clinical Tropical Medicine, and Chemotherapy. He had less success in dominating the Departments of Entomology and Parasitology, but his program of research into pathophysiology blossomed. His other great strength was his insistence that much of tropical medicine research should be undertaken in the tropics. His role was to lead in the buildup of a key program of postgraduate education for students from tropical countries, such as Thailand, as well as from England. With this, he began to establish a wide collaborative network of key overseas institutions and students. Several of them in time became heads of Institutes of Tropical Medicine in their own countries. However, the Department of Chemotherapy under Maegraith was doomed as he set his own seal on the academic structure of the LSTM. By 1949, the leading senior staff of that department had departed.

One of the staff changes instituted early in Brian's reign was to create several posts of Lecturer-at-Large. Their role was to be based in developing departments in tropical countries and to help build up local training and research programs. In 1948 Herbert Gilles, an exceptionally able Maltese-born physician, like Brian, a Rhodes Scholar, was appointed to one of these posts. By the time I arrived on the scene, he had succeeded in helping Nigerian colleagues develop an important center for community medicine in the fledgling University of Ibadan, before returning to the Department of Tropical Medicine in Liverpool. Meanwhile, under Brian's direction, the LSTM was greatly strengthening the Department of Hygiene and establishing a new Department of Tropical Pediatrics and Child Health within the University Department of Child Health directed by Professor John Hay. This came to be headed by Ralph Hendrickse who Herbert collaborated with in Ibadan. Ralph built up a very strong department and international reputation and was made a Senior Lecturer in Tropical Pediatrics and Child Health in the LSTM in 1969. In 1975, he became a Professor in the University of Liverpool. The department was housed in the new Nuffield Wing when it opened in 1978. Ralph's staff and the department's functions at home and overseas were expanded over the succeeding years and he was made the first Professor of Tropical Pediatrics and International Child Health in 1988.

Changing world economic conditions, particularly those associated with the disintegration of the British colonial system, were accompanied by a decreasing level of support for colonial affairs by the government; that included funding for both Schools of Tropical Medicine.

The Deans of both the LSTM and LSHTM spent much of their time seeking non-governmental finance. A few major sources, such as the Rockefeller Foundation, were supportive up to a point. In those days preceding the growth of multi-billion pound philan-thropic bodies, such as the Wellcome Trust and the Gates Founda-tion it was an uphill struggle to ensure the continued existence of the core staff of the schools, let alone financing the research they hoped to perform. When I started at the School, it was undergoing a revision of its academic structure. This included splitting the Department of Parasitology in order to reinstate sub-departments of Veterinary Parasitology and Medical Entomology, each directed by a Senior Lecturer.

The previous Professor of Parasitology, William Kershaw, left for a Chair in the Royal College of Advanced Technology in Salford. He took with him an Egyptian mummy that adorned his office when I first visited the School some years earlier. It was his intention to look for parasites in it, but I believe he never received permission to do so from the museum that lent him this relic.

As I was not previously given any indication of the pending change, I was initially rather put out; especially as the new sub-department heads quickly established their independence. Moreover, I suspect they disliked the idea of having an outsider installed over their heads. As it transpired, it proved to be a satisfactory change since it freed me to stamp my mark on the organization. What Brian did not foresee was that I, as single-minded as he, rapidly set about converting what I inherited back to a virtually new Department of Chemotherapy in all but name, while maintaining the vital teaching commitment of the LSTM in medical parasitology, and extending the establishment of scientific relations with institutions and individual scientists abroad, as he was doing.

On my arrival I fortunately inherited a very experienced parasitologist, Bill Crewe. Prior to joining the LSTM, he conducted important field studies on several diseases caused by parasitic worms that affect man in West Africa. Among them was one caused by a fly-transmitted blood parasite called *Loa loa*, and a large fluke that infects the human lung and is transmitted from wild animals, such as the African civet, through the intermediary of water snails. Shortly after, I fortunately received a new university lectureship and had the good luck to engage a young Welsh parasitologist, Robert Howells.

Bob was working in the Department of Pathology of the university but wanted to return to his main love, helminthology. Bob remained with me throughout my stay in Liverpool, was promoted to Senior Lecturer, and eventually received a Personal Chair in parasitology. When Bob left the LSTM some years later, he was appointed to the prestigious post of Scientific Director of the Wellcome Trust.

Although they were no longer under my jurisdiction, I enjoyed an excellent working relationship with an entomologist, Bill Macdonald, an expert on filariasis, and Michael Clarkson, head of the sub-department of Veterinary Parasitology. Both were later awarded Personal Chairs. Michael later moved from the LSTM to the newly expanded Faculty of Veterinary Medicine of Liverpool University where he became a full Professor. Bill's then Junior Lecturer, Harold Townson, whose personal expertise lay in the transmission of 'River blindness' (onchocerciasis), in due course succeeded him as head of the Department and also was awarded a Personal Chair. He ultimately became President of the Royal Society of Tropical Medicine and Hygiene. A great help was that the University of Liverpool backed my application to the Medical Research Council for funds to establish a 'Research Group on the Chemotherapy of Protozoal Diseases and Drug Resistance' in 1968. I took on board a young physician, Anthony Bourke, who worked on drug-resistant malaria in Vietnam and Thailand. He was a Lecturer under the Technical Assistance scheme. Creating my new group allowed me to seek graduates with special talent. One of the first was a brilliant biologist, David Warhurst. I managed to seduce him from his post with Frank Hawking. Frank, by then, was directing a large group studying antiparasitic chemotherapy and drug resistance in the Medical Research Council's laboratories in Mill Hill. David immediately set to work assisting the build-up of our laboratory facilities and our study program on the chemotherapy of malaria, while simultaneously maintaining his area of expertise, parasitic amoebae.

Other outstanding biologists who joined my department group were David Molyneux, an expert in the field of trypanosomiasis, Michael Chance who made major contributions to the development of biochemical taxonomy, and John Jewsbury, who had worked in the pharmaceutical industry on antihelminth chemotherapy. To my regret, David Molyneux left the department in 1976 to succeed Kershaw in Salford; he soon became the department Chairman. Later he worked for WHO in Mali, and then became Director of the LSTM.

In 1969, I went to Addis Ababa in Ethiopia. One of Brian Maegraith's staff, Charles Leithead, did excellent work there on adaptation to heat and heat-associated disorders a few years earlier. At the time I visited Addis, an old friend from the LSHTM, Bill Bray, was head of the Wellcome Parasitology Unit No.2 in the Haile Selassie I University. He was investigating the epidemiology of leishmaniasis. His assistant, Dick Ashford, was a young science graduate who I first encountered bottom first. His top half was submerged in a hole in the ground where he was collecting tiny sandflies that were suspected of transmitting parasites from a still-unidentified animal reservoir to humans. When Dick emerged I saw that he lacked his right arm, lost in an accident in his student days, This barely hindered his expert handling of scientific equipment, large or small.

Both Bill and Dick were excellent naturalists, and their Ethiopian studies revealed the complex nature of leishmanisis in that country. I was fortunately able to induce Dick to join my team in Liverpool. Years later he was awarded a Personal Chair. The teaching work of the department was underpinned by the school's senior technician, Jeff Friend and his very able juniors. My research was facilitated by a skilled, motherly lady, June Portus. She was joined shortly after by Brian Robinson who was working with the RAMC. He remained with me through thick and thin until I finally retired from laboratory work in 2004. June had a pet white rat named Star that sat on her shoulder while she worked around the lab. Little did Star realize how near she was to receiving a dose of the malaria parasites that we routinely used to examine antimalarial drugs in mice. Throughout my academic life, first in Liverpool and later in London, I had the good fortune to acquire an excellent technical staff and postgraduate students. I say more about some of them later.

The world of medical parasitology is relatively small, even at an international level. For those interested in the chemotherapy of tropical diseases it is even smaller. Thus, my attendance at many scientific meetings and visits to the clinics and laboratories of numerous physicians and other research workers created an invaluable network of friends, colleagues, and other scientific collaborators for me. Such a network expands exponentially when adequate communications are maintained. The development and rapid extension of the Worldwide Web and electronic mail enormously facilitated that process. However, during my Liverpool era, extensive travel was the best way to develop and maintain a productive and enriching familiarity with the health problems of people in the global family; particularly people in developing countries. A prime target for both the School and for me was to alleviate some of those problems. To give even a brief account of all my experiences during my work with the LSTM and the LSHTM is neither the aim of this biography nor realistic. From this point on, I write what will be a very inconsistent review of this period of my life. It's readable I hope, but sketchy, varies in depth and locations, reflective of people and events, probably too lengthy but, with luck, not too tedious.

It was in Liverpool that I became acquainted with an infection that until that period of my life had evaded me, leishmaniasis. The complex of diseases generally known as the leishmaniases is spread by tiny sandflies. They are estimated to afflict some twelve million people worldwide. Between one and a half and two million new cases arise yearly. The only regions free from leishmaniasis are

Oceania and possibly Australasia. The infections are caused by several different microscopic organisms in a genus that was named *Leishmania* after an Indian Army doctor called William Leishman. I was forty-seven years old when one of these diseases first stamped an indelible mark on my mind. Below I describe a journey I made to Brazil in July 1971 when I visited a hospital near the capital city of Brazilia. The physician in charge offered to show me the wards that housed patients suffering from a condition that I naively thought of simply as leishmaniasis. I knew that the causative organisms live in cells of the immune system. Some kinds invade the liver and spleen, others the skin and mucous membranes. Surprisingly, I encountered very few individuals with leishmaniasis during earlier travels.

In this hospital the first patient I was shown shocked me. He was a simple, black farmer. His entire nose and much of his face were destroyed. In their place was a gaping hole in which stood his upper molar teeth, many of them surprisingly sound and shining white. Above the cavity two deeply sad eyes gazed into mine. Over the previous years I had built a strong research team in Liverpool to search for novel drugs to treat malaria that no longer responded to older compounds. However, there was never a safe drug to cure this type of leishmaniasis called *espundia*. I saw other patients in the ward with lesions that, though less advanced, would inevitably progress in the same direction. I was so disturbed by this man's plight that I determined, there and then, to divert a major part of my research from malaria to seeking a way to prevent or treat this dreadful disease. Over four decades later Simon Croft, one of my former students who eventually succeeded me at the LSHTM, made one of the first discoveries of new drugs for this purpose.

Leishmaniasis brought me into contact with several other *leishmaniac* members of the camaraderie of whom I write later. In the 1970s, a global network sprang up including centers as far apart as China, through the old Soviet Union, the Middle East, India, East

Africa, Ethiopia, Europe, the United States, Central America, and South America.

The leishmaniases eventually grew to fill an expanded place in the World Health Organization (WHO) programs and in international meetings of parasitology and tropical medicine. The overall complexity and public health importance of these diseases were given recognition at last, although they still receive little funding for the study that they merit. During the same epoch, the devastating effect of parasites on human immunity caused by the newly recognized plague of AIDS was first revealed. This increased interest in leishmaniases still further, especially in countries bordering the Mediterranean, where parasites that commonly affect dogs increasingly cause both visceral and cutaneous leishmaniasis in humans.

At some stage in this era one of us coined the term *leishmaniac* to reflect our zeal in entering the leishmaniasis arena. A relatively small number who could claim equal membership of both clubs I came to refer to as *polyprotomaniacs*. Prominent among these is Bob Killick-Kendrick with whom I spent many years sharing several research projects in both fields as well as joint editorship of two books; one on malaria and the other on the leishmaniases.

My first visits to Latin America, described in Chapter 12, opened me up to a world very different from my former experiences in Africa and Nepal. Being established in the LSTM gave me further opportunities to go to Brazil. This was an especially apt place on which to focus my attention. The Amazon was one of the first places where an expedition was deployed by the LSTM. The namesake of my Chair, Walter Myers, went out to Pará in Brazil in 1900 with the 4th LSTM Expedition and died there in January 1901. As I recount later, a Canadian doctor, Wolferston Thomas, who was the Director of the school's Runcorn laboratory where he investigated drugs to treat trypanosomiasis, went to the LSTM's Research Laboratory in Manaus in about 1905. He preferred to go his own way in the work. He stayed in Manaus as the only member of the school. He died there in 1931. In the interest of continuity I have grouped my Amazon experiences in Chapter 15.

I enjoyed some contact with the WHO research activities in relation to antimalarial drug resistance while working with CIBA, but these were limited. That is to be expected as my work was in a commercial environment. After my move into academia, this situation changed and I became increasingly involved in the international environment. In 1967, I was appointed a member of the WHO Expert Advisory Panel on Malaria. I retained that post until 2005, long after my formal retirement. I was free to seek research funding not only from WHO, but also from pharmaceutical companies. I also established a close collaboration with the massive program on antimalarials of the Walter Reed Army Institute of Research (WRAIR) and later, with their leishmaniasis research program.

Money was extremely hard to come by at that period, so a significant portion of a department head's time was devoted to financial and administrative matters. This situation remained unchanged when I moved to London. More interesting was the opportunity my academic position provided to play an active role on various national and international committees that guided research. At the national level, I was privileged to serve on the Tropical Diseases Committee of the Royal Society, the Tropical Medicine Research Board, and on the Training Awards Panel of the Medical Research Council (MRC). In the spring of 1967, I debuted in the WHO Scientific Group on Chemotherapy of Malaria when I was invited to participate as a consultant in a key meeting in Geneva. In autumn of 1972, I was to attend another session of this Group that set the pattern for future laboratory and clinical studies on antimalarial drug resistance. It remains relevant to this day. From 1969 to 1975 I directed the WHO Collaborating Center on Antimalarials in the LSTM, was Chairman of the WHO Steering Committee on Malaria Chemotherapy (CHEMAL) from 1975 to 1982, then a member for a further year.

All these activities necessitated frequent visits to meetings overseas, especially in the WHO headquarters in Geneva, and in the United States. One of the invaluable and informative tasks I carried out for the MRC was on-site inspection of research supported by that organization in tropical centers. I made two such tours from Liverpool, one in 1974 to West Africa, and the second in 1975 from Egypt southwards as far as Tanzania in East Africa. The following section covers some of my 1974 tour. Some of my 1975 work for the MRC is incorporated in a brief account of my encounters with the Arabic-speaking world in Chapter 18.

At the end of January 1975 I flew from Khartoum to Addis Ababa. When I boarded the plane I felt rather tired but did not know that I was harboring a severe tummy bug. With great self-control I reached land and a toilet in the nick of time. Greeted by my old friend Bill Bray, I explained my predicament. As they say, the rest is history— but one I never wish to repeat. Eventually my problem resolved and I was able to enjoy an exceptionally fruitful visit to the Armauer Hansen Center for the treatment of leprosy. The distinction was first made here in 1969 by Anthony Bryceson between lepromatous leprosy and the disseminated form of cutaneous leishmaniasis. Now we know the latter is an unusual form of infection with *Leishmania aethiopica*, a parasite of hyraxes described by Bill Bray, his son Michael, and Dick Ashford in 1973. (See my earlier note on my first encounter with Dick and his recruitment to Liverpool.) At the time of my visit to Addis Ababa, poliomyelitis was also rife as mass vaccination had not reached that part of the world yet. As I note above, another Liverpool colleague who spent several years in the medical school in Addis Ababa was Charles Leithead. One of his specialties was the problem of so-called heat stroke.

Dick and Bill were expert ornithologists, as well as protozoologists. With his memorable wife Betty, Bill took us out one day to visit hippopotamuses and other wildlife that inhabited the upper reaches of the Omo River, about 100 kilometers west of Addis Ababa. It was a long and tiring journey, but very rewarding as we observed a wealth of birds and the lumbering hippos.

Four days later I flew on to Nairobi. I last passed through there on my way back from Tanganyika in 1953 during the Mao Mao rising. I stayed there a couple of nights with Frank and Lorna Schofield, old friends from Papuan days. When they took me out for the day to visit Lake Naikuru, I foolishly failed to wear a hat. The result was the most severe sunburn on my balding head that I have ever suffered. It left me forever after with an ugly-looking scalp. An old passport tells me that on 29th January 1975 I flew from Addis Ababa to Dar es Salaam in Tanganyika, where I spent time with Professor Wen Kilama discussing malaria control problems. I hoped I could return to my former stamping ground, Njombe, where I worked in 1951. I took time to telephone home to Ruth from Dar and learned that she was having severe abdominal pain, so aborted my journey and took the first available flight home via Nairobi. On my return, we found that she was suffering from endometriosis, which fortunately responded to hormonal therapy.

Memories of my next East African safari are clearer and far happier. I found a stamp in one of Ruth's passports reminding me that she entered Kenya on the 21st of February 1976. That was when I had just made another tour that included Khartoum and Ethiopia, from where I flew on to Nairobi as a representative of the MRC's Tropical Medical Research Board. Part of the time I was with a colleague from Cambridge, Bruce Newton. To me, the most important part of that stay at the start of 1976 was that I planned to follow it with a brief holiday, which included Ruth. It was to be her first, but unfortunately, her only visit to Africa. Prior to her arrival, I was due to visit Lake Turkana in the north of Kenya. It was a pity that she could not share that experience with me. I went to see the work of a medical center in that remote area of the Rift Valley where a large number of people suffered from a massive swelling of the liver known as 'hydatid disease.' This is caused by infection by a parasitic tapeworm found almost universally in dogs of that region. The Turkana villagers are very colorful herders of cattle in a harsh, dry environment bordering the south of the massive Lake Turkana. The women bear numerous necklaces of brightly colored beads, and metal rings which stretch their necks rather grotesquely, but little else. The men also wear bright adornments. It was a common custom among them to keep domestic dogs. One of the dog's functions was to help clean the numerous babies crawling around the ground by licking them. It was not surprising that the infants, in turn acquired infected eggs from the 'nurse dogs' from intestinal worms passed by the dogs which cleaned themselves with the same tongues. The eggs hatched inside the infants and passed through their bodies until they reached their livers. There they grew and formed cysts. Some reached the size of a full-grown baby or more as the children themselves grew. The only treatment for afflicted children and adults was surgery. A small hospital staffed by Kenyan and British nurses and doctors spent most of their surgical time removing cysts.

I flew to Lake Turkana in a Cessna piloted by a remarkable Swiss doctor, a sister of the well-known Professor Geigy who I met years earlier in Basle. Dr. Spörri of the East African Flying Doctor service based in Nairobi spent her entire life helping provide medical services to remote areas of the country. She was an extremely wealthy, large, bluff, and very jolly middle-aged woman and an excellent pilot. She could have spent her life in luxury anywhere in the world, but chose to live and work as a voluntary medical worker in East Africa, which like her brother she loved. We were warmly welcomed by the British doctor and his wife who were in charge of the center. I was invited to assist him in the series of operations he was about to commence on some patients. Although I had not carried out an operation of any kind for many years, I prepared myself for the ordeal, and his patients survived my interventions. Fortunately for them I only acted as the assistant, not the main operator.

With my official duties for the MRC accomplished, it was time to indulge in a holiday and one that Ruth and I could share, her first sight of Africa.

I booked us into the traditional old Norfolk Hotel in Nairobi. From there I rented a car to drive out to meet her at the airport with great joy. My plan was for us to explore some of the beauties of the Rift Valley and game parks of Kenya before moving on to Malindi to enjoy a further week in a glorious beach hotel. The car that Avis provided was a rather worn Toyota Corolla. The following morning we explored the wildlife of the Nairobi game park, a wonderland of nature just beyond the city boundary. Accompanied by a Kenyan guide, we saw a remarkable variety of big game, elephants, giraffes, rhinos, lions, cheetahs, leopard, zebras, and numerous species of deer and birds. The next day, we headed west along the Rift Valley to Lake Naikuru to see the vast flocks of flamingo that nest on the salt flats, as well as a superabundance of other waterfowl, including pelicans, before heading up into the hills to look for larger wildlife.

At the top of a high hill we came across a herd of buffalo. We stopped to watch them and they us. We did not leave the car, knowing how notoriously dangerous these animals can be. After enjoying this sight, I realized that the car headlights were still full on, even though the engine was off. I had dreams of the battery running down and of us being isolated indefinitely on the hillside. Luckily, the battery was still alive so I started the engine and we aborted our safari to set off on the long return drive to Nairobi. Nearing the city well before dusk, we were stopped by a police officer who wanted to know why we were driving in broad daylight with our headlights full on. I explained our predicament and assured him that I was hastening to return to the Avis garage in town while it was still possible, since there was no way I could find even to dip the headlights. We were allowed to complete the journey and, with great relief, return the hire car. The people at Avis were very apologetic. They immediately exchanged the faulty vehicle with a brand new Corolla.

The following morning we drove to the Amboseli game park at

the foot of Mount Kilimanjaro where we spent the night in a comfortable park lodge. We arose before dawn the next morning to witness the unclouded beauty of the snow-capped mountain as the sun rose. A park ranger joined us and we spent the rest of the day with him feasting our eyes on yet more magnificent game near the foot of the mountain before driving back to Nairobi. I returned the new car that had behaved perfectly and proved to be extremely comfortable to Avis. We were so impressed with it that, as a Toyota advertisement says, we never bought anything but Toyotas from that time onwards. From Nairobi we moved to the coastal resort of Malindi where we indulged in sun, sea, sightseeing, food, and drink for another week. Swimming among the abundant fish in the nearby Watamu national marine park was an unforgettable moment. That visit to Kenya was one of the happiest and most relaxed holidays we ever had in over twenty-five years of marriage. To find that I could still remember enough of the Swahili I had learned while living in Tanganyika many years before was a pleasant surprise. It gave me a smug sense of one-upmanship. I was even told by one Masai selling souvenirs that I had a Tanganyikan accent! Ruth was very impressed.

Whenever possible, Ruth joined me on my travels and we would attempt to combine work with pleasure. In May 1978, I was to participate in a WHO meeting in Manila so we decided to travel together and to extend the journey to Japan and the USSR on our way back. In Manila, which I visited on a previous occasion, we were hosted by a Filipina doctor who studied with us in Liverpool and her husband. Although we found Manila to be a threatening city, we risked going out from our hotel one night by taxi. We were somewhat soothed when we observed that the hotel porter noted the number and destination of our taxi. While in Manila, we met up with our friend Herbert who was on an assignment for WHO. By then a widower, he had met a Yugoslav lady who was attached to the regional headquarters of WHO in that city. Mejra invited us all to dinner in her apartment and Ruth, who had a sharp female intuition for such situations, said to me as we returned to the hotel that this was more than a casual acquaintance of Herbert's. She proved to be quite right and they subsequently married.

The next leg of our journey took us to Japan. Another of my former students, Mamoru Suzuki, who by then was the Chairman of the Department of Tropical Medicine in Gunma University, and his wife invited us to visit them and to give a lecture there. His former mentor and patron was a very well known and respected immunologist-parasitologist, Professor T. Sawada, who entertained us in his beautiful home near Tokyo. Among the highlights of the evening were the consumption of a seemingly endless number of pre dinner tots of sake by him and Mamoru, while our hostess, Ruth, Mamoru's wife, and I sipped Chivas Regal whisky. This prelude was followed by the serving of a huge, very expensive raw fish, the cost of which our host proudly informed us, and the demonstration of a superb, ancestral Samurai sword that he was able to retain in spite of the official ban on the private possession of such weapons after the end of WW II.

The Suzukis entertained us for a few days in a traditional country inn, a very attractive and popular holiday place on a mountainside near Gunma. That experience, which was quite unique, included a moderately severe nocturnal earth tremor, quaint pornographic films on the bedroom television, and a dip in the hotel swimming pools. These were filled with warm, rather muddy water from a natural spring. There were supposed to be one for men, one for women, and one for families. Mrs. Suzuki took Ruth to the women's and Mamoru led me to what was said to be the men's pool. It was the custom to swim nude in these pools, but I had no sooner entered the water when there was a babble of voices, male and female, from the far end of the pool, as a couple of Japanese families joined in, all similarly unclad, having mistaken it for the third pool which was their intended destination. I made a tactful withdrawal as soon as I could, much to Mamoru's amusement, explaining that such mixed nude bathing was just not something to which I was accustomed. Ruth and our hostess were greatly tickled by the event. Before returning to Gunma, we went to see a famous old shrine, which was very impressive. While we were admiring the architecture, an elderly Japanese approached Mamoru and spoke with him earnestly for a few minutes, all the time looking and nodding in our direction. When he had parted, Mamoru told us that this was a former soldier who had served during the war. He wanted Mamoru to tell us how welcome we were in his country, and to express his deep apologies for the way his compatriots had treated so many of the soldiers and civilians in countries that the Japanese armies had overrun. We were very moved by his action.

The next day I spent with Mamoru at his institute where I had the interesting experience of presenting a lecture to his students with simultaneous translation into Japanese by one of his staff who spoke excellent English. Ruth opted to remain quietly in our hotel that day. She was sipping a cup of tea in the lounge when it occurred to her that she did not understand a single word of Japanese, and none of the hotel staff appeared to speak anything but Japanese. She had no idea of the name of the city we were in, how to get in touch with Mamoru or his wife should the need arise, nor where I had put our passports. At that moment I was being shown around a very interesting collection of exotic monkeys by one of Mamoru's colleagues, but that would have been of little comfort to Ruth.

From Tokyo our return flight stopped in Moscow where I had arranged to visit colleagues in the Martsinovsky Institute. As we were disembarking, I was amused to note that almost every passenger except Ruth and me was steered in one direction to the transit lounge, whereas we were guided ceremoniously down another corridor. The faces of many of the other passengers looked at us with pity as if they thought we were being arrested. In fact we were passed without difficulty through the immigration and customs desks and met by two ladies from the institute. They drove us into the center of

Moscow where we were accommodated in the old Hotel Russia, a ghastly Stalinist construction that was almost the only hotel in town at that time. I was forewarned that the one essential piece of equipment we should take to Russia was a universal washbasin stopper and this proved to be valuable advice. At least there was hot water. There was also a telephone in the bedroom. No sooner had we unpacked than the phone rang and a young female voice spoke to me in English. She invited us to join her and her friends for a party in one of the hotel rooms. I made what I hoped was a polite excuse not to accept the invitation. From that time on, Ruth and I decided to converse in Swiss-German dialect while in our room.

Professor Soprunov, our official host, was a charming cosmopolitan Russian doctor who was a senior officer in the Russian army during the war. He and his colleagues, especially Margareta Strelkova, a specialist in leishmaniasis, and Susanna Rabinovitch, a researcher on malaria chemotherapy with whom I had earlier corresponded, entertained us generously, both in the institute and in the city during our spare time. Food was sparse in the USSR. This did not stop my colleagues from laying on a magnificent luncheon buffet at the institute complete with champagne and vodka. They managed to acquire tickets for excellent seats at a performance of Carmen in the Kremlin's Bolshoi Theatre and for the famous and hilarious Moscow puppet theatre. This we reached via the metro, surely the most truly beautiful underground railway station in the world.

One day when I was engaged in talks at the Martsinovsky, Ruth very bravely took off by herself for a sightseeing boat trip on the Volga, not speaking a word of Russian. As in Japan, she had no idea how she was to communicate with anyone should the need arise, nor was she sure whether the boat really was going to turn around in due course and return her to town, or whether she would be carried on forever, finally to be dumped at sea. However, all was well and I found her later that afternoon back in the hotel, very relaxed and very justifiably proud of her exploits. Another evening, Margareta and her husband invited us to a party in their home in a Moscow suburb. They occupied a fairly large and comfortable, if sparsely furnished apartment in a huge ugly complex of flats, typical of that part of town. They too, in spite of the obvious difficulties of obtaining food and drink, entertained us and other friends most generously and warmly. Happily, we were able to follow up the warm relationships that we established with our Russian colleagues after we returned to England.

I made a second visit to the Martsinovsky in the winter of 1986 in company with Geoff Targett, later to be my Senior Lecturer at the LSHTM, and a colleague from WHO to discuss problems of leishmaniasis which was, and remains, a serious public health problem in parts of Russia. Fortunately, two of our Moscow friends were later able to visit us in England, enabling us to return at least some of their hospitality. This included an overnight stay in Stratford-on-Avon where they attended a performance of the Royal Shakespeare Company, a special treat for their biochemist colleague, Leonid. He was a great admirer of the Bard and was involved in producing Shakespearean plays by an amateur theatre company in Moscow. We still maintain contact with some of our Russian friends after these many years.

Running concurrently with my administrative activities in Liverpool I had a heavy teaching and research program that involved supervising a succession of MSc and PhD students.

Teaching, in principle at least, was one of the main objectives of receiving professorial appointments in Liverpool and London. This topic does not lend itself to a brief résumé as it is intimately interwoven with all my other activities. Thanks largely to my interest in photography, a major contribution to teaching was the development of a book originally titled *Colour Atlas of Tropical Medicine and Parasitology* with two good friends and colleagues, Herbert Gilles and Geoffrey Pasvol. The book ran through six editions between 1977 and 2007. Shortly after my transfer to London, I developed a book, *A*

Colour Atlas of Arthropods in Clinical Medicine. It reflected my deep interest in medical biology and was published in 1992. It was hard work but great fun to produce these atlases, which taught students and graduates more than could words alone. They were originally the brainchild of an imaginative publisher, Peter Wolfe, who sadly died at a young age just as the atlases began to make their mark in the world of medical education.

I spent much time writing research and review papers as well as several major books. When Brian Maegraith retired in 1975, I was elected to serve as the Dean of the LSTM until 1978. During this period I was also the Vice-President of the European Federation of Parasitologists that I served later as Honorary Secretary until 1985. Some of the overseas tours I made necessitated my absence from Liverpool and home for weeks at a time. Examples were visits to the Amazon and to Borneo, which I have described separately. In the latter half of 1978, following the visit to the Southwest Pacific, I had to attend meetings in Geneva, Paris, Poland, Copenhagen, Turkey, Montpellier, Washington, and Holland. Fortunately, Ruth was able to join me on several of those occasions.

Not surprisingly, this frenetic existence placed a significant burden on Ruth who was reaching a difficult time in her life. This began to create a dangerous level of psychological stress on our personal lives that began to threaten our marriage. In early 1979, I was appointed to a committee on parasitology of the Pasteur Institute in Paris. This was an excellent opportunity to reinforce our links with tropical medicine in France and Pasteur Institutes overseas. At the end of February, I was invited to serve as a British Council-sponsored external examiner in the University of Malaysia, Kuala Lumpur. I arrived there safely although several hours late, but my baggage did not. It continued onward to Hong Kong. There it sat until it was traced and, from Hong Kong, it was flown back to Frankfurt! I learned from a stamp on a baggage label that it was screened in a vacuum chamber to detect any delayed-action time bombs that were designed to ignite at high altitude! Having passed that hurdle, it was sent back to meet me in Kuala Lumpur where I was busy examining over 100 students and their examination papers—an exhausting task. In the absence of my baggage, I bought more clothing courtesy of British Airways. Within forty-eight hours, I had a new tropical suit handmade by an excellent Chinese tailor. It was the best I had ever had, but I only wore it once. From Malaysia I flew back to Delhi in a rather dilapidated Aeroflot plane, the only direct flight I could find between the two cities. Once aboard I felt very thirsty and could barely wait for the stewardess to make her rounds, asking what passengers wished to drink. I was not very impressed by the sight of an old-fashioned samovar attached to the wall of the pantry as we came on board, so asked if I could have a glass of vodka and tonic.

"Ve only haf bottles," was her reply, so I ordered a bottle. Luckily, it turned out to be two flat half-liters. I made inroads into one enroute. The second I managed to get through Indian customs without difficulty as Delhi is less strict about alcohol than Bombay. I was in Delhi to discuss my long-standing collaboration with the All India Malaria Institute. I befriended the director and staff when Ruth and I went to India in 1954. It was a very enjoyable and informative meeting.

From Delhi I flew on to Lucknow to pay a follow-up visit to my good friend, Nitya Anand, Director of the Central Drug Research Institute (CDRI). Nitya, a leading Indian chemist, had worked with me on CHEMAL since 1975. He eventually replaced me on CHEMAL in 1982 when I had served my time. It was a rewarding collaboration enriched by challenging, but constructive meetings between an ever-evolving group of chemists, biologists, and malariologists. It took place several times a year, often in Geneva, but from time to time, in more exotic locations such as Lucknow, Panama, Washington, and Beijing. Our primary function was to review the global progress of the acquisition of resistance to antimalarial drugs by human malaria parasites, to seek solutions to the problem, and to help provide funds for research as well as the developments of new compounds with which to combat this rapidly growing problem. However, funds were very scarce and had to be spread thinly between meritorious research workers around the world. All of our laboratories worked on a shoestring budget. In spite of that, between us, we succeeded in making some seminal discoveries and taking at least the first steps in the experimental and clinical investigation of promising compounds. We hoped these would form the basis of a new generation of drugs to prevent and/or treat malaria in humans that no longer responded to our small armamentarium of previously active chemicals. With the help of the British Council, I was able to establish a formal link between the CDRI and my department in Liverpool. This involved a program of medium-term staff exchanges that proved to be very productive for both parties.

Whenever possible, I would visit Nitya. Time permitting, he would invite me home where his wife, a medical doctor, provided me with the most delicious vegetarian meals, the Anands being Brahmins. One such visit coincided with Holi, the Hindu Festival Of Lights that is a joyful occasion. Quite a few of the Anand extended family were present and I was accepted as one of them, especially by the small children who insisted that I should be the person who had to hold the fireworks, which nearly terrified the life out of me. The Anands also took me to a dance festival held in Lucknow for the holiday. I saw the most elegant performers dancing both individual pieces as well as parts of traditional plays. I will never forget the remarkable and stirring dances from Madras and other parts of southern India.

My hotel was situated right next door to the CDRI, itself an elegant old colonial structure from former days. Another memory that has always remained clearly in my mind was the sight of beggars living in their hovels that were constructed in a sort of open passage that lay between the rear wall of the hotel, just below my window, and the bank of the Ganges river that flows through Lucknow. Looking out I could not but help see the people going about their daily lives, women cooking, children playing, vendors selling their wares, all oblivious to the foreigner observing them from a hotel window high above, but waving cheerfully when someone happened to spot me.

One of the centers most prominently involved in the search for new drugs was WRAIR to which I referred above. For several years running, the current director of their antimalarial drug program, Colonel Craig Canfield, was seconded on to CHEMAL. I in my turn was invited to advise WRAIR on their activities and to test some of their compounds. WRAIR had also developed a working link with the CDRI and other research centers that included the Department of Tropical Medicine of Mahidol University in Bangkok. There Professor Tranakchit Harinasuta, a former student of Brian Maegraith, and her team carried out well-controlled clinical studies of promising new compounds in volunteer Thai patients who suffered from naturally acquired malaria. Indeed, she was one of the first to confirm that our best drug, chloroquine, was no longer fully effective against *P. falciparum*, the 'malignant tertian' parasite. This happened in Thailand as early as 1962 when I was still working with the CIBA company in Basle. Her report was one of the triggers for my launch into my own research program. The link with WRAIR was especially valuable because it was independent of CHEMAL. Both CDRI and Mahidol had large colonies of rhesus monkeys that could be used to examine new drugs in the later stages of their development before the compounds were given to human patients.

I admit that the meetings of CHEMAL were not entirely all work, since we were a sociable group of friends and spent several spare daytime hours and agreeable evenings together. On the occasion that we met in Panama in June 1979, I again lost my baggage. For some reason, probably following a visit to Geneva, I had to change flights in Paris where my baggage had to be checked out in transit, and then rechecked onto another airline. Unknown to me then, there is a city called Panama in the US, as well as Panama City which was my destination and, sure enough, the assistant at the Air France check-in desk labeled my baggage for delivery to the wrong place. Again, I reached my destination baggageless and was doomed to go shopping on the first available occasion. In my baggage was not only my brand new tropical suit but my Nikon camera that I had foolishly packed as it was quite heavy. Panama City proved to be not a good place to buy clothing that fit my unconventional figure. I ended up with a pair of mustard-colored trousers that Ruth insisted on giving away the moment I unpacked them on my return home. Outside our work time, my CHEMAL colleagues and I were able to organize a party one Sunday. We hired a boat and tackle to go deep-sea fishing, something that I only experienced on one other occasion; during the holiday that Ruth and I took in Kenya. Off the Panamanian coast, to my great surprise, I hooked a sailfish bigger than I was. I was able, with considerable help from my colleagues and the crew, to land it on the deck of the boat. It was a beautiful creature and I resolved then and there that was the last time I ever hunted such a victim. As was the local custom, the big fish belonged to the owner of the boat, but we also hooked a number of large and very beautifully colored parrotfish that made a delicious supper.

Although most of the time I was overseas Ruth was able to accept the situation, it was starting to be obvious that something had to change if we were to survive as a couple. In 1979, Russell Lumsden, who succeeded Cyril Garnham as head of the Department of Medical Protozoology at the LSHTM in 1968, was due to retire and the Chair was duly advertised. By this time, Ruth was beginning to feel the need to move away from Liverpool and persuaded me, rather against my wishes, to apply for the London Chair. It was a prestigious position and I was in considerable doubt about my chances. At the same time, I was generally content with my association with the LSTM. However, I acceded to Ruth's wish and applied for the post. In due course I was invited to Keppel Street for an interview with the Dean, a microbiologist named Gordon Smith, and members of the LSTMH

Council. Somewhat to my surprise, I was offered the post, to the great annoyance of other candidates whose names I will not mention. I could only assume that the advantage I had over them was that I was first and foremost, a physician with practical experience in tropical medicine but no formal qualification in parasitology. Whereas they were highly qualified and experienced parasitologists, but only would-be physicians.

I returned to Liverpool to break the news to Ruth and my colleagues and to consider plans for making the move to London. This would include transferring several of my research projects, and at least one member of my staff, Brian Robinson. Notices were put out seeking applicants to fill the Walter Myers Chair in my place. Ruth was delighted by the vision of moving south. I am not sure that she had ever fully accepted Liverpool as being a civilized and cultured environment, in spite of its historic museums, elegant Victorian civic buildings and merchants' houses, well-kept parks, and one of the best concert orchestras in England, the Royal Liverpool Philharmonic. Indeed, it has since been renamed The City of Culture. I do not think she ever recognized the Beatles, who emerged during our time in Liverpool and whose manager was almost our next-door neighbor, as quite civilized beings, although she changed her view on these musicians as they matured.

My appointment to the LSHTM was announced early in 1979, but we were not due to leave Liverpool until the end of the academic year. Nevertheless, it was necessary for us to go through the unpleasant procedures of selling our Liverpool home and finding a new one in or near London. This necessitated several trips up and down the M1, which culminated in our discovery of a house in Hertfordshire as I describe in Chapter 16.

In the interim, I still had to continue teaching and examining in Liverpool, conducting my research work on malaria and leishmaniasis, and visiting countries overseas. One of these was in the company of Gordon Smith who would be my next director as

Dean of the LSHTM. At the end of January, we attended a meeting of the US National Academy of Medicine in Washington. We shared a small apartment provided for us by our hosts near the center of town. It was a most important meeting at which I gave an equally important review paper on some aspect of malaria of which I have absolutely no memory—so much for its importance! However, I recall vividly an evening social event at which I met Senator Edward Kennedy, brother of the late President. He was a charismatic character, larger than life, and he knew it. My immediate and lasting impression was that I was glad to have met him but, for some reason, had no desire to do so again.

My close working relations with my colleagues Alain Chabaud and Irène Landau in Paris led to a suggestion that, together with Cyril Garnham, we should undertake an investigation on malaria in the lemurs of Madagascar. The idea was strongly supported by the director of the Pasteur Institute in Tananarive and his French associate, Dr. Coulanges. Between them they managed to obtain the authorization of the Malgache government for this project. In mid-April, Cyril and I set off via Paris for Madagascar where we spent about a week making preliminary plans for a collaborative study between our three institutes. Lemurs are fascinating creatures, as are many other of the animals that occur mainly in that country. Perhaps the most extraordinary that we saw was a coelacanth, unfortunately only a preserved specimen, but one that was rescued from a fisherman's net a couple of years earlier by a biologist from the local museum. This remarkable fish is a living fossil of which only a handful of live specimens have ever been found from this genus of fishes that are otherwise known only from fossils dating back millions of years.

Tananarive was also notable for its colorful, vibrant market, which is notorious for the number of pickpockets who operate there. In fact, I was busy taking photographs of the throngs on the market, my money tucked safely away inside the waistband of my trousers, when

I spotted Cyril in my viewfinder in the process of being deftly separated from the wallet that he innocently kept in his back trouser pocket. The thief was a small boy, about ten years old. He spotted me observing him, gave me a big grin, withdrew his hand full of purse, and disappeared in the crowd. I went over to Cyril who was bargaining with the woman stall keeper who I was sure also saw what was going on. I paid for his selection of gifts, fortunately modest ones, and extricated him from the crowd, to his great annoyance and embarrassment. He was a kindly, gentle man who could not imagine anybody robbing him so blatantly. In the end, we were unable to carry out our project for logistic reasons, but our Parisian colleagues later succeeded in transferring some lemurs to the Musée d'Histoire Naturelle in the rue Bufon, where they succeeded in obtaining and describing the malaria parasites with which they were infected. At the end of the month, Cyril and I attended a parasitology meeting in Mexico City but I believe, spent more time in the National Museum than in the conference. To my astonishment Cyril demolished an enormous fruit sundae full of cream in one of the sidewalk cafes. In spite of this he was a very slim man who was a great walker and climber in his earlier years. You will read more of him in the following pages.

My life in Liverpool was punctuated by two episodes very much in keeping with the early tradition of the Liverpool School to support field expeditions to tropical countries to investigate problems of exotic diseases. One that I undertook was closely linked with Cyril Garnham and my friend Bob Killick. It took us to Sabah to study not people, but orangutans. The second was a prolonged journey I made in Brazil along the Amazon. Both are stories in their own rights that I recount in Chapters 14 and 15.

The time came for Ruth and me to move to London in June 1979, but my obligation to Liverpool University expired at the end of August. I arranged to stay in one of the student halls of residence during this time, commuting home on Friday afternoons and returning on Sunday evenings. A friend and I went ahead a couple of days before moving day with a vanload of carpets to be laid, and then returned to assist Ruth on the great day. We had to drive both our cars to our new residence in Little Gaddesen and agreed that she would go ahead. Imagine my surprise when I caught up with her some distance from Liverpool, stationary at the side of the M6 near the junction with the M1. This was the time when her car broke down. In those days, we did not have mobile phones. I do not recall how we resolved the problem, but somehow, probably with the help of the RAC, we managed to do so. We arrived in our new house just before dusk, only to discover that our predecessors had removed every single light. Welcome to your new home!

Between settling into the new house and commuting to Liverpool, I squeezed in working visits to Jeddah, Basle, and one with Ruth to see her family in Herisau. The Jeddah visit was my last to the new university. From Jeddah I flew to Tabuk, the furthermost city in the northwest of Saudi Arabia, just short of Iraq. My attendance at a meeting of the Saudi Pharmaceutical Association was arranged by one of our Saudi students, Majdi al Tukhi. It was an interesting meeting, but particularly memorable for the opportunity to visit the relics of the old Hejaz railway that was constructed for the Ottoman army prior to WWI to convey their army from Istanbul to Mecca. Their attempt to reach the Holy City failed. The line only reached as far as Medina. All that remains today is a short stretch on which an ancient Turkish steam engine sits. The line was demolished by a band of Arabic irregulars commanded by Emir Faisal, who Lawrence of Arabia rode with during WWI.

Reflecting on our years in Liverpool I realize how privileged I was to acquire sufficient knowledge and experience of the malaria problem to write a tome entitled *Chemotherapy and Drug Resistance in Malaria* that was published in 1970. It was the first such widely embracing work and proved to be exceptionally timely. In order to draw together my work and that of my team, I produced another thesis for which I was awarded the degree of DSc of London University in 1975. I am reminded that, in the book I wrote, "In the treatment of tuberculosis, polytherapy has long been accepted as a rational approach to the avoidance of drug resistance. Today, the treatment of a fresh case with, say, streptomycin or isoniazide alone would not be seriously contemplated. In malaria, the danger of treating overt attacks with plasmostatic compounds such as proguanil or pyrimethamine has been recognized for many years. "

In 1987, I strengthened my gospel message by labeling monotherapy 'unethical' for treating either tuberculosis or malaria, but few people paid attention.

At the end of August 1979, Ruth and I returned to Liverpool to bid farewell to the LSTM. We were fêted by my old staff and colleagues, presented with a huge wine cooler that looked like the World Cup and, sadly, took our leave of the town and friends where we had spent the previous thirteen, mostly happy, years of our lives.

Chapter 14

Studies on Malaria in the Orangutan 1968–1974

This project was born indirectly in September 1968 when I attended the 8th International Congress of Tropical Medicine and Malaria in Teheran. That was a memorable occasion. In addition to some excellent scientific presentations, a virulent respiratory virus was circulated as a bonus to most participants through efficient air-conditioning units in the university's recently completed Congress Hall. Another phenomenon arrived to dominate the scene one evening. Many of us were enjoying a post-lecture drink in the cool evening in an open-air cafe, when there was a sudden silence. I saw that nearly every female head was turned towards the way into the center of the café. A quiet gasp went up as a tall, handsome, fair-haired man walked in, looking exactly like the popular Hollywood film comedian, Danny Kaye. It was my old friend Vincent Zigas of kuru fame.

Stamps in an old passport remind me that I traveled directly from Teheran to the Far East for a purpose I no longer recall. Nine days after I left Teheran I arrived in Sarawak via Singapore and Kuala Lumpur. From there I went to Djakarta in Indonesia, back to Singapore, and on to Bangkok where I spent ten days. From Bangkok

I returned to Delhi, then headed for my old stamping ground, Kathmandu. I stayed for nearly a week and finally flew home via Delhi to Liverpool. Life was rather complicated in those days.

The point of recording all this is to note that somewhere along the way; I met a young Sri Lankan doctor named Neville Rajapaksa, then working with the Sabah Department of Health. He showed me blood slides that he made from orangutans in Sabah. He collected specimens between 1968 and 1971, in some cases on repeated occasions. One of these animals also had an unidentified parasite in two different years. He spoke to me about this but I was by no means certain what they were. The slide's staining was not ideal, yet I felt they could be a species of malaria. One orangutan parasite was seen by Laveran in 1905. It was described by two German scientists, Halbastaedter and Prowazek in 1907. It was in a blood specimen from an orangutan from Java and named *Plasmodium pitheci*. In his classic monograph of the malaria parasites written in 1966, Garnham wrote, "It appears that infections have never been studied under natural conditions in the haunts of the orangutan, i.e., in the forests of the East Indies. This ape is now in danger of extinction. Unless investigations are started soon, the true characters of *P. pitheci* will never be established and preservation in deep freeze will be impossible. Nothing is known of the sporogonic or exoerythrocytic stages of *P. pitheci*."

In 1966, an American parasitologist, McWilson Warren, a graduate student of Cyril, observed malaria parasites, probably *P. pitheci*, in the blood of orangutans in the Sepilok reserve of eastern Sabah where we eventually carried out our project. His specimens were examined in the Institute of Medical Research (IMR) in Kuala Lumpur by Yap Loy Fong who found that ten of nineteen animals were infected and two types of parasite seemed to be present in at least one animal. This state of affairs clearly lay on Cyril's mind. When I returned from the Far East with news of the parasites shown to me by Neville, his eyes lit up.

His immediate response was, "Why don't we go to Sabah, try to find some infected orangutans, and complete the story of the life cycle of *P. pitheci?*"

Simple as that!

We mulled over the idea and brought Bob Killick into the picture. It was exactly the sort of project that he would delight in undertaking if the means could be found. This started the saga of our expedition to Sabah in 1972 to complete the study of the lifecycle of this strange ape parasite before it was too late. I wondered whether, in his heart, Cyril was more concerned about the disappearance of the parasite than its host. As we looked into the matter, it became obvious that the logistics of this investigation posed considerable problems.

We first had to search for infected orangutans. Then we had to find an anopheline mosquito to feed on one such animal that had malaria parasites present that would undergo a full development cycle. Then we needed to infect clean apes with a sufficiently large number of the infective stages from the mosquitoes, i.e., the sporozoites, to produce a primary infection in the recipient's liver. These had to contain enough early, pre-erythrocytic stages for us to find; no easy matter at the best of times.

Cyril and Bob had considerable experience in tackling this sort of problem when investigating the life cycles of malaria parasites of human parasites, of rodents, and of monkeys. They had shown that some human parasites could infect chimpanzees and that the early stages could be found in the liver both of human volunteers and non-volunteering apes. We knew that a number of monkey parasites could infect humans, whether volunteers or as accidental hosts in the wild. It was usually essential to remove the spleens of animals that were to be recipients of infected blood or sporozoites. This minimized the risk that their immune systems would eliminate the infecting organisms.

It was a logical idea to consider whether parasites from one great ape, the orangutan, might prove infective to chimpanzees or possibly to the small South American 'owl' or 'night' monkey, *Aotus trivirgatus*. This had recently been shown to be susceptible to both *P. falciparum* and *P. vivax* of man. By the late 1960s, the potential danger of humans contracting lethal viruses from simians was coming to the fore, so there was no question of any volunteers being inoculated with orangutan blood. In terms of selecting a surrogate host for the orangutan parasite, this limited the choice. It would be both unethical and illegal to attempt to infect orangutans, so we were faced with the choice of employing chimpanzees and/or *Aotus* monkeys.

That left us with two problems; one was to find orangutans that were infected in nature and, two was to find a species of mosquito that might be able to transmit this parasite and could be raised in large enough numbers for the purpose. Finally, we had to find one or more funding sources for what looked to be a very expensive project; all this for a rare malaria parasite in a rare animal. Who on earth was likely to back such a wild project? Could we persuade the Sabah authorities to give us permission to undertake the project? Who could collaborate with us to tackle some of the entomological problems that we faced?

After much discussion and exploration, this is how we resolved the problems during the next three to four years. When I visited Kuala Lumpur and Sarawak in 1968, I established excellent working and personal relations with the Director and staff of the Institute for Medical Research in Kuala Lumpur and the Medical and Forestry Departments in Kota Kinabalu, Sabah's capital city. That country is a part of Malaysia and medical research carried out there had to be authorized through the Directors of the medical departments in both Kuala Lumpur and Kota Kinabalu. Moreover, research involving animals had to be blessed by the Sabah Forestry Department. Fortunately, the Chief Game Warden of the latter organization was a very foresighted Sri Lankan, Stanley da Silva. He had already pioneered the establishment of an orangutan sanctuary in the Sepilok Forest Reserve of eastern Sabah. From its inception in 1964 up to 1974, over fifty young orphaned orangutans recovered from illegal human owners were settled there and two older females had borne infants. The unlawful timber cutting from the Borneo forests was, and remains, a major threat in relation to both the remaining orangutan population and global warming. Da Silva's plan was, to foster the young animals back to good health and gradually teach them to return to protected areas of forest where they could adapt to their normal way of life.

Adult orangutans are solitary animals; each adult requires about one square kilometer of primary forest in which to roam and feed to survive. They spend much of their life in the canopy where they sleep high above the ground in temporary nests made from twigs and leaves. The accumulation of so many young animals and a few mature ones in the Sepilok sanctuary, provided an excellent source among which to identify those that carried malaria parasites. The infants were quick to bond with their human caretakers and were easily persuaded to swap a drop of blood from a finger prick in exchange for a sweet. Once we decided to try to launch our project, I wrote to Stanley to explain what we had in mind. I told him it was important to determine to what extent, if any, malaria was affecting the health of wild orangutans. His response was enthusiastic. He was delighted to put his staff and the facilities of the Sepilok center at our disposal. Both Mac Warren and Neville had already taken sequential blood films from a few animals. As mentioned above, Yap in Kuala Lumpur found that a high proportion of the animals examined were infected. Sepilok was clearly the field area where we had to base our project.

The next question to consider was; which species of anopheline mosquitoes could be the vectors of orangutan malaria parasites? The first essential step was to identify individual orangutans that were parasite carriers, presumably *P. pitheci*. The second step was to attempt to infect surrogate simian hosts through the intermediary of mosquitoes that were allowed to feed on an infected carrier.

A considerable amount of entomological research was carried out over the years to identify the vectors of human malaria in Malaysia and Borneo, especially by staff of the IMR. All the evidence suggested that *Anopheles balabacensis* was the principal vector of human malaria in the north of the island of Borneo and that this mosquito could well be the vector of malaria in the orangutan. In the insectaries of the IMR, large colonies of this and other anopheline mosquitoes were being reared under the direction of W.H. Cheong, an old golfing partner of my Liverpool colleague, Bill Macdonald who spent several years in the IMR. Cheong readily agreed to involve himself and his staff in our project when needed. It was clear that we required the collaboration of an entomologist in the field. We were fortunate in enlisting David Lewis. He had a lifetime's experience of field entomology prior to his retirement and was well known to Cyril, Bob, and to me in England. Thus, it seemed that two of our potential problems were already resolvable. First, it was likely that we could use *A. balabacensis* as our potential vector. Second, large numbers of this insect were available if they could be transported from Kuala Lumpur to Sepilok.

Now we addressed which simian we would employ as surrogate host for the orangutan parasite. Remember that at this point that we were only thinking of this being *P. pitheci*. The first and obvious species was the chimpanzee. Over thirty years later, I doubt if this project would be considered. However, in the late 1960s the potential value both to science and possible human and veterinary medicine, appeared to us to justify any possible ethical considerations. Infant chimpanzees were available from reputable sources for such investigations; however, they were expensive to purchase and maintain. The same ethical question arose regarding the potential host species, the night monkey *Aotus trivirgatus*. They were being used extensively in the UK and US for research on antimalarial drugs and immunity against human malaria. Although numbers of these small animals were still being taken from the South American forests, especially in

Colombia, they were also being bred for medical research in several animal colonies in the US.

I had already visited Leon Schmidt. He was a pioneer in developing drugs to prevent malaria relapses in man and was at the Yerkes Regional Primate Research Center in Emory University near Atlanta, where a renowned primatologist, Geoffrey Bourne, was the Director. From these experts I learned a great deal of the husbandry requirements of these animals. By coincidence, Bourne was a fellow Australian of Brian Maegraith and both were at Oxford together.

After much discussion with my colleagues, we decided to try to obtain two infant chimpanzees and two night monkeys in London. We also felt it was advisable to have the chimps splenectomised by a veterinary surgeon in London prior to their transfer to Sabah if the time came for that stage of the project. We thought it better to fly the small night monkeys out prior to this operation. This idea was reinforced by word from Sabah that the surgeon in Kota Kinabalu, James Han, could perform this task.

So far, so good. Making travel arrangements to fly ourselves and the animals to Sabah was no easy matter. We needed to travel on the same flight, with the animals in a heated, pressurized hold. We found that Malaysian Airlines was able to deal with this matter. Cyril, Bob, and I planned to fly first to Kuala Lumpur where the animals could be housed temporarily in that institute's animal quarters. We could refine the plans for the project there with our Malaysian colleagues. David Lewis and his wife Lesley would travel later when both were free of other commitments. They would meet us in Sandakan, the airport nearest to Sepilok.

During this time, Cyril and I explored possible funding sources for the project. Cyril was to approach the Royal Society of which he was a Fellow. We would both apply to the Wellcome Trust. They were known to fund such occasional medical field projects. This was before the days when the Trust became one of the biggest medical philanthropic institutes in the world. We had doubts if they would think our project merited their consideration. To our surprise and joy both organizations agreed to back us. We received additional financial support from the World Health Organization and from the LSTM. I was left to assemble the necessary equipment, such as microscopes, small instruments, stains, and similar items that we would need in Sepilok. These were carefully packed and sent ahead by air to await our arrival.

We and our animals arrived in Kuala Lumpur at the end of January 1972. We spent a fortnight finalizing arrangements with the Director and staff of the IMR. There we encountered an American friend, Frank Cadigan. He was on temporary assignment to the IMR from the US Army in Washington to collaborate with the artist-parasitologist, Yap Loy Fong in virus research. Yap showed us some tiny chevrotains, pygmy antelopes, *Tragulus javanicus*, in which another species of malaria parasite was discovered. These animals are so small that a single one can be housed in a cage designed to hold a couple of rats. The technique that Cheong and his staff employed to raise their mosquito colonies was very tricky since *A. balabacensis* do not mate freely in cages. It was necessary to use the procedure known as 'artificial mating'. Single male or female mosquitoes hatched from pupae in the insectariums were transferred to individual glass phials about 5 cm long and 2.5 cm diameter. A male was stunned, decapitated, and held in place on the end of a dissecting needle. Its posterior end was then placed in contact with that of a very lightly anaesthetized female. This triggered a spontaneous reaction on the female's part. She clasped the male genitalia from which sperm were ejected to fertilize the female. The females were transferred to a small cage containing a bowl of clean water. Once they recovered from the anesthetic, they were fed sugar water for several days until their fertilized eggs started to mature. At that point the female would lay her eggs on the inside of the bowl of water. Once hatched, the young larvae were easily reared to the pupal stage and then to a new adult generation. While it is a tedious procedure, this technique yielded large numbers of mosquitoes for experimental work. Only half were of use to us since only the female anopheline feeds on blood in nature. They need blood to gain the nutrients essential for egg production. The malaria parasites arrive along with the blood. Once parasites mature in a female anopheline, they are available to infect a new vertebrate host when the female seeks another blood meal.

While waiting to leave for Sabah, we visited a village near Kuala Lumpur occupied by Malay aboriginals, the 'Orang Asli', to learn about their health problems from the staff of the medical center there. Malaria was still present, although much reduced as a result of national malaria control operations performed in the country for many years. On our way back to the city, we stopped in a primary rain forest area to examine the forest canopy. It was likely that the vector of malaria in orangutans would be a species of mosquito that spent much of its life in the canopy. Some time earlier, a group from the IMR investigating the ecology of virus diseases, constructed a walkway high in the canopy so they could collect and examine plants, insects, animals, and other creatures that live there partly or exclusively. This was like the tower I encountered near the Amazon, but more versatile. A site was selected in a small valley where tall forest trees rose from the slopes. A flimsy ladder was attached for the full height of a tree on each side of the valley. The walkway was a rope floor with wooden slats and rope sides; thicker rope served as a handrail. The whole construction, suspended over twenty meters above the valley floor, looked and felt extremely unstable and waved gently with the breeze. I had grave doubts about climbing up but had no choice when Cyril, my senior by twenty-three years, took off with great enthusiasm and speed. I tucked a small tape recorder into my shirt and reluctantly and slowly followed him up and out onto the swaying walkway. I did not dare carry the cine camera that I was using to record our exploits. I confess that this was not my most glorious hour. I felt great relief when my feet were back on solid earth.

Nevertheless, the experience of being at the same level as the canopy dwellers was a fascinating one. I hoped for another opportunity to make the upward journey one day. A couple of years later I did, but that is another story.

Back in the IMR we held long discussions with our colleagues to plan the integration of our fieldwork with support activities that we needed in Kuala Lumpur. If we succeeded in inoculating our chimpanzees and night monkeys with malaria parasites from orangutans, we wanted to return the animals to the IMR where their progress could be carefully monitored and further investigated. This included obtaining small biopsies in which to search for any stages of the malaria parasites that might develop in the animals' livers as these were the sites of initial development of species that infect mammals.

On 14th February 1972 we arrived in Kota Kinabalu with our night monkeys and chimpanzees. By then, we had named them Sandy and Khan, after Sandakan. We received a warm welcome from Stanley, Neville, and S.V. Rajah of the Veterinary Department. They had already arranged accommodation for our animals. Sandy and Khan soon began to bond with individual members of our team and were easy to handle, but the night monkeys were not as adaptable. They were kept together in a cage and were handled with thick protective gloves. The local climate was ideal and an appropriate diet was readily available so all the animals were in excellent condition.

After a few days, we were all flown to Sandakan where we met Peter Govind of the local Department of Health. Our animals and equipment were transferred by Land Rover to the Sepilok base, a couple of miles inland across a very rough, muddy road. At that time the buildings at the base, except for the laboratory, were very simple. They also housed a few young orangutans that required medical care and such animals as a gibbon that was rescued from the wild and needed attention. Only the Forestry Department staff and some forestry students were allowed in the base in those days. Later, it was enlarged and developed to enable it serve as a sanctuary for the orangutans and as a major tourist attraction for Sabah. In addition to wild orangutans, there were macaques, other monkeys, and gibbons in the surrounding forest. It was a constant joy to hear the latter from dawn to dusk as they swung elegantly through the trees, uttering their characteristic and unforgettable calls. Underlying the gibbon calls was a cacophony of sound created by woodpeckers, numerous species of songbirds, and myriad insects. Also in the forest were snakes and strange flying lizards. Wild orangutans suffer from a number of infectious and parasitic diseases in addition to malaria. They are especially susceptible to tuberculosis and a disease called melioidosis. Both are highly infective to humans. On my first visit to Kota Kinabalu, the English doctor there told me he had developed an unusual and chronic abscess. He asked if I would take a specimen back to Liverpool to have the infecting organism identified. I carried the specimen in a glass tube in my toilet bag for safety. I passed it to the Professor of Microbiology in the university to examine. A few days later, his call told me that the infection was with the very dangerous and highly infectious bacterium that causes melioidosis. It is often fatal in man. So much for carrying it in my toilet bag!

Cyril, Bob, and I were put up in a small hotel in Sandakan. We spent many evenings examining microscope slides on which we prepared and stained blood samples from young orangutans. The majority of these animals spent the day wandering freely and playing around the Sepilok base where they were fed by the forestry staff. Most of the youngsters were housed in wooden cages overnight for their safety or treatment if they were ill. We used their temporary lack of freedom as time to collect blood samples. We used the simple expedient of pricking one of their fingers with a special stiletto. Their payment for this minor trauma was a colorful sweet, a 'Smartie.' They rapidly learned that if they offered us one hand, they would receive a sweet in the other. Orangutans are very intelligent animals and quickly learn to create and use simple tools. A few hundred meters from the center along a forest path, a large metal-barred enclosure was constructed for temporary housing of larger animals. When we were there, the sole occupant was a very young honey bear that was being cared for until it was large enough to be released back to the wild. The door was kept closed with a latch that was secured by a twisted piece of wire rather than a padlock. Wandering freely around the base was a young female orangutan named Joan. She was reared from infancy, released when older, mated with a wild male, and produced her first baby. A few years later she wandered back to the base, bearing a very small, two-week old baby. Throughout our stay she hung closely, watching our activities. On an unforgettable occasion, Cyril, Bob, and I were sitting near the balcony of one of the huts. Joan approached us and held her baby up to Cyril as if offering it to him. Slightly perturbed, Cyril responded by gently patting the baby on its head. This seemed to please Joan who returned the infant to her breast.

Bob and I who were looking on in amazement, said to each other, "She must be mad! If she's not careful, Cyril will whip her baby off and splenectomise it to see if it has any malaria parasites!"

It was a rather unkind joke about a very kind man.

A few days later we went to the Sandakan airport to meet David and Lesley Lewis. David wore a smart trilby hat and dark brown suit and Lesley wore a bright floral dress and hat to match as if heading for the races at Ascot. David bore a large box that contained small containers full of adult mosquitoes he had collected from the IMR en route. It was too late to do any work with them that day, so we put them on a table that we stood in cans of water to protect them from ants inside the metal-barred enclosure. We transferred the young bear elsewhere for the occasion. As we were locking up for the night, we saw that Joan and her baby had followed us and sat quietly watching us. When we returned to the base, she as quietly followed us, but stopped halfway and climbed a low tree where she proceeded to make herself a twig and leaf nest for the night; the baby made the odd contribution by pulling off a few leaves. We continued on our way and left them to it.

The next morning we set out to inspect the mosquitoes and found the door of the cage wide open and containers of mosquitoes scattered all over the place. Joan not only remembered that she had seen something interesting and possibly edible the previous day. She untangled the wire holding the latch closed, opened the door, and helped herself to the contents that were especially bred and transported from Kuala Lumpur. It was difficult to construct the message back to Cheong asking for more mosquitoes because Joan had played havoc with the first batch. However, he generously managed to breed some more and got them to us safely. While we waited, we bought a strong padlock.

In the interim, we collected a number of wild mosquitoes to see which species fed on orangutans, as well as us. This involved sitting by cages containing the young animals at night and sometimes setting up traps that had to be examined very early in the morning. The daytime was accompanied by the gibbons' calls while the nights were enchanting with the variety of sounds made by giant cicadas and other insects attracted to our lights. Mosquito collecting was a tiring process. Bob and I felt we should take it on ourselves to spare our senior colleague in order that he could get more sleep. Senior he may have been, but Cyril was not at all amused as I think he misconstrued our move as intending to usurp his authority. Once reassured on this point, he was quietly contrite and made it up to us over drinks the next evening.

Our inspection of the orangutans' bloods on repeated days soon yielded very exciting results. I will never forget the look of exultation on both Bob and Cyril's faces when, one evening they suddenly realized that not only did a high proportion of the animals have *Plasmodium pitheci*, the parasite we were looking for in their blood; but a few had an entirely different parasite, either together with the first one or on its own. This organism had a quite different structure from *P. pitheci*, and looked very similar to *Plasmodium vivax*, which causes benign tertian malaria in humans. Had we discovered an unknown species of malaria? Was it something that was suspected but not confirmed by Mac Warren, Yap, and Neville? From this point on our attention focused on three questions: (1) Were the blood stages of either or both of these parasites directly infective to the chimpanzee or the night monkey? (2) Was it possible to obtain infective stages of either, or both, these parasites in any of the mosquitoes that were available to us? (3) Could such stages (sporozoites) that we might obtain in mosquitoes, infect clean chimpanzees or night monkeys, and develop into liver tissue stages?

To our disappointment, we could not infect either surrogate host species with blood stages of the original object of our project, *P. pitheci*. Neither could we infect the night monkeys with the new parasite. However, one of the chimpanzees, Khan, developed a heavy blood infection after receiving an inoculum of infected orangutan blood.

From that stage of the project, the plan was to return to the IMR in Kuala Lumpur where better facilities were available to complete the investigation. Unfortunately, I had to return to Liverpool where I had heavy teaching commitments. So I had to leave the termination of the study to Cyril, Bob, David, and our colleagues in the IMR. The transfer back to Kuala Lumpur passed uneventfully except when one of the night monkeys made a bid for freedom in the grounds of the Institute and took refuge in a tree. It required a lot of patience and the local fire brigade to flush the escapee out of his tree and back into captivity.

Together with Cheong, his team, and Frank Cadigan, Cyril, Bob, and David were finally ready and able to infect not only *Anopheles balabacensis* with the new parasite, but also several other anopheline species. On 8 March 1972, 3,000 mosquitoes comprising four species and containing the mature infective forms, fed on Khan. Twelve days later, many of them were found to have mature infective stages in their salivary glands. After a week, pre-erythrocytic stages were recovered from this chimp's liver. Glands dissected out of 140 mosquitoes were injected into Sandy from whose liver it was hoped to obtain liver stages of a different age but he unfortunately succumbed to an anesthetic. Superb paintings were prepared of all the stages of the life cycle of the new parasite. This was named *Plasmodium silvaticum,* to reflect the sylvatic nature of both its primate and insect hosts and to honor Stanley da Silva who was the father of the orangutan sanctuary.

Back in Liverpool, I was the delighted recipient of a telegram from Cyril and Bob saying, "One tissue form first fifty sections. You owe us champagne. Garnham."

Throughout the project, I took both film and still photographs, but left the cine camera with my colleagues to continue after my departure. Much background material was needed in order to complete the picture and I returned to Sabah in January 1974 for this. My visit that time coincided with that of a colleague from the Muséum d'Histoire Naturelle in Paris, Jean Claude Quentin, who was in Sabah to study parasitic helminths. He was accommodated in a small house at the Sepilok center where new buildings were erected and I joined him there. One day, news arrived that a rogue elephant was shot not too far away and Jean Claude was invited to go there to collect material to examine. He returned to Sepilok with a large plastic bucket full of elephant guts that he proceeded to dissect. They contained large numbers of very small worms about one centimeter long. It was necessary to look very closely to find them. He was a heavy smoker so for just this sort of occasion, he provided himself a cigarette holder at least twenty centimeters long. Watching him smoke hands-free and dissect stinking elephant guts at the same time was something never to be forgotten.

When my work in Sepilok was finished, I returned to Kuala Lumpur. I believe I was lecturing or examining in the University at the time, and wanted to pay another visit to the forest canopy walkway with the cine camera. However, I made the mistake of accepting an invitation for dinner the previous evening from an old student who was now a lecturer. He was determined to give the old man a memorable evening out and did that. The next morning I had such an unbelievable hangover that there was no way I could have put a foot on the first rung of the ladder. So, we believed, ended our saga of orangutan malaria, bar the gathering of material for a number of joint publications and a lecture at the Royal Geographical Society some time later.

Bob and I edited the film Frank and I made and wrote a commentary that Bob recorded. We added that in the LSTM in constructing a short film. This has survived as a video tape and several copies as DVD discs. Unfortunately, the original film and spare material disappeared during a series of changes of laboratory I was obliged to make after retirement from the LSHTM in 1989.

While we concluded that *P. silvaticum* was a previously unknown species of malaria parasite that occurred only in the orangutan, it clearly bore a strong resemblance to the benign tertian parasite that infects humans in the same area, namely *P. vivax*. In the years since 1972, sophisticated methods were devised to define the genetic basis of such organisms at a molecular level. In late 2008, thirty-six years later, I entered by chance into collaboration with two new colleagues, Balbar Singh, a young Professor in the University of Sarawak, and his scientist wife, Janet. They made the important discovery that another simian malaria parasite, named *P. knowlesi*, occurs in macaque monkeys and commonly infects humans in parts of Borneo and surrounding countries. It sometimes causes lethal infections. This indirectly reopened the questions of whether *P. silvaticum* can infect humans, or *P. vivax* the orangutan. As I write this in 2009, Bal and Janet are exploring this in Sepilok animals, with the delighted collaboration of Bob Killick and me.

"What goes around comes around!"

Chapter 15

Visit to the Amazon 1971

I based this section mainly on extracts from a diary that I wrote at odd moments during a particularly instructive visit to Brazil.

On 17th July 1971 I traveled to Brazil from Liverpool on a tour organized by the British Council. We covered an immense distance from Rio de Janeiro, Belo Horizonte, and Brazilia, as well as a long stretch of the Amazon. Most memorable was the journey on a small boat from Manaus to Coari and back to Belém.

Brazil is well endowed with highly talented tropical physicians and research scientists. From the inconsistent notes in my diary I find I started my travels on that occasion in Rio de Janeiro, then flew to Belo Horizonte which I visited previously for CIBA, from Belo to Brazilia, and then to Manaus. My stay in Belo Horizonte was especially interesting as Professor Mayrink was working enthusiastically on his leishmania vaccine. This had already received accolades from the local press, but was unfortunately not successful. I was able to hold long discussions on malaria with Leonidas and Maria Deane, two pioneers of tropical medicine in Brazil, and two younger medical scientists. Professor Zigman Brener was an expert on Chagas' disease and Pellegrino on schistosomiasis. That is when I organized an exchange visit for Bob Howells with a Brazilian veterinarian. Later in Liverpool, the vet suffered acute renal failure. On a later visit to Belo

Horizonte I met him again, fully recovered after a renal transplant from his father. By chance, years later when I gave a talk at Imperial College, Ascot, I met him once more as he was a participating senior student in a postgraduate course.

Professor Paraense met me in Brazilia and invited me to his house for Sunday lunch where I met his wife who taught biology. My notes from that stay in Brazilia were mainly technical concerning teaching and research in the University. From Brazilia I visited a hospital in a nearby town where I first encountered patients with advanced mucocutaneous leishmaniasis, 'espundia'.

(I wrote in Chapter 13 how this encounter radically influenced the future direction of my chemotherapy research in the LSTM. My team continued this work when I moved to the LSHTM. After I retired in 1989, it was further developed by one of my successors, Simon Croft. He originally joined me to study for an MSc in Liverpool and rejoined me years later in London. He eventually became Head of my former department there.)

As I continued my journey through Brazil I acquired more information about espundia and the less terrifying forms of leishmaniasis. These included relatively simple skin ulcers of a type that often healed spontaneously, and also the visceral form known as 'kala-azar'. It mainly afflicted young children and was commonly fatal. I learned that a major obstacle to any study of leishmaniasis was that it was observed that the parasites causing the various clinical forms had few minor morphological differences. These were hard to distinguish, even by an expert.

My next port of call was Belém at the mouth of the Amazon. I flew there on 29th July to spend time with two parasitologist colleagues, Ralph Lainson and Jeffrey Shaw, both prominent 'leishmaniacs'. They had been senior scientists in the Wellcome leishmaniasis research unit at the Instituto Evandro Chagas for several years. Their objective was to search for means to identify the different parasites responsible for the range of clinical forms of the disease in man and in wild animals, and also the tiny sandflies that transmitted the parasites. Until that time, little was known about possible wild animal reservoirs in the New World, nor of the species of sandflies that might pass the organisms between mammalian hosts. Moreover, it was very difficult to grow parasites from certain types of infection and especially from patients with espundia. If we were to start seeking drugs to treat the different forms of leishmaniasis, it was first necessary to find a reliable way to identify the parasites that produce them.

With Ralph, Jeff, Dudley Dumonde (an immunologist from Middlesex hospital), and Bill Bray, from the LSHTM, who were also visiting Belém, we flew in a small Cessna to the Serro dos Carajós. This mountain is composed of solid iron ore. The top of the mountain was sheared off to make a landing strip. As you step out of the plane, you can almost hear your feet clanging on metal. On each side of the strip the land falls sharply away. It is strewn with the wrecks of small planes that made poor landings. At the time, the mountain was starting to be exploited by a joint US-Brazilian combine named Compagnia Meridionale, formed by US Steel and Compagnia Rio de Valle Doce de Minas Gerais. I recall lunching in a sumptuous, bungalow-style rest house with the most magnificent view over the Amazonian rain forest one could wish for. I would have liked to stay there a few days and collect insects, but we had to return to Belém the same day. During my time in Belém I managed to climb the tall iron tower originally constructed by a team from the Rockefeller Foundation. They were studying yellow fever transmission in the forest canopy. From several stages of this tower and its summit, one could capture mosquitoes and small animals that never got to ground level, an important factor in unraveling the ecology of that lethal virus disease of which the animal reservoirs are various species of forest dwelling monkeys.

On another day, Ralph took me to catch butterflies on the banks of the Amazon. He was an avid and expert lepidopterist who amassed a unique collection during his extensive travels throughout the length and breadth of Brazil. We caught a few exotic butterflies, using his shiny little red and blue flags to attract *Morpho* butterflies. However, my most memorable catch was the side of Ralph's head that I hit with a tremendous swipe with his net trying to catch an unbelievably beautiful, swift Amazonian beauty. He eventually forgave me, but it took time! More seriously, I selected a number of *Leishmania* strains prepared for me by Ralph and Jeff to collect on my way back through Belém after my Amazon trip. These were for my return to Liverpool.

At the time I noted; "R.L. very contented here. A lifetime of parasitological problems. Well thought of by Brazilians. No reason, unless personal, why he should not continue in Belém. If not on leishmaniasis, many other subjects, including medical, e.g., Chagas' disease, malaria, and veterinary, e.g., *Trypanosoma vivax*."

In 1996 Ralph with second wife Zéa, a Brazilian scientist, retired in Belém where he is an Emeritus Professor in the University. He continues to work his way gradually through the hitherto unknown life cycles of numerous Brazilian parasitic protozoa. He is currently assembling a book on this subject that will include his magnificent paintings. Jeff, now married to a Brazilian doctor, is a Professor who commutes regularly between the Universities of Brazilia and São Paulo.

I flew directly from Belém to Manaus on 3rd August. I was met by Elizabeth Sender, a Voluntary Services Organization (VSO) nurse from Birmingham. She took me to meet Neil Murphy, the British Vice-Consul who worked in the local branch of the Bank of London and South America.

Of Manaus I wrote; "… an air of tropical degradation well mixed with attempts to make a quick buck. Streets, as in Belém, were badly cared for and taxi drivers grossly dishonest. Lord Hotel, the second best in town, is very dingy but air-conditioned. Service is very pleasant."

After a few days visiting the university staff, Elizabeth and I boarded a small boat, the Isaac, which normally carried about fifty local passengers up and down the river. Before leaving I tried to change dollar-denominated travelers' checks, but the US dollar had just been devalued, so on this unique occasion nobody was interested in that currency. The river journey from Manaus to Coarí was especially memorable.

I wrote; "The Amazon is still flooded. The helmsman steers a course westward to Coarí hugging so close to the right bank of the river that you feel you can put your hand out and touch the branches of the trees. Sometimes you can. Floating islands of grass and flooded farmland separate the houses. They stand silently on stilts in the water, moonlight gleaming bright silver on the corrugated aluminum roofs. Far away near the opposite bank are the lights of riverboats like the Isaac heading downstream to Manaus with their cargoes of patient farmers and traders stretched across the decks in their hammocks. To our port side the Southern Cross is obscured by clouds from which occasional lightning flashes remind us of the sudden electric storms that can spring on us from the clearest sky— unusual now in August but always possible. At last it is cooler and, apart from the intrusive throb of the engine, quieter except for the chorus of frogs and crickets that arises whenever we sail particularly close to the bank. I will try once again to get some sleep on my bunk. In the morning fishermen appear, silhouetted against the golden light of the dawning sun, its rays rippling on the boat's wake. Little groups of houses, patches of manioc are now seen to intersperse the undulating river's edge. Debris washed off the flooded, soggy land floats past us downstream. Islands of *Pistia*, water hyacinths, and tall sedges drift by in the dirty, muddy water. Hammocks open like chrysalides splitting down the center to reveal sleepy, tousled brown heads, and a queue forms for the smelly latrine and the solitary water tap. Behind them all in his cubbyhole of a galley, a wizened old man cooks coffee for us. Now the sun has risen to a glaring ten degrees over the horizon and already it is becoming warm again.

"As the day drags on and the sun rises higher it becomes an effort even to watch the houses on the banks, people fishing, bony cattle seeking pasture, hawks and kingfishers hunting. Lunch arrives, fejão, rice, spaghetti, and stewed meat. They smell tempting, but I have seen the galley and its attendants so tinned Spam and biscuits for me. Guaraná my drink. I put up my hammock and sleep successfully for a few minutes in spite of the loud put-putting of the engine. The swinging of my neighbor woke me, then the crick in my neck combined with the cramp in my left leg and finally I give up. Another hour passes and I go forward to sit in the breeze and shade and wonder if the duty helmsman—the young boy who helps the cook and serves our meals—will succeed in running us aground on each successive spit of land. All this, 300 miles of Amazon in forty hours, complete with full board for thirty cruzeiros, under £3! Anyone interested? Just now we pass floating islands of light purple-flowered water hyacinths, so close I feel I could stretch out my hand and touch them. Unwise to try though. If I fell in I might make a tasty dish for the piranhas. Here a small chapel—but no priest comes here except maybe once a year on the community's Saint's Day. Then all the year's crop of infants are baptized at once and the parents are married. The river is falling and you can see on the posts a dark mark rising a yard above their bases. We have gone just half way to Coarí, twenty hours—twenty hours to go. The houses are more frequent here, perhaps five, six, or more every kilometer of riverbank. We have crossed to the left bank going upstream, following the shorter curve of the river as it bends to the southeast, our left. Shades of green and brown predominate, blending with the broken blue of the sky full of puffy cumulonimbus all round but clear above. Here and there yellowing, massive leaves or bright red cotton tree pods or fresh, plum-colored mango leaves break through the green wall, but mostly we are now just too far from the bank to see more colored details of the plant life. Our new helmsman has just taken over, a more cautious young man. Perhaps this is a sign that coffee is brewing.

"Approaching Codajás 8:00 p.m. and night, still hugging the river bank, right bank this time. Charles Aznavour and the Beatles breaking the silence of the night. If you please! We reached Codajás shortly after, struggled through the milling crowd on the floating dock and made our way to the Casa dos Padres to deliver some cigars and receive a welcome beer. Half an hour out of Codajás the small auxiliary lighting plant failed, but the brilliantly shining full moon was more than enough for the helmsman to steer by. At Belém the entomologist had thrust a large three-battery flash lamp at me to do a night catch of sandflies. The captain borrowed it to fiddle with the faulty motor. By the time I lay down on my bunk the lights had flickered on and died again maybe half a dozen times. At 3:00 a.m. pounding rain on the cabin roof and a mighty flash and roar of thunder woke me abruptly from sleep. I slipped my trousers on over my pajamas, my shirt, and sandals. Still no light. In the dark broken only by occasional lightning flashes, I groped for my suitcase and my small rechargeable emergency lamp, cursing myself with each increasing roll of the boat for not having packed it in a more accessible spot. I stepped out of the cabin door into driving rain. The helmsman had headed, as far as he or I could see, away from the bank towards midstream. Two women and their boy, Bacari, on the deck outside were rolling up their wet hammocks to tie them against the center beam of the roof, out of reach of the rain. We all struggled into my cabin, the women on the bottom bunk where I had been sleeping, the boy and I on the top. Up there was just room enough to lie down, maybe eighteen inches space. I am sure I swallowed one of the many spiders living under roofing planks as I struggled up— but if so, tant pis! We lay there wedged in against the rolling and pitching of the boat until, maybe after an hour, the rain eased somewhat. My guests arose and returned to spend the rest of a cold, damp night in their hammocks after politely declining my suggestion that they stay in the cabin and let the boy and I sleep in the hammocks. Perhaps ten minutes later the motors stopped and I heard shouting. Again I got up hastily, this time I was sleeping in my clothes, my little flashlight in my trousers pocket. Two lights shone from the riverbank and men were shouting from there. The light of my Belém lamp in the captain's hand showed no break in the forest wall there, so we progressed a little further then pulled into the bank. By this time the lights were hidden by the last bend in the riverbank. The 'gangplank', a single plank with crossbars, was put down. To my astonishment two men eased their way down the plank, carrying between them a large, old-fashioned treadle sewing machine. This they deposited on the muddy bank in the rain. Then they stepped back on board, collected two bundles of clothes or goods, stepped back on the riverbank, picked up the machine and were swallowed up in the humid darkness of the forest. We had delivered a couple of shoppers to their front door. I undressed and lay down again on the lower bunk, my rolled up hammock in a plastic bag covered by my shirt as a pillow.

"Gratefully I saw the first faint predawn light appear at the window. I dressed again and stood at the soggy rail watching the frogs plop into the water at our approach. As the light grew, vivid king-fishers glided from their perches and herons flew up in alarm from their nocturnal perches close to the river's edge. A pink freshwater dolphin glided elegantly out of the water just astern and I watched for his second emergence—but he failed to appear. The captain handed back my flash lamp with his thanks. "Nada", I replied, "it's a pleasure." The batteries were quite flat. Exercising mind over matter I have willed myself to stay constipated until we reach Coari. It is all I can do to hold my breath when, twice a day only, I am obliged to release a small quantity of highly concentrated urine in the ship's stinking toilet. Gina, one of the VSO nurses, poor girl, I am sure has amoebiasis. I will check this microscopically in Coari and treat her before she gets a liver infection."

Coari was an interesting remote small riverside town, the center of an area with about 25,000 inhabitants. Eight to nine years before my visit the congress of Bishops of Brazil set up an organization called the Movamento do Educação do Brazil (MEB), mostly paid for by the church. With some opposition, the government of the day, accepted the MEB and the local Bishop requested that the UK send out VSOs to run a health boat. A nurse, social worker, an Australian doctor, and a radio technician came, but the project soon collapsed. Later VSO nurses came to run health clinics but these folded due to lack of support from the local administrators and poor attendance. Coari was finally left with a small, twenty-bed church hospital run by nuns. This closed at the end of 1969 for lack of funds.

Then Elizabeth started a clinic on her own as the Australian doctor left. The UK government and the Brazilians finally set up a number of prefabricated hospitals; one in Coari. They were constructed in the US and equipped from UK sources but took two and a half years to set up. The Bishops refused to run the hospital or let their nurses do so because the state failed to provide support. When I was in Coari, it was run by two doctors; a Peruvian and a Brazilian from Recife, a trained nurse, and a dentist. The dentist had an X-ray, but no plates, and a UK-made, high-speed drill, but no materials for fillings. Most of the drugs in the hospital were free samples as the government supplied very little, and then only after a long delay. Only the intravenous fluids seemed to be satisfactory. The small laboratory had a binocular microscope and micro-haematocrit apparatus, but instructions were solely in English. There were absolutely no chemicals or stains, not even Ziel-Nielsen or Giemsa. The refrigerator for the blood bank did not function. A room was available for physiotherapy but not used. In the well-fitted operating theatre there were no instruments such as a laryngoscope for use with intubation, and the only anesthetics for major surgery were pentothal or spinals.

Elizabeth and her colleague carried out a health education program with the MEB training junior nurses, running vaccination clinics, and teaching a ten-day course for local midwives from communities in the area. CESP had an ambulatory service with a good building but no qualified staff. There was a confusion and multiplicity of medical services in the area. SUSEMI was established to run a hospital project in Amazonas, then it appeared that all hospitals would be controlled by the Secretary of Health. Forty-three total units, ranging from first aid posts to bedded hospitals were planned. Expensive equipment was sent from the UK to Manaus but I suspect much rotted in storage. One health post and one hospital were complete when I visited Coari. The hospital had an electric generator, but no money to buy diesel fuel. The town Prefect wanted to cut off the hospital electricity supply because the government did not pay. In Coari, a brand new Watson M4 X-ray machine supplied from UK was not assembled and all instructions were in English, which no local people understood. I complained to our government when I returned to England.

Although the clinic in Coari was officially closed, numerous patients arrived at the girls' house for help because, even when they were given any prescription for drugs from the hospital, they had no money to buy them. There was a rumor that the government doctors were going to start charging fifteen Cruzeiros for a consultation, an impossible sum for impoverished people. The hospital receptionist allowed poor patients to be treated free but favored the local townspeople whom she knew over poor peasants from the interior. There was no pediatric center. For whatever reasons, attendance at the hospital was poor. Between 07:30 a.m. and 11:00 a.m. from Monday to Friday, two surgeons between them only saw about ten cases in addition to emergencies and late arrivals from the interior. This totaled only twenty to thirty patients a day, including those who needed dressings renewed. About a dozen 'cold' operations were carried out per week. I doubt if I would have liked to perform more under the circumstances were I the surgeon!.

However, the cases that arrived were often very severe. The

morning I visited I saw a child with a huge ascites, a man with a cold abscess of the hamstring muscles, a patient with carcinoma of the stomach, and one with cystitis and probably hydronephrosis. There was some leprosy in the area. Patients were given dapsone, but not regularly followed up. While I was in the girls' house a baby was brought in with diarrhea, which it released on the living room floor. Its older sister had a severe fungal infection called 'tinea favus', with secondary infection and large cervical glands which were severely aggravated by her local native medicine treatment. An old copy of the Sunday Times the girls used to clean up the mess had an advertisement for the Guernsey Zoo, 'complete with tea bar, gift shop, piped music and a car park for 250 cars'! Surprisingly the infant mortality was said to be low in this area compared with Brazil's poor northeast and malnutrition was uncommon. It seems that protein was plentiful and there was no shortage of water to grow food crops.

I left Coarí at about 11:00 a.m. on August 7th to return to Manaus on the good ship Cidade, a superior boat to the old Isaac, in the company of Father Daniel. The Cidade had a remarkable cabin for the captain at the front end, complete with fancy bed sheets and pillowcase. We reached Manaus at about 6:00 p.m. and made for the Casa Parochial de Aparaceda where I stayed. That Sunday evening I had a long meeting with Dom Mario Roberto Anglim, the Bishop of Coarí. It turned out he knew Bishop Arkveldt, the flying bishop, our neighbor in Wewak when we lived in Maprik, Papua New Guinea years earlier. The next morning I went to the University of Amazonas. I was keen to track down information on the old Liverpool pioneer, Wolferston Thomas, who worked and died in Manaus. However, the librarian contributed nothing on him. First, I made official calls. On Monday I arrived at 8:00 a.m. at the INPA headquarters to see the Director, Dr Antonio de Brito Bonates, but he had left for the university. In the medical laboratory I borrowed a microscope to examine stool specimens from Gina that I found full of *Entamoeba histolytica* as I suspected. I went to the six-year old Faculty of Medicine of the University of Amazonas to meet the Dean, Professor Bernades. He spoke little English but did manage to explain how hard it was to obtain any drugs, chemicals, or other supplies in the university. There was a shortage of teachers, yet they were just producing their first medical graduates. I paid my respects to Professor Dutra, the Rector and Dr. Jose Lopez da Silva, the Vice Rector and gave them a non-committal suggestion that Liverpool may help if possible at a vague time in the future if staff became available. I met a man named Murphy and a Mr. Davidson, a bank inspector, for lunch. During lunch they assured me that grandiose schemes for the development of Amazonia were largely paper tigers. The following day, Tuesday, I again tried to meet Professor Dourado, but with no success.

Tuesday 10th August. The faculty buildings are new, a dazzling gleaming white in the Manaus sun. Students, here as everywhere, stand about, chatting, discussing classes, professors, and affairs but here the impression is they do nothing but stand and chat. I tried to see a particular professor at least four times, but he is not here. Nobody knows where he is or when he will return! Everywhere I meet great courtesy. People go out of their way to find other people for me, even to the extent of abandoning their own work to take me downtown. There is a paradoxical air of indolent enthusiasm, tempered by the intensive heat and humidity of this strange town set in the middle of the Amazon River. In the offices most of the staff seem to spend their time sitting and talking—or just sitting. Occasionally I hear the chatter of a typewriter. Cigarettes are smoked and coffee is drunk. Everyone cadges cigarettes from everyone else. In Brazil nobody has matches! In spite of the high general cost of living, three things are very cheap; tobacco, alcohol, and transport. Until very recently the University of Amazonas was a family affair. Its finances and administration were dominated by the Marinhos, a single Manaus family.

Now their stranglehold has been broken and appointments of professors are no longer made in accord with the whims and fancies of the patriarchal old Rector. A government-appointed rector sits in his place, a gentle, benevolent elderly lawyer. Unlike the other Brazilian universities, few people here from the rector down, speak any language but Portuguese, although they may be able to read some Spanish, French, or English—in that order.

Few Brazilians want to come to Amazonas. Few know what it is like. For most it is a world apart, a world about which the politicians make speeches, talk big of development, integration, education, Transamazonian highways, and resettlement from the Northeast badlands. Who in the coolness of Rio Grande do Sul, the hustle and bustle of São Paulo or Belo Horizonte, the exotic buzz of Rio de Janeiro, or the futuristic dream of Brazilia gives a damn about the steamy forests and rivers of the Amazonian jungle? Who would dream of going to live there? The government shrewdly made Manaus a free port to encourage Brazilian tourists. The bait is tax-free cameras, radios, television sets, but damn it, not whisky. It is gradually luring the Brazilians into their own tropics. Big signs say, "The Amazon is not a green hell." Tourist shops sell stuffed piranhas and Indian artifacts manufactured on the mission stations. Amazon Adventures Ltd. offers a variety of boat trips up the rivers on each side of Manaus and mini-safaris for the more daring. Pan American airline drops off the occasional bold Americans who break their journey for a day or two between Rio or Brazilia and Miami. Few remain long. The Hotel Amazonas caters to their tastes with an American bar and air conditioning at excessive prices. The more modest Novo Mundo provides courteous service and air conditioning in small rooms, and a large breakfast without the trimmings for less than half the cost. Brazilians stay here.

Courtesy is the keyword in Brazil, at least outside the major cities. Even there, it is only lacking in the tourist haunts and hotels. Brazilians are basically well mannered and good-humored. A visitor rarely meets discourtesy or dishonesty, in spite of a virtually complete ignorance of their language. The crudest effort to speak in Portuguese is appreciated, though it offends their ears. A Brazilian smiles very easily and openly, the women especially so—yet not flirtatiously except the Cariocas. With them, it is second nature and very charming. Here on the Amazon simple people smile, except taxi drivers, but I wonder what it is like in the Northeast where people starve. Time is a strange commodity and its value fluctuates greatly.

In Manaus the price tag is low, "Hora Braziliera o hora Inglesa?" is a frequent question when an appointment is made. Rendezvous are readily made and readily forgotten. The Postal Service has a special character, such as the gum on the stamps. The practical authorities provide gum dispensers in each post office. When affixed with this gum, stamps are more difficult for dishonest postal clerks and others to remove. To be on the safe side, Brazilians pay a bit extra and send mail Registrado. From there on it is in the lap of the gods. If and when letters reach their destination, it is at least cheap, Cruzeiros 0.20, about 1½ pence, for an airmail letter inland.

Offering a 'cafezinho' is one of the many agreeable Brazilian courtesies. The little cup of hot strong sweet coffee turns up everywhere, waiting in the hotel lobby, talking to people in office or laboratory, sitting in airplanes, or simply as a token of casual friendship. One I particularly recall was offered to me by an unkempt, unshaven, wild-looking, but courteous old rogue who I met by the Coari waterfront one morning. He carried his pet boa constrictor coiled round his shoulders as he went from stall to stall in the street for no obvious purpose that I could detect. He was followed by a swarm of young children daring each other to touch the great snake. Having kept a pet boa of my own in Sierra Leone I was interested to talk shop with the old boy and to photograph his friend. This was relatively easy but talking was another matter. He decided to take me in hand and teach me Portuguese. So, surrounded by an amused crowd, he backed me against a shop door and commenced the lesson. I didn't want to hurt the man's feelings, but I had to get back to the mission for breakfast. I muttered something about 'café da manha' and started to move off. Nothing doing. Next thing I knew, a cafezinho was thrust at me and we drank to lasting friendship, good health, fortune, and I'm not quite sure what else before I finally made a decent orderly exit to the mission house.

I finally met a Sr. Helvecio Ramos Nogueira at the university. To my delight he produced a framed photograph of Wolferston Thomas and also a number of Thomas's old textbooks that he had presented to a Dr. Lira who gave them to me. I was delighted to take these for the Liverpool School archives. Thomas who originated in Montreal, studied tropical medicine, then joined the staff at the Liverpool School. From there he traveled to Manaus where he bought a house on the Praça da Congressa, now renamed Praça Agnella Bettancourt. In 1908, he set up the first hospital and laboratory for English people in Manaus. However, he accepted all comers. He lived alone with no wife; it is uncertain if he had one, He set about the study of anatomy, pathology, and entomology among clinical subjects. He was the first to perform smallpox vaccination and established a smallpox hospital during the second major epidemic in Manaus. This hospital was named the Hospital Dr. Thomas and became the first old people's home for the poor in 1925. I visited the home, now called Assil Dr. Thomas in Rua Recife. Thomas's house became a nurses' training school and housed some ninety-four nurses when I visited. It was funded by the Ministry of Health. In 1908 Manaus had a population of 100,000 with twelve doctors. When I visited it had grown to a city of 300,000 with 150 doctors. Thomas lived in a house in Teresina Street and died there in 1930. He died of overweight and alcohol. His favorite tipple was President whisky. He was never visited by family members and had no Brazilian wife or children. He was cared for by an old Portuguese servant. Dr. Lira who lived nearby, was a student of Thomas who taught him English and German. Thomas took care of the English expatriates and their families, among them the Deanes. Later Professor Deane gave me the smallpox vaccination certificate he received from Dr. Thomas who vaccinated him in Manaus. I tracked down Thomas's old house and his grave in the cemetery of São João. When he was buried on May 8, 1931 the local administration decreed that his grave would be maintained at the town's expense in perpetuity, in a Decreto no. 31 de 09-05-1931. On his grave is a simple, black marble stone. I read:

To the memory of
Harold Howard Shearme
Wolferston Thomas
Born Montreal, Canada
May 29th 1875
Died
May 7th 1931
"He builded better than he knew."

The cause of death was recorded unceremoniously in the cemetery register as alcoholic cirrhosis.

I was fortunate in being able to visit the new Assil Dr. Thomas. The original smallpox hospital was torn down. The new home was built by a foundation directed by a charming old lady, Donna Virginia Amorin. She presented me with two photographs of the old smallpox hospital as it was in 1946 when she took over. The residents of the home whom I saw seemed content and were well cared for. Some live in individual rooms but most are in dormitories, all of them were very clean. A clinic is held there regularly by doctors and medical students. The home is now supported by the State and private resources. New patients are examined to exclude infectious diseases before they are admitted, but I saw several cases among the inmates with old lesions of espundia as well various physical deformities. In Manaus there was also a center for tropical pathology run by a Dr. Antonio de Brito Bonates whom I tried to visit without success. It was started in 1970 in collaboration with the Museo Goeldi of Belém and with Professor Lacaz of São Paulo.

In the late 19th century Manaus was a boomtown thanks to the discovery of rubber. The town became so wealthy that the city constructed its own theater, which invited famous European performers, Caruso among them! This building must be seen to be believed. It is one of the great sagas of the tropics about which several books were written. I visited the theater one afternoon and the caretaker obligingly illuminated it for me. He pulled massive switches on an antediluvian switchboard. Huge sparks flew in all directions and I fully expected him to be electrocuted on the spot. The baroque decor was unimaginable with amazing painted ceilings, especially in the salon that was painted by De Angelis in 1899. It took him two years, working two hours a day. The theater is full of tapestries, chairs, and marble columns all imported at great expense. Outside the theater all the paving stones are solid, black rubber blocks that have been there since 1896.

From Manaus I returned down river to Santarém, a town of 100,000 with another 100,000 living in the surrounding country. At the time of my visit, there was a twenty-bed hospital run by Franciscan nurses and funded only three and a half years earlier with the help of US funds. There was also a hospital with fifteen beds belonging to SESPE. About 100 babies were delivered at the Franciscan hospital every month. These infants had a unique record of freedom from neonatal tetanus thanks to a maternal vaccination campaign run by a priest-doctor, Father Tucker. I was particularly impressed by my visit to the laboratory where routine specimens were examined from women attending the antenatal clinic. I never saw such a wealth of living protozoa in fresh fecal specimens! I was also very impressed by the refusal of the Catholic staff to accept papal doctrine on birth control. In the neighborhood of Santarém I saw a man about seventy years old with an appalling ulceration of his left axillary region that exposed a large part of his ribs and thoracic cage. His lung moved in and out between the ribs with each breath. This lesion had progressed over about twenty years. He treated it with anaconda fat to keep it clean! I also visited a factory that made hammocks. About forty people working in the factory and another forty-five at home produced some 3,000 hammocks per month selling for between ten and sixty Cruzeiros each. The workers earn 250 Cruzeiros a month, the technicians 400, and the manager 1300. Everything from spinning the ropes to dying and weaving was done on the spot. It must have been at the SESPE hospital where the staff ran a baby clinic, mainly for vaccination, that I also saw a neonate with acute lepromatous leprosy who was receiving no specific treatment except spiritism. In this area a doctor could provide an examination and prescribe treatment as an in or outpatient, but the individual had to buy any drugs needed. Since most had no money, they received no treatment as, with few exceptions, most people were very destitute. Among the surgical cases I saw two suffered snakebite; one an amputation, two had severe burns, one had hepatitis and *P. vivax*, in coma, one had a prostatectomy, one had a laparotomy for a tumor, and one had a gunshot wound.

For some reason I abandoned the Amazon to return from Santarém to Belém by air. I wrote;

"Santarém to Belém, Two hours of smooth flying almost due east along the Amazon in a Sumurai turboprop of Cruzeiro do Sul. Unlike my last hop, from Manaus to Santarém with the infamous Brazilian airline, VASP, we left right on time. The plane was half-full, mainly Brazilians and some Franciscan priests returning to their duty station in Belém. For some peculiar reason, the Franciscan order in this area has attracted an extraordinarily large number of giants. At the barbecue, which the nuns laid on for the last evening of the convocation, I felt like a Lilliputian in a world occupied by people at least ten feet tall. I, at five feet, four inches nearing five feet, five inches practically had to shout to make my voice reach elevated targets."

The contrast between the devoted care given by the nuns in the semi-mission hospital and the equally devoted care provided at the CESP hospital across the way was heartbreaking. The physical conditions in the two centers apart, there is a pathetic system by which the government doctors, competent diagnosticians, are obliged to prescribe treatment for their patients who then must go, or send relatives or friends, to the local pharmacist to buy the required drugs. CESP has a minimal stock for a few utterly destitute cases, in addition to those used to treat malaria, TB, leprosy, and one or two other endemic diseases of public health interest. Many people who neither have nor can beg the money to buy their drugs simply go without. Fortunately the drug companies are often liberal with their samples. At Coari, for example, the hospital pharmacists' store had a few basic supplies such as bandages, rubbing alcohol, disinfectants, vitamin pills—tons of these are consumed in Brazil, and chloramphenicol, the most popular antibiotic! However, the more sophisticated and up-to-date compounds in his cabinet were moestras gratuais (free samples). Big banners and big words, highly publicized senatorial visits and flourishing statements about Amazonas and Transamazonas are one thing. The reality is another.

So back to Belém for a little relaxation, perhaps a letter or two from Ruth, wash my clothes, collect a few butterflies, and talk and drink until my next port of call. From Belém I visited Macapá in Amapá State that had about 100,000 inhabitants. This fascinating town of 40,000 to 53,000 inhabitants, depending upon who tells you, lies north of the Amazon. A hospital and nurses' training center was established with the private funds of a larger than life, zealous Italian man, Dr. Candia. It had two outlying clinics, one at Santana and one at Pacoval. Patients arrive at these in large numbers by small boats called montarias (horses), sometimes paddling for days to seek treatment. They pay one or two Cruzeiros or give something in kind to buy a paper ('ficha') that lasts them for six months. The clinics were run by six lay staff who devote themselves entirely to the centers and live on the island where they were situated. A doctor from the hospital visited every Saturday or patients could be referred to the hospital. The main hospital, three kilometers south of the equator, was run by five doctors, two full and three part-time, who saw about fifty outpatients each day. Dr. Candia was planning to build a new center to be named the Hospital Escola São Camilo e São Luis. It would have 100 beds, a school for seventy-four nurses and a district service. His aim was to establish a radio education service and a research center. When I saw the hospital it already had well equipped wards, supplied with oxygen, well lit, and airy built on a Liberian model and designed by Candia's brother-in-law. It was a truly impressive establishment, well supported by European companies and funding agencies from both Europe and the US. The laundry was donated by Oxfam. An ex-industrialist ran the high-powered organization very successfully.

"Brazil is a country that has always inspired visions and produced visionaries, frequently from other lands. Here in Macapá is a vision realized; an ultramodern hospital set in the waist of the world at latitude zero—the visionary, Marcelo Candia. Through his inspiration, imagination, and drive he has concentrated the spiritual and practical help of many friends and collaborators in his country, Italy, and other countries of the Old and New worlds. He has welded them together with the active participation of the government of Brazil to produce here, in the capital of Amapá, the Hospital Escola São Camilo e Sau Luis. This work deserves to succeed. It will aid untold numbers of poor people in Amapá and help build a healthier, happier generation in this equatorial state. I will be honored to do whatever I can to see that this fine medical center, created and run in the true Christian spirit of love for mankind, continues to grow and fulfill its purpose. Good luck and thank you all for your generous hospitality. Ate logo."

I wonder to whom I addressed that speech. I meant it sincerely but doubt if anything came of my good intentions at the end of the day! I returned to Belém on Tuesday 17th August 1971.

"It's curious how each place visited and the nature of the visit evolved a character of its own. In Macapá I spent much of my time visiting individual patients in their homes and I was deeply impressed by the kindness and humanity that the simple poor people of the town show towards each other. This is something far removed from the ascetic academic atmosphere of my laboratory, the highly sophisticated experimental approach to what, in the end, are human problems. I dare not allow myself to become too involved in the realities, but I must be sure that I see them sometimes.

"Up with the birds, in fact a little before most of them. By the time the cocks were in full crow I was shaved, showered, dressed, packed, and rearing to go. It's remarkable how the mosquitoes bite just before the dawn, probably the newly hatched brood of early evening. Not everybody shares my enthusiasm for getting to the airport on time. We finally reached it five minutes before search time. The search is such a normal part of air travel today, thanks to the influence of a handful of fanatics and neurotics. We think no more of standing in a queue to have our bags and persons ignominiously searched than of walking down the street. This is progress in our civilized age! So, from the ramshackle hut of Macapá airport by Caravelle jet back to Belém. Just one more week to go."

I spent an enjoyable couple of days with Ralph Lainson and Jeff Shaw in the Instituto Evandro Chagas in Belém where we collected specimens of leishmania in hamsters to take back to Liverpool. On 19th August I flew south from Belém to Recife.

"Finally I began to feel that I was headed for home, traveling once more on my international ticket. Steered firmly by the robust figure of Donna Estella, the Brazilian administrator of the Institute, I made my way for the last time to the Cruzeiro do Sul desk. We slowly walked to the exit gate, the portly, dignified figure of my protectress opening a path through the crowd at the airport as if by magic. Ignoring the man at the gate we entered the waiting room and parked ourselves on a bench. I opened up my briefcase, actually an old Gladstone bag with the center cut out to make space for cages, to give some air to my six traveling companions, hamsters with various highly pathogenic strains of leishmaniasis. After a while an elderly man entered the room. Donna Estella with a satisfied grunt rose with her usual stately poise and greeted him. The two engaged in friendly banter, following which I and my bichos were introduced. The Chief Customs Officer, as he proved to be, peered into the briefcase amicably and inspected the hamsters. Six pairs of beady eyes looked up and inspected the Chief Customs Officer. All well.

"Next time," he said, "don't forget to bring passports for them as well."

"A kind man," said Donna Estella when he had left, "always very humorous. He gives me a lot of problems, but always in the end I am winning."

This I could well believe. Somehow I could not visualize anybody having the temerity not to let the indomitable Donna Estella win. Who should arrive as I was leaving but the inimitable Dr. Candia? He spat a warm greeting in broken French through the gap in his upper incisors and thrust another bundle of photographs at me over the barrier. Such a generous openhearted fellow. No wonder the Pope gave him a special benediction. I referred him to Donna Estella who stood steadfastly by the barrier determined not to leave until my plane was safely on its way. She was delighted to take another helpless male under her wing.

"Off we flew from Pará and the Amazon over the sandbanks to São Luis. A short stop and south towards the badlands of the Northeast and Fortaleza. I glanced up and there at last was the blue Atlantic stretching away to my left, waiting for me to cross its vast expanse and after these long, eventful journeying, reach home once more."

What would they be like, those first moments of reunion with Ruth? Six weeks at times can seem like sixty—and sixty is infinity. How can people stand separation for years, in wars, prisons, forced apart with no foreseeable reunions ahead of them? How much it must change even those most intimately entwined souls. Does it ever seem quite the same again? Surely there must be a scar somewhere in the mind and the emotions. Perhaps like scar tissue, the gap closes and tightens more firmly than before.

However, some scars weaken and the gap stretches wider. Dear God, never let this happen to us.

In Fortaleza I was welcomed by Michael and Rosaria Lacey of the British Council. Like all the British Council staff whom I have encountered in Brazil or elsewhere, they were a warm, generous couple who rapidly made me feel at home and went out of their way to give me all the help they could. They arranged meetings with the medical staff of various hospitals, government departments, and so on and saw to it that all my arrangements went as smoothly as possible. The British Council abroad certainly has never received enough credit for the contributions that their staff makes, often in very difficult circumstances.

"An afternoon off, marketing for family and swimming. Fortaleza, well-developed, clean, fresh-looking town."

The area inland from Fortaleza proved to be highly endemic for kala-azar. Much of it was very arid and semi-desert country in which cattle die from lack of water. What a contrast to the nearby Amazonian flood lands. From Fortaleza I flew on to Recife where I was received by Lucy and Peter Oakley of Oxfam.

"Weekend in Recife with the Oakleys—too tired really to care and somewhat depressed after a solid six week grind. I feel myself flooded with impressions following a kaleidoscopic view of Brazil from Copacabana to Coari, from the exotic beaches of Rio to the inferno verde of Amazonas. I am too close to it all now. I must put an ocean between all this and me, wait a while, then take a long, cool look back before I can recall the scene as a whole.

"Then what? My journeys never leave me unscarred, mentally more than physically. This is especially true of my visits to this continent called Brazil. Perhaps in a way it is lucky that I didn't discover Brazil when I was younger, say a quarter of a century ago, I feel this today! I believe I would never have left. How would my life have evolved then? Who knows, and what does it matter anyway? This ludicrous, portly little figure would still be much the same. I don't believe that the environment changes the personality. On the contrary, the personality warps and moulds the environment. After all, what is the environment? Just one pair of eyes! Today I made the inevitable discovery that I am middle-aged."

I made no notes of what happened when I finally returned to Liverpool from Recife on the 24th of August.

Chapter 16

In and Out of the London School of Hygiene and Tropical Medicine 1979–1989

Once Ruth and I decided to leave Liverpool and move to London in 1979 we needed to find a new home. We wanted to live near Hampstead, but learned that house prices in that part of London were far too high for a university professor's pocket. One attractive alternative was the area of Tring, a small Hertfordshire township within easy reach of London, surrounded by attractive countryside. Moreover, Tring had a small but excellent natural history museum that was established by Walter Rothschild to house his exotic animal and insect collections. I was already acquainted with of some of the staff, in particular Neville Bennett who specialized in small butterflies of the family *Lycaenidae*. I collected many of these in Africa and consulted him between visits back to Europe. He found several previously unknown species, some of which he and our French friend, Henri Stempffer of Paris, whom I mentioned earlier, named after me in 1956. Thinking ahead, it seemed a good idea to look for a house near the museum, then in the years to come, I could perhaps spend time in Tring doing entomological research on a voluntary basis. Rothschild's collectors had amassed one of the world's best collections of butterflies. What I did not foresee was that before long, he bequeathed his entire butterfly collection to the Natural History Museum in South Kensington and physically transferred it there. A small token collection remained in Tring for the benefit of visitors.

By 1979 I had established a working relationship with parasitologists in the Wellcome Research laboratories in Beckenham. That organization had a veterinary research field station near Tring in a village called Little Gaddesden. While reconnoitering the Tring area, I learned that one of the Wellcome veterinarians lived in Little Gaddesden. I got in touch with him and he offered to show us around the local area when we drove down for the day. The village and the houses he showed us looked very attractive, but very expensive. A few days later, as we were about to leave Liverpool to drive down again and have another look around, the postman delivered a letter from an estate agent whom we contacted for information on possible housing near Tring. The letter directed our attention to a small house in Little Gaddesden. We discovered later that it was neighbor to part of the Wellcome field research station.

It was snowing heavily as we approached the house from Berkhamsted. We passed a large field beside an extensively wooded area. We later found it was part of the Ashridge National Trust forest. A small herd of deer were scratching for forage through the snow and the setting was very attractive. When we first set eyes on the house the weather was bleak, the garden bare but full of trees—and nobody was at home. Ruth immediately fell in love with what appeared to me to be a small, dilapidated old semi-detached cottage. It was called Pulridge House East. We approached the immediate neighbor's house called The Bailliffs for information about the owners. We were warmly welcomed by a charming couple of about our age who told us the people we sought were at work, but would almost certainly return that evening. We decided to stay in a hotel overnight and call on them next day. The outcome was that we decided on the spot that Pulridge House East was what we wanted. We bought it in spite of my misgivings that it was far too small even for our modest needs. We lived happily in that house for the next twenty-eight years and developed a close friendship with Barbara and Jeremy Day, our new neighbors.

Pulridge House East proved to be smaller than we wished. It was three years before we had an extension built to provide us with a room to accommodate guests and to provide Ruth with her workroom and studio. This annex was designed by a young and imaginative architect named Paul Burdess. He lived at the far end of the village and it was constructed by a local villager, a gentle giant named George Catchpole who lived with his family at Paul's end of the village next to the village store cum post office. George and I immediately struck up an excellent rapport. He was originally a thatcher by trade who hailed from Norfolk. He had migrated south and married a local girl, Minnie, with whom he raised a family. George was mostly self-taught but, with his skill and exceptional physical strength, he was equipped to take on almost any job. With the help of one young lad, Matthew Dixon, he built that annex in about six months, completing it in 1983. The completion was marked by a blue wall plaque made by Paul's wife, Vicky. It was inscribed as built by George Catchpole "almost to the plans of Paul Burdess." The annex was great and Ruth spent much of the next three decades in her studio reading, writing, painting, and producing beautiful, imaginative embroidery. When time allowed, I spent it on writing and entomological pursuits in a small upstairs bedroom that I converted into my study. I later installed a series of computers to communicate with the outside world. From Little G., as we called the village, I commuted to work in the LSHTM for the next ten years.

September 1979 was special. On the 18th Ruth and I celebrated our silver anniversary. On 27th September, the week before I took up my Chair in the London School, my father celebrated his 100th birthday.

While our commemoration was spent quietly, Henry's was the occasion for a splendid luncheon party at a luxurious and very private Mayfair hotel. It was attended by many family members including our American cousin Hal, his latest wife, and two young daughters. They were accomplished musicians who were destined to follow outstanding musical careers. Especially memorable were the photographs that Hal took of the occasion, only to discover that he forgot to put a film in his camera. Hal's delightful daughters entertained us with a superb private concert later that evening in their hotel nearby; cello and piano if my memory is correct.

David Warhurst's arrival and my own at the LSHTM in 1979 were warmly welcomed by the Senior Technician in my department, Peter Sergeaunt. He had a long-standing reputation for his seminal contributions to the diagnosis of human amoebiasis. For some reason the Dean of the LSHTM, Gordon Smith, was very antagonistic to the principle of permitting junior employees to engage in research. My predecessor, Russell Lumsden, likewise gave Peter little or no encouragement. I took exactly the opposite view. For Peter then, the arrival of David and me was a breath of fresh air. After my colleagues in Liverpool and London developed novel laboratory procedures to identify parasites by such biochemical techniques as the characterization of enzymes specific to each species or strain, 'isoenzymes', Peter and his junior assistant, John Williams, adapted the techniques to amoebae. They gained a universal reputation for this contribution to clinical science and Peter later received an Honorary Doctorate in London and the Brumpt Prize of the Société de Pathologie Exotique in Paris. I received the same prize in 1999.

Although our home in Hertfordshire was only about fifty kilometers northwest of the LSHTM, the journey down the M1 motorway was tiresome as this is one of the most congested in the country. I generally traveled by train to Euston station, a forty minute journey, and then two kilometers by foot.

One homeward train journey in December 1984 stands out in my memory. It was probably the nearest I came to serious injury. As we neared Wembley Junction, I saw another train approaching us on my right side at an unusual angle and suddenly realized that it was about to hit us. Seconds later it did but fortunately for those in my compartment, it struck several carriages ahead of us. There was a screeching of brakes, a massive shuddering, and sound of shattering glass before the two trains ground to a halt. I was in the last carriage and saw someone behind me push his way into the rear driver's compartment that was empty. He picked up what looked like a large strap, opened a door, and placed the strap across the railway line adjacent to ours. Later I learned that the man was an off-duty railway employee and this strange act had cut power to all tracks close to our own and set nearby signals to STOP. The adjacent tracks were continuously busy with rail traffic and many terrified passengers were heedlessly spilling out of the train onto the adjacent tracks to escape. This very fortunate intervention probably saved many lives. The carriage in which I was traveling remained upright but when I descended clutching my Gladstone bag of documents I was taking home to study, and walked forwards I saw that the engine and leading carriages of our train were derailed and lying on their sides. I heard calls for help and decided to see if I could provide first aid for anybody. I handed my bag to another passenger with no idea how I would ever retrieve it, found an inter-carriage door that was open, and made my way along the first carriage. I walked over seats and on doors and windows, a strange sensation.

The first casualty I encountered was a man who was half thrown out of a door that then trapped him. He was clearly dead. I moved further and heard a woman call for help from outside the carriage. She had escaped from a door or window on the side that was on top and was sitting outside with a bad wound on her arm. By then the rescue services were arriving, so I decided that the best help I could give her was to talk to her until I could get the attention of one of the ambulance men. Her main concern was not her wound although she was badly shocked, but who would feed and walk her dog that was waiting for her return home. I took her name and address, as well as those of close neighbors and assured her that somehow I would get the message through. I did manage to contact the police shortly after and learned later that they took the situation in hand.

Once the rescue teams were in full operation, there was nothing more I could do. I heard later that four people died and a large number were injured. I walked to the nearest station platform a couple of hundred meters further along the line. My first priority was to locate a telephone and call Ruth. Those were the days before mobile phones were widely used. It was essential to reassure her that I was intact in case she heard of the accident on the radio or TV and let her know that I would find a means to get home even though I might arrive late. By that time, nearly all the uninjured passengers had left the station and it was strangely quiet. As I left the phone, I saw a policeman walking along the platform carrying my Gladstone bag that somebody had handed to him.

All trains on that busy main line were stopped. I left the station, walked along a row of shops outside, and came to a chemist shop that was run by an Asian family. When I went in and explained what I was doing there, they provided me with that reliable British remedy, a nice cup of hot sweet tea, for which I was very grateful. While waiting, I telephoned the police to inform them about the injured passenger's dog. Later that evening, after I reached home by taxi, they called me back with good news. Had I been seated further forward in that train, I might not have survived. Over the next decade there were several other serious rail accidents between Euston and my home station of Berkhamsted but I was fortunately not involved.

From my second official day on the London School staff I was inundated with overseas travel commitments. The first was to the Pasteur Institute in Paris where I was a member of the Parasitology Research Board. This was a challenging and stimulating position that I held for several years. It gave me an exceptional insight into the

French approach to the problems of research in tropical medicine. In addition to visiting the Pasteur, I was invited by my colleagues, Professor Guy Charmot and Dr Jacques Le Bras, to give a number of lectures on malaria chemotherapy in the Institut Léon Mba at the famous Hôpital Claude-Bernard. In spite of my poor French, I was privileged in following years to be a member of juries to adjudicate doctorate presentations by research students from this institute, from the Muséum d'Histoire Naturelle, and other French academic centers, including Montpellier and Bordeaux Universities.

This was an excellent opportunity for Ruth to accompany me. We enjoyed visits to the wonderful museums and art galleries of a vibrant Paris. As time passed, my French became less primitive. For Ruth, French was originally her second language, so it was a chance to enjoy a series of mini holidays among good friends. By the 1970s I extended my activities in the field of leishmaniasis. This gave me opportunities to visit the team of Professor Rioux in Montpellier and consolidate our collaborative research on the biochemical taxonomy of those parasites. Added to my overseas work were increasing responsibilities in London. For eight years, while still in Liverpool, I served as a member on the Council of the Royal Society of Tropical Medicine and Hygiene. I was reappointed for the duration of my first three years at the LSHTM, then was elected as Vice-President for five years, and finally as President to succeed Herbert Gilles for the last three years of my University life.

Nineteen eighty started off with a visit to Calcutta for an international meeting held at the School of Tropical Medicine. I was the Lady N. Brahmachari Reader. I had visited the school two years earlier when I had the privilege of being the J.H. Chowdhury Memorial Orator. I was looking forward to seeing more of that historic center of tropical medicine research. The following notes are extracts from letters that I wrote home.

Tuesday 15th January 1980

". . . After a long delay at the airport in Delhi I finally arrived yesterday and spent half of the day sleeping so that I would have a clear head for today's paper. In fact I got up early to do some work on it and in the event I think it went over quite well.

"Afterwards I lunched with A.B. Choudhuri and some of his staff and we were joined by his wife who is a pediatrician. Now I am working on the paper for tomorrow's oration and waiting to see if any of the conference delegates turn up. . . Calcutta fortunately is much cooler than I expected, only about 2° C, and Delhi was 5° C at night, but it is still as dusty, noisy, and overcrowded as always. Holes in the road that I remember from two years ago are still there only bigger. The Tropical School is two years dirtier than it was, but otherwise unchanged.

"The main conference starts on Thursday and about forty people are coming from overseas. I do not know yet who is coming or what is happening as they do not yet have the program out. The excuse is that all the printers are blocked by the elections. Of these there are still plenty of signs around in the way of posters, graffiti (in Hindi!) and suchlike, but everything is completely peaceful and normal."

Wednesday 16th January

"Well, my second 'Oration' is over thank goodness. It was rather like a Jacques Tati comedy, my arrival in the middle of a long speech in Bengali by the new Minister of Health where I was sat down slap in the middle about two feet away! Most embarrassing.

"Anyway, after a coffee break it was my turn to bore the audience instead of the Minister. Perhaps after all it wasn't too bad since Frank Hawking who suddenly turned up and took his usual place in the first row did not go to sleep, which he usually does when anybody except himself is talking. . . Other people are beginning to arrive for the meeting. I met Garnham briefly as I came in this afternoon, looking very tired as he had not slept on the plane. Then I bumped into Irving Kagan and Mike Schultz, your friends from C.D.C. Atlanta.

"This morning I was handed a card inviting me to a dinner to be given to all the Congress on Friday by Pharmitalia, and find myself the Guest of Honor and Director of the London School of Tropical Medicine! So much for the reputation of Gordon Smith."

In mid-February 1980, under the auspices of WHO, I paid my first visit to the People's Republic of China. It was a valuable moment since the news had very recently been published in the *Chinese Medical Journal* that Chinese scientists had discovered that a widely distributed weed, commonly known as 'qing hao' was extremely effective against malaria infections that were strongly resistant to the few other drugs then currently available. China was obviously a country that, just emerging from the bleak period of the cultural revolution that ended in 1978, merited a visit. It was not just out of curiosity, but more to help reestablish cultural relations with the West. With regards to medical problems of mutual importance, China shared two of my major interests; drug-resistant malaria and leishmaniasis. The first of these conditions had surfaced during the war with neighboring Vietnam. Little was known at the time of how this impinged on the inhabitants of southern China. The second condition was leishmaniasis. Parts of northern China were notorious hotspots of the visceral form of this disease, 'kala-azar', as well as being endemic for a form of cutaneous leishmaniasis. At that time relatively little was known of the epidemiology. What I and the outside world later came to learn about qing hao is a story in its own right. I devote a separate section to it in Chapter 17. Here I give a general account of my brief experiences on this voyage, and a second visit to China that I undertook with my colleagues of CHEMAL in October 1981.

Monday 17th February

"With the help of a Nembutal and a large whisky in place of supper, I managed to get five hours of sleep—not too bad. I woke up when breakfast was being served, just before Bombay. From here on, the plane has few passengers. Next stop is Peking in five hours or so. It is -12° C and snowing! (Tell Mother I will be glad for her socks that I have in my overnight bag—and for Marija's pullover!). I think my Tsipfullkappe (a Swiss wooly cap with a tassel that once belonged to my father-in-law) will come in handy too.

"A man from the British Embassy whom I met on the plane tells me that the hotels are heated, but offices, etc., frequently not! It will be interesting to see what it's like lecturing at freezing point. At least it should keep my audience awake.

"Wouldn't it be nice if I could just stay at home and do the gardening with you."

After a long journey via Delhi I reached Beijing. formerly Peking, where I was met by officials who drove me to the city. A vicious wind was blowing, it was snowing, and the temperature was -15°C. I was ensconced in a small old, but comfortable hotel; probably long used for visiting business people. From the bedroom window overlooking a fairly busy main street full of bicycles and taxis, I heard music blaring from loudspeakers to accompany thickly clad passing pedestrians who stopped on the grass verges and moved solemnly through their Tai Chi exercises as a short break on their way to or from work or home. The sight made me feel very guilty for not joining them.

That morning the director of my host institute, an interpreter, and one of the institute staff who it transpired hoped to come to work with us in London, greeted me. It was the first day of the spring holiday. Seeing how poorly equipped I was for the cold, my hosts insisted on lending me a heavily padded overcoat for which I was quite grateful. Throughout my stay my hosts took great trouble to feed me scientific knowledge and also excellent Chinese food and drink. They also shared some of the unique cultural features in and around Beijing. That day, perhaps inappropriately, they took me to see the Summer Palace. A visit to the palace and Kunming Lake, constructed in 1750, even in the cold of February leaves one with a deep impression of the range of Chinese art and architecture. In 1998 this area was declared a World Heritage site. The gardens are very popular with the ordinary citizens of Beijing and I saw many family groups, well padded against the bitter cold, wandering through the gardens and taking endless photographs of each other. In those days before digital cameras, it must have been quite expensive for the proletarian population. The pressure of children in some spots was considerable in spite of the national one-child policy that was statutory at that time. The pressure was so strong that one poor youngster found himself accidentally pushed into the near-freezing water of a small pond. The buoyancy of his padded overcoat kept him floating like a cork in a bottle until he was rescued by one of his family who waded in waist deep to haul him out, dripping profusely, onto dry very cold land.

I soon discovered fuel was scarce. The laboratories and lecture rooms in Beijing and those in Shanghai were not heated. I felt sorry for the seventeen million inhabitants of the capital and the eighteen million of Shanghai. The laboratories I saw in Beijing were not only unheated, but almost unequipped. Even the simplest apparatus was either obsolete or absent. Chemicals were freely available and technical expertise much in evidence. This situation changed rapidly. Within eighteen months after my first visit, the scientific potential of the Chinese was increasingly recognized by international and unilateral donor agencies that started refurbishing their major academic and industrial research centers. The staff were quick to learn how best to use their new facilities. When I revisited Beijing and Shanghai, the new equipment and furnishings and the skills to deploy them were very noticeable. Today, the rapid pace of development in the PRC has led to the total conversion of several

Chinese cities including old Beijing and Shanghai as I first saw them. They are ultramodern, thriving metropolises with populations to match. No more dreary blue-uniformed workers trudging about on their old bicycles, but smart young cosmopolites driving around the abundantly filled shops of the modern, skyscraper-filled city centers.

On my first visit to China I gave a number of lectures and attended numerous discussions. My colleagues overwhelmed me with their desire not just to learn from my experiences, but to share their own exciting discoveries in the field of malaria chemotherapy. Much of this related to their research on traditional medicinal plants, especially qing hao, the herb known widely outside China as 'Sweet Wormwood'. In addition to spending time with Chinese colleagues in the Institute of Materia Medica, I was taken to meet other research workers in the Military Medical College. A number of innovative chemical structures synthesized there showed significant activity in models of malaria infection, similar to those my team was working on. The staff there were very free in discussing their data with me. They also showed a readiness to provide me with samples to take back to London where I could examine the novel substances in my own laboratory. The willingness of members of both institutes to share their knowledge with me was quite contrary to the preconception of a number of western investigators and other westerners who view the Chinese with mistrust. I devoted quite an effort in the following years to convince colleagues how misguided they were. The open publication of much Chinese data and then clinical reports convinced many outsiders of the high level and integrity of the Chinese workers. Recent reports reveal the potential value of several novel Chinese drugs against drug-resistant malaria, both on their own and in combination with some of the artemisinin series (see later).

Some research workers were carrying out studies on the epidemiology of cutaneous leishmaniasis that they discovered was common in many of the wild gerbils in northwest China near the border with Russian Kazakhstan. By then, the major role of dogs and wild canids as animal reservoirs of the visceral disease, kala-azar, was known. It occurs as epidemics in China. By the time I visited a special license was required to possess a pet dog. However, feral dogs were common and a potential source, not only of leishmaniasis, but of other serious diseases such as rabies and several major worm infections that destroy the liver.

When visiting a city previously unknown to me I always asked to be taken to the local market. A stroll through these centers can be extremely educational in many ways. The type and availability of different types of food was one feature that taught me important things about the local people. The markets in China were no exception. Some odd-looking pieces of meat hanging on hooks caught my attention. They turned out to be smoked dog, literally the hot dog of American fame, but not quite the same species. Chickens and ducks were very popular. I later learned that no part of these birds was discarded during their culinary preparation. This put me off Aylesbury duck in later years—but not totally I am happy to say.

When time permitted, my hosts took the opportunity to show me other cultural heritage sites. The wonders of the unique Forbidden City with its 980 buildings provide an unforgettable insight into the splendors of ancient China. In the immediate aftermath of the cultural revolution, China was not a popular destination for tourists from the outside world. The first view many from the west had was in the magnificent film *The Last Emperor*, the life and times of the Emperor Puyin, made by Bertolucci in 1987. That year the Forbidden City was declared a World Heritage site by UNESCO. Up to that time UNESCO included thirty-seven sites in China. The 4,000 mile-long Great Wall of China is a sight that staggers one, even on a frosty day. Part of it north of Beijing is readily reached from the capital. The glimpse obtained there, and construction vanishing into the distance as it winds up and down the hills, once seen is never forgotten. Fortunately, with the opening of China in the past twenty years and the incredibly rapid rate of its economic and social progress, sites such as these are readily accessible to a huge influx of visitors from the outside world, as well as many of the Chinese from outside the major cities. My great good fortune was to be privileged to get a short glimpse of these wonders before the tourist hordes arrived.

My mission in Beijing completed, I flew an internal Chinese airline to Shanghai, already a relatively large city and one that positively reeked of long-ago international commerce. The temperature was milder, but still much colder than I would experience further south. My first hosts in Shanghai were members of the staff of the 2nd Chinese Military Medical College, an organization that I knew was engaged in the search for novel antimalarial drugs. I would soon study many in London. My welcome was as warm as times permitted. I was housed in a large hotel that was better equipped for visitors from the outside world. My room had a small color television. The main program appeared to be somebody giving English language lessons. I encountered a number of young Americans in the lobby all speaking what sounded like fluent Mandarin. I learned later that they were university students who volunteered under US government auspices to teach English in Chinese schools and universities, somewhat akin to our VSOs. The visitor facilities were quite acceptable. I encountered several noisy groups of tourists from Hong Kong, Japan, and Yugoslavia in the lobby. In the hotel I was even able to have my Kodachrome film processed overnight.

My program was full as I had to visit three institutes and present five lectures during my three-day stay. As in Beijing, the facilities in the research institutes and in university laboratories were still very basic. Only during my next stop in Canton did I consider taking off my overcoat in the buildings. By then the teaching and research centers in Shanghai were being refurbished and the staff was able to rapidly expand their research programs. The crowded schedule did not prevent my hosts from tending to my cultural needs; on a Sunday evening they took me to a performance of the famous Peking Opera.

It was a non-stop, traditional Chinese play that, in the course of three hours, encompassed a spectacular range of drama, comedy, opera, acrobatics, juggling, and slapstick that enthralled the audience. In an odd free hour I visited a large store where I bought two heavy marble statuettes of typical guardian dragons. These were skillfully packed for shipment home by sea to Little G. where they spent the next twenty-five years guarding the small fishpond that Ruth had made for my birthday. It contained several generations of colorful, Chinese-looking Shubunkins.

In February much of China can be very cold; fortunately this was not the case in Canton, now called Guangzhou, my last port of call. It is pleasantly subtropical. Before the cultural revolution there were close contacts between Chinese scientists of that region and Chinese and western colleagues in Hong Kong, then independent of mainland China. I had the good fortune to encounter several of these scientists whose names I do not specify for one or two reasons; First, it may not be in their best interest to be mentioned here if they are still alive. Second, I no longer possess my notes on the journey and cannot recall their names. One elderly doctor, whose home and family I visited, was well known as a specialist in tropical diseases. He had received some of his early postgraduate training in England, a country for which he had a great affection. In spite of his medical expertise and high cultural level, he was hauled before a local revolutionary committee and sentenced to an indefinite period of reeducation. That meant working as a simple laborer on the land. He survived this and ultimately was reestablished in the university where he carried out pioneering studies on the epidemiology of malaria. He focused on the endemic island of Hainan where chloroquine-resistant malignant tertian malaria was becoming an increasingly serious health threat.

My hosts arranged a visit to the nearby city of Fujian, which is well known as a center for producing ceramics and traditional-style scroll paintings. It was fascinating to see a score of young artists all engaged in painting delicate copies of a scene containing birds and trees, complete with a poem in classical Chinese script; each one was virtually identical to the next. I also recall trays of very solemn Chinese officials modeled in clay, patiently waiting their turn to be placed in the kiln for baking. Sitting by their side was a pretty little Chinese girl solemnly doing her homework, while her mother tended the patient clay models.

My first assay into China was finally over. Weighed down with a selection of interesting books given me by my hosts, including an excellent and invaluable illustrated text on traditional Chinese medicinal plants, an alarming book on acupuncture, and a delightful work on Chinese pottery I was put on an internal flight back to Beijing. From there I flew an international airline home on March 4th. The demand on my time was such that a week later I had to fly to Basle for a joint meeting of the Royal Society of Tropical Medicine and Hygiene with the Swiss Society of Tropical Medicine and Parasitology of which I was an Honorary Member. Fortunately with Ruth this time.

The following February I flew to Lucknow in India where the CDRI, whose staff we were collaborating with, held a special international symposium on antiparasitic chemotherapy to coincide with our next scheduled CHEMAL meeting. Along with my colleagues of CHEMAL, Nitya Anand, also a member of the group and the Director of the CDRI, invited a number of other scientists who were prominent in the field of antiparasitic chemotherapy. This included Bob Howells who replaced me in Liverpool and Ralph Neal. Ralph was then working with the Wellcome Research laboratories. He later joined my team in the LSHTM. It was an excellent high-powered conference. Presentations were made by such prominent figures as Lord Todd, Cyril Garnham, and Lawson Soulsby, to become Lord Soulsby. Nitya flatteringly invited me to present the 6th Mellanby Memorial Lecture on *Chemotherapy of Malaria And The Host-Parasite Interaction*. I also presented a review on the chemotherapy of leishmaniasis. I then flew to Lucknow via Delhi where, already planning my homeward journey, I wrote the following to Ruth.

Friday 13th February 1981

"...At the moment it looks as if I will have to stick to my schedule and return as originally planned. All the flights from Lucknow to Delhi are full and I want to get a guaranteed seat even on the plane from Delhi to London on Saturday/Sunday night—but I'll still try.

"Yesterday I had dinner with Tom Buchanan, British Council, in order to meet an Indian research worker with whom I had more detailed discussions today. Actually this morning I went to the malaria HQ, and learned how the situation is, in some ways, deteriorating. I also visited briefly the old research center next door, which is going rapidly from bad to worse!

"After missing lunch I went straight to the All India Institute of Medical Research, one of the key places in India, where they are a bit better, but the people very unimaginative. When I have finished this letter and a bag of peanuts saved from British Airways I have to make contact again with the British Council, but I hope to get a quiet, early night and bed since I leave here for Lucknow at 05:20 a.m. tomorrow.

"Yesterday as I got back to the hotel in the afternoon I bumped into the WHO Japanese malariologist whom we met in Manila. He was waiting for Ade Lucas, head of the TDR program in Geneva, who I find is also coming to our meeting in Lucknow. According to Lucas, with whom I had tea there is more money for the TDR program than we believed, so perhaps I can direct some towards London... It is relatively cold here at the moment, all the locals walking about in pullovers—but not quite as cold as Little Gaddesden."

My second visit to China, which I write of in the next chapter, was in October 1981 when I headed the CHEMAL team to Beijing for discussions on antimalarial drug development. I was charged by Ruth with doing some shopping there.

Friday 9th October 1981

"... This evening for the first time we were taken to do some shopping. I have managed to get your two dogs—but they are in marble, not porcelain that are not made any more—and they are so heavy that I am having them shipped home. With luck we may have them by Christmas, and I think they will look very nice by the fire.

"So far no luck with the blouse—wrong color, size and shape, and jackets are all too rubbishy here. Tea I have, but the words I so carefully copied from our tin at home mean Best China Tea, so that didn't get me very far! Anyway, I hope to look in some more shops on Monday.

"The husband of Li Ze-Lin, the Chinese scientist who was due to join us in London, came to see me yesterday. He proved to be quite young, very pleasant, and laughing or giggling most of the time. Apparently he has made a major advance in virology here and is very well known in the world of medical research. On leaving he presented us with an attractive bottle of a ubiquitous and smelly rice liqueur called Maotai. I am not sure what to do with it, but at least will keep the bottle.

"The meeting itself has gone well, with good humored exchanges on both sides which I hope will lead to a productive collaboration and, maybe a valuable new drug—only time and more work will tell."

It certainly did. The new drug was artemisinin.

While I was in China a dramatic political event was occurring elsewhere. At the end of that letter home I added,

"... The news does get through here and I was very sad to hear of Sadat's assassination. What a cruel world when one man who I believe really tried to lay the foundations for peace was murdered by his own people."

In 1982 I found myself once again in Lucknow, this time en route for a Workshop on Leishmaniasis that I helped to organize in Patna. I traveled via Delhi.

Wednesday 1st December 1982

"... My own flight here was comfortable enough if long, and we arrived an hour late. Then came the chaos! Delhi airport has never been very well organized but this morning was really hellish. To top it all my suitcase was the last to arrive. I had just about given up when I spotted it—two hours after we landed.

"Better late than never. Fortunately the driver did not give up and I finally arrived in town where I am staying with one of the British Council people, the hotels being full with the Asian Games!

"Tomorrow I get the 07:15 a.m. flight to Lucknow, then on to Patna on Sunday. This evening I am the guest of honor at Prof. Ramalingswami's house for a semi-official dinner to finalize arrangements for the Workshop."

Professor Ramalingaswami, a charming man who was a Rhodes Scholar in Oxford and a good friend of Brian Maegraith, was the Director of the All India Institute of Medical Research and one of the foremost Indian medical scientists of those days. He spent much of his time fighting against government bureaucracy in order to promote the highest standards of research in India.

The state of Bihar was one of the epicenters of 'kala-azar' in India and was devastated on more than one occasion in the past by massive epidemics of this killing disease. The parasite that causes it in that country, *Leishmania donovani*, only infects man. Because the visceral disease it produces was still a serious problem, I collaborated with my Indian colleagues and, with the aid of the British Council, I set up an Indo-UK Workshop on Leishmaniasis to evaluate the current situation and to explore new avenues of research aimed at its treatment and control.

In addition to parasitologists and physicians from major Indian governmental and academic centers, we recruited a team of leading experts from England. These fellow leishmaniacs included Anthony Bryceson, a clinician with considerable experience of kala-azar from the Hospital for Tropical Diseases in London, Bob Killick Kendrick with whom I was working in Saudi Arabia, Ralph Neal, an expert on experimental chemotherapy, Dick Ashford, a parasitologist and naturalist from my former department in the LSTM, and Ralph Lainson, who was directing the Wellcome center for leishmaniasis research in Brazil and others. I see from old records that I presented a joint review with an Indian colleague on "Kala-azar in India—its importance as an issue in public health." Indeed, it was an important issue at that time, partly because of the high rate of infection by local sandflies, known as *Phlebotomus argentipes*, but also since there were very few drugs with which to treat it. The most widely used one was a very toxic organic derivative of antimony called sodium stibogluconate. Treatment with it was nearly as hazardous as the disease itself. Moreover, a high proportion of treated patients relapsed.

In reviewing the current situation in endemic villages in and around Patna, it was clear that much work was needed along several lines. First was to develop new simpler and more accurate means of diagnosing the disease. Second was to develop safer forms of treatment once the diagnosis was made. Third was to develop better means of preventing infection. The only useful method then available was the application of insecticides to destroy the vectors and the use of fine mesh bed nets. There was no protective vaccine available and there is none to this day. The extensive spraying of interior house walls in India with DDT was an integral part of the antimalarial eradication campaign of the 1950s and 1960s. This initially led to a remarkable, coincidental reduction in the incidence of kala-azar as well as malaria. This was because the vectors fed on humans mainly indoors. The disease exploded dramatically in 1975 when the campaign against malaria slowly stopped. In passing, it is interesting to note that kala-azar in China is caused by a different parasite for which humans and also canines are the reservoir. The Chinese health authorities in the 1970s and 1980s succeeded in reducing the incidence there by combining the treatment of infected people with a radical campaign aimed at the total destruction of the majority of domestic dogs within all known endemic areas of the country. As I noted elsewhere, some of these animals found their way into the local meat markets.

During my ten years in the LSHTM I had numerous occasions to travel within and beyond Europe. To give even a summary of these would occupy too much of the reader's time. Simply stated, I devoted many days and weeks to participating in international field and teaching programs aimed especially at managing such diseases as malaria and leishmaniasis, and also onchocerciasis, or river blindness, and other worm infections. After my official retirement in 1989, I continued to play a part in many of these activities, as I note in following sections. Moreover, the laboratory research on which my teams and I were engaged in Basle, Liverpool, and London occupied much of my time on writing up and publishing our data.

In between, I worked with my co-author Herbert Gilles and later, Geoffrey Pasvol, on new editions of our *Color Atlas of Tropical Medicine and Parasitology*, no mean task. It is one that I only recently abandoned after the publication of the sixth edition.

Meanwhile there was life to be lived, holidays to take with Ruth, mainly in Switzerland where we could recuperate in the Engadine and visit some of her family in Herisau and Zurich. As the years passed after my retirement from the LSTMH, we indulged in a few cruises, the most memorable taking us through several Middle East countries.

Once we settled in Little G., Ruth devoted much energy to her inventive painting and embroidery. She actively participated in a small, select group of fellow stitchers called 'The Closed Circle'. From time to time they exhibited their work, which was widely appreciated. She was inspired by the collection of tribal artifacts that we acquired during our residence in Papua New Guinea. Many of her imaginative works were based on tribal folklore that she became familiar with when we lived in the Sepik area. Fortunately for me, she also took up golf, a sport that neither of us had ever indulged in. In 1980 she was admitted to the excellent Ashridge Golf Club close to our home. Unfortunately, it soon became apparent both to her and the pro who instructed her, that a long-standing back problem would never permit her to play well. She was allowed to become a social member; something from which I profited thereafter as Ruth invited me to the club for excellent Sunday lunches. She was the one who had an inherent ability to make friends. We were fortunate in gradually coming to know a small circle of local residents whose company we greatly enjoyed over many years.

One simple question that we were often asked was: While living and traveling as we did for so many years in often primitive conditions, did we catch any exotic diseases? Our answer is only relatively seldom other than the occasional intestinal infection with bacteria and once in Ruth's case, amoebiasis. Apart from once acquiring a simple infection with benign tertian malaria in Nepal, Ruth remained free of such problems. I did better. I managed to develop malignant tertian malaria in Liberia and benign tertian in TPNG, tungiasis (chigger fleas), in my feet in Tanganyika, hepatitis B from a contaminated syringe when the fleas gave me a severe bacterial foot infection against which I received penicillin injections, severe bacterial intestinal infections in New Delhi, Santiago de Chile, Khartoum, and Geneva from food in first-class restaurants, creeping eruption from the larvae of hookworms that invaded my legs in Borneo, and severe sunburn on my scalp in Kenya. We managed to survive them all.

After we were in London for about three years, I began to record some of the events of our lives and some intimate thoughts on my computer. I was not at all sure why I was doing this. As I stated before, for several years I had the habit of making brief notes during my overseas journeys in small diaries mainly to remind myself of factual events, meetings with various people, and sometimes of places and atmosphere. I probably always had the notion that I would write something in the nature of an autobiography one day in the future. For a reason I now find it impossible to recall and probably while I was still working at the LSHTM, I destroyed nearly all my handwritten notes, something that I later came to regret. A few notes survived when I first started to keep them on the computer. They were sometimes composed with long intervals between. Only much later did I start to write more regularly and at greater length at certain times.

1982
Wednesday 13th January 1982

"In the airport on my way home from a visit to Riyadh to discuss with the Saudi Arabian National Council for Research plans for a major program to investigate the problem of leishmaniasis in the Eastern Province, I telephoned Ruth who told me that my father had died on this date. Henry was in his 103rd year and it seems he passed quietly away. He never did want to make a fuss. I was unable to reach home in time for his funeral which was held on 14th January but it was well attended and somebody, I still do not know which of my relatives this was, read a very warm eulogy in his memory."

(See Chapter 21. In 2009 I learned that I had total amnesia for this event and rediscovered the name of the writer of that eulogy.)

Sunday 11th April

"Not long following my father's death, life took another unexpected turn for Ruth and for me. Early in the morning of Easter Sunday ten days after my fifty-eighth birthday I was baptized and confirmed in the University Church near Bedford Square by Bill Westwood, the Anglican Bishop of Edmonton. I had received instruction from Peter Hughes, the young priest in charge during the previous four months. It was an extremely emotional occasion for both Ruth and me as well as a major change in the direction of my life that I had long felt I owed her. After a post-service breakfast everybody gathered in the square which was mercifully empty at that time of the morning, except for a passing postman who witnessed, with obvious astonishment, the sight of a Bishop in full regalia and assorted participants dancing in the street."

1986
Monday 17th November 1986

An encounter en route to Saudi Arabia. London-Riyadh-Jeddah Dept.12.30. In Terminal 3, London Heathrow.

"I would put her age at the mid-to-late sixties. She resembled the caricature of an elderly Scandinavian spinster you would expect to see in a vintage Danny Kay comedy, grey hair in a bun, steel-rimmed spectacles, tinted hair, and accent to match. The Saudia executive lounge was at the far end of the pier and I left it to catch my plane before most of the passengers waiting there and after all the tourist class passengers were aboard. It flashed through my mind as soon as I glimpsed her that she had lost her way. As she approached me, carrying only a letter in her hand—perhaps also a handbag but I didn't notice—I assumed I was right.

"'Excuse me Sir, are you going to Saudi Arabia?', she asked me shyly. 'Yes, I am.' 'I wonder, Sir, if you could possibly help me. I have to send a message very urgently to a relative of mine in Libya. It will take at least three weeks from here and I thought if it could be posted from Saudi it would save a lot of time. The post is much quicker that way.' She half opened the airmail envelope to give me a glance at two folded, partly handwritten sheets of paper. 'It's only a letter you see. I used to work here sometimes and I thought if somebody would kindly take this with them and post it for me.' Her voice trailed off. Quickly she added 'I have a dollar for the stamp.'"

"Warnings not to carry parcels for strangers flitted through my mind. *Libya—of all places! What was she doing there, without baggage, not where she was to catch a plane, nobody else about?* We approached the Saudi desk where three of the staff were waiting for the first class passengers. 'If it is so urgent, why don't you ask one of these people?' I asked, indicating the check-in counter. 'Oh thank you very much Sir', she replied eagerly and, as I crossed the lounge to enter the plane, I heard her quiet, Scandinavian voice repeating its request to the check-in clerks. 'I used to work here sometimes'. Her voice faded into the distance.

"Uneventful routine journey except for mad scramble at Jeddah International. Met and warmly embraced by Mohammed and his boss, Dr. Ali Al-Gamdi, General Director of Medicine from Medina at 01:30 p.m. and driven to Intercontinental Hotel."

In July 1989 Geoffrey Targett and my other colleagues in the Department of Medical Protozoology organized a two day 'Anti-protozoal Chemotherapy Symposium' at the LSHTM in honor of, or maybe thanks for, my impending retirement after ten years there and thirteen years at the LSTM. It was attended by an impressive group of colleagues and students, a number from overseas, and the program lasted for two days. We enjoyed an excellent reception at the end of the first day's sessions and Ruth was presented with a superb bouquet when the symposium closed the next day. It was a touching and unforgettable occasion. Two months later I emptied the drawers in my office, shook hands, and departed to catch a train home from Euston station. My official career was over. The next one was to commence. I was only sixty-five years old.

Chapter 17

The Evolution of 'Sweet Wormwood'
0340–2009

The medicinal value of the weed popularly called 'Sweet Wormwood', 'Sweet Annie' or 'qing hao' has ensured its place in traditional Chinese medicine for nearly 2000 years. Since 1972 its modern development and exploitation as one of the most potent antimalarials ever known, became the focus of a number of scientific papers and theses. The first to come to the attention of scientists outside China to this research appeared in English in the *Chinese Medical Journal* in 1979. This remarkable paper immediately drew my attention to the revived study of malaria in China and stimulated me to visit in early 1980. During the Vietnamese war of the 1960s, resistance to the best antimalarial drug available at that time, chloroquine, became increasingly common in the malignant tertian malaria parasite, *P. falciparum*. The lives of large numbers of non-immune indigenous people in Southeast Asia, and others such as American soldiers, were threatened by the lack of an alternative treatment. While their infections usually were cured by quinine, supposedly the oldest known antimalarial drug, it is a toxic compound only obtained from trees mostly grown on Indonesian plantations and supplies were scarce.

In southern China adjacent to North Vietnam, chloroquine resistance was becoming a threat. The Chinese Maoist government ordered its scientists to seek an alternative antimalarial to chloroquine to treat their soldiers and the general populace. For this work, the People's Liberation Army Research Institute joined with scientists of the China Academy of Traditional Chinese Medicine. A Qinghaosu Antimalarial Coordinating Group was formed for the project. China has a long, successful tradition of herbal medicine. Chinese scientists began searching in the old writings on traditional medicinal plants. The therapeutic value of the weed called 'qing hao', *Artemisia annua*, was used to treat such disorders as fevers, diarrhea, and several skin ailments including boils and other infectious conditions. Although the nature of the agent causing malaria was not recognized until the late 19th century, the intermittent fever it produced was well known, and Chinese texts of materia medica, dating from the 4th century AD, described the value of concoctions made from qing hao for the relief of such fevers.

An active compound subsequently called 'qinghaosu', with potent antimalarial properties, was extracted with difficulty from qing hao. This widely distributed common species of wormwood grows in many countries in Asia and Europe. The botanical identity of qing hao was the subject of learned debate. Now it is acknowledged that two different members of the genus *Artemisia* (Family Asteraciae) contain a chemical, a sesquiterpene lactone at first called 'arteannuin' after the Latin name of the plant. Now it is known as 'artemisinin'. Of the two species, *A. annua* has a higher yield and *A. apiacea* a lower one.

On my first visit to the China Academy of Traditional Chinese Medicine in Beijing I was shown a collection of plants derived from seeds of different varieties of *A. annua*. This plant has spikes of very small, yellow, mimosa-like flowers, and the leaves have a delicate, pleasant, aromatic odor when touched or squeezed. The tiny dust-like seeds are collected in small paper sachets placed around the spikes once the flowers are mature and have been either self-pollinated or pollinated by insects. My experience with growing the plant in a closed greenhouse in my home leads me to suspect that self-pollination is a common reproduction process. The institute's scientists discovered that a simple aqueous infusion of the crushed whole plant produced the maximum yield of the compound. However, it is poorly soluble in water. In mice experimentally infected with malaria, the maximum activity level came by injecting an oily solution of the chemically purified substance. In subsequent clinical trials, an oily solution also gave the maximum activity level in patients naturally infected with malaria. The action of this preparation proved to be very rapid, even against infection with strains of *P. falciparum* that were highly resistant to chloroquine. Animal experiments confirmed the lack of cross-resistance between the two compounds. Before leaving Beijing, I asked to visit a typical herbalist store where I could see and purchase some dried medicinal plants. In the store I visited, the shop assistant showed me a large drawer and several glass jars containing dried qing hao. I purchased a small packet to take home with me. By then I recognized the Chinese symbol for qing hao and the shop assistant explained to me, through my host, the wide range of ills for which this plant was a popular remedy.

Qing hao has spread beyond Asia and Europe to other countries with temperate climates. In May 1982 I visited the Walter Reed Army Institute of Research (WRAIR) near Washington to discuss studies I was carrying out in association with their massive antimalarial program. Our conversation naturally turned to qing hao, by then a hot topic among everybody searching for new antimalarial drugs. On a pleasantly warm spring day, a colleague took me outside the main building where I saw bunches of a plant spread out drying on a trestle table. The plant was qing hao. One of my hosts was a Boy Scout troop leader in his spare time. While taking his group for an outing along the banks of the nearby Potomac River, he spotted an unusual plant growing in abundance. A brief inspection told him that this was *Artemisia annua.* He and his scouts gathered as much weed as they could carry and took it to WRAIR to confirm its identity and study its antimalarial activity.

Within days they knew they had struck gold. How qing hao reached the Potomac River is unknown. It is likely that Chinese immigrants years ago had, like me, brought traditional medicine with them. That seed was dispersed accidentally and the plant colonized in that area. I was already aware of the ease with which this can happen. In our small conservatory Ruth and I raised a number of plants over 1.4 meters tall from the dried qing hao I brought back from Beijing. As far as I was aware, *A. annua* did not occur in England. Not wishing it to run wild around our garden, I took the precaution of destroying the plants as soon as I photographed them. Two years later, in early summer, a plant with a familiar leaf about thirty centimeters high grew at the foot of my garage wall. It was qing hao. I searched around for any more plants but found none. Therefore, I uprooted the sole plant and transferred it into a small plant pot that I took next day to my laboratory where it was out of harm's way. I was away for some days and my staff forgot to water it. All that remained when I returned was a sad, shriveled, flowerless weed.

For practical reasons it is far better to use a water-soluble drug than one that must be injected in oil. The Chinese chemists devoted much effort to studying chemical modifications of artemisinin (called for the sake of brevity, QHS) and discovered several that were water-soluble, although rather unstable once they were in solution. One was a compound they called artesunate. In a freshly prepared aqueous solution injected intravenously it had a potent, although short-lived, action. The result was a dramatic rapidity with which it killed malaria parasites in the blood stream and organs of infected patients. Many would have died otherwise.

At the time Chinese laboratories were very poorly equipped and they were keen to develop a working relationship with appropriate centers in other countries where further studies could be made with the QHS compounds. However, they were wary of unscrupulous methods used by some in the pharmaceutical industry and academic centers, when exploiting the products and intellectual rights of individuals and research centers in less well-endowed institutes. I was a bit surprised when my Chinese hosts expressed their eagerness for one of their research staff to come to work with the team I had established at the LSHTM by late 1979.

Through the newly formed UNDP/World Bank/WHO Special Programme for Research and Training in Tropical Diseases (TDR for short) I was able to organize two fellowships. The first went to Li Ze-Lin, a biologist from the Department of Pharmacology of the Institute of Chinese Materia Medica in Beijing. At a later date, there was another for Gu Hao-Ming. At the time he worked in the Shanghai Institute of Materia Medica where I originally encountered him on my second visit there. It is a Chinese custom to place the family name before the personal name of an individual as we did for Dr. Li. Somehow we always referred to Dr. Gu as plain Gu.

Ze-Lin arrived in London just before Christmas of 1980 and Ruth and I met her at Heathrow airport. We waited so long at the arrivals exit that we feared she had missed the flight. As far as we knew, it was her first venture outside China, even though I believe her husband, an oncologist, was working on a fellowship at the International Cancer Research Centre in Lyon. Finally a very tired and bewildered Chinese lady turned up and we took charge of her. We drove her to Bloomsbury and booked her into a typical small hotel near the LSHTM. We went in with her to check the accommodation and settle her in. However, we both immediately agreed that we could not leave this poor stranger alone for the coming holiday period. She spoke relatively poor English and knew no one in London. We left her there that first night to get some sleep, then came back the next day, and drove her to our home in Hertfordshire where she spent the first couple of weeks of her stay in England. I had experienced the simplicity of life in Beijing; the sad near-uniform clothing worn by most people, and the frugal living. Ze-Lin could not get over the fact that we had running hot water, central heating plus a small wood fire, a good variety of food and drink, and nobody to look over her shoulder. It was a joy to host her. She was anxious to help Ruth with domestic matters so Ruth took her under her wing. One day Ruth discovered that Ze-Lin had come across a winter pullover that she was knitting for me and decided to contribute to its production. Ze-Lin added a few rows, albeit it in a somewhat different stitch. It added a certain charm to the garment that I still wear to this day, a quarter of a century later.

To my pleasant surprise, the Ministry of Health of the PRC permitted Ze-Lin to bring samples of a number of the best QHS analogs that were designed in her institute. We examined them together in my laboratory under the WHO CHEMAL project in which we were engaged. When Gu joined us the following year, we were able to extend the range of our research. As far as I know, this was the first research carried out on QHS and any analog outside China. The Li-Gu members of my team were among the first Chinese scientists allowed to work outside China after the end of Mao's Cultural Revolution.

In 1985 we published our first paper on a joint study I carried out with my colleagues David Ellis, David Warhurst, and George Tovey together with Ze-Lin and Gu. It was on the changes QHS produces in malaria parasites observed with the electron microscope. The following year Ze-Lin, David Warhurst, my chief technician Brian Robinson, and I published the results of our studies comparing the action of QHS with four of its analogs, including artesunate, against a large range of malaria parasites of mice. Among them were strains that were resistant to all currently used and some new antimalarial drugs of different chemical types. This consolidated our knowledge of the enormous potential of the Chinese compounds.

The Chinese government wanted to ensure that its research establishments were acknowledged as the discoverers of the anti-malarial potential of one of their traditional remedies by the outside world. They had already started to manufacture QHS for medicinal use, but recognized that they lacked the expertise to supply a drug that was acceptable outside China and other Southeast Asian countries because they lacked knowledge of internationally acceptable production methods and standards. They were anxious to acquire this knowledge and approached WHO for help.

In October 1981 I set up a joint meeting of the CHEMAL team with the Chinese scientists in Beijing. My team included the current director of the WRAIR antimalarial program, Craig Canfield. His colleagues acquired considerable experience in developing novel drugs to meet international standards of production with their own compounds. By this time they also gained experience with some of their novel derivatives of QHS. Contrary to uninformed rumors circulating outside China at the time, our hosts were very frank in regard to their program, problems related to QHS, and the analogs they were developing. On Craig's initiative, arrangements were made to let one of his staff go to Beijing to advise the Chinese how to modify their program in order to manufacture QHS at internationally acceptable standards.

Following this move, production soared at one of the Chinese pharmaceutical factories. At the present time, they supply a significant part of the global requirements of QHS and several of its analogs, such as artesunate.

After Ze-Lin returned to Beijing we lost contact. About five years later, Ruth and I were in Paris where I was attending a conference. One bright spring morning we bumped into an elegant, smartly dressed young Chinese woman walking along the Champs-Elysées. It was Ze-Lin who had joined her husband in Lyon.

The late 1970s began an epoch when interest stirred in the pharmaceutical industry outside China in the commercial and practical potential of novel compounds, either derived from QHS, or based on the chemical structure of these compounds. Through my role in both the CHEMAL research program and my association with several pharmaceutical companies, my small team worked on a shoestring budget with WRAIR and individual chemists from industry and academia. We became a focus for the primary screening in mice infected with rodent malarias. This is one of the basic steps in antimalarial drug development.

Direct test tube screening of drugs against cultures of the human parasite *P. falciparum* had been possible since 1976 when Americans, Trager and Jensen, first demonstrated a method of growing the parasites in continuous culture. Testing novel compounds in mice has major added values that include low cost, ease of use, the demonstration of activity in the intact animals, metabolic effects, and toxicity or lack of it in the rodent hosts. Moreover I was able to pursue my specialty which was to explore the potential value of drug combinations of various sorts in slowing down or preventing the selection of resistance that inevitably occurs when parasites are exposed to antimalarial drugs used alone, i.e., monotherapy, over a length of time. I was agreeably surprised to read a paper by two staff members of WHO in 2004 who gratifyingly acknowledged; "The idea that drug combinations can be used to delay antimalarial drug resistance came from Peters."

The accompanying reference was to a paper I published in 1980 in which I suggested that artemisinin was a promising component for this purpose. From 2006 this became globally accepted policy. However, by then, nobody remembered who originated the idea of deploying what is now referred to as Artemisinin Combination Therapy, (ACT).

During the early 1990s I met an English chemist named Charles Jefford who worked in the University of Geneva. He was one of the first to explore the mode of action of compounds with structures similar to that of QHS. For several years we enjoyed an interesting, productive collaboration that later led him to synthesize a very promising compound, somewhat related to QHS. We hoped for adoption by a pharmaceutical company with the means to carry out the costly developmental steps that new medications must undergo up to and, hopefully, during clinical investigation. Not surprisingly, Charles was not the only chemist to take on the challenge. I was fortunate to be involved with others over the years, including Gary Posner and Richard Haynes, who also successfully produced highly promising lead compounds. The confidential manner in which we managed all the data we produced from various competing sources meant that my team and I rarely enjoyed the publication of our contribution to the development of any of these compounds. Ultimately, a number of them reached us from CHEMAL and WRAIR sources. It is very difficult to overcome all the hurdles involved in new drug development. It is sad that Charles' most promising candidate compound never reached the clinical trial stage. However, that has been the fate of all the others to date. As I write this in 2009, no other truly novel compound of the QHS or similar chemical type has found its way into clinical trial.

My interest in the artemisinins was not limited to discovering new and more active analogs. Prior to my retirement, the main thrust of the final stages of my research program continued to be the study of the extent to which it was possible to deploy carefully selected drug combinations to impede or prevent the selection of drug resistance in my rodent malaria models. Before this we first had to see whether malaria parasites could become resistant to the QHS type of compound.

This was a long arduous task. It turned out that parasites could become resistant to such compounds, but the rate was much slower than we were accustomed to see with any other antimalarial drug. However, the parasites did become resistant given enough time. Once we established that, we needed to see if we could influence this process by combining any of these compounds with drugs of a different structural type. We had already produced interesting data with other types of combinations. Some were very effective in slowing down the selection of resistance and we finally produced data showing that this should be possible by combining a QHS-type compound with something else, such as one of the relatively new types of antimalarial called mefloquine. The concept of administering them in combination with other antimalarials, like lumefantrine, was being explored under the partial guidance of CHEMAL.

A joint Thai-British team, supported by the UK Wellcome Trust and Oxford University, was prominent among groups carrying out this work outside China. Clinical trials were set up in naturally infected patients in several centers led by experienced clinical staff of Mahidol University in Bangkok in close collaboration with Nicholas White and his Oxford colleagues. Trials were conducted in Bangkok and Cheng Mai on the Thai-Burmese border.

Nick made a groundbreaking mathematical analysis of the likely effects on the rate of cure of malaria infection of QHS alone or in combination with another compound such as mefloquine. Unfortunately the combination failed, possibly because an underlying high level of resistance to mefloquine already existed in that area.

In 2005 one of my last papers was Part LXIII of a series we published in the *Annals of Tropical Medicine and Parasitology* from 1968 onwards. It describes the potential value of one combination put into clinical trials in East Africa by the pharmaceutical company, GlaxoSmithkline. Unfortunately, it was withdrawn due to toxicity caused by one of the components, dapsone, in a small number of individuals. Paradoxically, this was one of the first drugs used to cure leprosy. It continues in use for that purpose.

As I write, another ACT is being prepared for clinical trial. Early on in my collaborative work with Chinese chemists, I received a sample of a very active new compound called pyronaridine. They issued promising reports on its action against chloroquine-resistant

P. falciparum malaria in Chinese patients. In a paper we published in 2000, Part LVIII in our series, we first recommended use of this combination. Prior to its publication, I presented data on this and the Chinese work at a special meeting held by WHO in Geneva late in the 1990s. I strongly promoted the idea of putting a pyronaridine-artesunate combination to the further stages of drug development that had to precede its possible introduction into clinical trial. It reflects both the politics and cost of drug development that more than a decade elapsed before this combination, under the name of Pyramax®, first entered clinical trials. I doubt if future literature will mention the pioneering contribution made to the progress of Pyramax® and its evolution by our team over many years.

It was soon evident that a shortage of QHS compounds and the high cost of their production were serious obstacles to their deployment, especially if they were administered in combination with a partner compound. Based on the success of clinical studies in Thailand, the principle of deploying QHS with a second drug became generally accepted. As mentioned above, in 2001 the use of an ACT became dogma at the international level. However, a problem remained; how to produce enough of the parent plant, *A. annua* and how to do so at a cost that was affordable to the most needy, often impoverished countries?

Mass *A. annua* cultivation was extended in Southeast Asia and also in such areas as the relatively temperate highlands of East Africa where large plantations and extraction plants were organized with support from international funds. American agriculturist Dana Dalrymple recently reviewed this interesting saga. The final product is still costly and means are still sought to produce QHS at a significantly lower price.

International awareness of the grinding burden of malaria, especially on the African continent, has finally brought massive infusions of money on an unprecedented scale from philanthropic individuals and organizations like the Gates Foundation. By 2008 they provided the previously unthinkable sum of $1.2 billion dollars for malaria research to underpin plans not to *eradicate*, but to *eliminate* malaria. The UN Secretary General proposed this target in a speech given on World Health Day in April 2008. Plant geneticists and molecular biologists were enrolled in the search for novel means of production. One of these is the ingenious transfer of the genes within *A. annua* that are responsible for the plant's synthesis of QHS into yeasts that can be cultured en masse in fermentation chambers by long used techniques developed for mass production of such compounds as penicillin and beer! A recent and most ingenious avenue being explored is modifying a biochemical pathway in chicory. It is a widely cultivated vegetable that synthesizes a natural precursor of QHS that is readily and cheaply extracted for simple chemical modification into QHS.

Meanwhile my forebodings, equally ignored for decades, of the exceptional ability of malaria parasites to produce drug-resistant mutants, even when appropriate combinations are used (not always the case) and correct doses given, seem to be justified with some of the first publications that hint of the emergence of resistance to certain ACT combinations in that epicenter of drug resistance, Cambodia. My hope is that the Pyramax® combination might arrive in time to extend the future of ACT combinations. I have no doubt this will include some novel QHS derivatives or other compounds with a similar mode of action. Only time will tell. In the meantime one hopes we can reduce the huge burden of malaria by applying other means for controlling malaria transmission such as; mass protection by insecticide-treated mosquito nets, which big finance is now promoting. Moreover, good progress is finally being made on developing an antimalarial vaccine. Sadly, man is an unreliable and often unscrupulous creature. The world's pharmaceutical markets are flooded with fakes and unacceptable, often useless products, that masquerade as antimalarials, antibiotics, anticancer drugs, and so on.

Fortunately there is hope that artesunate, or an analog compound, may have an alternative and exciting future. Recent reports by investigators in China and elsewhere show it possesses remarkable activity against certain types of tumor, both in the laboratory and in a number of human patients suffering from advanced cancer of widely differing types.

Sadly, several of my colleagues and I were so focused on the antimalarial action of artesunate for years, that we only recently learned of its anticancer potential. Meanwhile, five of our spouses succumbed to cancer. This included my wife, Ruth, who died from the devastating effects of a malignant tumor at the end of 2007.

Chapter 18

Glimpses of the Arabic Speaking World
1975–2000

My first direct exposure to Arabic speaking countries was at the start of a journey sponsored by the British Council from Liverpool early in 1975. It was a memorable occasion, not only for the opportunity to see the practical problems of tropical medicine with which I was not yet familiar first hand, but to make new acquaintances. I also encountered a few of the inevitable hazards of international travel. With a passport full of impressive visas, I set out on 18th January for Cairo. I anticipated being met at the airport by a representative from the British Council as I had no idea where I was to stay. I arrived after midnight, collected and cleared my baggage, and went to the main reception area. I wondered how I would know who I was meeting. An hour later I was still looking. Not being able to contact somebody, I found a taxi with a driver who understood a few essential words of English and asked him to find me a hotel in town.

Once in the car and driving through deserted streets, I began to wonder if this was such a bright idea after all and what to do if I found I had delivered myself into the hands of an unscrupulous scoundrel! To my great relief and that of my wallet, the driver stopped outside the door of a modest hotel in a quiet square somewhere in the middle of what I presumed was Cairo. The driver took me inside where a sleepy receptionist, whom the driver had obviously informed of my predicament including the fact that I spoke no Arabic, took me plus my baggage upstairs to a small, but clean and comfortable room overlooking the square. In a few minutes he returned with a welcome pot of sweet tea and left me to settle down for what little remained of the night.

A clear bright sky awoke me early and I went to the window to see the bustle of life in the attractive square outside. Once dressed, I went downstairs where I found a hotel employee who understood a few words of English. He provided me with breakfast served by a very attractive if skimpily clothed young woman with a broad welcoming smile. After breakfast, I found the British Council telephone number and was finally put through to the individual who was supposed to have met me. It seems that, he not having a means of identifying me, abandoned the search at the airport. He decided that I must have either missed the plane or headed direct for Cairo. Even more interesting was his reaction when I told tell him where I was. My enterprising taxi driver had assumed I sought company for the night and drove me to a modest brothel in a notorious district of the town. Had I but known!

Later that morning, my British contact collected me and transferred me to a large luxury hotel near the Nile. The name was familiar; it was partially destroyed by a bomb some years earlier. This was one of only two evenings I ever spent in a house of pleasure. The second was with Ruth when we first went to Basle together, many years before. Having never visited that city, we inadvertently checked into a small hotel on the side of the Rhine at the edge of the old town. Like most Swiss hotels, it was perfectly comfortable and discreet.

I have strayed from my memories of early encounters with the Arabic-speaking world. These, and nearly all later experiences from Libya to Arabia, leave me with an impression of warm, open, and friendly people. This despite many social limitations imposed in some communities by narrow religious and legal restrictions. There have been exceptions, but I was most fortunate over a period of intermittent contact of some thirty years to make many friends and acquaintances among numerous levels of society from peasant to prince.

Understandably, my medical and academic background means the people who I came to know are generally well educated. However, most were from simple or unsophisticated family backgrounds. Luckily it is not one of my characteristics to go through life wearing rose-colored spectacles. I met many maliciously bigoted individuals in my time, but I did not befriend them. On reflection, most of these people were not of the Arab world, but they often disparaged those who were.

When I was young, but not too young to be critical, I passed through a racist phase. Long ago I realized that bias is blatant ignorance and hastily shrugged it off like an ill-fitting skin.

During my introduction to Egypt, a country where my sister Ronnie lived and worked several years, I saw the great difficulties that the leading universities faced because of large numbers of students and minimal facilities. These were particularly hard on practical medical and scientific teaching. So a majority of students were deprived in many hands-on teaching subjects that are the norm in equivalent institutions in the western world. The few lectures I gave in Cairo were attended by comparatively huge numbers of students. All were eager to scize on the few crumbs of knowledge that I had to offer. When visiting patients in hospitals I was embarrassed by the paucity of the information I could supply compared with the wealth of practical knowledge I gained from their teaching staff. Admittedly I saw cases and diseases that were relatively new to me, but the enthusiasm that my Egyptian colleagues and their students invested in the patients under their care was outstanding.

My hosts went out of their way to ensure that I did not leave Cairo without seeing some famous cultural attractions. They took me to visit the pyramids and the sphinx at a time when the air was still crisp and bright. Sadly, today smog tends to cover everything. They took me to the Cairo museum where I could spend as long as I wished gazing at the remains of Tutankhamun without being distracted by hordes of tourists and flashing cameras. I had to wait twenty-five years until the year 2000 before I was able to revisit those sites, this time with Ruth. During that visit we had the thrill of crossing the desert from Safaga on the Red Sea coast to Aswan to spend a day in the Valley of the Kings and among many other incredible ruins of that region that are almost beyond description.

My first brief visit to Cairo lasted only four days. Then I flew on to Khartoum where my arrival was less adventurous. Many Sudanese physicians received their primary medical training in British medical schools and formed lasting links with their alma maters. One of our former Liverpool PhD students was already working in Khartoum. He was Alan Fenwick, who with Sudanese colleagues was researching the epidemiology and control of schistosomiasis ('bilharziasis'). Thanks to them, I got an excellent introduction to that very debilitating infection caused by small worms in the gut, liver, and bladder. It occurs in very large areas of the Old and New World tropics and subtropics. It is acquired when minute worm larvae penetrate the skin of people who enter the water in which intermediate hosts of the worms, various species of aquatic snails, live and breed.

In countries such as Egypt, the Sudan, Brazil, and China schistosomiasis is very common where the population uses freshwater canals and lakes for agriculture. In the absence of preventative weapons such as vaccines, control of schistosomiasis still depends largely on destroying the snails along with diagnosing and drug treatment of infected people. The search for novel antischistosomal drugs was an objective of my colleagues when I worked with the old CIBA company in Basle. Although a few relatively new drugs are being widely deployed, there is always a threat that the worms will become resistant to them. In the past few years the world has directed attention to the possibility that a superhuman effort can eliminate schistosomiasis. For the first time, a massive injection of funds is available for this purpose, especially from the Gates Foundation. Alan Fenwick is the individual mainly responsible for managing this program. Since then, he became a Professor in Imperial College, London. Besides schistosomiasis, Sudan is endemic for numerous other parasitic infections including malaria and leishmaniasis. I discuss the second below. Moreover, it is home to some of the most devastating fungal infections to afflict humans. I saw a number of sufferers from these in hospitals in Khartoum.

In the Sudan some years later I again came face to face with leishmaniasis, my second obsession. Mainly in the cutaneous form, it is rampant in parts of that country. Professor Ahmed El Hassan, a senior British-trained physician carried out much research in association with an American team formerly directed by a renowned and charismatic character, Harry Hoogstraal. I think almost every parasitologist knew Harry, a plump, extremely hospitable bachelor, who resembled the film director, Alfred Hitchcock, and was always preceded by a large cigar. Harry's home was a luxurious house in Cairo where he headed one of the US Navy's famous, highly productive medical research units. Harry's and Ahmed's teams carried out pioneering studies on the epidemiology of cutaneous, mucocutaneous, and visceral leishmaniasis in the Sudan, a country notorious for epidemics of these infections. I first met Ahmed in Khartoum and later renewed his acquaintance when we worked in association with the King Faisal University in the Eastern Province of Saudi Arabia (more later).

On his recommendation I accepted a Sudanese graduate, a young woman doctor named Sayda El-Safi, to carry out a clinico-epidemiological study of cutaneous and visceral leishmaniasis following an epidemic in and around Khartoum. The investigations by

Sayda and her Sudanese colleagues revealed that, during a period of six months from the end of 1986, about 10,000 people living in or near Khartoum suffered from severe forms of cutaneous leishmaniasis. Using the techniques my teams in Liverpool and London developed to identify parasites, she showed that the infections were caused by one known as *Leishmania major*, and the epidemic was probably associated with a massive increase in the wild population of a local rodent, *Arvicanthis niloticus*. This animal breeds on the banks of the River Nile and its population exploded in 1986 because of exceptionally favorable ecological conditions. Infections of *L. major* were identified in these rats, in patients with skin lesions, and in a wild cat-like mammal, *Genetta genetta.* However, in spite of their presence in large numbers, surprisingly no *Phlebotomus papatasi* were found with infections of that parasite and the vector remains undefined. A surprising and important finding was that this parasite was causing large numbers of cutaneous lesions, and probably complicated forms known as mucocutaneous leishmaniasis. The organism causing this was previously in doubt. (In 1980, my Saudi colleagues and I observed this parasite for the first time in Saudi Arabia, in a baby with mucocutaneous leishmaniasis in Hofuf.) At the same time, Sayda and her colleagues only recorded a handful of patients with the visceral disease which they identified as being caused by a form of *Leishmania donovani*, a species that at other times was known to cause massive epidemics of kala-azar in that country.

When Brian Maegraith retired in the autumn of 1975, I was elected to take the mantle of Dean of the Liverpool School for the coming three years. His policy was always that a major impact of the School should be in developing world countries, not just in Liverpool. In 1976, we were approached to send one of our staff to discuss teaching parasitology to medical students at the University of Tripoli. I seized this opportunity to familiarize myself with that country, as I had no first-hand knowledge. We already had two important contacts in Libya, in spite of the touchy political nature at that time of relations between Colonel Muammar al-Gaddafi and much of the rest of the world. The first was the temporary assignment to Liverpool of a Libyan doctor, Dr. Ashour Gebreel, to receive training in Public Health. I was unaware then that the North African region, known as the Maghreb, was distinctive both in its culture and the variety of Arabic spoken there. Maghrebi Arabic differs considerably from the language spoken by most of the Arabic world further along the African coast and in the Middle East. Moreover, a large part of the population is of Berber, rather than Arabic descent. I suspect Ashour's temporary assignment was engineered by Herbert Gilles. His mother tongue is Maltese, a variant of Maghrebi Arabic.

Our second contact with Libya was through visits of Bill Macdonald, head of our sub department of entomology, to assist the Ministry of Health resolve some problems with vector-borne diseases. Sometime later, Bill Beesley, one of Macdonald's colleagues in the Liverpool School, played a leading role in the frightening discovery of the deadly New World screwworm, *Cochliomyia hominivorax*, in Libyan cattle. His role in its eradication by releasing irradiated, laboratory-bred male flies, was a groundbreaking international achievement.

I had misgivings about undertaking the journey. The initial hint of political tension came when the Libyan authorities insisted that the only wording on visas they issued, apart from the visitor's name, had to be in Arabic. The second was the country's strict ban on alcohol. It is not that I was an alcoholic, but this was a new situation to me in my naivety. Just for the hell of it, I arrived on a Libyan airlines flight with a plastic half-liter flask of Scotch in my loose-fitting jacket's inside pocket. Luckily an official from the university met me and nobody searched me! Once I emptied the flask my concern was how to dispose of it. I had no idea how tight their security was so I dumped it in somebody else's rubbish bin. Security in Libya at that time was tight.

My first duty was to check in at the British Embassy where I passed through a series of locked and barred doors and armed guards. After that formality, I encountered no more problems. I received a warm welcome at the university. I found it very well endowed from an architectural point of view, but badly lacking in appropriate teaching materials. In this case it was not for lack of funding. Libya is an oil-rich state and enjoys one of the highest average personal incomes in Africa. It was a simple matter to set up an arrangement whereby the Liverpool School would acquire or prepare materials for teaching parasitology, then send out its senior teaching technical officer, Jeff Friend, to assist its installation. Moreover, I was able to help Dick Ashford both teach and assist the Ministry of Health in establishing procedures to eliminate the rodent reservoirs of cutaneous leishmaniasis in the coastal areas.

When my work in Tripoli was complete, I was informed I should collect a fee for my efforts. I was amused to observe the disdain with which the government officials who handled this matter dealt with it. I and several visitors were invited into a room to receive our fees. A man arrived with a sack of large Libyan banknotes and dumped them unceremoniously onto a mat on the floor. A man counted out a sheaf about a foot thick, tied them with a piece of string, and handed one to me. He asked me to sign what I presume was a receipt in Arabic. I was not quite sure what to do with this mountain of paper. Later that day, a university colleague took me to a bank where I exchanged it for a small wad of sterling notes to take back to the Liverpool School.

All that accomplished, several Libyan colleagues and I were driven by car to visit the monumental Roman city of Leptis Magna, about 150 kilometers east of Tripoli. The excavation of this magnificent city came to a halt when Al-Gaddafi decided that, "History starts with me."

Nevertheless, previous explorations were maintained well and an interesting museum was erected on the site. It housed fascinating artifacts from the time of the Roman occupation some 2,000 years ago. Although nothing was supposed to be removed from the site, I salvaged a few small shards of Roman pottery and mosaic fragments from the shallows at the water's edge. I still have those to remind me of that visit.

Leaving Tripoli, I traveled a long drive east by car towards Egypt to Benghazi. We passed through the Jabal Al Akdhar to the Green Mountains, the wettest part of Libya. Italian colonists had lived and planted excellent vineyards there. I discovered that my smuggling a flask of alcohol into Libya was absurd to say the least. I learned that most of my Libyan colleagues made their own wine or, if they were in the know, purchased excellent old stock that was hidden in a number of stores left over from the Italian occupation of the Green Mountains area.

In Benghazi, I was warmly welcomed by Ashour in his home. I was wined and dined like a lord; the drink of the day was a sort of Sangria made with locally produced wine. At the time, Ashour's wife was living in England. He planned to return there to continue his studies in Public Health, but he had to remain in Benghazi a while longer. Would it be possible for me to take his young son Amro, then about eight years old, with me when I flew back to London? It sounded to be a daunting task given the tense relations of the day between Libya and most other countries, but I rashly agreed to do so.

I underestimated Ashour's powerful position in Libyan government circles. The little boy and I were delivered at Benghazi airport with all the necessary documents and baggage in hand. The aircrew gave the child and me a warm welcome and we had a comfortable and uneventful flight back to London. There I succeeded in passing him through immigration controls without bother and delivered him to waiting family members. Ashour, on completing his training in Liverpool, obtained an important public health appointment with the WHO Regional Office in Cairo and he remained a good friend of the British Ministry of Health. I was recently surprised to receive news from my friend Herbert that Ashour now lives permanently in this country where he continues to be involved in international public health. He and his family have obtained British citizenship and his son, now a grown man, still has happy memories of flying with me to rejoin his mother. Moreover, Ashour was awarded an MBE for his services to this country. Small world.

It appears from the entry in one of my old passports, that the first visa I obtained to visit Saudi Arabia was issued on December 14 1975 and the next on May 5 1976. The latter includes a footnote to the effect that, "Void if bearer obtained thereafter an Israeli visa." This passport was, "Gratis. With the Compliments of His Majesty's Government."

My first visit followed a request from the developing medical faculty in the newly formed King Abdul Aziz University in Jeddah to advise them on organizing aspects of their curriculum. This was the first opportunity for the Liverpool School to develop academic links with the Kingdom of Saudi Arabia. It was the start not only of that association, but collaboration at several levels that carried over to my later position in London University and beyond. It lasted for thirty years. The Saudi government was averse to issuing multiple entry visas. I ended up with a large proportion of the pages of a succession of passports filled with large green stamps, at least thirty-six of them.

The first intake of medical students for the medical faculty in Jeddah received their preliminary education in Riyadh while facilities were constructed in Jeddah. Indeed much of that city was being developed in 1976. It cost a large part of the historic and picturesque old town with unique house structures that served as natural air conditioners. The international airport was a simple affair in the center of town, another interesting feature of Jeddah. Most of the embassies and diplomatic missions were still in Jeddah or were being transferred to Riyadh. A new diplomatic suburb was under construction on the outskirts of that city. The Jeddah souk was a traditional and picturesque area. The approach allowed a blind man to find the souk by scent as the characteristic aromas of numerous fragrant herbs permeated the surrounding streets.

Beyond the busy port of Jeddah the city extended a short distance, but a tarmac road continued north along the shore of the Red Sea. A few kilometers along this road, some wealthy residents of Jeddah constructed beach bungalows. I was invited by my new colleagues from the university to spend a number of weekends relaxing with their families and friends in their beach homes. In this situation, it was a delight to find that much of the formality of everyday life was shed. The womenfolk abandoned their all-concealing cloaks and headwear and shook out their dark tresses, even in front of such strangers as me. We indulged in enticing barbecues and the men abandoned themselves to the pleasure of swimming among the unpolluted coral reefs of the adjacent sea. It was idyllic. Sadly over the next few years, like all major Saudi cities, Jeddah expanded exponentially along the coast road eastwards to join a new and dramatically designed international airport. Large new housing and commercial areas were established along the way. In fact, two separate airport terminals were built; a private one for the Royal family and one for everybody else. Part of the second was reserved for the vast numbers of pilgrims who visited Mecca via Jeddah yearly for the Haj. After a few years the city elders and government realized how much of their architectural heritage was being lost. They forbade further demolition of old buildings in Jeddah, but sadly large portions were already destroyed.

My introduction to Saudi Arabian university development included participating in a series of roundtable discussions with members of the medical faculty, on appropriate building facilities, teaching requirements and curricula. I was in one of two groups of overseas consultants; one from British universities, the other from a middle-rank university from the United States. It was evident from the start that the latter were hell bent on selling themselves to King

Abdul Aziz University. While the atmosphere between the two groups round the table was not antagonistic, neither would I say that it was particularly friendly. Our Saudi colleagues clearly sensed this. The Dean of Medicine was a young man educated in Germany as I recall, as were a high proportion of the first generation of Saudi medical professors. In addition to his team members, we frequently met an older, very agreeable, and shrewd man. He was a bit of a father figure to staff and students alike. I believe his background was in Public Health. He was a valuable counter to the pushy Americans.

A source of great concern was how to arrange the buildings for pre-clinical teaching such that each lecture room had two well-separated entrances, one for males, and the other for female students. There also had to be two separate residential areas that included practical laboratories. A couple of years later I was invited to serve as an external examiner for what would roughly equate to a first MB BS. This took place in the Women's College one day and the Men's College the next. To enter the women's premises, we had to pass through a guardroom entrance presided over by an old Saudi watchman and accompanied by several senior female lecturers. As I entered the 'holy of holies' I was greeted by a mixture of gasps and giggles; the former arising from the conservative girl students who hastily covered their heads and faces with their scarves, and the latter from the more daring girls who accepted my presence with equanimity.

This division in their decorum continued throughout the oral exams. I remember being impressed by the overall intellectual superiority of the latter group—or perhaps I was subconsciously biased by the attractive features of many of the latter.

For some lectures, including those by guest lecturers, both sexes attended using separate doors into the large lecture theatres. These rooms were divided down the middle by a double screen, one running from each door and converging just in front of the lecturer in a fashion that totally hid female students from the males, while the lecturer had a full view of the whole audience. It was a bizarre scenario. The two sexes only met, officially, for the first time when they commenced clinical studies. Even then the women were fully veiled in their junior clinical years.

I watched the Faculty of Medicine develop during the next few years. It was a rewarding experience as I became friends with my Saudi colleagues. I had the opportunity to attend excellent medical meetings held annually in one or other major city. These attracted numerous well-known speakers from other countries. The scientific standards were on an international level. The economy of the country at the time was on an upward slope and hospitality was on a lavish scale. This became such that it eventually aroused criticism even in Riyadh circles and was reduced to a more reasonable level!

From 1981 on I found myself involved in a major research program on the problem of cutaneous leishmaniasis in the Eastern Province. This National Leishmaniasis Research Project ran for five years and is a story in itself. I give a special account of it in Chapter19. Later two Saudi students joined me to work for PhD degrees. May Al-Jasr was one of the first female Saudi students given permission to work outside her country in the absence of her husband. He was a member of the Saudi delegation to OPEC. I committed her to a project to study a severe form of cutaneous leishmaniasis that we believed was caused by *L. major*. It was endemic in villages near her home in Riyadh, so she had easy access to her field center. After receiving her PhD, May became a lecturer attached to the Medical Faculty of the University of Riyadh. She subsequently published important papers on her investigations of the pharmacodynamics of antileishmanial drugs in Saudi patients with *L. major* infections. Moreover, May was a source of the famous Viennese chocolate cakes called SacherTorte that she and her husband brought back for Ruth and me from Austria where OPEC often met.

The second student was a short, sturdy son of the mountainous region around Abha in the southwest of the country. In 1986 the opportunity arose to investigate the problem of leishmaniasis in two other areas of Saudi Arabia; the cool, fertile mountain region of Al Baha, and the hot, drier coastal area of Asir bordering the Red Sea.

While attending an annual meeting of the American Society of Tropical Medicine, I was approached by a jolly, young bearded Saudi who introduced himself as Mohammed Al-Zahrani. He was studying for a Master's degree that involved parasitology and public health at an American university. He wanted to obtain a position in his home country with the chance to carry out research that would enable him, ("inshallah Allah" or "God willing"), to obtain a PhD. Could I advise him? Mohammed was clearly a capable man with ambition and I immediately felt he would be a good candidate to work in some capacity on my London team on a study of leishmaniasis in Asir. This was his home territory, the Zahranis being one of the dominant tribes of that region. The cool climate in the mountains is delightful and a fairly heavy, year-round rainfall ensures that the area around Abha is ideal for agriculture. It is also ideal for many kinds of biting insects, including species of sandflies not found in the dry desert areas or lowland oases such as that of Al Ahsa. In due course we acquired a research grant from Saudi sources including the General Directorate of Health of Asir Province. A research laboratory was established in the highland city of Abha, Mohammed's hometown. Laboratory and field staff were hired and trained.

For the following three years, under my direction, Mohammed and his team carried out extensive epidemiological surveys in the highland and lowland areas in collaboration with physicians from the General Directorate of Health. Their joint investigations demonstrated that here, as in the Eastern Province, cutaneous leishmaniasis was highly prevalent and increasing rapidly year by year. However, in contrast to findings in the Eastern Province, it affected people of all ages, most being indigenous Saudis. Visceral leishmaniasis was generally limited to infants and was far less prevalent. The cutaneous disease proved to result from a different organism, *Leishmania tropica*.

It was transmitted by a different species of sandfly, *Phlebotomus sergenti*, essentially from human to human. From Abha, which is over 2,000 meters, an excellent but winding tarmac mountain road descends to the coastal plains. I had the hair-raising experience of being driven down the mountainside by Mohammed. He was an inveterate cigarette smoker as are many Saudis. He insisted on turning to chat with me, cigarette in mouth, just as we approached hairpin bends. About halfway down the road, much to my relief, he pulled over to a grass verge, stopped the car, got out, and spread a small prayer carpet for morning prayer. I felt tempted to join him. I devoted many words trying to persuade him to stop smoking in vain as had his father. Al-Zahrani père was equally unsuccessful as I knew from an unforgettable visit to his simple family home. I was royally entertained by him in company with a huge circle of half his male family members and relations plus a hoard of small children. Veiled ladies popped their heads in from time to time with more and more dishes of delectable food. I was enthroned in a comfortable armchair while everybody else sat cross-legged around me. Mohammed's oldest son sat on the arm of my chair acting as my interpreter.

Along the coastal littoral, a small number of infants were found with kala-azar, the visceral disease caused by yet another parasite, *Leishmania donovani*. The number of cases was highest towards the Yemeni border in the region of Gizan. Feral dogs were common in the lowlands and a high proportion had clinical signs of leishmanial infection. Because of practical difficulties, isolates from only three animals were identified. All harbored yet another species, *Leishmania infantum*, a parasite that is widespread in countries bordering the Mediterranean region where it also causes human kala-azar. However, near Gizan a number of black rats caught in houses where infants with kala-azar lived were infected with the same *L. donovani*. Surprisingly, one rat was infected with the same variety of *L. infantum* that infected the dogs. We found no evidence of the vectors of either species of parasite in that area.

Mohammed drove me from Gizan up into the hill country adjacent to Yemen where fertile terraces were laden with bushes of khat, *Catha edulis*, a plant with leaves that contain a mild, amphetamine-like stimulant. Chewing khat leaves is the favorite pastime of inhabitants of southeastern Saudi Arabia and Yemen. It is also very common in neighboring countries in the Horn of Africa and the Arabian Peninsula. Alcohol consumption is prohibited in most Muslim countries, so Khat chewing is the basis of social life, especially among men, but also women and children. Surprisingly, khat leaves are imported into the UK where there is a big demand for them from Middle East immigrants. An unusual but typical architectural feature of hillside villages in the khat-growing area, are square-shaped, tower-like houses about three floors high topped by an open terrace. These buildings stand singly, well apart and dominate the landscape. They are ideally suited for life in this very hot, humid corner of the country. Returning from the hills towards Gizan we saw a large dead animal suspended from a tree by its hind legs. It turned out to be a full-grown caracal, a beautiful wild cat that survives in small numbers in the hills. A little further down the road, we were stopped by a police patrol who searched our van for khat. The use of khat is officially illegal. Fortunately we had none. On another visit to Gizan with a colleague from the LSHTM, I was offered a post-lunch chew with our hosts who included most of the senior members of the local Ministry of Health. We gracefully declined and took a siesta instead, knowing that our hosts were not likely to surface for three or four hours at least. We were right!

Mohammed Al-Zahrani, PhD was made a senior administrator in the Department of Public Health in the Ministry of Health, Riyadh. A third Saudi student joined my department in London. He studied under the guidance of one of my senior lecturers, John Ackers. He gained a PhD for research on another protozoal disease, giardiasis, before returning to Riyadh. He served there for years as a senior figure in the Saudi army medical services.

By coincidence, my Saudi Arabia contact was reinforced through a philanthropic organization called the King Faisal Foundation (KFF). This well-endowed foundation's Director General is HRH Prince Khalid Al Faisal bin Abd-Alaziz Al-Saud. It was established in 1976 and is based in Riyadh. It is one of the world's largest such organizations. Its fundamental objective is to "promote the search for truth that will benefit mankind." To this end, its reach is international. In addition to the inauguration of a Centre for Research and Islamic Studies, in 1979 three prestigious King Faisal International Prizes were established in subjects directly related to Islam. Two years later two more prizes, one each in Science and Medicine, were created to be awarded annually in each field. For the latter two awards the precise topic changes every year and a prize is only awarded if the nominated individuals are considered to be of sufficient global standing by an independent, international committee. The first prize for Medicine was awarded in 1982 for Primary Health Care to a British pediatrician from the University of London. It was announced that year that the 1983 prize in Medicine would be for malaria.

Gordon Smith, then Dean of the LSHTM, proposed that the University of London nominate me for the award and set the wheels in motion. I wrote earlier that the philosophy of the Liverpool School of Tropical Medicine was that one's engagement with their subject should be undertaken as much as reasonable in the tropics. Gordon took a different view, so at that time I was surprised by his action. In my usual rebellious manner, I was having a serious disagreement with him concerning the proportion of time I should devote to teaching and research in the school, and the proportion I should occupy with international activities that necessitated overseas travel, sometimes for weeks at a time. Ruth and I felt that he put my name forward more in anger than hope, anticipating that my nomination would fail. I was inclined to reject the nomination. However, Ruth with her usual commonsense persuaded me to accept Gordon's proposal so I did.

Near the end of 1982 I was astonished to receive a telegram from Riyadh, informing me that I was selected to receive the 1983 King Faisal Prize for my research on malaria. On March 1 of that year, I became the bemused recipient of the second King Faisal International Prize in Medicine. The recipients of prizes for the three Islamic subjects were also present, but there was no award made for Science that year. Of the two people selected as co-winners for Service to Islam, one was Sir Tunku Abdul Rahman, a Cambridge-educated lawyer who became the first President of independent Malaysia in 1957. He was one of the least pompous and most humorous men one could wish to meet, but a masterly politician. The former British colonial administration of Malaya soon discovered this when he served as the First Minister of the old Federation prior to independence. The ceremony, held with great pomp and ceremony in the Riyadh Hilton, was presided over by Prince Khalid. The late King Fahad presented the awards. Each prize consisted of a document, hand-inscribed in Diwani calligraphy, a large gold medal in a baize-lined case, and a check. All the proceedings were held in Arabic. Each recipient was invited to make a brief speech to acknowledge the award and briefly explain the basis of the contribution he made to his field of study. In my case, my speech was translated and presented on my behalf by a Saudi scholar with a fine speaking voice while I stood nervously at his side not knowing quite where to look. When the interpreter finished speaking, King Fahad shook my hand and offered his congratulations in English. A KFF official handed him the box with the medal. In doing so, he let the heavy object slip to the floor where it made a loud and embarrassing clang. Nobody turned a hair. He hastily replaced the medal in its box and passed it to the King who smilingly handed it to me.

Once off the podium I took my place in the front row of the large and crowded auditorium with walls lined with sword-bearing bodyguards from the King's tribe, the House of Saud. To my amusement, I spotted Gordon Smith and one of the LSHTM's senior staff, Patrick Hamilton, seated among the international invitees behind me. Both happened to be visiting Riyadh. The speech I prepared in English and that was translated into Arabic before it was presented was just a little risqué. My theme was the need for greatly enhanced funds for research that might lead towards the reduction of malaria, hardly a surprising topic since that was why I received the Prize. I hoped to point out that the money paid for the purchase of a single modern fighter aircraft, which Saudi Arabia was ordering in numbers at that time, would make a major contribution to that research, and hence be a potential "benefit to the welfare of mankind," the declared objective of the Prize. Luckily I realized that such a confrontation was indiscreet on this occasion. To quote from the script that I finally prepared;

"... I would like to leave you with this message. To fight disease it is not enough only to improve our tools by scientific research. We must also use them. This requires money and social organization. To get rid of malaria we must use all the weapons at our disposal, including not only new drugs and insecticides, but also vaccines. To develop these in the laboratory is now relatively easy, but to produce vaccines on the massive scale required to control malaria and to build an effective organization to apply these and other control measures to the millions of people who need them, is another, infinitely more difficult, and costly problem. Financial considerations at the present time (this was 1983) are proving a barrier to research and development of antimalarial drugs and vaccines. I believe that a special international fund is needed urgently to support this work."

I never heard that funds for malaria research were provided by the country. But then I do not know how accurately my speech was translated.

After the 1983 award I was invited to visit the KFF on a number of occasions. I was consulted about such matters as which were suitable topics for future medical prizes and how best to make the work of the Foundation better known to the outside world. My passports show that I made an annual pilgrimage to the KFF and continued collaborative field studies on leishmaniasis with the NLRP and my students until the year 2000. The high level of many of the King Faisal International Prize winners is reflected in the fact that, by 2008, twelve subsequently received Nobel Prizes in Science or Medicine.

One of my contributions to the KFF was to assist with organizing the tenth anniversary of the first award of the Prize in Medicine in 1992 in a joint meeting with the Royal Society of London. It was an international symposium entitled *Science and Medicine in the 21st Century—a Global Perspective*. Sixteen previous winners of Prizes in Medicine and Science presented reviews on their individual subjects, including some who had become Nobel laureates. This occasion was especially memorable for me; first, since participants' spouses were invited to the proceedings, and second, for the lavish hospitality that our Saudi hosts provided in London. My personal award ceremony years earlier was marred by the hesitation of the KFF, at the time of the initial awards, to invite the recipient's spouses to attend the ceremonies in Riyadh; a gaffe at the international level that they remedied in later years.

Just before I paid my final visit to Riyadh in 2000, I was given a conducted tour of the future home of the KFF, the thirty-story Al-Faisalia Tower. It was designed by a leading British architect to be the tallest building in the Middle East. My visit to it was certainly an impressive one. My guide was the Supervisor of Works, a British engineer who showed me the developing structure from top to bottom. It was a terrifying, but awe-inspiring visit. I regret not being able to attend the opening ceremony. I saw later from a DVD made of the occasion, it was a super-spectacular affair. A two-story, rotating, globe-shaped restaurant was at the peak of the tower below the summit of a spire that is 267 meters above ground level. A team of Pakistani construction workers was installing glass panels during my visit. They were suspended perilously from the central spire on the summit. I shuddered to think how the window cleaners perform their task. The basement of the tower on which everything else sat was the largest single-span room ever designed. The room serves as an auditorium or banquet room for hundreds. Still under construction, it was extremely imposing. The tower was to house a large hotel and all the administrative offices of the KFF. During these oil-boom years, money was no object in Saudi Arabia. Construction of the Al-Faisalia tower, which cost $320 million, was barely started before another Saudi organization started to construct their own architectural state-of-the-art building, the Kingdom Tower, two blocks down the main thoroughfare. These modest contributions to Middle East architecture are currently put into the shadows of monstrous constructions like the grandiose hotel complexes of Abu Dhabi and Dubai. A partner building, the Al-Faisalia 2 tower is planned for the near future. It will be adjacent to the first and may exceed even those in height.

I cannot close my comments on my long association with the King Faisal Foundation without noting two light-hearted memories. As the Royal Society meeting was being planned, the Secretary General of the Prize organization, Professor Abdullah Al-Uthaimin and one of his senior colleagues came to London to discuss plans with Prince Khalid who was in London at the time. We arranged to meet one morning at the Prince's home in Kensington. After our discussion we were served coffee by one of his staff, probably an ex-SAS man, and then walked a short distance to a nearby hotel for lunch. Our host was casually dressed in a smart leather jacket and tieless whereas the rest of us were more formally dressed. I was greatly amused when the maître d'hôtel declined to give us a place at the lunch table in the main restaurant because the Prince had no tie on and referred us to an alternative room. Our host who could, without blinking an eye, have bought the entire hotel, was totally unperturbed. A few days later, Abdullah and I accompanied one of the younger princes, who was responsible for assuring some of the detail arrangements for the meeting, to meet the then President of the

Royal Society, the Egyptian-born mathematician, Professor Sir Michael Atiyah. None of us had met him before. The young prince was very informally clad with a smart open-necked shirt and sports trousers. On our arrival at the Society we were directed to the first floor where the President had his office. Somehow we lost our way. We bumped into a middle-aged man in shirtsleeves and asked if he would guide us, which he did. We entered a secretary's room to await the arrival of the President. He soon arrived, but this time wearing a tie and jacket.

Chapter 19

Fighting the 'Little Sister' 1971–2000

Let me explain 'Little sister' clearly from the start before I create a family split. The Arabic expression 'Al Okht' translates as 'Little sister', the name given in parts of the Middle East to a skin disease spread by tiny insects called sandflies—cutaneous leishmaniasis (CL). Why is it called that? Friends tell me it is because everybody has one. True or not, CL is a condition that is spreading dramatically in many arid areas, in parallel with increasing development of rural housing. It occupied a surprisingly large part of my life in the last two decades of the twentieth century. What follows is not a medical treatise, but anecdotes of experiences of colleagues and me in Saudi Arabia. My story does not start in the Old World, but in the New; Brazil in 1971. Recall in Chapters 1 and 15 my key encounter that triggered my interest in leishmaniasis and turned me into a 'leishmaniac.'

In 1975 I was invited to visit and advise on establishing a medical curriculum at the new Medical School in the King Abdul Aziz University in Jeddah. I summarized these experiences in Chapter 18. From that visit through the next twenty-five years, I made a number of visits to Saudi Arabia. I gained experience from and participated with other universities in academic and research meetings in cities as far apart as Tobuk, Jeddah, Abha, Riyadh, Jizan, and Dammam. My medical parasitologist reputation spread as, in 1980, the year after my transfer from the LSTM to the LSHTM, I was invited to a '*Medical Symposium on Leishmaniasis*' held at King Faisal University (KFU) in Dammam. I presented three papers there. In many ways, this was a turning point in my career. In a letter home I wrote the following:

March 23rd, 1980

"... The conference is going better than we expected and I am having to give several demonstrations in another center some 120 kilometers inland tomorrow. In a few minutes I'm going off to see a baby in the hospital with a terrible leishmaniasis of the face, the worst I have seen yet, and will try to isolate the organism to help guide the treatment. It makes me realize how serious a problem this really is..."

Based on a rapid increase in cases of leishmaniasis arising in the country, revealed at this symposium, the Saudi Ministry of Health sought assistance in dealing with what was becoming an epidemic-sized problem. In June 1981, I was invited to visit the Saudi Arabian National Centre for Science and Technology (SANCST) in Riyadh. This relatively new organization funded the establishment of research programs associated with universities throughout the Kingdom. In the Eastern Province, cutaneous leishmaniasis was increasing so rapidly that a high proportion of young children in rural communities had active skin lesions or healed scars of ulcers caused by a species of *Leishmania*. Little was known about the species involved, the epidemiology of the disease, or the best way to treat it. A number of limited clinical studies on cutaneous leishmaniasis were done in different areas of the country. They were mainly led by Egyptian scientists. Sandfly vectors were studied by European entomologists. One of these was a Swiss, William Büttiker from Basle, the other my old friend, David Lewis. He worked with us during our orangutan malaria project in Sabah. Both were authorities on the sandflies that transmit leishmaniasis. In certain parts of the country two other forms of leishmaniasis were recognized in increasing numbers. One of these, mentioned earlier, was visceral disease affecting the liver of young infants in the lowlands of the Asir Emirate to the southeast and the neighboring territory of Yemen. The other was a different cutaneous form in Al Bahah, the highlands Emirate north of Asir.

SANCST was considering funding a National Leishmaniasis Research Programme (NLRP) to be based initially on the College of Medicine and Medical Sciences of KFU near the east coast, together with the College of Veterinary Medicine. The latter is located in the large oasis of Al Ahsa, south west of Dammam, where it was readily accessed by road or rail. I had visited KFU for scientific meetings and was involved with the Dean of the College of Medicine and his staff in discussions on teaching. It was a thriving center with excellent staff. Several, like those in Jeddah, received their medical education in Germany, the USA, or England. A number of expatriate staff included some from the Sudan and India. The outcome of the discussions following my first contact with SANCST was that I was to draw up, in collaboration with colleagues in KFU, a program to investigate all aspects of leishmaniasis in the Eastern Province. The vision was that this program would involve extensive field, laboratory, and clinical research to run over a five-year period. Generous funding would be made by SANCST through KFU. Some of their staff would be heavily committed in running and directing the program. In view of my personal interest in the problem and the ongoing involvement of my department in the LSHTM, I could not refuse this offer.

David Evans, a colleague at the LSHTM, and I attended the Sixth Annual Saudi Medical Meeting held in March 1981 at the King Faisal University in Jeddah. Under his direction we had the facilities in London to identify the responsible parasites and I was open to recruit other experts from England. Their role would be to guide the epidemiological and parasitological research while I would collaborate with our Saudi and expatriate colleagues in the clinical studies.

It was my good fortune that another 'polyprotomaniac' scientist, my friend Bob Killick-Kendrick who was associated with the Department of Parasitology of Imperial College in Ascot, and with whom I had collaborated in several research areas, including the Sabah malaria project, was available to join the team on a part-time basis. He hoped he could recruit Tony Leaney, a young parasitologist from London, to establish and run a laboratory for the NLRP in Hofuf, the main town of Al Ahsa. Professor Yusuf Al-Gindan, a young German-trained physician, who loved classical music by German composers, headed the KFU team in Dammam. My old friend Professor Ahmed M. El-Hassan, a clinician with much experience of leishmaniasis in his home country, The Sudan, and Indian dermatologist, Raj Kubba and others worked with him. Sabir Elbihari, a young Sudanese professor of Veterinary Medicine led the veterinary team. He sadly died shortly after the project ended.

1981
June 10th

". . . Riyadh from the little I have seen of it, is like Jeddah, but without the sea, and consequently the daytime temperature (at least 40°C) is much less uncomfortable than you would expect. So far, apart from catching up on my sleep, I have sat in the hotel room marking exam papers, an exercise I shall have to indulge in again today. In between I have been trying to make phone contact with various people I need to see to try to organize some collaborative teaching and research work for the future. . . so far of course I have had no chance of getting to the shops which are, in fact, at the other side of town. This is a new hotel (aren't they all ?) in a section of Riyadh near the airport and the provisional University area. A new medical school is under construction some way out of town. I will probably see it tomorrow when I go to visit a small town to the North of here where there is said to be a lot of leishmaniasis."

June 12th

"... Here at 10 a.m. the sun has been blazing for hours and it is probably already 40°C outside. In this dry heat, however, it is not uncomfortable, and of course the hotel is air conditioned... Apart from work I am, as usual, having a quiet (and dry) time. I have been asked to give an impromptu talk at the Military Hospital during Sunday lunchtime so I will prepare some notes for that later using some slides I have borrowed from the department here. Guess what! They are ones we prepared ourselves with my Dutch colleague Folmer for the MEDDIA series, so they really are serving a useful purpose after all! It seems they are regularly used here for teaching.

"... Wednesday evening I had a quiet meal with my old colleague Dr. Büttiker of CIBA who after seven years here is shortly being recalled to Basle. He has travelled widely and made some very interesting observations on the natural history of Saudi Arabia, which are appearing in a series of books that he is editing. He is going to spend a few days in London in July so maybe we could both meet him there for lunch... Later today I will think about having a swim in the hotel pool if I can raise the energy to do so. I must say that one is not too inclined to do too much moving in this heat, but I suppose it will do me good. Also I have brought some chapters of the malaria book to edit, so this is more than enough to occupy me until I start the oral exams tomorrow."

My next visit to SANCST was the following winter. The previous morning there was heavy snow over the whole of Britain and the taxi I ordered had great difficulty delivering me to Heathrow airport. We heard on the car radio en route that all of Wales was completely cut off from England.

1982
January 9th

"... We did not actually leave Heathrow until about 6:00 p.m. because only one runway was open, and all planes taking off had to wait in the queue for de-icing equipment to clean them before takeoff. Once away the flight was of course uneventful, but we arrived much too late (at Dahran) for the connecting flight and have spent a comfortable night at the airport hotel instead. We leave again for Riyadh at 10:20 a.m. . . The weather at home looked absolutely appalling and I heard that the temperature was—28°C at Grantown! . . . There's of course no news yet. I will try to phone my contacts here to tell them I am around since I should stop here to see them on the way back from Riyadh. This after all is where the work is supposed to be going on."

By 1982 the NLRP started operating. A leishmaniasis clinic was established in Hofuf. Patients from there and the surrounding rural area were examined and treated on a regular basis by members of the Dammam team. The latter also made numerous surveys of villagers for evidence of existing or past infection with *Leishmania*. We had two methods available to isolate parasites from man or animals so their identities could be confirmed by biochemical and immunological techniques. The first was direct inoculation of culture media with material obtained from skin lesions or for visceral infections, liver, or bone marrow punctures. With specimens obtained from wild rodents and other animals, the alternative was to inoculate laboratory mice that were susceptible to many species and strains of *Leishmania*. Our problem was that the best animal for this purpose was the 'Balb-C' inbred strain of white mouse and none were available in Saudi Arabia. It was my lot to arrange the purchase of a hundred of these animals from a breeder in London, then take them with me by air on one of my flights to Dammam. The animals were housed in special boxes, which were placed in the heated, pressurized hold of the Saudi Arabian airlines plane in which I travelled.

There was consternation about my baggage when my animals and I reached customs at Dammam airport. Fortunately I carried a document in Arabic explaining the purpose of my importing these unusual passengers. However, we arrived late at night and nobody was at the airport to accept the two boxes containing my travelling companions, so I kept them with me in my room at the plush French Meridien hotel.

I was weary, but I had to ensure that my mice had water to get through the night; I knew they had food. I made a small hole in each box lid to pass a straw through. This let the mice drink their fill from a water container I placed on top of each cage. Thoroughly tired by our journey I went to bed. In the middle of the night I awoke to a strange noise, turned on the light, and discovered, to my horror, that a group of enterprising rodents had enlarged the hole in the lid of their box and escaped. My bedroom floor had excited white mice scampering about looking for fresh pastures. I spent the rest of the night recapturing the little brutes, one by one, until I told myself I surely have them all back in their box. I sealed the hole with adhesive plaster from my toilet bag. The next morning we checked out of the hotel as soon as my colleagues arrived to drive me and the mice to my veterinary friends in Hofuf. I left wondering how many animals I failed to find. I also wonder what the reaction of the next guest was if he or she was aroused from their sleep to the sight and sound of squeaking white mice. I never found out!

Once we succeeded in obtaining *Leishmania* cultures from whatever source, the next person who was returning to London would convey sealed specimen-tubes to hand over to David Evans and his team to grow and identify. For security, the best way to carry these specimens was in one's overnight bag. That was easy to do in those days, but would be extremely difficult in the current era of super tight airport security.

However, that was still easier than returning isolates of *Leishmania* from Latin America, as I did years earlier (see Chapter 15). They did not grow readily in culture, so we had to transfer them in live hamsters or cotton rats that were susceptible to them. One time, I carried several cages of infected animals, in individual metal cages, inside an old Gladstone bag with the central dividing panels removed to provide adequate space. I obtained several animals from a laboratory in Caracas, Venezuela and took them to Belém in Brazil where my friends Lainson and Shaw supplied more infected animals. I boarded a British Airways flight to London with the bag between my leg and the side of the cabin. During the night I surreptitiously peeped into the bag to make sure all was well and to slip small pieces of apple into each cage as food and moisture. I expected the passenger next to me would summon a steward to investigate my strange behavior. However, he either slept during the long overnight flight or decided that I was harmlessly crazy.

In that age of innocence I passed the scrutiny of British customs without difficulty and delivered the animals into the care of the staff of the animal house and David Evans in the LSHTM. What an age of innocence! On another occasion, my colleagues asked me to take two canvas bags from Brazil to Paris. Each was the size of a small overnight bag. One contained a medium-sized harmless snake, the other a small collection of lizards. All the animals bore infections with fascinating and unknown blood parasites to be studied by my associate, Irène Landau, in the Paris Museum of Natural History. They also travelled at my feet, but fortunately did not need food or water en route. I dread to think of the commotion had one or more creature escaped in mid-flight.

Another time I took a well-sealed cage about sixty centimeters cubed on a flight from Paris to London. It was covered with nylon mosquito netting and the whole contraption was covered in brown paper tied with string. The cage held several hundred live laboratory-bred mosquitoes infected with a species of small worm that causes a condition called 'elephantiasis' in humans. They were destined for use in a research project by one of the helminthology staff of the LSHTM. On my way to the departure lounge in Charles de Gaulle airport I was stopped by a security man who enquired what I was carrying. I explained exactly what I had, a cage full of living mosquitoes for scientific research. He enquired politely if he could inspect the cage. I gingerly moved one corner of the paper aside so that he could examine the contents. One view and he was convinced that I meant what I said. He told me to replace the paper quickly so that the poor insects would not get too cold, which I did before making my way hastily to the descending escalator. On reaching Heathrow the process was reversed and I and my mosquitoes reached the LSHTM with no further problems. Such was life two or three decades ago.

October 25th

". . . Just to show how shortsighted British government policy could be about admitting overseas students to our universities, I learned yesterday that the young Vice Rector of King Faisal University (about the same as a Vice Chancellor) was one of my DTM&H students in Liverpool in 1970. (He passed !). As soon as he and I learned this the atmosphere immediately became very cordial.

"My negotiations here seem to be going ahead very well. We are meeting with remarkably good cooperation and flexibility from both SANCST (the funding agency in Riyadh) and the university here. They have agreed to fly in our candidate for the full-time entomological post (a young Englishman) immediately for our visit and to give him a chance to see and be seen here before signing a contract—a very exceptional concession.

"Tomorrow morning we will go by train to Hofuf (about two hours I'm told) where we will start some field studies, examine patients and organize the next stages of the program. Willie Büttiker will also join us there. We spoke to him on the phone yesterday and he sends you his greetings.

"Yesterday evening just before I phoned you we walked to a pharmacy to buy Bob some medicines that he forgot to bring with him (antihypertensives!) however, the 'fifteen minute walk' ended up as five miles there and back. We couldn't see a single taxi ! However it did us good to get the exercise."

October 29th

"Here (in Hofuf) we are certainly making full use of our time. We have spent two evenings so far trying to collect sandflies on a farm some fifteen kilometers away, but the weather was too windy. The incidence of leishmaniasis is very high there. For example, seven out of nine Thai laborers we examined were infected, one with over sixty lesions. Yesterday morning we saw about twenty cases in the local hospital. I made biopsies from six new cases and five of these were positive. There must be several thousand new cases every year in this small area alone. Our Saudi colleagues seem to be delighted that we are working with them because we stir things up when we come and everybody begins to get into the swing of the research. There are many practical and administrative obstacles to be overcome, but we are very frank about them and not so reluctant as people who live here to find ways of overcoming them. Willie Büttiker and a Saudi entomologist from Riyadh will join us on Sunday, and the university has agreed to fly Killick's man here from Nairobi especially to join us for this visit in the hope that we can recruit him to work here in Hofuf for a couple of years. (I hope he will accept!).

"On Tuesday we will take the train (quite comfortable, air conditioned) back to Damman where we have the main 'Workshop' on Wednesday. Also on Wednesday and probably on Thursday morning I hope to get my own administrative questions cleared up so that I can return over Thursday night via British Airways to reach Terminal 3 early on Friday morning.

"Yusuf and the rest of the team joined us here yesterday but returned to Damman in the evening. Yusuf has sought our help to edit the Proceedings of the leishmaniasis symposium which was held here in March 1980(!) and is still waiting to be published. So that will be our daytime chore over the next day or two, apart from going to the hospital where there are some babies I have to examine who may have visceral leishmaniasis."

1983

On Tuesday March 1st I attended the award of the King Faisal International Prize in Medicine in Riyadh (see Chapter 18), but only stayed a couple of days. All this took place during the time that I was working in Saudi Arabia with the NLRP. My award was greeted enthusiastically by my colleagues in KFA who feted me in style on my next visit to Dammam. I flew out of Heathrow again on Friday March 18th to Dahran to continue with the leishmaniasis work.

Our studies on leishmaniasis in Al Ahsa were in full swing. Tony Leaney and his wife Cindy coordinated field studies around Hofuf. Bob Killick and I spent several weeks each year studying the ecology of the infection in the farms and villages in the area. Bob, an expert on the collection, colonization, and dissection of sandflies, set up a series of efficient light traps in sundry dwellings, as well as in buildings constructed for commercial chicken breeding which served as useful insect bait. Bob and his wife Mireille were experts on breeding sandfly colonies for research in their laboratory. At times is was necessary for a small batch of sandflies to be offered a meal of human blood. Bob would rise to the occasion. I remember one evening we were reclining in his bedroom in the small, friendly Hofuf hotel, listening to a CD on Bob's portable player while a small cage of hungry, wild-caught *Phlebotomus papatasi* fed on the back of his hand. The next day, their bite marks were clearly visible, but fortunately it appeared that none of them was infected with *Leishmania*. Out on the farms, which were mainly devoted to the culture of dates, we spent many hours with our team and the local inhabitants, drinking endless cups of sweet tea or coffee and consuming large quantities of delicious fresh dates. We were on our guard when moving at night to avoid the many feral dogs that roamed the area round the villages. We did not wish to risk exposure to bites from what could be rabid animals. Our veterinary colleagues trapped several of the dogs and found some were infected with *Leishmania major.*

During 1983 and 1984 it was shown that over 50 percent of adult expatriate workers (mainly from Southeast Asia) who lived in Al Ahsa and at least 10 percent of all Saudi children, had evidence of active or healed cutaneous leishmaniasis. Epidemiological studies showed that the rapid growth and extension of villages and farms in Al Ahsa that followed the oil boom of that period, brought a massive ecological change to the region. The habitats of wild gerbils, mainly *Psammomys obesus* that lived in large colonies scattered throughout the sandy soil of the oasis, were invaded by new building construction, so the rodents came into increasing contact with the humans. The majority of the rodents were found to be infected with *Leishmania major*. It was transmitted by the sandfly named *Phlebotomus papatasi*, which bred in the gerbil burrows. However, these sandflies were also content to feed on human blood. From dusk and through the night, large numbers of these tiny flies roved the area where many people slept in the open because of the intense heat. Most severely afflicted were the non-immune foreign workers. On many we commonly found fifty or more bite marks and many developed severe chronic sores caused by infection with *L .major.*

March 20th

"It already seems a long time since I left you, but at least this time I have managed to pass the time usefully. My affairs from last year are now resolved and I hope that at least some of the business from this visit will be sorted out by the time I leave. The big fly in the ointment here (forgive the pun) is the young Vice Rector who is loathed by everybody including many of the Saudis. (This is the man who had been my student. We had been on good terms but power seemed to have gone to his head during the past year.) At the moment I am here on my own as Bob is in Hofuf with our French consultant mammalogist, Francis Petter. He returns to Paris tonight, Bob bringing him back from Hofuf to the airport. I hope they will meet me here in the hotel sometime this evening. They should also be bringing Willie Büttiker with them as he was due to fly in to Hofuf today.

"Tomorrow I may be lecturing here, then we have a big meeting in the evening which will include people from the Ministry of Health. It seems we may after all be going to the Southwest of the country near the Yemeni border. It we do go it will probably be on Saturday and we would stay there for a couple of days.

"I am just expecting my Chinese-American colleague to come and pick me up to go 'shopping'. It's one way of passing the time. Actually I expect to go to Hofuf on Tuesday for a few days in the field. The weather here now is very pleasant but they had a very exceptional storm last week that lasted three solid days. Everything was flooded and a lot of damage was done—not quite what you expect in the desert!"

October 24th

"Here things are going as usual, i.e., slowly. The Vice Rector is away until Saturday so we will go to Hofuf tomorrow and I will return here on Friday.

"Among other things this morning I went to see the man in charge of the whole police force for the Eastern Province, the one who was supposed to come here earlier this year. He is obviously not at all well and I am arranging for him to see one of my medical colleagues when he next visits London. On Friday I am going to his house for dinner to sort it all out.

"Saturday morning I hope to see the Vice Rector and get some other matters arranged, then fly to Riyadh in the late afternoon. While I am in Riyadh I intend to find out from SANCST (as non-commitally as possible) whether they still feel that it is worthwhile my coming out here because, if not, I would rather prepare to ease out of this position if, at least, the Dean in Riyadh has a more useful alternative to offer. Don't worry, I will be very discreet and diplomatic in anything I say.

"I have seen a preliminary program for next week's meeting and it looks as if I will give my paper on Tuesday or Wednesday, so please think of me and wish me luck! Now I am going to prepare for dinner (here in the hotel). George Brooks, the American we knew in Nepal may be joining us for a working dinner—it's about the only way we can catch up with each other."

October 25th

"6.30 a.m. We are planning to make an early start to Hofuf. There is now a new and very good highway all the way and we have a new, big, strong station wagon for the journey."

October 29th

"Yesterday morning I returned here from Hofuf by a combination of buses and taxis—not too bad. There is now a very good motorway between the towns. The only danger is when driving in the towns which are full (Hofuf at least) of small children driving small American-style bicycles all over the roads. They shoot out from all directions and are an absolute menace.

"In Hofuf the work is going well and Tony Leaney has settled in admirably. The main problem here is the Vice Rector who makes as many administrative difficulties as he can for everybody in the University, not only us. He has been away for weeks and only returns today. We have come here (i.e., Bob and Tony are coming this morning) specifically to see him, but whether we succeed in doing so is another question.

"Yesterday I was supposed to dine with General Othman, the chief of Police in this region, but he was called to Riyadh and I had a meal at the nearby Meridien Hotel with his assistant instead. It was still a useful meeting and gave me a good insight into certain aspects of Saudi life and thinking. I will probably see the General when I return here from Riyadh next week. Now I must get myself ready for this morning's confrontation and make some notes so that I remember to bring up the important things. This afternoon I get a flight to Riyadh at about 5 p.m."

1984
April 29th

"The atmosphere here has completely changed since they retired the last Vice Rector. The new man, a pediatrician, is charming and most helpful. You may meet him later as he is coming to the UK in the summer to do some training so as not to get too out of date while he does his administrative chores.

"Trying to put together the program's 1983 report (due last December!) is fairly easy, especially having my machine here, but time consuming. I make a first draft then give it to an Indian clerk to retype—he is remarkably quick and efficient. On Wednesday I intend to visit the vet in Hofuf to go over his work with him, but the entomologist, Tony Leaney, is Killick's man and he can look after himself. I am also seeing patients in the clinic near Hofuf and the dermatology clinic here with Raj Kubba (once a student of my old Liverpool colleague, Andrew Griffiths), a very competent and agreeable Indian. Tomorrow he and his wife have invited me to dinner—my only social occasion so far. Apart, that is, from finding to my surprise that Frank Shattuck is now here having given Liverpool up in disgust at not getting the Chair (in Public Health. Frank had been one of my fellow students when I was studying at Barts in the 1940s.) We had a meal together and he told me all the gossip about his rival for the Chair, (Ken Newell) which I will tell you about next week.

"I have only succeeded in having one swim, on Thursday, and the wind was surprisingly chilling. Friday (= Sunday) seemed a good day not to go as I understand the pool gets crowded, even though there is no mixed bathing. Since I do not want to eat (a) in the restaurant and (b) too much, I have brought in cheese, crackers, and fruit that formed my evening meal the past two evenings, and I work all through the lunch hour, so I certainly shouldn't gain weight. In this climate I don't even feel hungry, no need for calories for warmth I suppose."

1985
February 12th

"As I said, apart from my flight out here being delayed by a strike of catering staff, it was uneventful and I arrived in the hotel at about 11:30 p.m. local time. My friend Yusuf was here at the hotel when I arrived—actually he had come to meet the Dean from Riyadh and some external examiners who are here for the medicine finals. Anyway, so far nothing interesting has happened but nothing bad either. The Vice Rector is in Ireland and only coming back to the office on Saturday. In his absence most things come to a grinding halt. I am trying to pull in all the reports from the departmental heads. As usual those who have done the least are making the most fuss and complaining the loudest. The exception is Killick who only just got his data before I left from Leaney who has returned to the UK, so I still won't be able to complete the whole report before I come home (I'm certainly not waiting here for it to arrive!).

"To my surprise I received a personal invitation to have dinner with one of the external examiners (an old chap from Edinburgh) from my old sparring partner, Al-Torki, the former Vice Rector who gave everybody so much trouble. It was a typical Arabic dinner, held in his house with about a dozen other Faculty men and ourselves. All very congenial but uncomfortable, squatting on the floor, something I'm not very good at! Tonight the Department of Medicine has an invitation for us at the hotel next door—all helps to save money I suppose, and makes a change from the dreary restaurant in our hotel.

"Tomorrow I will go to Hofuf with Yusuf to see patients in the clinic. They are getting over fifty cases a day, so it should be interesting. There is not much I can do here at the moment anyway. I finally managed to track down Asem Bokhari in Riyadh and have arranged to go and see him there on Sunday. I will fly there and back the same day as it's only an hour's journey, and then I won't have the bother of changing my hotel, etc. I have to get him to finally authorize my amended program so it is important that I do see him.

"I can't say that there's much else exciting going on. By and large this aspect of my work here is rather dull and time wasting but it's all part of the job and helps us in the long run. The worst part is of course Friday. We might talk about 'Sunday, bloody Sunday!' but it's not a patch on 'Friday, bloody Friday!' I can tell you. This time I didn't bring any swimming trunks because there's still too much of a cold wind to enjoy the pool, so I expect I'll have a long walk somewhere instead."

1986
April 29th

"Up to now I have had no opportunity of looking for a carpet for you or in fact doing any shopping. I have been flat out with meetings, my lecture, yesterday's visit to Hofuf, etc. Tomorrow I will go to Hofuf again with Mohammed's boss from the Ministry of Health, Dr. Al-Jeffery. If you happen to phone him you can tell him that I am doing my best to get his fieldwork organized.

"In Hofuf I had the pleasure of identifying the first infected sandfly of the new season which is just starting up there. Unfortunately Riyadh ben Ismael (a Tunisian parasitologist who worked with Bob) has had to fly to Tunis tonight because his mother is ill, otherwise I would probably have spent a night or two there. This evening

I hope to have a quiet meal on my own in the hotel and an early night in preparation for a 7:30 a.m. departure tomorrow morning. Raj Kubba is cooking a meal for me tomorrow night. I will leave on the Friday afternoon plane direct for Jeddah and hope there will be someone there to meet me since I have no idea where I am staying. However there is now an abundance of hotel rooms everywhere since the number of visitors to the country has fallen off enormously over the past months.

"Fortunately my administrative arrangements have gone without a hitch—quite a change from the early days of this project. Actually the former Vice Rector came to my lecture and was very friendly and chatty. The present incumbent unfortunately will soon yield the post to another and you never know how things might change, but I have only another eighteen months on this project anyway.

"It seems to have stopped raining but there are still deep lagoons on several of the main roads in town—quite spectacular when some cars drive through them at speed. Fortunately the motorways are better-designed and quite dry."

The NLRP work continued for the rest of 1986 and until 1989. We assembled the scientific data acquired as the studies continued and published them from time to time as appropriate. In June 1987 I was elected as President of the Royal Society of Tropical Medicine and Hygiene. For my presidential address in October I chose as my subject, *The little sister—a tale of Arabia*. The tale continued, however.

In spite of decades of research to produce a vaccine against leishmaniasis, to this day no success has met efforts to vaccinate against any of the species that infect humans except the inoculation of living cultured *L. major*. That procedure has one advantage. The active lesions it produces, once healed, give the host a solid immunity against later infection with the same species of parasite, but not against other species. Moreover the lesions produced by the vaccination are often as severe as those following natural infection.

Therefore, it is best to select an inoculation site that will not leave an unsightly or damaging scar.

Part of the NLRP program was to investigate possible ways to prevent or treat cutaneous leishmaniasis and a clinical study of novel anti-leishmania drugs was an integral part of that program, but not vaccination. From the Balb C mice that I brought into Saudi Arabia, Sabir El-Bihari succeeded in raising a thriving colony in his laboratory in Hofuf. These proved invaluable for making new isolates of parasites from wild rodents, and for studying the immunological responses of hosts. During the project, David Evans discovered that some gerbils were not infected with *Leishmania major*, but with a previously unknown parasite we later described as *Leishmania arabica*. In Hofuf, the team found that a prior infection with *L. arabica* produced a self-healing skin lesion in the host mice and left the animals with a modest level of immunity against subsequent infection with the more virulent *L. major*. *L. arabica* was not isolated from a human case of cutaneous or any other type of leishmaniasis, yet many local schoolchildren, who had no scars of healed lesions from *L. major* infection, were still found to bear a high degree of immunity to that parasite by immunological skin testing.

In London, Bob Killick, I, and the LSHTM team discussed this paradoxical observation with Anthony Bryceson, a very experienced clinician in the subject of leishmaniasis, with other staff members including the immunologist Jenny Blackwell and with experts in outside organizations, including F.Y. Liew, an immunologist in the Wellcome Research Laboratories. The hypothesis was that many small children in the Hofuf villages were bitten by sandflies carrying infections with *L. arabica*, and this parasite was not able to induce skin lesions, but was sufficiently immunogenic to give the children a level of protection against subsequent bites with sandflies carrying the virulent species, *L. major*. The question was; if this form of active immunization against a pathogenic parasite by infection by a harmless parasite in the same ecological situation was a reality, could one utilize living *L. arabica* to vaccinate previously non-immune humans visiting or living in areas highly endemic for *L. major*? This phenomenon is known as 'zooprophylaxis'. Since *L. major* infection was a serious public health problem in Saudi Arabia and numerous other countries of the Old World and no vaccine was available, we decided it justified launching a project to explore this hypothesis, provided all relevant ethical considerations were fulfilled. David Evans could produce cultures of *L. arabica* for this purpose and a small select group of volunteers was among our immediate circle. All would have to demonstrate no previous exposure to infection with *L. major*. This excluded Bob Killick who was bitten by numerous sandflies during our Hofuf studies. My student Mohammed, mentioned earlier in this chapter, who was shown to be immunologically negative and had no known prior exposure to *L. major*; two other non-immune colleagues and I volunteered to receive the live *L. arabica*. One volunteered to be an unprotected control and my Sudanese student, Sayda El-Safi who had a clear history of prior infection with *L. major*, volunteered her blood for immunological studies.

After an appropriate interval following a single vaccination, five of us were inoculated with live *L. major*. All developed large, active lesions that self-healed with no drug or other treatment. Less severe acute lesions developed in the unvaccinated control volunteer. A thorough immunological investigation suggested that the vaccine permitted those who received it to develop an accelerated immune response to the challenge, but clearly further work was needed. Unfortunately, lack of time and considerations including my retirement from the LSHTM, brought a premature end to the study. Nobody has followed up this promising lead.

Such was the volume of new information collected by the NLRP team in the Eastern Province that it later was the basis for more than a dozen major scientific papers. A large field and clinical investigation was conducted in the area around Al Kharj, a short distance south of Riyadh, where a severe epidemic of cutaneous leishmaniasis was in progress. My second Saudi PhD student, May Al-Jassr, showed this was due to infection with *L. major*. During that busy period when our joint experiences immersed us deeply in research on leishmaniasis, Bob and I rounded up our fellow leishmaniacs. In 1987, we edited a two-volume collection of their writings on *The Leishmaniases in Biology and Medicine* that embraced the state of the art in that rapidly expanding field. In 1991, Bob and I published an annotated bibliography of leishmaniasis in Arabia that contained over 250 references.

2009

I suspect that those who had the patience to read this far may ask, "After all that, what on earth did anybody actually find out about CL and what to do about it after five years' work?" As I assured readers at the start of this section, it was not my aim to set out a scientific treatise here. All we learned was published in various medical journals—and we did learn a lot. However, among the salient conclusions were the following.

1. A major contributing factor to the annual increase in the quantum of infection with CL in the Hofuf area, was the increase in the population of the reservoir rodents that nest in communal burrows associated with wild plants (xerophytes) that grow around farms and villages. With the increased wealth of many human inhabitants of the peri-urban desert areas, the potential breeding sites of both reservoirs and vectors were increasing steadily.

2. The elimination of xerophytes from around human habitation may contribute to a reduction in reservoir rodents and their accompanying sandfly populations. We recommended that a campaign to destroy these plants be organized as soon as funds were available. Unfortunately, we were unable to follow up whether any action was taken on this after the NLRP was brought to a close.

Yes, we learned a lot about leishmaniasis, but it still exists in Arabia and many parts of the world. There is a long way to go and I believe that it will remain with us in one form or another for centuries.

PART IV

"Listen carefully, old man! From here on your lives changed gear; each day took on a new dimension."
Peters, 2009

Chapter 20

Retirement with Ruth— Confronting Our Demons 1989–2006

What brings two people together, what cements this relationship, and what can threaten it? Obvious and facile explanations present themselves and are those we offer to the outside world, family, friends, publishers, solicitors, priests, and, perhaps most important, ourselves. Beyond them however, lie deep-rooted ghosts in our hidden psyches, childhood conditioning, long-forgotten physical or psychological traumas, secrets often unrecognized, buried prejudices, and phobias, loves, hatreds, jealousies, and shameful memories.

From time to time the calm of a long-standing partnership is shattered. Trauma is triggered by a minor event, as most are, and the pieces are rapidly and readily put together again. Some fractures heal but leave permanent scars. Others, the least common, are irreparable. Of these I will say no more. To the observer little is evident. Yet if they are honest enough, the major part of a couple's life is often a permanent state that compares to 'walking on eggs.' We become quite adept at this way of life, so a skilled, egg-walking pair can live out a mainly harmonious coexistence for much, if not all of their lives.

Contrary to the traditional aphorism, I believe that every man and woman *is* an island. Each individual builds their own private world within the framework of the partnership. If all else fails, they build their world outside it. As the years advance edges may smooth over. Or they may be too frayed to hold together. The middle years of one's life are particularly fraught with emotional traps and pitfalls.

The fates decided that Ruth and I would lead an unusually peripatetic life. This worked for me, but was not always to her taste. Consequently the comings and goings without her gradually developed into a source of increasing friction. The scenes of our partings were one-sided conflicts. I felt that I was almost inevitably the loser in conflicts from which I emerged more and more scarred. Age finally caught up with us, and as the years increased the need to travel decreased radically. So, by and large, we evolved a state of truce—you might call it a peaceful coexistence.

The following account tells of a long period in our lives that was emotionally traumatic to say the least. In retrospect, it is hard to see how we both survived as well as we did. I reflect our mutual travails in an interwoven account that mingles recent, retrospective reflections, with contemporaneously written commentaries that I recorded intermittently. I had doubts as to why I composed these records. These doubts are clear in the following pages. Some are repetitions of my self-questioning, totally introverted 'conversations with myself.' I do not like what you are about to read, but it all happened. I reveal a radical change in our lives, expose weaknesses in both of us, bitter emotional conflicts, unforeseen reconciliations and the underlying, vital interdependence of two very different persons. Judge for yourself—but please, do not be too harsh on us. At times the important things of life faded and the trivia became overwhelming.

I took my official retirement from London University in 1989 and moved, with the agreement of my successor, into my former laboratories at Winches Farm, the field station of the LSHTM. It is just outside the cathedral city of St. Albans, a comfortable car drive from home. In the laboratory I retained the services of Brian Robinson who was my senior technical assistant since he joined me in the LSTM in 1969 from the RAMC. I also kept two female junior technicians, Jo and Mandy. This permitted me to continue researching antimalarial drugs, as well as doing some photographic work and microscopy. The latter were associated with a new edition of the *Colour Atlas of Tropical Medicine and Parasitology*. The first edition was developed at the LSTM with Herbert Gilles in 1977. I published a new book in 1992, *A Colour Atlas Of Arthropods In Clinical Medicine*. In addition to these activities, I was still engaged with international work, especially with WHO, and with field research on leishmaniasis in the Middle East.

Nevertheless my lifestyle change filled me with misgivings as to how to utilize my energies over the coming years. Whatever benefits retirement confers, it is also fraught with the dangers of introspection and reflection. I was not exempt from these dangers as this chapter makes clear. While we were at last free to arrange to share our lives more closely than was possible during my academic career, this introduced inherent challenges to meet. Fortunately there were lingering tasks about the house that I never seemed to have time to address. One was to construct a simple woodshed adjacent to our garage. During my first days of retirement I drew up a plan for this job, purchased the materials and equipment, and finished the task in a couple of weeks. This crude woodshed survived intact for over twenty years.

After finishing that task, misgivings about the future began to dwell on my mind. The following mainly contemporaneous memoirs reflect some of the stages of mental turmoil that both Ruth and I endured, and our mutual interactions over the next months and years.

In spite of my presence around the house, Ruth was able to pursue her interests with a selective circle of friends who shared her love of art and creative embroidery. In the warmer months of the years, I turned some of my attention to entomology. I noticed a remarkable variety of hover flies in the garden. I began to collect and identify these and accumulated a useful, representative series of detailed records. I donated them to those who drew up a national data bank for these interesting and important insects. I no longer collected butterflies but kept a record of all the species in or near the garden and photographed as many as I could. I also recorded the names of birds that appeared in our garden. When a *Millennium Book* was being prepared for Little Gaddesden, I provided records of both butterflies and birds for that publication in addition to some insect photographs. Once more I recorded my thoughts on my computer. I show them in the following pages as 'conversation.' In a very short time I saw that the greatest challenge and adventure in our lives was going to be to learn to accommodate to each other—not to the world around us.

1989
September 29th

"Five hours ago I glimpsed, for the first time, the darkness at the end of the tunnel—we were given a farewell retirement lunch. It was a pleasant, informal occasion. A speech was made, a splendid bouquet of flowers for Ruth, a large card filled with good wishes and signatures from colleagues and students. I gave a return speech, appreciative, jocular, avoiding solemnity. Then it was over. Handshakes, kisses, plans for future meetings—but not too soon— the end of a lifetime's employment. From here on, a slow phasing out, some work, catching up on the saved up odds and ends, an increasing awareness of the autumn. And, at home, a bottle to celebrate the happy occasion.

Perhaps tomorrow will seem a happy day."

September 30th

"It was."

1990
February 15th

"So much for retirement. No time even to add to this saga in the last four-and-a-half months. Am now launched on a new '*Atlas*' which keeps me occupied whenever I have time to work on it—and in three day's time I am off to Vietnam and Thailand. Perhaps, one day, I will have time to continue my 'pensées.' "

In the latter half of February I was to visit Ho Chi Minh City, the former Saigon, to discuss problems of malaria control in South Vietnam with staff of the Ministry of Health. It was my first visit to Vietnam. The city was full of traces of previous colonialist rulers. Their presence was conspicuous in the style of buildings in the city with many signs in French. There was French food alongside Vietnamese cuisine in the restaurants and wine in abundance. Two Dutch colleagues joined me. I knew them from my time in Papua New Guinea when their base of operations was in Hollandia, just over the border from Wewak on the northern coast. Vietnam was of particular interest, not only because of the history of American and Australian troops' involvement in the appalling conflict in the 1960s, but because that was the time when resistance to chloroquine first raised its ugly head in people infected with malignant tertian malaria. Apart from being able to review the current control measures being taken against malaria by the Vietnamese, I saw why virus diseases, such as dengue, were such a threat in that area. In most villages drinking water was stored in large earthenware pots that bred hordes of the mosquitoes that transmit this infection. A clear major need was to provide piped water supplies throughout the countryside. This was one of the messages we sent back to WHO.

From Vietnam I flew to Bangkok where I was to chair a meeting of the CHEMAL team. On arrival I learned we were one member short. Our colleague, Peter Trigg, who was to attend on behalf of the WHO secretariat, suffered a heart attack on the flight from Geneva to Bangkok. He was fortunate as our friend David Warrell was on the same flight, a few seats back. David, a highly skilled physician based in Oxford, recognized that something was wrong with Peter. He went forward, rapidly diagnosed the problem, and informed the pilot that he had to land as rapidly as possible and arrange an ambulance to transport Peter to a hospital for intensive care. Meanwhile he applied what immediate first aid he could. The happy outcome of this intervention was that Peter survived the ordeal, thanks to David's fortuitous presence and rapid response to the emergency.

On a less fortunate note, after I returned home to continue my studies in the Winches Farm lab I learned that Ralph Neal, an old friend who joined me there on his retirement from the Wellcome Research Foundation, died while giving a lecture in New York. On the 29th of that month I had the solemn task of delivering a eulogy for him at his church in St. Albans.

Between March and December 1990, I travelled overseas less than in previous years but was not always able to remain home. Fortunately Ruth and I enjoyed two visits to Europe together. The first was to the University of Verona at the invitation of one of my former students, Giovanni di Perri, on the excuse of giving a lecture. He and his colleagues were very hospitable as Italians can be. They arranged for us not only to sightsee in Verona, but to spend a short time in Venice on our way home. On August 2nd, Iraqi forces invaded Kuwait. Later that month Ruth and I went to Paris where I attended the 7th International Congress of Parasitology. The following month we made our annual pilgrimage to Ruth's home-town and from there to our favorite hotel in the Engadine where we celebrated Ruth's birthday. On our way home we visited a German colleague, Gunther Wernsdorfer, and his family in Nuremburg. Gunther was the brother of my colleague Walther. He and I were long associated through our joint work for WHO and Gunther was an expert photographer. He generously lent me some of his excellent pictures to include in the Atlases I was working on. All in all, it was a much needed and welcome interlude.

At the end of October, I was invited to WRAIR in Washington, not long before 'Desert Storm' erupted, to advise the US military on the problem of leishmaniasis in the Middle East. In mid-January the following year, a combined task force including over half a million US troops under United Nations authority, pushed north from Saudi Arabia to expel the Iraqi army of occupation from Kuwait. The war continued with massive destruction in Kuwait and Baghdad until the end of February 1991 when Kuwait was freed of its invaders. Many of the coalition forces acquired cutaneous leishmaniasis while on active duty during that campaign. I flew across the Atlantic to present a paper to the American Society of Tropical Medicine and Hygiene (ASTMH) at their annual meeting held in November in New Orleans. This is a fascinating city that I had never had the opportunity to visit.

Almost immediately after my return, I developed an attack of flu, which I acquired while dining with a friend from WRAIR, but recovered in time to give another paper at a meeting of the Swiss Society of Tropical Medicine in Thun. On November 28th I went there for a week to attend the annual meeting of the Swiss Society of Tropical Medicine of which I am an Honorary Member. While I was in the town I dropped in to a jeweler to see if I could buy Ruth a ring for her next birthday, even though that event was in September of the following year. My idea was to give her a signet ring and thought it would be special if I could have one engraved with her family crest. I had no idea if such an object existed, so was delighted when the jeweler produced a brief history of the Scheidegger clan going back to the year 1317 complete with family crest from a large Swiss genealogy tome. This was a very fortunate find. I arranged for him to deliver the ring to a colleague from Hoffmann-La Roche who I would meet later in the year in London. He offered to bring it to me. Ruth was extremely surprised and delighted when I presented it to her in September 1991, complete with a colored drawing of the family crest that she did not know existed, plus a copy of the entry in the genealogy book. (See Chapters 1 and 8).

Two weeks later, while pruning bushes in the garden at home, I pulled some branches out too abruptly. The next morning, while shaving, I saw what appeared to be red blood cells in my left eye as they would look through a microscope. It was a hemorrhage from a retinal tear that I had to have sealed by laser by a local eye surgeon, Kim Wang.

December 27th

"Christmas is always a bad time—and not only for me! Everybody gets sick, our cat Minou has G.O.K. (God only knows what), goes off food, constipated, coughing (is it cat flu?); Ruth has spinal arthralgia, grumpy, nagging, and other symptoms. Then I get a retinal hemorrhage just before Christmas Eve. One solution is to get slightly blotto and hope that tomorrow will be another day.

"Then what happens the day after tomorrow? Probably an extension of the war in the Gulf."

This turned out to be true.

1991
January 4th

"What also happened two days later was that I developed a retinal hemorrhage in my right eye! Another visit to Mr. Wang was called for. As usual at this time of the year, I was invited to join the KFF Prize committee in Riyadh, but had to decline because of my eye problems. I suspect that my hosts thought I declined because I was not willing to fly there, with the Gulf War in Kuwait being in full force. In spite of this, I continued to receive invitations to Riyadh at about the same time every year until 1997."

January 12th

"So where are we today? 95 percent into a new World War; 30 percent into a new book; 30 percent blind? So much for retirement and 1991! Better to get at least 30 percent sloshed!"

Late January to August

"In spite of the international turmoil, we managed to join a big party organized by Bill Bray to celebrate Cyril Garnham's ninetieth birthday. It was a grand affair, typical Bray, at a hostelry tucked away in an obscure village off the M4 motorway quite close to the Thames. Fortunately, Ruth and I made a reconnaissance some days earlier as we agreed to collect the Garnhams on the way to the party. Their house in Farnham Common was on our route. When the evening arrived it was intensely foggy, but luckily everybody arrived more or less on time. My only problem was that I had to resist the excellent wines as we were to make the return journey through the fog. Nevertheless, it was a great occasion and the last with Cyril who was to die on Christmas Day, four years later. The remainder of 1991 was relatively tranquil. Ruth and I spent a short time in Rome where I gave a lecture, this time in a prefab in lieu of a lecture theatre, for a reason I forget. We paid our first visit to the Vatican, which both impressed and depressed us.

"At the end of May, I spent a short time in Abidjan where I was asked to give a lecture to promote the use of combined drug therapy to reduce the development of resistance of malaria to a new antimalarial drug called mefloquine. I had worked on this with WRAIR, CHEMAL, and the Swiss pharmaceutical company, Hoffmann-La Roche, for several years. The combination was called 'Fansimef' and it had a promising future. Unfortunately, its development was abruptly cut short for all the wrong reasons that I will not enter into here. However, it was a good example of the difficulties faced in new drug development. It especially demonstrated the ability of one or two ill-informed 'experts' to destroy years of work. Ten days later, I gave another lecture at a meeting in Pharo, the French military medical center in Marseilles. I had not been there for many years and was once more able to indulge in a delicious bouillabaisse."

August 24th

"Saturdays are always bad and this, being August Bank Holiday weekend, is even worse. So let's take inventory of the past two years— my God, already all that since I retired?

"World news? Only a war in the Gulf over and done in about six months, except that half of Kuwait was left in a pall of thick, black smoke which is still there, and Saddam Hussein sits it out in Baghdad. A second Russian revolution, all over and done in a week, last week—Gorbachev almost out and nearly for keeps, in fact! Yeltsin in and Communism is sliding rapidly into history. John Major is in the ascendancy and Bush Senior is still playing golf. Better that than Gulf.

"The Peters? Going back yet again to glorious Pontresina next week. Wonder if that will do anything to stop the invidious, progressive alienation that we seem to be developing for each other. Is it, as usual, all me—increasingly distanced from the few remaining friends and colleagues and becoming too conscious of leading a life style that I do not like, hence nursing a deep resentment that I cannot throw off? Or is it just banal, both tired and needing a break from the daily routine? What is true is that I am becoming more and more morose and touchy. Ruth grows increasingly touchy and critical. Since the *Atlas* went to press I have lacked any serious objectives. The past weeks have been occupied in moving from the old lab I had, to rooms in the main building at Winches Farm, but knowing it to be for months only. The future from there? G.O.K. as usual. Still struggling to obtain a small amount of money to keep the work going, partly to keep my assistant Brian in a job and, to be honest with myself, mainly to keep me from dying of boredom at home in complete isolation. Was infuriated, having recently had to spend a ridiculous amount of time and effort in getting funds from Spain for past work and a new, very modest contract, to be told by my Ruth that I was prostituting myself for money. Who gets the benefit of my income, anyway? Certainly not me!

"No, I seem, firstly, not to be doing any of the things that I thought I would like to do when retirement gave me freedom from work obligations. Secondly, I feel ignored, forgotten, unappreciated by my peers—never, for example, any award or even a kind word from my recent institute, the government, the tropical societies, while all around everybody else seems to be getting honors and awards, except Gordon Smith who, poor man, got cancer instead of a Knighthood! Thirdly, am getting to the stage when I do not really know what I would want to do, even if I were entirely free to do what I liked in a purely selfish way. Sex of which we seem to share no more on the home front, begins to call less and less, regrettably, perhaps for lack of stimulus, but more likely lack of the right hormones in us both, damn it. Creative writing? Fine, but where are the ideas (of which I never had many, outside captions for atlases and a bit on malaria) and, most important humor of which, according to Ruth at least, I never did possess any anyhow—she's usually right I'm sorry to say.

"I suppose that ultimately what holds a frayed old marriage together is the dread of solitude and a deep residual affection. Love? How do you define it, especially after thirty-seven years as it will be in a fortnight? Heaven help me if Ruth ever sees this. I don't believe that she would ever understand herself, or us—but perhaps, as usual, I have it all wrong and she would understand far better than I ever could, with her sharp feminine insight into people, other people. I wonder though how much she understands of herself. It is very hard to be self-analytical, and at the same time completely honest with oneself. So how much harder to share the analysis with someone else, especially one's nearest, dearest and only fellow human being?

"Already two years since retirement! Is it possible?"

August 28th

"All packed and ready to leave in the morning on our annual holiday to the Swiss mountains. How we love the blue skies, clear air, the mountains and walks on the wild side, endless lengths in the indoor-outdoor swimming pool, and those exhilarating evenings after dinner in the Grand Hotel Kronenhof, Pontresina (altitude 2,000 meters and more). And, of course, a visit to Ruth's niece, husband and son en route through Zurich where Ruth can pass a little while browsing through the shops on the Bahnhofstrasse."

September 28th

"We have survived it all and returned several kilos heavier and many pounds lighter. Net result, we are on diet and that is no easy matter. Today I have lost more weight than Ruth who has been taking it out on me ever since she stood on the scale, which depressed her greatly. In fact, she now weighs over a kilo more than me—and when I recall the sylph-like figure she had when we married (how many years ago?) and my own gross corpulence at that time, it seems unbelievable.

"I am still searching for inspiration for a theme on which to base my first new book. There appear to be two weekend courses for would-be writers at the adult education center in Great Missenden. One is called *Writing For Money* and the other just *Creative Writing*. The money motive is not the one I need, but how to become creative by spending a weekend at Missenden escapes me—unless, that is, one of one's fellow students were to provide an unexpected stimulus. (At my age?)

"Perhaps I should make an effort to go through the scribbled notes that I made over the years when on my various journeys to far flung places and type out what might be of interest to someone. Who knows, I might prove to have been a budding Maugham without ever realizing it all these years, although it hardly seems likely. On the other hand, I have visited a few interesting places, the Amazon, Fushan, Lucknow, and all the others. Travelogues per se, however, are deadly missiles in the hands of most authors and autobiographies even worse since they expose just the parts that the author wants to show, and as a rule not the bits that lie under the surface, unless they happen to escape when the author is not looking.

"As to writing an autobiography, there are so many memories tucked away in my head, if only it were possible to bring them to the surface in an orderly fashion. All rather kaleidoscopic. I wonder if one can ever be sufficiently honest with oneself, in the strictest confidence of course, to dredge up *all* the memories. Just how many of the painful or shameful ones are truly so suppressed that only deep psychoanalysis can bring them to the surface and, even then, do many remain hidden forever?"

October 25th

"Yesterday was my time to visit Mr. Wang for an eye check up. Not very encouraging—I have more floaters than before."

"Over the past six weeks we have both been on diet following our holiday and each has lost about eight kilograms. This has entailed the usual dietary restrictions but hardest of all has been a serious restriction on alcohol. Tonight the tension demands a relaxation of this."

1992
January 10th

"On a high today, for no particular reason. On the radio is music from Prokofiev's Romeo and Juliet—some of my favorite pieces. Christmas and New Year have passed reasonably trauma-free, and life is settling back more or less to a normal and moderately tranquil pattern. Ruth who went back on her hormone patches to survive Christmas has now gone off them again, and she has returned to an interesting mixture of painting and embroidery. The major move from Winches Farm to the CAB International Institute of Parasitology (IIP) across the road is now imminent as the LSHTM has won its appeal to sell the site for a housing development and we will have to move out by the end of September. All depends on my being able to establish a new animal unit in the IIP, but we have agreement in principle at least, and hopes of raising extra funds for it.

"A big question now is what should I write next? I had thought of something autobiographical but cannot imagine who could possibly be interested. Perhaps a good start would be to make a sort of inventory of my past, an unofficial *curriculum vitae*. The formal one looks not bad but is a bit stodgy. One approach is to list all dates I can find in my passport. Let's try this approach.

"The first, No.404996, was issued 3 Feb 1947 in London when I had reached the tender age of twenty-two, coming twenty-three and was already a qualified but grossly inexperienced quack. Incredible to think that this was forty-five years and about six passports ago. The passport stamps are, of course, not all legible and in recent years there are less and less of them since one does not have one's passport stamped any longer in many European countries. This does make it a bit hard to recall all the visits, for example to Switzerland and France to which I have travelled so many times during the past decade. Moreover, I regret having no stamp from the USSR, which I visited twice, or was it three times, especially since that country ceased to exist about one month ago! Now there's something incredible, if you like. First, the Berlin Wall cracked and since then there has been a positive cascade of falling political walls. Not only was this unthinkable only about two years ago, but the rate at which walls and heads have been falling has been positively terrifying—not excluding my favorite woman, Margaret Thatcher!"

February 1st

"Today has been a beautiful cold, but sunny day, with intermittent mist blowing up from below the Ivinghoe ridge. Ruth and I went on our usual walk across Ashridge and back up the Golden Valley before lunch, collecting a few sticks for kindling at the top of the last hill, before taking to the Nettleden road and home the last few hundred meters (which always seem the longest). Perhaps because of the exercise, perhaps because I have not only lost about twelve kilograms since starting dieting after our autumn (fattening) holiday in Pontresina, but have not put any back since before Christmas. Perhaps I feel reasonably euphoric because I am going again to Riyadh next Friday, have already my tickets, and will collect my visa on Monday. A great pity that Ruth does not feel more energetic and ready to share the more enterprising, but more demanding things of life. She could, of course, easily have come with me to Riyadh for example, even with all the limitations in Saudi Arabia on the movements of women. At least she could have shown some enthusiasm to try, just once. But no! Stop complaining. Accept that she simply does not like flying, the Middle East, novelty, effort, for whatever physical or mental reasons. Just accept it and be sympathetic."

February 17th

"Just back from another visit to Riyadh to sit on the medical committee for the King Faisal Prize. I thought I would look at this encrypted file, but I forgot the password! Finally realized it was my own name, written in capitals. Had I not come across it, these scribblings would never have seen the light of day ever again."

March 28th

"Have been fairly busy since Riyadh. First of all, we both had a bad dose of flu. Ruth had it worse than I did. Her fever lasted for nearly a week. Had to cancel my visit to Paris for Irène Landau's doctoral thesis, much to my chagrin. Then busy with general affairs including planning for move to CAB at the end of September—if there are no last minute hitches.

"Visit to Madrid for meeting with Pharma Mar, Charles Jefford, and Craig Canfield. Ruth came with to do some tourism and we saw the Prado, but tour bus drivers decided to go on strike, so our visits to Toledo and Segovia were cancelled. Cut our losses and returned home a few days early. Now preparing for visit to Yaoundé in mid-May (if there is not an insurrection there in the meantime.)

"To pass the time, have just backed up all the hard disks on this computer. Not a very difficult operation now. Haven't been to the Cameroun for some eighteen years, and this will probably be the last time."

Some years later, after several changes of computer, I was unable to reopen any of my old backup files because many of the software programs had changed and I could not trace new versions that would operate on my current PC.

March 31st

"I will be sixty-eight years old in four hours time. April Fool!"

April 1st

"Proved in the event. Biggest row for years!"

June 20th

"My half-sister, Sophie Alice (a.k.a. 'Pete'), died at six o'clock this morning, at the age of eighty-five, from complications due to her lower aortic aneurysm. Expected as it has been since this was discovered, she had been living on borrowed time for several years, and was reasonably happy ever since her husband Harry died. Ruth's spontaneous reaction when she heard that the funeral might be next Tuesday—'Oh s***!'—we were going shopping on Tuesday. Today's kind thought. 'Well, she was nasty to me.' Probably true—but nevertheless!

"So we drank what we intended to drink anyway, Saumur followed by a bottle of '82 Chateau d'Angludet with dinner, and I consumed more than I realized. Managed to fall backwards into the bath later in the evening (but certainly didn't tell anybody) and had quite a hangover for church in the morning. Found ourselves in the middle of the baptism of the local fishmonger's daughter with 100 guests. C'est la vie. We come and we go, all in our good time."

August 1992

"In 1991 the LSHTM had made the decision to sell our historical field station at Winches Farm, to bolster the funds that would then be available to add to the facilities in Euston, a great mistake in my opinion. In mid-August 1992, my team moved over the road from our laboratories in Winches Farm to the premises of the Commonwealth Agricultural Bureau (renamed CABI Bioscience, International Institute of Parasitology,) by invitation of an old friend, Ralph Muller, a helminthologist who was then its Director. He was able to let us occupy a small laboratory on the first floor of the IIP and a Portakabin just outside, and to share all their facilities including the excellent accommodation for experimental rodents. We literally carried our possessions with us, a magnificent achievement all round. Luckily, we had only to carry everything a distance of about 200 meters, but that was enough. My associate, Simon Townson, had been running a major WHO-supported research program at Winches Farm in parallel with mine, to search for new drugs with which to treat common worm infections of man such as 'River Blindness' and lymphatic filariasis. He and his team were invited to join us in IIP. We were all to remain there, enjoying a very amicable and fruitful collaboration with our IIP colleagues, for the following seven years."

August 26th–September 5th

"Annual holiday to Switzerland, starting with two tropically hot nights in Versoix where we had one very agreeable day with our old friends the Siebolds. Then on to the Hotel Kronenhof at Pontresina. All passed reasonably well with some walks (including all day with the Defilas, an elderly couple whom we met there in previous years) and Ruth's sixty-third birthday. Returned home after rather a short time away because of the need to empty the Winches Farm laboratory and move over to the IIP. Definitely distracted by the idea and that didn't go down too well. However, the forthcoming visit to Paris and the Sorbonne in December, followed by the King Faisal symposium in London, may help to make the rest of the year tolerable."

September 18th

"Wedding anniversary, thirty-eighth. I got too blotto to write properly. Made one faux pas at 09:30 a.m. and didn't buy a present (having been told not to—never believe such a comment—the dew-sprinkled red rose collected at 06:00 a.m. and handmade card were not quite enough!). Day ruined. Tell you another day. Wanted her to look at some nice colors on a tree, but car arrived unexpectedly! And that was it. Why try?"

September 26th

"Returned late last Thursday night after a tiring two-day visit to lecture in Brescia, then in to pack the lab on the Friday morning. Today a quiet and peaceful one, gardening, moving a cupboard, and similar duties. Hope that peace will continue to reign."

December 8th

"An amazingly tranquil but busy two and a half months. Having moved lab into a Portakabin, have been very busy writing papers on new trioxanes, chapter for Royal Society meeting next week. Talked on leishmaniasis at the Swiss Society of Tropical Medicine in Ascona. Then gave a paper at the annual meeting of the ASTMH in Seattle after visiting WRAIR briefly en route. Did not plan to go to the Congress of Tropical Medicine in Thailand early December because of visit to Paris to collect Dr. Hon. Causa of the Université René Descartes. Went there with Ruth and was well entertained, wined, dined, and such, including lecturing in bad French to the Faculty of Pharmacy (my sponsors), up to climax of presentation of awards at the Sorbonne. Very impressive ceremony but it went on a long time and I had a sore behind before it finished! Was pleased to see my old colleague Rioux (all the way from Montpellier) and Nicole Léger—and amazed to see June Rollinson, British Council Paris, ex-New Delhi. That took a bit of explaining, but she was reasonably discreet—not that there was anything to be indiscreet about. Tomorrow, back to France to see Chabaud, Irène and Schrevel, then on to Montpellier to sit on Jury for Fréderic Gay (from Dominique Mazier's group)."

1993
January 1st

"Somehow we have managed to survive nearly two weeks of holiday, including Christmas and New Year—but this evening I blew it. I put the remains of my cranberry sauce onto my purée of potatoes and fennel!"

March 20th

"A combined force of British and United States troops invaded Iraq which was accused of hoarding weapons of massive destruction (WMD). The Iraqi leader, Saddam Hussein, was overthrown and executed after a prolonged trial but, six years later at the time of writing this entry (January 2009,) the Iraq war continues. No WMD were ever discovered."

April 20th

"Drove Teddy and Peggy Cusdin, elderly friends from Little G., for a short stay in the picturesque village of Chipping Camden where we met up with other local friends, Owen and Rosemary Williams, to celebrate a Cusdin wedding anniversary. On the way back we visited a stone-deaf retired doctor called Eason who was a world authority on centipedes and millipedes, so quite an interesting day."

May 15th

"To Paris with Ruth to join a jury at the Museum examining a presentation for a doctorate by one of Chabaud's students. Gave us a good chance to revisit some of our favorite old haunts, and to eat and drink too much."

July 26th

"The best we can hope to do is to keep one jump ahead of Nature. Malaria as a public health problem is very likely to remain with us for the foreseeable future. In the final analysis, no country can afford not to fight the problem of malaria within its boundaries. The indications are that chemotherapy will play an increasingly important role in this fight.

"I wrote those words in 1970. I quoted myself again at the close of my final chapter in the second edition of my compendium on antimalarials, which was published in 1987. Two years later I 'retired.' One of the joys of retiring is supposed to be that one does not have to feel obliged to keep up to date, to compete with one's successors to know the last word on one's specialty, leave it to the younger generation.

"When in the fourth year of my retirement I was asked to write a review of new antimalarial drugs and rational targets for drug design, I looked around, as one does, for recent published reviews of the field but rather to my surprise in view of the considerable agitation that antimalarial drug resistance is causing, I could not trace any of any significance. Then I was asked by a kind friend if I would write just such a review for a renowned international abstract journal.

"The great pleasure of retirement for me had been to permit myself rapidly to abandon the ever demanding task of keeping up to date with the literature, of attending as many as possible of the relevant national and international meetings in my chosen field, to retreat into a modest world of domesticity, gardening and long-abandoned hobbies, in my case entomology and philately.

"However—and there is always a however in most people's lives—the stimulus of being asked (at my venerable age, guaranteed to flatter the most modest amongst us) to present a review paper on *New Targets For Antimalarial Chemotherapy* was a sure way of winkling me out of my shell. An earlier surge in this direction was quelled by the polite refusal of a former publisher of mine to condone a third edition of my book on antimalarials. This was the basis of serious doubts on my part whether I should ever even try, culminating in a decision not to do so, but this latest challenge proved to be the stimulus for the present work. I hope that whoever happens to read that review will find it of some use."

July 31st

"Six months of the year already gone.

"I could easily become intoxicated with the Bossa Nova. I have always had a special feeling for Brazil that Ruth could never understand even if she tried. While she was slaving away in the kitchen creating a delicious three-meat (?) dinner, I listened to a TV presentation on the Bossa Nova. Brought back memories of my brief visits to Brazil. One day I must put my diary notes on them, on to this record."

(Which I did—see Chapter 15.)

"Now back to a routine Saturday evening TV watch. I begin to feel that life is slipping past and that I am not doing any of the things I really want to feel free to do in my retirement."

August 1st

"Swiss national day marked by a profound depression that was revealed as a grinding, aggressive antagonism following last night's revelation that I like Bossa Nova, and Ruth does not—she considers it common! Finally, during a walk over the Ivinghoe Beacon she admitted that she was going through a period of depression, so what could I say.

"This evening following an entirely wasted day, watched an exquisitely dull Poirot. I cannot help thinking that in spite of having all the physical comforts of life provided by Ruth I am deeply unhappy. I suppose that her withdrawal from all physical contact plays some role in this, not that I am exactly over desirous for sex at my advanced age—but a little warmth and physical love now and then would help, I am sure. All this is meaningless unless I am prepared to do something radical about it but the truth is that I just don't have the guts for it!"

August to December

"For much of August we lived quietly, occasionally visiting London or local events such as Music Society concerts. At the end of the month we returned to Pontresina for our annual visit and to celebrate Ruth's birthday. The stay was interrupted by a lecture I was invited to give in the University of Brescia, a short distance across the Italian border. We were collected by a taxi, driven across the winding pass and down the other side to Brescia where our host had arranged a comfortable hotel. Next morning I gave a lecture in my broken French to a largely Italian audience of students of tropical medicine. Many of them understanding even less French than English wisely slept throughout my excellent and well-illustrated presentation, but some then woke up in time to pose a few questions. Ruth and I were delighted. The next day we were driven back to Pontresina to resume our holiday.

"The remainder of September and October once more saw us leading a relatively tranquil existence in Little G. The break in Switzerland had obviously gone some way to enabling us to return to a more normal emotional level. However, in November I went alone to the annual meeting of the ASTMH in Atlanta where I gave yet another lecture and, in early December, returned to Paris to attend a conference at which I probably gave the same lecture again. That set the problem off once more."

December 26th—Boxing Day

"Christmas 1993—an unmitigated disaster! Ruth sick and furious, all presents wrong, even packed wrongly, could not possibly have been worse. Last night I had a vivid dream about being deeply in love with a beautiful, tender young woman—not a sexy dream but telling me how much true love and affection I have missed for over forty years—a lifetime. When I lay back in our mutual bed after bringing Ruth her tea, there were slow tears on my cheeks. Ruth has been profoundly depressed for days and making the best of an undiagnosable complaint for all that time. It is of course all my fault and, of course, again I have no sympathy, am too thick-skinned to see what is what, true to my upbringing by a mother who spoiled me all my life, etc., etc. After visiting an old people's hospice on Friday though she returned all contrite for her harshness and apologized in tears for being 'such a foul-tempered cow.' All forgotten five minutes later.

"Perhaps if I could see us with another's eyes I would be able to understand how much is me, how much she, and how much forty years of us? What a mistake it all seems now, all these years wasted and nowhere to go now—it's far too late at sixty-nine years and nine months of age! Happy New Year. Why can't I for once have something happy to say in this record?"

December 27th—Black Monday

"This proved to be another unmitigated disaster, so much so that I could not bring myself to include here the account that I wrote about it at the time."

1994
January to August

"The year started quietly with my annual pilgrimage to Riyadh in early February followed by a conference with Hoffmann-La Roche in Basle in March. On my seventieth birthday on April 1st, Ruth organized a surprise luncheon party for me at our favorite restaurant, the King's Head in Ivinghoe. It was a true surprise since, instead of lunching with her tête à tête as I had anticipated, we arrived to be met by a guilty-looking Georges de Maison, apologizing that he had overbooked. Would we mind lunching upstairs where he assured me the menu and accommodation would be up to his usual standards? Having no choice we agreed, to be met when the door opened by a roomful of friends and relations, some of whom had travelled a long way to be with us. Ruth had planned everything meticulously, transport, accommodation, food, and drink. It was a total and wonderful surprise but for some reason I omitted to record the event on my computer until much later. (See later, duplicated entry for mid-August 1994.) It so happened that my birthday coincided that year with Easter during which we enjoyed the company of Ruth's niece Marija and her husband, Aldo, who had joined us from Zurich for the occasion. The rest of April and May were tranquil and for a change, I did not have any journeys to make or papers to read. We took a couple of days off at the end of May to stay at Rick Stein's famous fish restaurant-hotel in the West Country and greatly enjoyed it. June was very peaceful, the major event being my delivery to our publisher of the manuscript of the 4th edition of our *Color (sic) Atlas of Tropical Medicine and Parasitology* months ahead of schedule. July proved to be another peaceful month as was the first half of August. I could not remember such a long period for several years past during which it seems we lived in peace and harmony once again. It was obviously something we both had needed badly."

August 12th, 1994

"Astounding—seven whole months passed without the desperate need to write in this diary (that is what it is becoming, in a way)."

"On the positive side, I was able to exert a superhuman effort and finish the new edition of the *Atlas* which I delivered to the publisher about three months ahead of schedule. It was in fact due about now. Work continues reasonably well at IIP where we now have a new assistant, Dr. Sue Fleck, thanks to further funding from Pharma Mar for Charles Jefford's B07, which really does show promise as a new generation antimalarial. He retires next month but the University of Geneva clearly does not intend to keep him on and he has managed to obtain a Chair in the University of Singapore. Meanwhile there is a good chance that we may obtain a further contract with WRAIR that would keep me occupied for another five years, all being well. The IIP, however, will have to move sooner or later, probably in 1996, but where to is not yet known. If it proves to be somewhere reasonably close, I will go along but not if it is on the other side of Ascot. Even I have my limits, never mind what reaction it would arouse in Ruth.

"Basically life progresses reasonably smoothly for the most part with occasional bouts of fury from Ruth for no good reason (usually). However, I have to admit that all in all I am not happy. Fundamentally, I feel that I am not actually doing the things I would really like to be doing having retired and not having to worry too much about income. I have to admit sadly also that Ruth and I after forty years have very little left to say to each other, and this becomes all too obvious day after day. However, what to do about it is another matter. When we heard I was to receive a medal from the American Society of Tropical Medicine I immediately asked Ruth to come with me to Cincinnati to receive it this coming November. She sounded quite pleased, although I suspect that she was, and remains, horribly jealous of me for it. She probably she does not realize this. Her own work on creative embroidery has produced some very interesting pieces including a large wall hanging for which she has used ethnic Papuan motifs. Her problem, and this she does know, is that she cannot get away from being over-elaborate in her designs. This makes her angry but there is unfortunately nothing I can do to help there being a complete ignoramus when it comes to art. I have to admit that one cause for my unhappiness is that I begin to feel that I cannot sustain enthusiasm for anything I do now, a sure sign of approaching old age.

"All in all I suppose that I should count my blessings. We have a comfortable home, sadly now without our old cat Minou who I had to have put down just after New Year. At Ruth's insistence, we now have a small fishpond, which is quite interesting, and two rapidly fattening shabunkins to feed. Ruth provides all the material comforts of home and usually tolerates my going part-time to the IIP. We occasionally see old (i.e., our generation) friends of the village, dine together or lunch at the King's Head. Rarely we go to London to see an exhibition, or shop. Never do we go to the cinema which I would like to do sometimes but we 'watch the box' every evening which becomes a duller and duller pastime for the most part. We do not read much for some reason or other. Sometimes we walk in the neighboring woods and this summer, which was exceptionally hot and dry we sat in the garden under the apple tree, and did not much else.

"Such is life in August 1994, almost five years of retirement and still surviving. I should be able to say that we are adjusting to a quieter way of life and of mutual understanding and tolerance. Up to a point I suppose we are as witness the long delay since the last entry in these notes. However something is lacking and I sometimes think that, if I were only just a bit more of a man, I would give it all up and do something entirely different, just on my own. Meanwhile the tropical world is falling about our ears, millions are dying or refugees in Africa, even parts of Europe are in flames. Why cannot we be content, count our blessings and just relax?"

Mid August

"Strange, but I forgot to mention that I was seventy on April 1st and Ruth gave me a surprise party at the King's Head. (Refer back to previous entry for January to August 1994, and below.) Her organization was magnificent. People were invited from as far afield as Zurich (Marija, Ruth's niece and her husband, Aldo), Inverness (Sonya, Ruadh Ross's widow), the Fryers from Epsom, Davidsons from Regents Park and, among local guests, Owen and Rosemary Williams. Transport and accommodation were arranged, a menu selected with Monsieur Georges, and a good time was had by all. If only she didn't throw her party back in my face every time we had a row over the next few months, it would have been one of my happiest souvenirs of our long marriage. However, in a few weeks she will be sixty-five, in Pontresina and, two weeks later, we will celebrate our Ruby Wedding by having a couple of days in Chipping Camden and a night of Shakespeare at Stratford-on -Avon.

"Why did I not write about April 1st before? (See above— apparently a Freudian slip.)".

Late September

"Pontresina came and went at the end of August—beginning of September and a very agreeable break it was, for the most part. Birthday lunch was at Champfer in the excellent Buntner restaurant run by the Rohri family. We both enjoyed it and bought his cookery book, which Ruth now uses extensively.

"We celebrated our fortieth wedding anniversary at Chipping Camden on our own, plus flowers and champagne in the suite waiting for Ruth. It was a successful weekend, with a superb performance of *Twelfth Night* by the Royal Shakespeare Company, and a reasonable dinner to follow at the theatre.

"At present all is on a fairly even keel. Ruth has gone for the day, Sunday, to join other women in an embroidery session, while I cleaned various bits of the house, threw out old pot plants, and similar tasks. In a fortnight we will fly to Zurich where Ruth will go on to Herisau for a primary-school reunion, and I will go to Leysin to the Swiss Tropical Medicine Society, thence to see seventy-nine year-old sister Ronnie for an evening. We meet up again in Zurich for Sunday evening with Marija and Aldo, then return Monday. Mid-November, we will fly to Cincinnati as the American Society of Tropical Medicine has kindly decided to award me the Le Prince medal for malaria. More on that later."

October 26th

"In mid-October we did return once more to Switzerland, Ruth for her school reunion, and I to kill a couple of days at the annual meeting of the Swiss Society of Tropical Medicine in Leysin."

"The annual meeting of the ASTMH was held in Cincinnati in November and for once Ruth agreed to accompany me. It was the occasion when I was presented with the Le Prince Medal of the Society for my work on malaria and, I suspect, in particular for the contribution I had made over many years to the antimalarial research program of WRAIR. That great American malariologist, Le Prince, had been one of the pioneers who helped to make possible the construction of the Panama Canal. I was very pleased to join the ranks of those medalists who had preceded me, the first after LePrince himself being Brian Maegraith and the latest Cyril Garnham. Moreover the meeting gave us both a chance to see once more many old friends and acquaintances."

Christmas Day

"We received the sad news that my old friend and mentor, Cyril Garnham, had died after a brief illness on Christmas Day."

1995

January—September

"The year started quietly with my attendance at a meeting of the Royal Society of Tropical Medicine at Northwick Park Institute of Medical Research, the center that was five years later to become the location for my laboratory. As usual, I went to Riyadh this time in mid-February to assist with the KFF Prize selection committee. March was memorable for my being asked to present a eulogy for Cyril Garnham. It was held in the ancient Church of St. Bartholomew, which stands just outside the main gates of the medical school of which both Cyril and I had been graduates. The Garnhams had a large family, including as one of his son-in-laws the priest who led the memorial service, and many were there. So too was an assembly of many of the great men and women of tropical medicine including several from France where Cyril had been much admired. Alain Chabaud, who was a special friend of Cyril, was represented by our colleague Irène Landau who had been one of Cyril's favorite students thirty years earlier. I spent many hours and consulted several of Cyril's old friends and students, drafted and redrafted the text, until both Ruth and I agreed that it would befit the great man. Finally, I asked his son-in-law to give my eulogy his blessing, which, thank God, he did.

"At the end of May, Ruth and I decided to drive to France in our new car, a very comfortable Toyota Camry, to visit several friends in Brittany. From the ferry we drove to St. Peran where we were invited to spend some time with Bill Bray and his wife Betty who lived in an old building that had once been something like a riding school. It was an interesting structure that fit the Brays who had always had a tendency to eccentricity in the nicest possible way. Betty unfortunately had a relatively serious stroke and was not able to indulge in the activities that she adored including gardening. Bill being the gourmet that he was we were overindulged with excellent food and drink but, alas, it was the last time we saw Betty. From the Brays, we drove to Rennes where we were invited to spend some time with a French parasitology professor called Jean Doby. He had been a great friend and admirer of Cyril. He and his wife offered us the hospitality of their spare house which was situated a couple of miles away from their main residence in St Peran and was where they stabled their horses, Jean being a very keen rider. Doby was an imposing figure with a remarkable resemblance to General Charles Degaulle for whom he was often mistaken. He and Madame Doby were also very generous hosts and insisted on taking us around Brittany where we saw for the first time such sights as the Mont-St-Michel (outside which we ate an over sufficiency of delicious Normandy oysters), the extraordinary megalithic circle of Carnac and the tapestries in the cathedral of Angers. Not least of interest were our visits to a selection of vineyards along the Rhone where we indulged in once-in-a-lifetime personally guided wine tastings. Luckily Michelle Doby who kindly resisted the beverages was an excellent driver and got us all safely back to the Doby residence, but not without a couple of cases of excellent white wine that would accompany us on our return journey home. To accompany them Doby presented us with a superb bottle of calvados that did not survive long in Little G.

"For the next few months we passed a remarkably sedate life, Ruth continuing to occupy herself with her increasingly ambitious embroidery and I with the study of antimalarials and the writing of papers for publication on our work. Only in June did I venture abroad once more, this time to Basle where we held a WHO meeting in the Swiss Tropical Institute. I recall two special features of that meeting. First it was the only one I have attended where one of the principal participants, Irwin Sherman, had to be addressed lying flat on his back on a desk—he had an acute attack of fibrositis but was not going to be put off participating in the proceedings. The second feature was a superb meal one evening, arranged by our hosts of the Institute, at an excellent restaurant just a few yards from the first home that Ruth and I had occupied when we originally went to live in Basle in 1960, thirty-five years before. Once again at the end of August we went up to Pontresina which had become our habitual holiday resort."

September 24th

"I am now aged seventy-one and a half, have been retired for just six years, have a new and very fast computer (at least compared with my first, CP/M-based Epson) and, give or take a few minor signs of aging, am in reasonably good physical shape. My PSA is only 1.6ng/l, even though I have to pee rather early in the morning. Part of the reason for continuing this saga is to help ensure that my mental faculties remain equally active!

"At about this time, the most recent edition, the fourth, of my *Colour Atlas of Tropical Medicine and Parasitology* should be appearing in the bookshops and, I hope, reviews. The problem now is that I am rather at a loose end for something substantial to write. ('Have computer—seek topic' syndrome).

"Ruth is just finishing doing her hair before we make lunch. Note the confident we. Our recent and, for a number of years, annual pilgrimage to Pontresina was marred this time by several factors. Firstly, a shortage of breath at nearly 2,000 meters due, in part at least, to increasing weight, severely limited both the speed and distance that Ruth could cope with, which left me, as usual, frustrated. Moreover, I never have had the courage to do the things I would have liked to do, such as going higher and walking along some of the high plateau trails to view the country around, the fauna and the flora. As it happens, an accumulation of minor irritations have put Ruth off the five-star Grand Hotel Kronenhof to which she no longer wishes to return. Since it has been costing us a small fortune to go there each year and we have not enjoyed it that much, this will be something of a relief for future vacations, except that we will now have to find out where else we can go—maybe Scotland in a B and B for a change! Why not, indeed?

"Hairdressing seems to be finished, so I will also close down for the time being.

"Mid-afternoon and have just finished mounting a small, metallic, delightful bas-relief over the sitting room fireplace. Ruth has one of her regressive, lazy moods where, on the excuse of feeling very cold, she has taken to her studio settee under a blanket with the electric fan heater full on. Far too hot for me in there, so I have had to leave her to it with a cup of tea. No doubt she will raise herself in time. The problem is that one never knows whether her moods are essentially due to boredom and a need to draw attention to herself, or whether she has some underlying problem, e.g., mild thyroid insufficiency, incipient congestive heart disease. Since she flatly refuses even to discuss the suggestion of having a thorough health check and loses her temper at the mere mention of it, there is little I can do to help her."

October 24th

"Today has been windy, with a mild easterly blowing birch seeds and small leaves about like snow, so a good moment to tidy the fish pond for winter and cover it before too many leaves pollute it. Sadly, a number of baby shubunkins are dying, whether from the fall in temperature, infection of some sort or just what I don't know. However, there are still about twenty around, some very tiny and others, especially the all-black ones, achieving about three to four centimeters in length. I hope both parents are well as I have not seen what we think is the male for a few days."

Mid-November

"In the event, in spite of my not attending the annual meeting of the ASTMH, I was made an Honorary Member of the Society for outstanding contributions to the field of tropical medicine. I regretted not having been there to collect the award, partly because I had never been to Texas and indeed have not been since.

"Now I intend to take a look at one of my encrypted files to see whether I should add some more diary notes to it. When I changed computers, I had a serious problem with the PC Tools program that I had used to encrypt it and, for a ghastly moment, feared that I might have lost all the files. However, I finally managed to sort out the problem. Showed how hazardous encryption can be."

In the end I found that I had copied very few of my handwritten notes on to the computer.

1996

"This year seems to have passed like a flash, the main events being summarized in notes for 1997. Once again, I went to Riyadh and in mid-April to Montpellier to sit on another PhD jury with Rioux. In June, I was in Paris probably for yet another thesis jury at the Museum. During the year I was also preoccupied with my role on the Universities Higher Education exercise. For this panels of academic experts sit in judgment on the research and teaching outputs of British universities in order to advise which most merit government support, not a comfortable task. In September, Ruth and I visited Glasgow where I attended a meeting of the British Society of Parasitology while she enjoyed her first visits to some of the excellent museums and art galleries of that city. We just managed to tolerate a society dinner where we were duly entertained in a traditional but deafening Scottish style. She also had the unforgettable experience of listening politely to an enthusiastic student thinking that he was talking in some little known, archaic European tongue. It was just broad Glaswegian. In the light of her experience at high altitude in 1995, for the first time in many years we did not go to Pontresina in September to celebrate Ruth's birthday but to Zurich at the end of the month. I always felt that an annual return to her homeland was the least compensation I could provide for her loyalty in accepting from me what must have been a trying and often lonely life. In the following sections I have filled in some of the other events of 1995 and 1996 as they were recorded during the following year."

1997

"Apart from a few brief visits to Switzerland to attend committee meetings of WHO and one that we made together to a meeting in Louvain and Herisau in May our lives were unusually tranquil until the autumn when I went to Hyderabad for an international gathering in commemoration of Manson's discovery that mosquitoes transmit malaria. As usual, our Indian hosts organized an excellent program that included a visit to Manson's old laboratory, but we ran into difficulties when the early onset of the monsoon disrupted nearly everybody's arrangements for returning home. Some of us in the English contingent managed to reach as far as New Delhi but from there back to Europe it was very hard to obtain a flight on any of the international airlines. The British Embassy doctor, whom I already knew, offered us his hospitality while we tried to sort ourselves out and fed us on pizzas brought in by a local home-delivery service, which I thought, was hilarious in such a city as Delhi. Geoff Targett, my successor at the LSHTM, was particularly anxious to return home as he was about to remarry, (having lost his wife some years earlier from illness), and still had to complete his and his fiancée's wedding arrangements. I was more fortunate in that I was able to obtain a seat on an American airline with the help of American Express although this meant that I had to invest in a new ticket. I was determined not to leave Ruth alone a day longer than necessary. Moreover, we had arranged to go to Italy at the end of August for Ruth's birthday. We were recommended a smallish hotel tucked away in a quiet corner of the coast just east of Naples. It proved to be a typical holiday place for many residents of that city.

The swimming and sun bathing were excellent provided one could put down a couple of mattresses early enough in the morning but the sound level in the evening was sometimes a bit hard to endure. From the hotel we arranged to visit Pompeii, which we had not seen before, and to visit much of the beautiful Amalfi coast to the east.

"The local hotel shop was by chance run by an English girl whom we had come to know. One morning as we were lying on the beach she came up to us looking very somber and broke the news that Diana, the unhappy Princess of Wales, and her Egyptian friend Dodi Al-Fayed had been killed in a car accident in one of the Parisian riverside tunnels. The tragic accident cast a remarkable shadow over everybody in the hotel of all nationalities, and numerous guests learning that we were English offered us their condolences. Most people there spent many hours watching the subsequent course of events on the television and we returned to an England over which a pall of sadness had spread. We were to have other reasons to grieve as the month of September wore on."

September 19th 1997

"Yes—amazing, but two years have gone by since I last added to these notes. A glance at my old daily diaries reminds me that the end of 1995 saw intensive negotiations going on with Pharma Mar to try to convince them to pursue work on B07. All to no avail. An option was taken on it by SmithKline Beecham who then put the compound on the shelf. However, they then decided to sponsor work at the IIP on some of their own compounds thanks to John Horton, an old sparring partner, but one of the last in the pharmaceutical industry to actively support research on tropical diseases. The end of 1995 and 1996 were punctuated by the deaths of neighbors and colleagues. Now we are faced with a death in the family with Aldo's diagnosis of pancreatic carcinoma. This has hit Ruth very hard because of her great fondness for Aldo's wife, her niece Marija.

"Several more cheerful things have happened since the end of 1995 however. First, we two seem to have achieved a reasonable balance in our own very long marital relationship. In fact only yesterday we celebrated our forty-third wedding anniversary with a lunch à deux at the King's Head—as Ruth said, a cod lunch! (But a very nice one). At the end of 1996, the fourth edition of *A Colour Atlas of Tropical Medicine and Parasitology* won the BMA prize for medical books. I have an embarrassing photo of Herbert and me receiving the certificate like two boys at the end of school term. Then earlier this year George Cowan nominated me for an Honorary Fellowship of the RSTM along with Herbert and Ralph Lainson, prior to George's retirement as President. I must admit that this sits well with the Le Prince Medal of the American Society that I received in 1994.

"In January 1995 and 1996 I paid what is becoming my annual visit to the King Faisal Foundation in Riyadh to select winners for the Prize. Each time I land up there during Ramadan, which is becoming a bit tedious but is not too distracting really. It is always nice to see my old students, Mohammed Al Zahrani and Majdi Al Tukhi again, although in 1997 I did not catch up with May Al Jassr.

"Having written two book chapters this year, one for *Advances in Parasitology* and the other on methods in malaria chemotherapy research, I am beginning to feel rather directionless and badly need another gripping topic on which to write. I really do not feel that there is the remotest interest in my writing anything autobiographical."

October 21st

"I was pleased to receive a letter from Professor Peter Smith who was then the Head of the reformed Department of Infectious and Tropical Diseases of the LSHTM, telling me that I was now an Emeritus Professor in the newly formed Unit of Pathogen Molecular Biology and Biochemistry, the head of which was one of my former junior lecturers, Professor Michael Miles."

December

"It had been several years since I had attended one of the ASTMH annual meetings and as I had been invited to give a lecture I agreed to go to the one held in Orlando, Florida early in December. Most participants stayed in Mickey Mouse land which was exactly what I had anticipated but nevertheless comfortable. The conference facilities were all one could wish for and I fortunately managed to avoid going to see Disneyland. Unfortunately, I did not find an opportunity to see the nature reserves in the Everglades. My journey home with Virgin Airlines was spectacular. My long-time friend Karl Rieckmann had been at the meeting and came to the hotel exit to bid me farewell while I was awaiting a taxi that the airline was sending to drive me to the airport. A white vehicle seemingly about 100 meters long appeared and the driver came over to greet me. The stretch limousine had no other passengers and I felt very vulnerable. Karl and I were equally impressed but I assured him that as this was my accustomed form of transport all would be well. Which it was. I arrived back in London safely, to find another taxi waiting to convey me back to my humble home in Little G. and Ruth, but it was only a five-seater."

1998
March 15th

"The pace of decay accelerates with age, and additions to these jottings have become rarer and shorter. Six months have passed since I last put fingers to computer keyboard, Christmas and New Year have come and gone, which was not the case for Riyadh. For some reason(s) of which I am unaware, my place was taken by a colleague, Martin Taylor, on the KFF Medicine Committee. I had mixed feelings about this, as well as curiosity to know what underlay the change. Since then we have narrowly missed being launched into another Gulf War, but the battle continues intermittently at home.

"It is obviously high time that both Ruth and I took up new tasks. Not long ago she succeeded in obtaining an award from the famous City and Guilds Institute in London for her embroidery, a remarkable achievement. However, since she completed her embroidery for an exhibition, theme Rouald Dahl, which is currently displayed at the Aylesbury museum, she has lost heart in this work and has a complete creative block. Unfortunately, I am going through a period of dullness and am in need of a new theme. Maybe the grey and excessively mild weather following a completely untypical winter with few really cold days has something to do with it. At least we have booked to spend a couple of days doing plays at Stratford-on-Avon, as well as a week in Madeira next month which Ruth says she is offering us for my forthcoming seventy-fourth birthday on All Fool's Day.

"I have now demolished all my travel notebooks and extracted a few notes, from which I hope to pick out some that are worth recording when the mood takes me. Now I will check my email (more in hope than expectation), then go down to watch the *Antiques Roadshow* which I generally find very boring."

April 28th

"As promised, Ruth arranged for us to spend a week in Madeira, an island that we had never seen. The plane had to land on a short runway suspended perilously over the sea, which did not appeal to either of us, but it was a clear day and we survived the ordeal. A car collected us and drove us up the hill away from the center of town to a reasonably good tourist hotel that was next to the historical Reed's hotel, the only one in which Teddy and Peggy Cusden would ever deign to stay. There a short time before the youngish second husband of a lady we knew from Little G. had succumbed to a sudden heart attack. Madeira, touristic as it may be, was an attractive island with superb flowers, a splendid orchid center and some hair-raising motor roads with magnificent views from the cliff-hugging coastal route. It was an enjoyable week but we did not feel that we had to make another visit. On departing we noted that the plane had to land on a nearby island to refuel before heading back to England as it was too dangerous to attempt a takeoff from such a short runway with a full load of passengers and fuel. Ruth never enjoyed flying and this time I could sympathize with her."

August 29th

"In retrospect we made an unwise decision to take our annual autumn holiday not in Pontresina but at a slightly lower altitude at the base of the Matterhorn in Zermatt which neither of us knew. From the window of our comfortable old hotel we enjoyed a superb view of the mountain and, of course, intended to take the local train line to the hotel yet higher up. It was while walking up there that Ruth realized how short of breath she was becoming. Only after we returned home did her GP find that she had a very elevated blood pressure for which she needed intensive treatment. For the next year or more, she underwent a series of trials of a wide range of antihypertensive drugs, most of which she tolerated badly until eventually, we found a regimen that gave her reasonable control of her blood pressure. Several of the compounds that she tried had severe psychological side effects that did not help the state of our general interactions and, in retrospect, I now see how badly she suffered during the following months. We decided that our stay in Zermatt would have to be the last time that we would holiday at such a height. In September, we ventured only as far as Bad Ragaz to celebrate Ruth's birthday at a very comfortable hotel with thermal baths, good food and easy but attractive scenic walks. We returned from Bad Ragaz via Geneva where I had to attend yet another WHO meeting before flying back home. From the lack of notes in what remains of my diaries, it would appear that the remainder of the year was fairly tranquil."

1999
January—August

"The first half of the year was a quiet one for us both apart from my having to attend other WHO meetings in Geneva in January, June, and July, as well as to sit on another PhD jury in Paris in April. Ruth attended several weekend courses at Missenden Abbey, which she always enjoyed, and I was busy trying to arrange laboratory accommodation so that I could continue to follow my research work on malaria. At this time, the urgent need to develop drug combinations was slowly being accepted and this was exactly the area on which my small team focused. I gave a lecture on one such combination of which one component was Charles Jefford's novel, artemisinin-like compound, at a meeting in May, but sadly this combination never reached an advanced trial."

September 20th

"During 1999 when we had enjoyed its hospitality for seven years a decision was made by CABI to close down the IIP premises adjacent to Winches Farm which had, by this time, been converted almost completely into a small housing estate. Once more Simon Townson and I were faced with locating a new home for our teams. At the suggestion of a young polyglot friend of mine, Georges Snounou (who was, incidentally, a link between me and our colleagues in Alain Chabaud's unit in Paris) I went to visit Geoffrey Pasvol who was the Professor of Tropical Medicine and head of the Lister Institute laboratories based near Harrow to the north of London.

"In addition to his medical unit which was part of the Imperial College—St. Mary's Hospital organization, he was also associated with the Northwick Park Institute of Medical Research (NPIMR), an independently funded unit with excellent laboratory, library, and other supporting facilities. The NPIMR was directed by Colin Green who was also a Professor of Veterinary Medicine in University

College, London. If we could pay our way, Colin was prepared to find accommodation for both Simon's and my teams. This was an extraordinary offer that we were both delighted to accept. Our sources of funds were rather shaky but we hoped that we could continue to attract international support from such organizations as WHO and its Tropical Disease Research Programme for the next few years at least. We gratefully accepted Colin's offer and, at the end of September, moved lock, stock and barrel from St. Albans to Harrow.

"Unfortunately not all our young technicians could join us in the move but we were lucky that some could. One of them was a tall, strong Glaswegian girl called Lindsay Stewart, and the other a young man, Andy Freeman, an expert animal caretaker who had been with us for several years and agreed to join Simon's team. Thanks to Geoff's reputation and recommendation, I was offered the title of Honorary Professorial Research Fellow in the Division of Medicine of Imperial College at Northwick Park from June 2000 with an honorary attachment to the North West London Hospitals NHS Trust at Northwick Park Hospital. I continued my laboratory research there for the next three years until 2003, when we finally transferred what was left of our activities and possessions to the LSHTM (see later). At the suggestion of Brian Robinson who had remained with me for better or for worse since he first joined my department in Liverpool in the 1960s, we called ourselves the Tropical Parasitic Diseases Unit then, later, the Centre for Tropical Antiprotozoal Chemotherapy (CTAC) to distinguish the work of our team from that of Simon. We continued our research there on behalf of WHO until 2002 when somewhat to my annoyance (but to Ruth's relief) the director of the antimalarial drug research program decided that I was getting too long in the tooth to receive his further support. My association with WHO in various capacities had lasted since 1953, but I never received as much as a 'Thank You' letter from anybody in that illustrious organization when I was finally discharged.

"In September we returned to Bad Ragatz for a second break there for Ruth, this time to celebrate her seventieth birthday. We returned home in time to commemorate our forty-fifth wedding anniversary together at the King's Head. At the end of October, Ruth and I flew again to Switzerland so that Ruth could attend another school reunion in Herisau to which I was also invited. It was almost the last one at which she was present. I still had one more journey to make to Paris shortly before Christmas."

2000

"In mid-January I flew to Brussels, but the reason for my journey there escapes my memory although I believe it was a final mission for WHO. I paid yet another visit to the KFF in Riyadh for their Prize committee in February returning for some reason via Zurich. On March 30th we set off on our first cruise (see next entry). From the time of our return sometime in May I have no notes or diaries to remind me of the course of events, until I recorded the following section."

October 3rd

"Two and a half years on since my last jottings and time for a cystoscopy, since I have now all but completed the Fifth edition of the *Colour Atlas of Tropical Medicine and Parasitology*. (This was the first edition for which I invited Geoff Pasvol to be my co-author, perhaps to Herbert's relief. It proved to be a good move.)

"Quite a lot has happened in the interim period, the main things being that Ruth and I are still together and most of the time closer than before and, second, that my laboratory has been relocated to the Northwick Park Institute for Medical Research where we have been installed for the past year.

"Funny that my last entry saw me going down to watch the *Antiques Roadshow*. It was on again yesterday evening.

"For the first time ever, we went on a cruise this spring to Jordan, Egypt, and Israel on the SS Minerva of the Swan Hellenic Line.

Would not have been bad except that Ruth developed a severe intestinal infection for which she refused to accept proper treatment. After our return home, I went down with acute prostatitis followed by spectacular reactions to ampicillin, then ciprofloxacin. Having now been going through a prostate assessment (PSA still normal) I go for a cystoscopy tomorrow and, later, a second ultrasound, to be followed most probably by a transurethral prostatectomy in a couple of months. This I am *not* looking forward to.

"I was stimulated to reopen this saga because I have been asked for some funny stories about my field experiences by Duane Gubler who is the incoming President of the American Society of Tropical Medicine and Hygiene. It was hard to think of any and even worse to try to write about them, so I consulted some of my earlier notes from Brazil. Now I am considering whether to write up any more old notes from the remains of my notebooks. Probably I am too lazy now to bother." (My Amazon notes here form the basis of Chapter 15, Visit to the Amazon.)

2001
January 21st
"Before Alzheimer's and anger set in, I feel a deep urge to set the record straight. If anybody is ever requested or, very unlikely, feels obliged to write my obituary, he or she would find little beyond the bare bones of WHO's WHO to guide them. It is only fair, then, that such a skeleton is fleshed out with some honest detail. A truly honest look at oneself is rare, as Burns noted;

'O wad some Pow'r the giftie gie us,

To see oursels as ithers see us!'

"I have tried to do this but, rather than producing an auto-biography, since most such works are an immense bore and unreadable, have decided to compose some biographical sketches. My life has, after all, been by no means a humdrum existence even if I have failed to take advantage of it as events would have merited."

(This was written long before I had come to the simple, but evident, conclusion that what I was really doing was writing an autobiography.)

March 28th

"After all, it seems that I will not need a prostatectomy, at least for the foreseeable future. It is coming up to my seventy-seventh birthday when we will, by chance, be spending a long weekend in Brussels. This is mainly to make a break for Ruth whose morale has not been the best in recent months. When we return, the page proofs of the Fifth edition of the *Atlas* should be waiting. It will be interesting to see how this edition compares with its predecessors.

"Since the last entry of these notes life has taken a sharp change of direction. I have felt obliged to agree with Ruth to cut back my attendance at Northwick Park to a level where I feel I can no longer justify calling myself the Head of anything. Negotiations are now under way for me to hand over the responsibility for the unit to Simon Croft whose group at the London School is thriving, especially now that the Gates Foundation has donated a huge sum to the school for malaria work. This seems to be the best solution to saving the integrity of the unit, which for various practical reasons I could not leave in the tender care of my long-time assistant, Brian.

"To compensate a bit I now have a new and faster computer, scanning equipment for slides and bigger objects, and a fax with a dedicated telephone line. However I now need a new and major project in order to make good use of these facilities."

2002
(Addendum November 1st)

Such writing inevitably gets put aside for unforeseeable periods. I note that the same theme of age and decay recently has brought itself to the forefront of my mind. Perhaps in a depressed moment a week or two ago I scribbled the following:

"What Ruth accuses me of is true. My memory is beginning to fade at the early age of seventy-eight. Well, to be honest, I have noted the signs for the past few years, losses of short-term memory, and erroneous actions such as making coffee in the machine without first putting water in the reservoir, and so on. Life has been generous with us. There have been so many interesting episodes in our modest lives that many would envy. So why not exercise what remains of my ability to recall the past as a means of stimulating whatever part of my cerebral cortex stores, or used to store memories of long ago or recent times as a means of delaying the inevitable decline of my thought processes. Logically I suppose one should start at the beginning and progress from there, but I prefer to look around me at the present and work backwards—more difficult in some ways since it is a curious fact that the oldest memories linger while the recent ones rapidly fade.

"It would be useful if we could consign unwanted or superfluous memories to the waste basket as one does with a computer, and then press the *Empty waste basket* button!

"Recently I received a reprint of a review on the contributions of biomedical engineering to medicine and surgery written by my American cousin, Hal. It is a well-researched, comprehensive, and interesting review. Hal was ninety last year, has had radical surgery for bowel cancer (ironically, his own surgical specialty) and is nearly blind. So perhaps there is hope for me yet, genetically speaking. After all, my father (his mother's brother) died in his 103rd year and my surviving sister is eighty-seven and pretty fit."

2003
July 11th

(Email circulated from Northwick Park. Simon Croft had been one of my best students at the LSTM in the 1980's.)

"Dear friends and colleagues,

"After many years of engaging in studies on the chemotherapy of malaria I have decided that the time is ripe for me to step down from active participation in laboratory research. The continuity of the team who worked loyally with me at this institute, some of them for many years, is I am pleased to inform you assured by a pending change of administration. From the end of this academic year CTAC will be integrated into the research group of my colleague, Professor Simon Croft, of the Department of Infectious Diseases, London School of Hygiene and Tropical Medicine. The CTAC team will continue to work in the present facility within the Northwick Park Institute of Medical Research under the directorship of Simon and the day-to-day management, for the time being, of Brian Robinson. The address and other contact details will remain unchanged.

"We all look forward with enthusiasm to the establishment of an enlarged chemotherapy group which will provide a unique center for the investigation of antiprotozoal chemotherapy in very well equipped laboratory and staff facilities in London and Harrow.

"I would like personally to express my thanks to all the friends and colleagues with whom we have collaborated over the years. It has been a great challenge but also a privilege on the part of the CTAC group and me to have been able to contribute to the development of novel antiprotozoal drugs and to explore the problems of drug resistance and its prevention. For some time I hope to retain contact with Simon and his group as an honorary consultant and I will, of course, be delighted to remain in contact with you if ever I can be of help."

September 30th

"Tomorrow is the day. Between this and my last journal entry, I have been giving thought to what parts of my life can now be disposed of, what must be disposed of and what I cannot live without. So far I have only decided on one immediate disposal, my collection of African butterflies. A few weeks ago I made contact, or so I believed, with a Mr. (or is he Dr.?) Phil Ackery who I believed is based at the Tring Museum, the offspring of Walter Rothschild's natural history collection. About fifty years ago I first made contact with the Tring Museum through Neville Bennett who was a lepidopterist specializing in lycaenid butterflies. Unfortunately, the world-class collection was transferred from Tring to the main Natural History Museum at South Kensington about thirty years ago and remains there to this day. My idea was that through Tring I would (a) ensure that my collection would be looked after as I believe it should be and (b) have a good excuse to visit Tring from time to time as it is only a few miles from here. Having received the agreement of Phil to accept the collection for Tring I realized a little late in the day that he is based in London where he is the Collections Manager, Department of Entomology, so next week he and a colleague will come here to transfer my modest collection to London. Still, I am glad it will have a good home. Yesterday I went through every case on my shelves and picked out over sixty containers that I would guess must together hold around 3,500 to 4,000 butterflies. Many of those are about fifty years old and I wonder now how I found the time and patience to set them, or at least about 90 percent of them. However, of course they were all from my tropical bachelor days. I have in my general collection also perhaps 800 to 1000 British and other European specimens, the oldest going back to my early WW II time as an evacuee billeted on a long-suffering but kind, simple family in Buckden, a few miles from Huntingdon. (One thought leads to another. The area around Buckden in the early 1940s was one that was rich in insect life. My evacuee days evoked other memories many, but not all pleasurable, a selection of which I have mentioned earlier.)

"Sorting letters and other never discarded papers, disposing of unwanted material, and transferring home from the laboratory at Northwick Park a selection of documents, books and other things that I simply cannot discard will take many visits, but they will take an indefinite period. My reasons are; (1) Ruth's determination to cut my umbilical laboratory cord, and (2) my belief that one must not breathe down your successor's back. To be honest, I was never a good administrator nor did I enjoy a position of power. What appealed to me, as far as practical, was to be my own boss. (I refer to work, not domestic matters that are based on more complex and subtle arrangements in life!). I have no doubt that much needs improvement in the working of my old team. From what I have seen of how he works, I expect that Simon will make many changes in the coming weeks. I certainly hope for the better.

"However, I have given little thought as to what else I cannot live without and how I am going to fill the void between my 'work' and my domestic, everyday life. The satisfactory disposal of over sixty cases of insects will restore shelf space for more general use—storing my postage stamp collection perhaps.

"I don't believe I have broached this topic before; but it is something that may be worth enlarging on at another date? I have already strayed somewhat from my initial theme. Not long ago, I received a photograph from a long lost cousin in California. It showed both of us as small children. It reminded me of parts of my life long before WW II, so perhaps I will also add some early reminiscences—but then, perhaps not!"

2003–2006

"In a strange way the years between 2003 and 2006 have slipped below my radar. Even worse, I failed to retain daily diaries that made passing mention of where we were and what we did during that period, nor did I make computer entries. They may have been ones that I discarded long ago and in files with no readable backups. We continued living in Little G. but leaving my laboratory in Northwick Park in 2003 was a cultural shock. How did we occupy ourselves during those three years?

"I finally recalled events of 2004 that had evaded my memory when I initially wrote of this period. During the year we decided to mark our golden wedding that was on September 18th by going on a Swan Hellenic cruise to the Mediterranean that month. As we only landed in European countries there no stamps to mark the occasion in our passports. We did not announce the event but invited some passengers we befriended on board to join us for champagne and nibbles on the great evening without offering any special reason. Only when hard pressed did we admit our guilty secret.

"It was indeed a strange period in our lives.

"Five years later, on 11th December 2005 at 6.00 in the morning we were awoken by an enormous bang, accompanied by the whole house shaking. From the bedroom window we saw flames hundreds of feet high, vast clouds of smoke rising over the fields, accompanied by further bangs shooting yet more flames and smoke into the air. The window gave an uninterrupted view across open fields that sloped gently down towards the northern suburbs of Hemel Hempstead, less than ten kilometers to the southeast. At first I thought this terrifying sight was the product of a major terrorist action, and then realized that a fuel depot lay in that direction. On the television I learned that the Hertfordshire Oil Storage Terminal at Buncefield, the fifth largest in the UK holding sixty million gallons of inflammable fuel, had mysteriously exploded. Unbelievably, nobody was killed and few were injured. The explosion caused an earth tremor that recorded two point four on the Richter scale. No wonder we woke up and even luckier that there was no damage to our house.

"The emotional turmoil we both went through in the first years following my retirement reflected earlier in this chapter slowly subsided. It was replaced, to a degree, by accepting the deep need we felt for each other. Ruth continued to devote energy to creating embroideries, full of color and fantasy. I spent long periods at my computer following the current literature and preparing the draft of yet another edition of our *Atlas*. (This sixth edition, was published at the end of 2006 and awarded two prizes in 2007; one in the Medical

Book Competition of the British Medical Association - our 4th edition received one of these awards in 1996 -, and the second from the Society of Authors and Royal Society of Medicine.) The absence of stamps in my passport between 2003 and November 2005 when it expired implies any journeys we made were within Europe where British passports are not marked. In my recent passport, a small collection of date stamps were inserted during a cruise we made round the Mediterranean and the Black Sea in August 2005. I am sure we crossed the Channel a few times to visit Switzerland but have no clear memories of when. Life was becoming quite sedate. With effort I recall some highlights of that last cruise, but we took few photos to remind us of people or places and this is not the place to indulge in a banal history.

"Sadly, during 2006, Ruth became unwell. However, by the end of the year her condition seemed to be improved. In retrospect, I admit that we were both suddenly getting older, maybe even old. But at least we were not alone.

PART V

Chapter 21

The Departure 2007

This book originally started as a series of reflections or *Conversations With Myself*. Subsequently it took on a life of its own and expanded in a retrospective direction to incorporate fragments of my early memories and a few outstanding events that were recorded, subconsciously and sometimes in writing—hence the possible appearance in this chapter of a few duplications and perhaps some contradictions. This is how life was and remains. The memories of some of our experiences stay near the surface; others sink deep into our neurons or mysteriously vanish. As I grow older, in place of broad mental pictures of our past life and adventures, my attention and writing increasingly focus on mundane daily events. This radical change of outlook and time frame are reflected in these pages. The trivia of daily living take on a magnified importance and one becomes increasingly self-centered and introspective.

To return to the major events, on the night of December 15, 2007 my life changed irrevocably. The sense of solitude that immersed me from early childhood until my marriage returned overnight. Then from June 10th the following year, my life's tempo suddenly slowed dramatically. I sank into a state of limbo that required several months to overcome.

Here are the events that brought these changes.

For some months from mid-2006, Ruth suffered from increasing back pain. Examination by her GP failed to reveal any specific cause for this and she prescribed simple analgesics. However, these did little. Her GP referred her to a rheumatologist but he was unavailable. She was eventually seen by an old colleague, Robert Davidson, at Northwick Park Hospital, the location of my last research unit. Rob made an instantaneous diagnosis of polymyalgia rheumatica, a chronic condition of unknown etiology that is very common in older women and to a lesser degree, in men. He started her on the classical course of high-dose steroid therapy that evening. Although she made progress that was quite spectacular and continued to improve almost to the end of 2006, it was impossible to reduce her steroid dose sufficiently.

Meanwhile we made the decision to leave our Pulridge House East home that sheltered us for the past twenty-eight years. We sought a simpler place to live that would be easier to manage. Ruth had her eye on a newish residential center for elderly people named Castle Village. It stood on top of Berkhamsted Hill, only three miles from Little G. The main administration building, now known as The Mansion, is a majestic block constructed during 1905 and 1906 as a private home for Sir John Evans of the Dickinson paper clan. Sir Richard Ashmole Cooper bought it in 1937. His family established a pioneering company that produced pesticides in Berkhamsted during the mid-nineteenth century. In 1947, the Coopers converted the building to a research bureau. In 1953, they moved their field research station for veterinary medicine and pesticides from Home Farm, next door to our house in Little G., to the large site that was once more known as Berkhamsted Hill. In 1999, it was sold to a retirement home development company. Over the following years, the research laboratories were replaced by attractive bungalows and blocks of flats.

During the autumn of 2006, a pleasantly warm dry one, Ruth and

I passed hour after hour playing Scrabble at a table under our silver birch trees in the garden, while estate agent representatives showed endless viewers our home, much to our discomfort. We, in turn, inspected potential properties in Castle Village. A major consideration for Ruth then, and fortuitously for me later, was the need to find a home on a single floor so she was spared having to climb stairs. It was against my personal wishes at the time, as I could not envisage being surrounded by a large number of old pensioners. I was soon brought down to earth by Ruth who correctly reminded me that I was an 'old person.' This move proved to be a blessing in disguise because first, we were old pensioners and second, the Castle Village community proved to be extremely supportive and young at heart.

We viewed several bungalows but none attracted us. One day our attention was drawn to a first-floor apartment in The Mansion that was currently occupied by a widower whom we knew when he resided in Little G. Peter was not well and considering moving to a care home. We let him know that we were interested in his apartment should he decide to move. Sadly, Peter died at the end of 2006 but not before giving us his blessing as the new owners. With good fortune, we sold Pulridge House East to an exceptionally agreeable, youngish couple and arranged our move during the coming spring of 2007 provided we could complete negotiations for each property in time. Ruth was very happy at the prospect of making our new home in Number two, The Mansion. I was less enamored at the prospect of living in a flat in a center for old people.

The move took place on April 5, 2007 at the eleventh hour. That was a mini-saga in itself. A technical hitch in the banking arrangements left our buyers and us sitting outside each other's new homes awaiting the formal exchange of keys, while the moving vans holding our possessions lined up outside. From late morning until late afternoon we killed time impatiently. Just when the movers were preparing to up anchors and depart with our goods and chattels, the word came through via telephone at each end and said, "Go!" Fortunately, I had the foresight to arrange our use of one of the guest rooms in The Mansion. This let Ruth pass the night in peace. I wanted to protect her from the further stress of our move, not foreseeing for a moment how traumatic that would be.

A tragic irony is that by the time we moved Ruth's condition was deteriorating. She was never able fully to benefit from her new environment or the amazingly supportive community of some 200 residents, most of our vintage, who surrounded us. That spring and summer, we walked slowly in the beautifully maintained gardens, sat by the fishpond with its enormous Koi carp and chatted with other folk on the terrace below our windows, which offer a magnificent view over the gardens. On the day of our arrival, we lunched in the restaurant, but never again as Ruth felt too unwell to make the effort to socialize. From then on, without recognizing my role change, I became Ruth's carer and served in this role until the end. On fine days, for a change of scenery, I would drive her out to sit in the car park overlooking Dunstable Downs and the Whipsnade lion carved onto the hillside. On occasion, she would accompany me when I shopped in Berkhamsted. She waited patiently in the car park while I fussed about inside trying to think what might tempt her declining appetite.

By Christmas 2006, Ruth became very unwell. Her response to steroid was failing. Rob referred her back to her GP to consult a specialist rheumatologist. She did that at the beginning of 2007. Unfortunately, he turned out to be incompetent. He prescribed an immunosuppressive that interacted with another compound that Ruth took as a prophylactic against chronic gout for years. The net result was that she became acutely anemic with an extreme fall in her red and white blood cells so that she had to have a large transfusion. She changed to another, younger rheumatologist who initiated a series of further examinations including a CT scan and bone marrow biopsy to look for possible unrecognized causes of the steroid failure and elevated inflammation markers. He prescribed a succession of alternative immunosuppressant drugs, none of which yielded any improvement. She had further scans, including one with radioactive fluorine at Mount Vernon hospital, and blood checks, but no specific pathology was revealed. Meanwhile she gained weight, partly from the cumulative action of the immuno-suppressants, and her back pains increased in severity.

Suddenly, early in October 2007, she developed an excruciating pain in her *right* pelvic area. On October 16th, she was admitted as an emergency case to the West Herts hospital where she had a further blood transfusion and another CT scan two days later. This time a solid mass was detected behind her *left* femur and small shadows were seen on her liver and lung. Their significance at that point was indeterminate. Ruth was referred to an orthopedic surgeon at the Royal National Orthopedic Hospital in Stanmore where a biopsy was taken on October 29th. The pathology report on November 5th revealed the presence of a poorly differentiated liposarcoma in her left thigh, a very malignant type of cancer. She was seen first in London on November 9th. Within a few days, she was returned to Stanmore where the surgeon removed a massive tumor on November 14th. She was scheduled to follow up the operation with a prolonged course of radiotherapy at Mount Vernon in December and returned meanwhile to the West Herts hospital on November 24th, paradoxically with the operation site well healed.

Ruth's last weeks were marked by continuous and severe pain in her right hip for which no cause was found. However, a new CT scan made it clear that she had secondary tumors in her liver and lung. A conference took place between the oncologists from Mount Vernon and physicians at Hemel. I was shown the scans and gently advised by a young woman oncologist, on December 10th, that Ruth would not benefit from, or even be able to tolerate, the course of radiotherapy planned to start in December (as I had already feared). With my agreement, the same doctor broke the news gently to Ruth.

From then on, she lost her will to live. I tried desperately to help her keep going, to feed her, assist her with basic hygiene, and encourage her in any way I could. Friends and neighbors kindly came and joined me in my vigil while she was given increasingly potent analgesics in ever-larger doses. On December 12th, Ruth was admitted into the gentle and expert care of the staff at the Hospice of St. Francis in nearby Berkhamsted.

December 15, 2007

Just after 9:30 p.m. after a long painful illness, finally freed of pain Ruth died at the age of seventy-eight. At that moment, I became an old man. My good friend and neighbor, David Grigsby, joined me that night. We went together to say goodbye to my loved one. She looked very peaceful at last.

A few hours after Ruth died I finally went to bed, exhausted, and slept. About three hours later, around 4:00 a.m., I awoke, turned on my table lamp, and picked up a pen and paper. The following words flowed from my heart. I hardly ever read a poem before, much less composed one. In the morning, I changed about two words. This is what I wrote:

"The Departure

In the quiet night my darling Ruth
slipped silently away, so tranquilly, so calmly.
Next to her bed in my armchair, restless, unable to sleep,
I felt a coolness in the air, listened
for her quiet, rapid breathing.
A silence penetrated my consciousness.
I stood up and went to her side.
In the dim light of the hospice, in her bed she lay still,
her lips pale, her skin like the smoothest alabaster,
her beauty surpassing the finest of statues.
Her eyes no longer were aware, but peacefully closed,

her veiled gaze looking down.
Through her softly closed lips no breath passed;
her pulse was silent.
I kissed her darling, tender brow and wept my goodbye
in the so peaceful room. My tears fell down our faces as I
bade adieu to the love of my life, my Ruth.
I said 'Thank you God, for lending her to me all these years
and now taking her back to you so gently.'
At a half past nine of a cold, mid-December evening, my darling
passed softly from this world into the silent night."

"My Love, it was not you who disappeared behind that curtain in the crematorium this Christmas eve. It was only your shadow. Every year at this time you and I would sit down with a glass of champagne, candles on the table, and presents waiting to be unwrapped. You would serve the blinis you prepared beforehand; we would add smoked salmon, soured cream and mock caviar and wish each other 'Happy Christmas, my Love'. Tonight you are gone. With a few kind friends, I half heard the lady vicar recite prayers to bid you farewell, to thank God for your life, to comfort those who mourn you. We said the *Lord's Prayer*, sang a last hymn for you, the words barely passing my lips. My shoulders shook as I fought to hold back my tears and remain on my feet.

"We filed out of the crematorium. I did not know what to do but thanked the vicar and moved down to the flowers brought by our friends. Then a 'Thank you' to them, an embrace, and away. It was all unreal. I felt emptiness and heartbreak. Our friends departed to their families, their Christmas carols, and their lives. Soon we will meet them again when we celebrate your life. I will exchange the black tie that David lent me, for the bright Gucci tie that you so liked, and try to smile again. But I will never love again."

It was very cold that night.

On Christmas morning it rained.

That afternoon Ruth's niece Eliane phoned from Bern. She and her dogs were lonely, poor woman. I remembered her sitting on my lap when she was a small girl in Geneva. Now she was sixty.

My neighbors Joyce and David Grigsby, both of whom I barely met before the last few weeks, dropped in that evening bearing a tray of supper for me, then returned for an hour's chat. What a fabulously kind couple they are. David has been a pillar of strength since Ruth became gravely ill and was with me when I parted from her. Without his support, I would have been totally lost. I never knew that people could be so kind.

December 26 was Boxing Day. Notices had to be prepared for the newspapers, the first of formal letters drafted to start settling some of Ruth's affairs. I had to force myself to do these things.

Pat and Ian Catchpole and David and Joyce came round in the evening of the following Saturday. We discussed details of the memorial service that we would hold for Ruth on January 11th. We decided with David's help to move from the church to the Golf Club for the wake. He and Joyce invited me there for lunch Sunday but I was not ready to face people yet. They still brought me supper every evening, guessing that I might not bother to eat otherwise. They were probably right.

"It is Sunday December 30, two weeks since you left me and I could weep all day my Love."

I walked to the fishpond, very unsteadily, but could not stay there.

Could not remember what I did on New Year's eve but, at a quarter to midnight I asked myself, "How could I have known how to help you? If I had not been so blinkered in my narrow line of research, would I have known that something I had worked with against malaria for nearly thirty years, artemisinin, might have helped to stop your cancer—or was it sheer exhaustion and pain that made you give up after suffering so long and so much?

"Can I really find the desire to go on without you when the future looks so meaningless?"

Chapter 22

Filling the Void 2008

"This was the first Saturday of 2008. At nine fifteen at night, in bed, three weeks less fifteen minutes before you left this world, I lay and thought of you. I wanted my eyes to pour with tears. Only a few fell and dampened the pillow before I dozed. I woke up time and again in the empty night; still could not cry as I wanted to do. Airplane lights and the space station passed across my vision through the bedroom window in the clear, cold night."

"A brilliant, sunny wintry Sunday morning and all I want to do is see you walk in a door, hear your voice, touch you—and now my eyes fill with tears again and again. I cannot believe that you have gone forever. I look through photo albums and see snapshots of our life together. How ungrateful I was for all you did for me, your tolerance, your kindness, your love. How little I deserved you and how badly I sometimes treated you, how selfish. The day before you left me, when you were barely conscious but at last finally without pain, I stroked your hand and said, 'Here I am my Love.' I saw a flicker of your eyelids and a trace of a smile. Did you feel me after that when I kissed you with all the tenderness in my breaking heart?"

"I watched a replay that evening of the unforgettably joyful concert by the Simon Bolivar Youth Orchestra of Venezuela. It was the last concert that Ruth and I saw of the 2007 Proms on the TV and one of the very last things that we enjoyed together. It left me in tears."

On Friday January 11th, we held a Memorial Service for Ruth at Little Gaddesden Church. I could not write anything then or for some weeks later. Over seventy people came to the church including old friends and colleagues from Liverpool. As the congregation arrived, we played part of the *Fourth Movement*, the heart-rending *Adagietto of the Symphony No. 5* of Gustav Mahler whose music Ruth so loved.

At the start of these memoirs in Chapter 1, I included part of a eulogy I wrote for Ruth. Our old friend Jeff Fryer read it at the beginning of the service. The essentials are in Chapter 8.

Following the first hymn, we heard a piece to remind us of the theme of the last creation on which Ruth was working, but alas, never completed. It was the humorous Mahler song about Saint Anthony preaching to the fishes. Following it was this tribute written and presented by her friend and mentor, Alison Shreeve.

"Before she became ill Ruth was working on a large wall hanging decorated with fish. She probably had in mind the words of the song we have just heard. It was these kinds of things that inspired her embroideries, images of the natural world around her, and the subtle ironies of life. Her embroideries are distinctive for their particular vision and approach to life; a gentle humor and a quirky vision.

"In fact I met Ruth's work before I met her. She was a somewhat reluctant candidate for a City and Guilds exam in Creative Embroidery and I was acting as the external examiner. I say reluctant because I did not think Ruth really needed certificates and pieces of paper to validate her interest and her expertise in this area. I think she went to classes to meet other people with similar interests and to learn new things; the examination may have been an unnecessary extra, but an achievement all the same! The piece I particularly remember from this first encounter was brought to my attention by her tutor. It was an indigo dyed, small piece, hand stitched and figurative. There were trees, and ducks featured on a lake. What struck me was the very distinct quality of the embroidery; it was very different to the standard, rather abstract work of most students at that time. Here was an individual voice with an assured, but unassuming handwriting. As I got to know Ruth herself through classes at Missenden Abbey, where a group of us met up to explore embroidery and textiles, I realized that she brought to her work a very distinctive character, one that she would perhaps have been too modest to recognize. She was true to her vision for each piece, no matter how small. If something wasn't right she would not be content until it was all resolved and worked as she intended it to. She wasn't afraid to tackle larger projects or to try something new and different. In her hands, pieces lovingly came to life, imbued with her own gentle sense of humor, a lively but controlled sense of color and pattern and woven throughout with subtle meanings and significance.

"Her appreciation of textiles extended to a wide range of eclectic objects from all corners of the world and from traditional cultures to modern times. She valued the workmanship and the design whether produced with the latest technologies or evidencing the most ancient and disappearing traditional techniques. When we met at Ruth's to organize work for group exhibitions, as avid embroiderers we could be assured of excellent food for the mind and the spirit as well as the body. We would discuss new acquisitions as much as progress and work in hand. These sessions were hosted by Ruth with the generosity she always showed and were occasions where our collective obsessions were fully indulged. We sometimes stitched or shared new techniques in her workroom, but more often than not chatted and laughed, caught up with the news and feasted on embroidery in every sense.

"Embroidery was central for Ruth. She stitched for love and for those she loved. There was nothing grand about her attitude to her work; it was just a wonderful necessity to express her creativity in this way. Many people benefited from her generosity as well. She hated to sell her work and would rather give it away. This church, as well as many of her friends, has examples of her work and they will be treasured for their singular vision. Her embroidery encapsulates her qualities; they are modest, humorous and gentle; skilled creative pieces made with a vision unique to Ruth herself."

It would have been impossible for me to read my poem for Ruth, *The Departure*, but our friend Anthony Bryceson kindly agreed to read it for me. Finally, at the conclusion of the service we played the uplifting *Finale from Mahler's Symphony Number two in C Minor*, The *Resurrection* as the congregation left the church. If Ruth was listening, I think she would approve our choice.

"The next Friday was five weeks after Ruth, for the last time, went to sleep. That afternoon I had a filling replaced in my tooth. Returning from the dentist to pick up my car, really our car but she never got to drive it, and drive home, I bumped into the young, blond South African physiotherapist who had treated Ruth in the West Herts hospital. She had been surprisingly insensitive to Ruth's difficulties. "

"How's Ruth?" she asked.

"Sorry to say she died on December 15th."

"Oh, I'm so sorry."

"Do you live here?"

"No, in Northchurch. It's my day off. My little boy is sick."

"Sorry, I won't hold you up."

"Take care," patting me on the shoulder.

Dummkopf!

Joyce, David, and then our Swiss friend Eva called before supper. Eva brought photos of church, flowers, and cemetery. She will go to Switzerland next week and will phone Ruth's niece Margrit in Herisau to explain what is happening.

I had a Swiss-made cervelas sausage for supper that we bought from a Scottish butcher months ago to enjoy together. It's not quite right with just a tin of warmed-up beans.

Ruth's Swiss passport was lost in the Christmas mail in spite of being sent Recorded Delivery. I phoned the embassy to cancel the passport. However, the letter also had a copy of her death certificate that I did not wish anybody else to get hold of for any purpose whatsoever. The same day I received my invalidity car permit with no fuss and returned Ruth's.

I felt very lonely tonight.

"Must do crossword, as I did so many times sitting by Ruth's bedside.

"I still don't know if I want to go on. I hear Ruth's voice every time I see her photo. I'll have a brandy and an early night; heavy rain outside, heavy heart inside. "

I had to get an ingrown toenail dealt with by our chiropodist Helen the following Monday morning. Our solicitor Nigel was to call on me in the evening to talk about sorting out Ruth's affairs.

"We kept space for two caskets of ashes."

On the Classic FM radio station they played the *Adagietto* from Mahler's 5th Symphony—wouldn't they!

That weekend a letter arrived from Ruth's niece Eliane who enclosed two old black and white family photos of Ruth, Marianne, Eliane, and Margrit. They were taken about 1952 when Ruth would have been twenty-three, about the time we first met. Another was of Ruth's mother and father, Marianne, Eliane, and Ruth taken a year earlier. I scanned and enlarged them.

"In about one hour from now, Ruth took her last breath five weeks ago.

"I cannot remember how it was that David came to the hospice. Maybe I called him on my mobile. I don't remember, but he was there. I asked him if he would come with me to say goodbye to Ruth. He did and he gave me strength. He drove me back to what was for a very short time, our home. Our car stayed at the hospice that night keeping vigil for me.

That dreadful night I went to bed, slept an hour or two. I awoke, got up, and turned on the light. I wrote what was in my head, corrected a word or two, and went back to bed. I wept again and slept. I don't know for how long.

"The next day was a world apart, unknown, black and empty."

I wrote these words five weeks later. Nothing had changed. People were very kind; letters were written and received, phone calls were made and emails exchanged. Services were carried out and condolences were sent. Now Ruth's ashes are buried forever in the corner of a field at the edge of the graveyard, waiting for a post to mark them and a stone to be set. Our good friends Pat and Ian Catchpole planted daffodils to keep Ruth company. I cannot go there to weep by her side yet. Through health and sickness, Ruth was the meaning in my life. Now it is empty. I make myself eat as everybody tells me I must do. Why the emphasis on eating? I drink little now. That used to be in case I suddenly had to drive to be by Ruth's side at one hospital or another. Now it is because drinking would serve no purpose and certainly give no pleasure or relief. The emotion is far too deep for that.

"I play classic FM on the radio and rarely look at television apart from the news. I listen to sensible, and usually rather somber music, but it is more or less soothes me in my present state of mind. I turn on the computer first thing each morning. Sometimes an email from a friend or my sister Ronnie helps a bit, but the mornings are especially hard. I rarely shave without shedding tears. I cannot bring myself yet to return to our big bed. Instead, I sleep on the uncomfortable bed in my study. I would ask a young neighbor, 'Handy Guy', to put up the mirrors in the big bedroom, but cannot bring myself to change anything yet.

"People will want to visit and to invite me here and there. Our old friend Herbert spent the night of the Memorial Service with me. His daughter Marija in Australia sent me an email recalling how kind her 'Aunt Ruth' was to her in her young days. She is now about sixty. I asked one or two colleagues to visit me but hope they do not come too soon—I am not yet stable enough, either mentally or physically.

"I will have a final drink, and then go to bed and think of our last time together five weeks ago.

"Today is Monday January 21st. One hundred and ten days ago Ruth went into hospital, never to return home.

"The following week I went to see my GP, Lesley Hallan and had my first general examination in twenty years. Net result; come back Monday to give buckets of blood for umpteen tests, to try to find out why I am so thin and have so much muscle stiffness in my legs. I also need X-rays. All that for starters and then we'll see where we go next.

"The next day I finished writing 'Thank You' letters to kind friends who wrote to me and to others who sent End-Of-Year greetings cards but didn't know that Ruth was gone. I probably sent eighty letters in all, but cheated a bit on the computer to save writing the same thing time and again.

"As most evenings, David and Joyce dropped in and shared a glass and chat, before returning with fruit salad to keep me healthy. I never encountered such a genuinely kind couple. I wish we had seen more of them while Ruth was still with us. David was with me when I said my last farewell to Ruth and at both ceremonies afterwards. I asked him how it was that he appeared at the hospice to drive me home the night Ruth died."

My mind was completely blank on this point. He told me I called him at about 10:00 p.m.

"Yesterday it was six weeks since Ruth departed.

"I needed to finish some fruit this morning so put washing into machine while I ate breakfast. Afterwards I looked in the drawers of Ruth's dressing table and took out half a dozen small hairbrushes. Decided to wash them, but removing trapped hairs was painful—

she lost so many while she was ill. I made coffee and read yesterday's paper, but felt the need to move as my legs are so stiff that I can barely bend them enough to walk up a step. The sun shone, so I went out at midday and sat by the carp pond where Ruth and I used to sit, and cried. Returned to be greeted by David who delivered a bottle of sherry and two glasses to the flat. The marvelous man must have extremely sensitive antennae. Sat and chatted about old times and people, sailing at Herne Bay, trout fishing in the River Gade, and other past events. How could he know that I was suddenly feeling so low?

"I decided I was not hungry but would have a cup of soup and an apple.

"There's a coincidence! Sometime last summer Bernard Peters, an elderly man, moved into Castle Village. He is a very sad widower who David tells me, lost his wife not long before he came here. I learned from Val, the senior nurse, that his son David's wife Pauline is the younger daughter of Gerald and Brenda Siegler who lived opposite us during our thirteen years in Liverpool! He was an ENT surgeon there. Pauline and David live in Amersham, not far from Castle Village—closing a circle of coincidence. What a small world!

"Today Pat and I will go to plant a temporary cross in the cemetery. I have to decide soon on the format of the permanent stone and the wording.

"February has started with a bright but very chilly winter's day with bad weather forecast so I managed a walk round the main garden at midday while it was still dry. In addition to having very cramped leg muscles, I suffer a lot of dizziness and find walking up three steps from the garden to the terrace difficult. Spent time in the afternoon sorting papers for Ruth's affairs and getting rid of unwanted paper. There is still no news of her missing Swiss passport.

"I make myself eat, but have no appetite and keep it simple. I bought in a few things I thought I would like, but cannot be bothered to take them out of the freezer and heat them in the oven.

I eat fruit and take in liquids, but light on alcohol. I have a glass or two of wine, usually with David and Joyce in the evening. One of their sons, Sam, who is staying with them, comes on occasion.

"Half a hundred nights since my darling passed away after more than 19,000 nights married.

"Restless day today, the first Sunday in February. Ronnie phoned in morning. She will visit her donkey sanctuary in Devon in May, and then come here afterwards. David, Joyce, and bottle of sherry plus Japanese nibbles arrived before lunch. We were later joined by their son Sam, a very likeable man.

"I force myself to behave quietly and rationally all day. Had a simple lunch of fruit and soup, checked email and at last found one from our old friends, the Rieckmanns, then read papers. Losing appetite more and more, but will make lentils and Swiss sausages tonight. The Rieckmanns just returned from a vacation in New Zealand, hence no response from them earlier about Ruth. They invited me to meet them somewhere in Europe or visit them; or go to New Zealand with them. Karl comments on excitement at ASTMH meeting in Philadelphia about malaria eradication! Quite rightly, Karl sounds skeptical about it all.

"Weekends are especially bad for me. I just printed another photo of Ruth, this one at 1983 party for the Catchpoles to celebrate George's completion of the annex he constructed for us in the old house. I put it near computer to add to my favorite of Ruth in a red dress. I could weep every time I pass that photo that was printed in black and white on the cover of the memorial service sheet. I like to have her with me so we could talk.

Pat Crowhurst from Little Gaddesden will bring her neighbor Rosemary Williams, Owen's widow, for coffee on Wednesday morning. That afternoon, I will have X-rays taken in the West Herts hospital, one floor down from where Ruth was. I arranged for David Warhurst and his dog Rhum to have lunch with me in Number two February 17th. He seems to be recovering well from his wife

Rosemary's death with help from his family. She died about a month before Ruth.

"It is already mid-February and the days slip by, but I have really accomplished nothing. Yesterday, I tussled with making backups of various files and concluded that my computer D drive was recording but not reading. Got the problem solved miraculously online by the efforts of two Dell technicians somewhere in India. They opened my PC and downloaded upgrades or something—all under warranty so I did not have to pay a service charge. Today I updated my subscription to McAfee security program for another year.

"I invited my neighbor Dorothea, whom we knew from our early days in Little G., for coffee tomorrow afternoon. I failed to make contact several times over the last few days. David Warhurst and Rhum will join me for lunch on Sunday. I must defrost things tomorrow.

"Recently I skipped through my old encrypted files and will make an effort to sort out the contents one day. I have not found my new path in life but I suppose it is early. Anita and David Molyneux sent me some more photos they took in Pulridge House East two years ago. There is one of Ruth with David and me and the shot of Ruth is delightful, so I selected and enlarged that bit. Now it sits on the sideboard in the study so I can greet her when I pass. I seem to hear her greet me back and it brings tears to my eyes every time, even as I write this.

"My hands as well as legs are getting very stiff and I am beginning to get trigger fingers on each side. I'm still waiting for results of X-rays of back and pelvis, but do not expect they will help much, certainly not with hand problems.

"The sun just came out, so I will do my walk round the garden before lunch, but have little appetite these days.

"It has been a strange weekend. The weather has been superb since Saturday, starting each morning with a heavy overnight frost followed by brilliant warm sunshine. Saturday, just before lunch,

Nurse Melanie brought up a man of about my vintage to introduce to me. She felt we might have a lot in common and she was right. Oliver turns out to be another tropical doctor, a man who qualified about the same time as me, spent some time in West Africa, and then returned to study for the DTM&H in the London School one year after me. We had a short chat. I invited him to come over with his wife for a drink and more chat in the near future.

"Dorothea, who is an artist, came across for coffee and cake on Saturday afternoon. She is a strong, no-nonsense personality who is interesting to talk to. She showed a special interest in, and appreciation of Ruth's talents, as indeed she should! I did not get around to asking her advice on where to hang which pictures—they are all still sitting up in the passage, faces to the walls—but she did suggest hanging the scrolls along the passage itself. I may well do that in time.

"On Sunday morning, David Warhurst arrived with Rhum and a bag of old newspaper to clean up after her as required. That's very thoughtful of him—I believe this is what one is supposed to do when walking a dog these days! We had a pleasant and relaxed, if emotional, day and the three of us shared lunch. In spite of my prior misgivings, it turned out not too bad. Talk turned to our late wives. We expended many words discussing old colleagues, the condition of the malaria world, the London School from which David just retired from his Chair in my former department, and other memories. He first joined me in Liverpool in 1968, quitting his post with Frank Hawking at the National Institute for Medical Research in Mill Hill, to do so. Later he moved to London. A few years later, he worked with me again when I moved there to take up the Chair of Protozoology in 1979. He is an exceptionally talented man, a very kind, and generous one. He was devoted to Rosemary and his two families, with a son from his first wife and two with Rosemary, plus their offspring.

"Saturday I received a letter from Peter Paterson telling me that his mother, Anna, had died. She was over ninety, but a very vivacious woman. She was a niece of the late Dame Marie Rambert of ballet fame. In our Liverpool days, we were good friends with Anna and her late doctor husband, Horace, but had not seen her for many years.

"I feel exceptionally low today in spite of, or possibly because of, the bright sunshine outside. Death seems to be around me. Our cleaning lady, a very kind, middle-aged woman who originates from a nearby village, was here this morning as she normally is each Monday. We had a brief chat when she arrived. Her daughter recently lost a pregnancy and I have tried to console her by explaining that nature often intervenes if something is not right with the fetus. She is always supportive of me so I said nothing about how I felt. Around midday, I only wanted to sleep, but forced myself to get up and make a simple lunch. I'll check my email, which is functioning again. Last night AOL seemed to break down and I had to abandon it until this morning. So far, it is working again. I would feel isolated without email even though I am not left alone for long. Usually somebody pops in or rings sometime during the day or evening.

"I will soon force myself to do elementary tasks like taking my empty bottles to the recycling center, and walking round the garden. I do not have the heart to go shopping, or in eating for that matter. I have plenty of things in the freezer, but none tempts me.

"I read a *British Medical Journal* review of a book about grieving by a writer named Dannie Abse. I may buy it even though the reviewer wrote, 'This is perhaps not a book for the recently bereaved; no, Abse is alert to the 'cool stranger', that is to say the rest of us—those who soon enough will be.'

"In the end, I did not walk round the garden, but went to see Ruth's tree planted in the meadow behind the Japanese garden. It is a red flowering crab apple and I look forward to seeing the first blossoms.

"David and Joyce dropped in during the evening with some fruit salad and ice cream and we watched a superb Attenborough documentary on reptiles; lizards, chameleons, skinks, and others. In the middle of this, Pat Catchpole phoned to say she had broken her ankle. Of all times, just when Ian is about to retire and she and he were booked to have a celebratory dinner with us here in the restaurant. Such lousy luck.

"I made a 'Get Well' card for Pat and will phone to see if I can do anything to help. Luckily, she has Ian's sister Hillary nearby who can keep an eye on things so she is not stuck on her own.

"Kosovo is independent since yesterday. Castro announced he is stepping down. I anticipated sour grapes comments from some, but I hear general admiration for his achievements from most open-minded people.

"I decided to take the plunge and order the stone for Ruth's ashes. At the last minute, I changed the wording. It will be like this, chiseled into rough grey granite and with the lettering painted black:

RUTH PETERS-SCHEIDEGGER

4.9.1929 – 15.12.2007

Beloved wife

ever in my heart

"Not a good day on the whole due to gloomy thoughts. An email from my nephew John in Australia says he put his late wife's portrait photo into storage. He 'Couldn't cope with seeing it every day.' I note that the passage of time permits him to refer to 'it' and not 'her.' I wonder if this will happen to me.

"The rest of the day is gloomy in spite of good sunshine. I finished off last few days' newspapers superficially until David came in for a short chat and a glass, again bearing fruit salad and ice cream from Joyce.

"The following morning was very foggy, but I arose early as I ordered a car wash at 9:00 a.m. It is the first since we bought it in September 2006. A young man named Martin offers a car valet service every Wednesday morning at C.V.

"I went through old photos and found two of father's 100th birthday, so scanned them on to PC and printed them. He certainly did not look his age. Nor did sister Pete who is standing with him in one of the photos.

"This morning the new book I ordered two days ago arrived from Amazon. It is '*The Presence*' by Dannie Abse. It turns out he is a well-known poet as well as a physician. He found himself in much the same position as me. A few months after his wife died, he started to write a diary about their life together. It should be interesting reading, but not too sad I hope. It seems to be common for old people to write their autobiographies. I think a former colleague from Liverpool days, Mike Service, mentioned not long ago, that a number of my extroverted contemporaries were writing theirs. I recall that both Brian Maegraith and Cyril Garnham were fervent diarists, but nothing of their lives has been published. Brian once said he would never dare distribute his while he was alive since he was so candid in his comments on the people around him and their families would probably sue. Garnham never retired for the night until he finished writing his diary for the day. However, the odds are that nobody could interpret his writing well enough to convert his words into a readable, much less printable form.

"Ronnie sent an email suggesting that our niece Jennifer and I might like to visit her in Geneva around the end of March for a triple birthday family celebration as our birthdays are all within a couple of days of each other. As I feel at present, both mentally and physically, I don't believe I could make it so soon. I will think about it after I get my X-ray results and have another talk to my GP. At the beginning and end of each day, my legs and hands seem to get stiffer and stiffer for some reason.

"After supper, the remains of precooked chicken bits and frozen peas, read half the new book by Dannie Abse. It mirrors some of my own sentiments. He started a diary when his wife was killed in a car accident, then began to turn it into this book within months. It is very moving in places and he is clearly a sensitive individual. I may write to him when I have finished reading his account. (I never did.)

"I shopped early and met Ian's sister Hillary. Pat is feeling very low at the moment, but we still hope she and Ian are able to come for lunch next week. Then I bumped into an acquaintance from Little G. He's now about ninety-four, but very sprightly. Tells me he is enjoying his Pilates classes, but not walking quite as much as before! He's pleased that three of the schoolchildren he teaches chess are up for the national championship. He's an amazing man who looks about seventy with sparkling intellect to match. That reminded me that I stumbled on a photo of Henry reading his telegram from the Queen at the luncheon party for his 100th birthday in 1979. He looked remarkably robust and smart for his age.

"Today I received an invitation to join Oliver and his wife for tea. We swapped yarns about the good old colonial times in West Africa and he lent me a brief summary of their days there. I'll read it quickly when I return home. That made me wonder whether to put together some of my own memories, but doubt if I really will. We will see. David dropped by for a glass of wine and a short chat before he and Joyce go downstairs to watch a film. I just finished supper of tasty mussel and smoked salmon chowder from Waitrose and a slice of bread. Today I discovered a section of the frozen food cabinets in Waitrose that has a number of small helpings of what look to be interesting meals. The trouble is, when I buy these things, I put them in the freezer but rarely have the heart to heat them up to eat on my own.

"After the talk with Oliver and wife, I will look for any pictures on the computer worth showing them from Africa. I doubt if I have.

Nepal and TPNG are another matter as well as a collection of clinical cases from around the tropics. I hope to finish the Abse book tonight or tomorrow.

"Tomorrow will be seventy days. It feels like seventy years.

"Did not succeed in reading any more of Abse last night. Rather, I finished off old newspapers and journals. I also looked up the location of Oliver's base in the Gold Coast. It turned out to be not too far northwest from Takoradi, one of the towns in which I worked in my RAMC days. I looked at old slides on my computer but little of interest from most places in Africa except natural history and clinical subjects. Checked to see if I still have any old Word Star files, but seems not to be the case.

"Vicki and Paul Burdess came to tea the next day. We talked at length about this and that and the afternoon passed quickly. Fortunately, the huge lemon meringue tart I brought in for them passed as well.

"Later on I read an article in the family section of *The Guardian* on bereavement, by a seemingly young oncologist at the Great Ormond Street children's hospital and her interviewer. I was so moved by it that I wrote her a letter of thanks to which I never received a response.

"Frankly, I cannot recall if I watched something on TV or not. I checked and I did not watch anything. No appetite, so ate a couple of biscuits and cheese, finished the cake, and went to bed by 9:30 p.m. I wanted to think about Ruth at 9:35 p.m., but went out like a light until 2:00 a.m., as usual.

"Every morning I seem to be stiffer and stiffer and can barely walk until I have taken my fix of paracetamol. After three weeks, I'm still waiting for X-ray results. Mornings are bad, but Sunday mornings are the worst as I get very sad very easily and today is no exception. I forced myself to change the bedding in preparation for the ritual Monday laundry day by the ladies downstairs. I should take my garden walk and go to Waitrose to bring in food for Pat's lunch tomorrow, but do not feel like doing either. Maybe later. I understand how people become anorexic; it is lunchtime and I don't even want to think about food. I could join in the C.V. restaurant meals, including Sunday, but just do not feel like doing so. I had arranged to invite Pat and Ian with Joyce and David next Thursday for lunch, but that now has to wait until Pat is able to walk again.

"Vicki and Paul brought the suit I bought with Pat from M&S. Hillary took in the trousers to shorten, but they still seem to be too long. That comes from not having Ruth to pin them for me before alterations. I may send them for further shortening, but this time will ask someone to pin them for me first! I don't know who to ask, so will probably end up doing it myself by trial and error. (This did prove to be an error).

Not a good night and a worse early morning, but that has become par for the course. Others are worse off. Poor Pat was lying on her couch, leg in the air and commode at her side, when I called at lunchtime. Ian was busy clearing his office desk on the last day at work in Harrow, prior to his retirement, and he is dining with colleagues this evening, so she will depend on visits from friends all day. I fished around in her kitchen and fiddled with her microwave to heat up lunch for her. As usual, I did not leave it in long enough! At least she had something reasonable to eat thanks to Mr. Waitrose.

"David dropped in for a quick glass of red wine, bearing fruit and ice cream from Joyce for my supper. We had a general chat until he left to play snooker with Sam, bridge with the old ladies, or something like that. As he was leaving, I encountered Margaret from Number one, taking her exercise up and down the corridor. I invited her in for a sherry and a talk about old times that lasted over an hour. She is a very sweet, sensitive, frail lady. She was widowed quite a few years ago but has a large, supportive family. She knows how to listen which is a great help. She drove a Red Cross ambulance in London during the war.

"Still no report on my X-rays so I wrote a note for Lesley Hallan. I'll leave it with Val tomorrow morning as Wednesday is surgery day and there is always a queue to see Lesley. I still stop to say, 'Hello

Sweetheart, to Ruth every time I pass her new photo and hear her say, 'Hello Love,' back. I always want to cry.

"Next morning I dropped the note for Lesley Hallan to Val in the surgery. To my surprise, she stopped me to introduce Pauline née Siegler who was waiting with her father-in-law to see Lesley. I barely recognized her, but she knew me. I felt embarrassed at encountering them and agreed to meet on another occasion. After getting home, realized it would be impolite not to invite them up for coffee, so I phoned the message back. They did not come because Bernard lost his hearing aids again and Pauline had to take him to get new ones. We agreed that she would get in touch next time she is at C.V.

"David arrived a few minutes later and wanted to back out when he spotted the tray ready with coffee and biscuits that he guessed, correctly, were for a lady's benefit. I reassured him and we had coffee together.

"Nice mild sunny day but felt despondent and lonely, so I drove out to visit Ruth, taking the camera to make a few more shots of her flowers. I stopped at the entrance to Pulridge House East on the way back but did not go in. I finished the film in sitting room where the sun shining on Ruth's latest photo gave it a spectacular 3-D effect. I hope it comes out when the film is developed and printed.

"Email from Lee and Tilly Schnur who are coming from Israel in May and would like to call here. I lost the use of my PC mouse as I was considering reply. I resolved that problem by turning everything off. It worked perfectly when switched back on. I hope I am not running into serious PC problems. May could be a busy month since Ronnie and the Killicks are due here. Lee forty years ago was one of my first post-graduate students in Liverpool. He invited me to visit them when I am fit. I have to think about all such travel when the time comes, which is certainly not now. Apart from getting physically fit again, there are important legal and tax things to sort out over the coming months, as well as the most important matter of setting Ruth's stone. I put this in motion with the undertakers.

"I took a short nap, had coffee, after which Dorothea dropped in to invite me for tea this weekend. She made an amazing recovery after fracturing her femur, then having a hip replacement almost immediately after. After what seems like only a few days, she is marching around without even a stick. I wish I could do the same without having had any breaks or repairs yet.

"Joyce and Sam came for a glass and chat. I lost my appetite tonight.

"I was despondent next morning. I feel that I am drifting through life aimlessly, and I am. Then I remembered that I should have invited Sam to join Joyce and David for lunch on Sunday. I must make more effort to pull myself together, but still cannot see where I am going.

"The lunch went well and we all ate lamb kidney casserole with an acceptable glass of house red.

"Joyce and Sam came round in the evening. We learned that she and I share a childhood memory of the airships, perhaps the R 101, flying over London. We must have been about five years of age—one of my first vivid childhood memories.

"I waited for delivery of wine this Leap Day but the postman arrived first bringing a letter from a German friend, Gunther Wernsdorfer, about his experience with treating cancer patients with artesunate. I passed the news, but not the details, to colleague of mine at St. George's Hospital. He called back after lunch with the good news that he is well on the way to getting his clinical trial of artesunate against cancer set up. He will try to come see me the week after next. I look forward to meeting him as we have only spoken on the phone or emailed.

"I took my film for processing to Berkhamsted and collected new trousers that were shortened for the second time. Any more cutting and I will have shorts in the summer. I keep buying things for the freezer, but don't know why. I don't feel like eating any of them.

"Later I phoned to ask for a fax of the X-ray report. I have to wait until next week to discuss it with Lesley Hallan. Here is the good news: 'XR Pelvis. Status: Painful hip with reduced range of movement and muscle wasting in both thighs. There are severe degenerative changes affecting both hips, worse on the right with total loss of the joint space superiorly, flattening of the femoral head as well as subarticular cystic change and sclerosis. Sacroiliac joints and symphysis pubis appear normal.'

"That will preoccupy me for a while. Perhaps this will give me a chance to get back at BUPA for their meanness over Ruth's hospital accommodation. I could not face surgery at this stage if ever. There is always an alternative.

"On my way back from emptying waste paper into yard bin, I bumped into a lady with her Scotty dog. We often meet when I collect my paper in the morning. I don't know her name but she has a Northern accent. She asked where we live and how long I had been here, so told her. She said she didn't think she had met my wife. I explained why not and she was quite sympathetic. She lost her husband ten years ago but still misses him and often hears his voice. I well understand that as every time I pass Ruth's photo and say hello to her, I hear her answer back. It invariably brings a tear to my eyes, even as I write these words. I must see if I still have that small hand recorder and if she said anything on the tape. That is unlikely. Why didn't I keep such a record, in addition to photographs, all those years? How stupid can one be?

"While looking for pen refills that I know I have, I came across the small tape recorder. Now I'll see if there is any recording of Ruth's voice. I succeeded and was rewarded with a very quiet, unforgettable, sweet voice, reading from a French book, possibly Proust. It is probably from one of her French weekends at Missenden Abbey. I forgot what excellent French she spoke and I never heard this recording. The batteries were nearly flat so I will try again with new ones tomorrow. It's a good reason to go shopping again. I do hope the recording survives and is readable. I'll try it on the radio tape player.

"Quel joie! I can still hear Ruth on the radio tape player, a poor recording but never mind. Pity I have nothing in English or German as well. I could hear the full range of her voice, which is soft and melodious. I wonder if it is possible to copy it and the quality improved digitally. I'll ask Sam if he knows.

"I phoned Ronnie to tell her about my X-rays and confirm that I cannot visit her in Switzerland in the near future. I will probably have at least one hip replaced first. I confirmed that she will come here on May 11 Whit Sunday, from her donkey refuge in Devon.

"The sun was still shining so I went for my walk round the C.V. garden, but the wind was too strong so I returned home after saying, 'Hello,' to Ruth's new tree near the entrance to the walking meadow. On the way back I saw a police car. A few yards further on, David told me poor old Bernard had backed his car out of his parking space straight into another car, badly damaging it. Fortunately, he only slightly damaged himself.

"Seventy-seven nights ago at this hour of the evening, Ruth's pulse was ninety-six, her respirations a rapid forty-per-minute, but she was peaceful. It is getting late and I have been crying on and off for the past half hour. I brushed my teeth and went to bed as tears flooded my eyes.

"In spite of it all, I went straight to sleep."

"The next morning it was a nice sunny day, so decided to have a walk in the garden once I contacted David G.

"The days and nights slipped by fairly quickly. That is partly because I started trying to put some order into practical affairs. Pat Crowhurst came to collect many of Ruth's clothes for the Hospice shop, mainly woolens. I did not want them to be damaged by moths in the cupboard. I made a start on setting her tax affairs straight, a simple matter that had to be done.

"On Wednesday, Lesley Hallan saw me at C.V. surgery and we agreed that I needed to have my right hip replaced before long, so I made an appointment to see an orthopedic surgeon next Monday at the Harpenden hospital, with which I am too familiar. As if that was not enough for one day, I woke up about 11:30 that evening having to pee. I discovered, to my consternation, that I produced urine heavily loaded with fresh blood. I remembered that, on retiring Tuesday night after a lone curry supper, I noticed that the last bit of my bedtime pee was pink. I attributed it to a coloring agent in the food. There seemed to be no abnormality on Wednesday.

At 6:00 a.m. the next morning, things seemed normal. I produced a specimen at midday which Val, our senior nurse, checked for abnormalities. She confirmed what was seen in the pot. There were red cells present. I got a telephone call from Elizabeth Ponsonby as the other practice doctors were not available. She will arrange for me to see a urologist. My PSA, taken a few weeks ago, was normal. Therefore, she is not worried and thinks it may be a one-off bleed from my chronically enlarged prostate. We will see in a couple of weeks. It seems it never rains but it pours.

"David G. has been very helpful and offered to take me for any hospital visits when required. I may accept his offer when I go for a cystoscopy. Ronnie offered to come over and help me post hip op not hip-hop. I prefer to spend a week or two in a convalescent home with expert care, rather than troubling her. I have not yet told her about problem number two.

"Good news from Pat Catchpole whose leg is mending well after all. She may be able to have the plaster off or changed in three weeks.

"Before bed at 10:00 p.m., I passed a pea-sized blood clot followed by fresh blood in my urine A couple of days later I passed a new clot with fresh blood. I phoned the surgery for appointment with Dr. Ponsonby. It seemed a long time to wait; two weeks to see a urologist about a bleeding prostate. (It must be that.) I was greeted warmly by her and examined. We found I have a very large prostate. I was told an appointment was being made for me urgently at West Herts and I should hear something from her secretary by this evening. Once diagnosis is made, if it is prostate and that seems likely, transurethral laser surgery is now the thing to have. We will see.

"I called on David on return to C.V. and had coffee and a chat with him. He offered to act as information contact if I have to go in for operation or anything similar. This seems likely now. I told him I need this new problem now like a hole in the head, hardly an original statement. I already had it in mind to ask if he would take on this role but he suggested it before I could. What an excellent and human friend to have found!

"The next morning David dropped by at 9:00 a.m. to see if I was still alive and kicking—I was. It was a gloomy morning with no newspaper as deliveryman messed things up. I could not be bothered to go out to buy one, so I slept a while. Then I decided to use up a packet of prepared vegetables I bought. As I was on the way to doing so, Herbert phoned to see how I was. The true answer would have been, "Bloody miserable." Instead, I told him about forthcoming meeting with orthopod and now a urologist. I asked how he was and learned that his wife Meyra fell and fractured the neck of her femur, which meant she needed a new hip. She is recuperating in hospital. I can imagine the effect on her already precarious mental state and how that affects poor Herbert. He cancelled his planned visit to Malta. I suppose some people have much more misery than I have.

Tonight, however, was the eighty-fourth since half my world died.

"That night I dreamed I was stranded in London on a damp night, with snow on the ground, only partly dressed, with a few strange coins in my pocket, and wondering how to get home. I figured the best thing to do was to find a police officer and explain my predicament. However, I was not sure where home was or even my name. It was very disturbing and symptomatic of my current drifting through life from day to day.

"I'm extremely stiff again this morning, but no more haematuria at present. Tomorrow I should go to Harpenden to see orthopod, but do not yet have referral letter from Lesley Hallan. Forecast is for worst winter storms of the year, so I'm not looking forward to the journey. I am nervous of travelling anywhere beyond the Berkhamsted shops at present.

"A dull day, but David and Joyce dropped by in the evening for a glass.

"On the Monday I received an appointment for cystoscopy for the following Friday and asked David if he would drive me to the hospital for this examination. This afternoon I will see the orthopod at Harpenden. My cleaning lady came this morning and I gave her Ruth's leather coat, which pleased her. I thought first to give it to her daughter, but seems she is too big for it.

"I can't say I am very enthusiastic about the rest of today, with the worst storms this year! Our water went off briefly this morning and I don't care about eating, so I'll stick to soup and sandwich. Got a nice Easter card from Pat and Ian and will make one for them.

"My appointment to see the urologist was not until Friday at 12:30 a.m. for cystoscopy. Earlier that week, after a marmalade sandwich and packet tomato soup for lunch, I went early to meet my orthopod, Brian Bradnock, at Harpenden. I arrived an hour early but he saw me immediately. I saw the new X-ray that looks like a bomb blast and agreed to exchange my right hip for a new one on June 10th at Harpenden. Now I have to find out what happened to my prostate. Maybe it will also look like it was bombed. I gladly accept David's offer to take me there on Friday. I gave him as 'next of kin' at Harpenden. They still had Ruth and the old address on their records.

"David spotted me on my return home and wanted to know my news. Told him I got on well with Bradnock and agreed we would celebrate with a malt whisky this evening. I will do likewise with Bradnock after he does my hip. I suggested to him that he might like to deal with my prostate as an encore but he didn't take the hint. I'll stop taking aspirin tomorrow to minimize bleeding from both sites.

I phoned dentist to postpone my June appointment for a month.

"I received a late afternoon call from Marika Clark of the Swiss club. She will bring George and Ursula, also club members, with her tomorrow morning for coffee. She is baking a cake, bless her. Maybe some will be left over for our former neighbor Barbara Day who is coming from Little Gaddesden on Wednesday. Next was a phone call from the St. Francis Hospice family support group. A kindly but rather hesitant lady named Mary wanted to know how I was getting on. I think she was a bit overawed by having to phone a Professor. She just called to offer friendly support, so I told her my woes, but also the great support I receive from old and new friends. I told her how much I appreciate the work of the hospice. In response to her question, I said she could call me 'Wallace'. I think that was a great relief to her. I believe these good souls on the support group are volunteers, a bit like the Samaritans.

"I'm waiting for David for our drink. He came after supper with Joyce. We had a nightcap and celebrated forthcoming operation by opening a new bottle of Glenmorangie.

"I bled more during the night for no obvious reason. I'll stop aspirin this morning.

"My legs are very stiff all day. Marika and Ursula came at 11:30 a.m., but without George. Marika had made a nice orange cake. When they left, I went to shop and dump empty bottles. I parked in Waitrose only to find I left money behind, so had to return to C.V. for wallet. I bought more food than I needed, but found I had no appetite by the time I returned home or in the evening, so I spent time reading papers. First Sam arrived for a chat and a glass of wine, then David and Joyce.

"I felt headachy and went to bed early with my lunchtime sandwich for dinner. I woke up at 4:00 a.m. to produce urine with much blood again. My legs were painful so I took more paracetamol.

"Next morning up as usual, i.e., reluctantly. Now I wait for a visit from Barbara. We talked about this and that, all very inconsequential. I can't remember what happened the rest of the day, except for a visit from David and Sam.

"What happened to fill the next day?

"On Friday March 14 David took me to West Herts Hospital for a cystoscopy which was performed by a young Kenyan Asian doctor. On the TV monitor, I had a good look at my prostate. It looked vascular and bloody and has bled slightly ever since. However, nothing in bladder or hard lumps. I'm waiting for ultrasound scan and flow test. Meanwhile I started on Finasteride, an anti-androgen steroid said to make benign prostate shrink, but it takes at least six months of daily treatment to do so. Meanwhile it may make my hair grow, or so it says in the package. I have a sore urethra and mild bleeding in the afternoon and night. I'm supposed to drink at least six pints of liquid daily; that's four liters!

"The next day I drove out to do a reconnaissance of the new Royal Entomological Society premises at Chiswell Green before the rain started and got a bit lost. I finally located it down a narrow lane, not far from where we once bought a Toyota near St. Albans. However, the gates were closed for the weekend.

"I drove home and was checking the email when Margaret from Number one put her head in to see if I was still alive. She had not seen me for some days. She is a dear old thing but so frail. After her visit, I made sardines on toast and soup for a late lunch that I forced down reluctantly. I watched a sad film on TV about clinical trial of new drug for post-encephalitic Parkinsonism that had me in tears. David came in, but Joyce is not well. I made the same supper as yesterday, Swedish meatballs and frozen peas; four-and-a half minutes in the microwave. Then I read papers before early night.

"Sweetheart, I talk to you every time I pass your picture. Life is so empty and meaningless without you. Living is just a farce and I wonder how long I will bother about it. I already told our solicitor Nigel the wording to add to our stone when the day arrives.

"Sunday, bloody Sunday. Only good thing is my urethra is less sore and not bleeding at present. I do domestic chores, wash clothes, change bedding, and eat breakfast. I spent time looking for information on university courses on creative writing, e.g., East Anglia. It looks like a non-starter but I'll check for anything at Great Missenden this year. David and Sam came in with bottle of sherry before lunch.

"After lunch I remembered I won £10 on National Lottery, so bought another couple of tickets. Cleared up a few things of Ruth's and found her long-lost tweezers, exactly where they should have been.

"I'm back to the weekend papers. I've had a mild, right-sided headache about this time every evening for some days, maybe hypoglycemia. However, I could not face eating much, so stuck a potato in the microwave to eat with goat cheese and Cenovis—not nice at all. I could not be bothered to watch TV.

"The next day I'm sad as on most mornings. I realize I am afraid, very afraid and very, very empty. It's essential that I find a new raison d'être before too long. I go downstairs to collect the paper every morning, say hello cheerfully to the usual men and women in the queue, exchange a few words, sometimes manage to remember the name of one or other, and then retreat up the lift to home again. However, the apartment feels more like a refuge than a home these days. I must not be too miserable when my cleaning lady arrives for her 10:30 a.m. Monday session. I'll check the email and phone Missenden Abbey for a brochure of this year's weekend sessions in case there is one on creative writing.

"After a miserable meal, a cheese sandwich and soup, I decide to work on papers for tax returns instead of moping and did this all afternoon. Elisabeth Ponsonby phoned for news at 5:30 p.m. We agreed I would try Finasteride as I do not want an operation unless necessary. In that case, she suggests I approach a better urologist. I suppose she means one who uses a laser TURP procedure to deal with my vascular prostate.

"I learned that LSHTM received something like forty-nine million dollars for work on malaria! A huge amount will be available for studies with ACT's. I bitterly remember Ruth accusing me of prostituting myself when I struggled to get a miserable few thousand dollars from WHO and WRAIR to support my small team on basic research on drug combinations! Why did I bother? I mustn't be bitter about such things, but it was not something I enjoyed. It is hard, even in retrospect, not to be bitter; especially when I see how some of the young geniuses climbed on my back. I suppose it was ever thus.

"Jeff Fryer phoned to see how I was getting on. I am afraid I was very negative and admitted I could not even think of joining them in London or anywhere else at present. I am too nervous to drive further than the local shops. Before hanging up, he thanked me for his birthday card. Bloody fool me; I completely forgot that this was his birthday and that was probably the reason he phoned me. I felt stupid about it, but he is a good man and I think he understood. In Chapter 8, I inserted parts of the eulogy to Ruth that he so kindly read for me at the Memorial Service. In some ways, it seems like months ago but it has only been two months.

"David and Joyce came, she is much better than she was yesterday. They left early, so I put my Waitrose meal in the oven. As usual, I did not leave it long enough, so ended up eating half-warmed pasta. I watched a bit of a program about Iraq, one of two on the fifth anniversary of the start of the Iraq war that the two geniuses, Bush and Blair, initiated.

"That night I had a worrying, apocalyptic dream of Ruth and me in an anonymous place with enormous black clouds and sky surrounding everything.

"The following morning I got busy preparing coats and handbags for Pat Crowhurst, a friend from Little G., to take to the hospice shop. I left it so late I had no time for lunch except an apple and a cup of bouillon. I had no appetite anyway. Now all saleable clothes and handbags are gone, plus a large bag of old clothes hangers and such that Pat offered to dump for me. All that is left is a drawer full of underwear, stockings, nighties, and lingerie that I have to bag and dump. It seems such a waste.

In any case, I could not think of doing this today. However, Pat tells me that the first lot of dresses, woolens, shoes, and other clothing are selling well. No wonder; Ruth had excellent taste in clothes; they were about her only indulgence. Nevertheless, disposing of them even for a good cause, St. Francis Hospice in this case seems almost like treachery. Her empty clothes cupboard looked so accusing that I transferred some of my clothes there to fill it up a bit. I discovered the rain jacket I thought was lost among the coats in the coat cupboard.

"I made myself sit down with coffee and biscuits to do the crossword but could hardly find a word today. It must be an effect of the stress. I noticed previously that simple thoughts evade me. I also have an increasing problem with trigger fingers, now on both hands. I cannot arouse any enthusiasm for anything at present.

"David came early today and was joined by Joyce who is much better this evening. Had a chat and wine until suppertime.

"After shopping next morning, I darned holes in my new cashmere pullover, a present from Ruth. The moths started eating it before I could wear it. It's too late for a proper lunch.

"In the evening I joined David and Joyce at a poetry reading session in C.V. The compositions of a number of residents were read and prizes given. Some were very good and others remarkably moving. It was interesting to compare the authors where known, some were anonymous, with my impression of their personalities. However, I knew almost nothing of any of them so it was hardly surprising. That is not to mention my total lack of appreciation of poetry or enthusiasm for it until very recently.

"I returned for a final glass with David and Joyce but too late to eat by the time they left. I settled for a couple of miserable cheese crackers and jam. It doesn't bother me if I eat less and I have no enthusiasm for food.

"In late March I received a request from Balbar Singh in Sarawak to read the manuscript of his new paper on simian malaria and one from Irène to translate a paper for her. I was surprised to receive a statement from Elsevier indicating that the fourth, fifth, and sixth editions of the *Atlas of Tropical Medicine and Parasitology* sold 16,500 copies between them. I assume that the first three editions may have sold half as many. That makes around 25,000, which is not too bad.

"It has been a bizarre Easter, snowing on and off every day including this morning. Now at 5:00 p.m. the sun is shining brightly. Friday and Saturday passed in the usual blurred haze and I barely remember what happened, apart from the usual kind visits of David and Joyce. Easter Sunday morning, it was snowing hard but I had arranged with them to go to the family communion at Little G. church so we went, snow or no snow. From the first hymn, I was hit emotionally and could barely sit or stand throughout the service without having to struggle to hold back tears. Several old friends and acquaintances greeted me including some whom I never thought of as being either. We arranged for all three Grigsbys to be my guests at lunch in The Mansion and we joined others there in the bar while waiting for our table. It was an agreeable lunch and good company, but I spent the afternoon and evening very quietly.

"Now I remember what happened on Saturday. (How stupid of me, but typical in my present disturbed state of mind. I have frequent brief memory losses of things that I should know the answers to without hesitation. I get stuck on simple clues in the *Guardian* 'Quick crossword.') Jennifer and Richard drove over from Gloucester in the snow and took me to lunch at the King's Head in Ivinghoe. It was oxtail stew, one of George's better lunches that his chef does very well. The last time I was there was with Ruth and the Christoffersens on Christmas Day 2006. It was shortly before we moved and when

Ruth's condition was beginning to go downhill. We decided then that we could not face any more such Christmas lunches at the King's Head. George greeted us warmly, even called me, 'Professor' for the first time ever. He must have been impressed by the people who attended Ruth's memorial as he also came, much to my surprise. I was touched by his welcome. We returned for coffee in Number two and a long chat about nothing in particular until it was time for Jennifer and Richard to return home in another heavy snow shower. I was glad they had Richard's Land Rover for security.

"I spent too much time this morning watching the BBC report on the interruption of the official start of the Beijing Olympics, the opening ceremony being held in Olympia, by pro-Tibetan protesters. The BBC managed to show the incident repeatedly, so the protesters had a good start to their campaign.

"After a short snooze following a miserable lunch, I remembered to check my phone and found that Suzie Banerji called yesterday morning to wish me 'Happy Easter' and invite me to join her, Arnab, and the family for an Indian meal in Berkhamsted this evening to celebrate her birthday. I phoned her to wish her a late birthday and Easter greetings but regretfully declined the invitation as I still do not feel up to even informal occasions among friends just yet. Anyway, we agreed we would meet here before long for a chat. They are such a 'sympathique' couple and it is always nice to see them.

"In my email today, I found a nice greeting from Anthony Bryceson who read my poem for Ruth so sympathetically. Also one from David Warhurst who wants to come over and see me again soon, with Rhum of course. That will be nice. I had a long message from Irène who asked me to translate a critical paper on structural versus molecular taxonomy of malaria parasites that she is writing. I agreed to do so as I entirely agree with her viewpoint. Finally, another message from Balbar Singh about the review he and his wife Janet are writing about the '5th malaria parasite of man' for *Trends in Parasitology*. I look forward to his visit in a couple of weeks' time.

Now I'll try to respond to these messages by which time I expect David to drop in for a quick glass.

"I must remember to read up about trigger finger on E-Medicine before doing anything else as I am beginning to seize up badly in both hands. Even eating is a painful process all of a sudden.

"Later that week the sun shone clearly, although there was still a cool wind. I made myself take a walk around the garden and carp pond, but my walking is now such an agonizingly slow shamble that I was glad to return to the flat and sit down.

"I see through the study window that two elderly enthusiasts are playing table tennis in the garden. Last summer when Ruth was barely able to get out of bed we used to hear and see a pair playing early in the mornings—a poignant contrast to my poor wife. In the mail just now, a nice letter from Frank Cox. I recently wrote him condolences on losing his wife who died some time ago, though at the time the news did not reach me. Frank wrote 'Whenever I come home I expect to hear Valerie's happy greeting and I miss her terribly; things do not get better they only get easier to come to terms with.'

"I hope he is right but, just now it is hard to imagine this. I get a card from Rosemary Williams just returned from Spain where she stayed with her oldest son Richard and his wife Rosa. They have a home in Barcelona and one in the Pyrenees. Rosemary said her daughter-in-law cried when she read my poem for Ruth. That brought tears to my eyes again.

"To occupy my mind I translated the manuscript on avian malaria from French into English for Irène. I got a trigger finger on my right hand for my pains. I cooked fish cakes in the oven and baked a potato in the microwave, then watched an interesting film on life in Tibet under the Chinese. It did not seem quite as bad as one would think from the recent protests related to the forthcoming Olympic Games in Beijing.

"By this time next week, I will be eighty-four. I thought of having a few people in for a glass of champagne on my birthday but do not feel sociable. I hope nobody knows the happy event is pending. In a drawer that was just mended, I came across some photos taken at the King's Head on my seventieth birthday when Ruth gave me a surprise party. It seems amazing that it was fourteen years ago, almost to the day. How she managed to arrange it all is astonishing. I don't wish to celebrate it this year.

"Almost the end of March, - 105 nights since Ruth's departure. The clocks went forward one hour but did not symbolize anything for me. Ronnie phoned me just as I was about to phone her and wish her a 'Happy Birthday'. She has a very full social life this weekend with parties every hour it seems. Not bad for ninety-three.

"The first spring-like morning and I did some dispirited shopping. I am as stiff as hell today and it is a job getting about. I am studying a catalog of aids for old people that David Warhurst brought me yesterday along with a useful long-handled pincers to pick things off the floor and elsewhere. I will call it my 'picker-upper'. It belonged to his wife Rosemary. It is better than the long medical instrument forceps I salvaged from the RAMC in 1950 and use in Number two to pick up the mail when the postman drops it through the letterbox.

"Yesterday, All Fools' Day I was 104, or at least felt like it. I got five cards and a phone call from Jeff Fryer. To celebrate my birthday I went out and bought a new pair of slippers for when I go into hospital for my new hip, and a pair of sandals for when I come out.

"We had a glass of champagne and olives instead of usual wine with David, Joyce, and Sam. Then heated up rice in microwave, ate and to bed. I get a lot of pain in bed so sent a message to Lesley Hallan this morning for advice, as her surgery list was already full.

"David and Joyce were having our usual glass together this evening when Lesley phoned back with some good suggestions, including spending a week or so at Ashlyn's Care Home after my operation. I'll visit the place soon to discuss things.

"I visited Ashlyn's the next morning to make my interest known, but came away unconvinced that I could bear to stay there, comfortable as it may be. I made no commitment.

"On way back I stopped to say 'Hello' to Ruth. Still some dwarf daffodils flowering by her stone.

"It is one calendar year since we moved here from Little G. I remember asking myself then if we would survive here until the end of 2007. My answer now has to be 'No'. I had to get a prescription so I went to Waitrose. Walking was extremely stiff and I was glad to get home.

"Tonight is the one hundred and twelfth night since '*The Departure*'.

"I don't feel very bright today. I carelessly smashed a large wine glass in the kitchen while preparing them for this evening's drink with David and Joyce. I'm not hungry at all tonight. I may be influenced by new tablets for pain, paracetamol-codeine, so will have a second glass of wine and maybe bread and jam for supper.

"I try to be bright and not talk all the time about Ruth, but it is all a façade. I am desperately lonely and lost without her. I hope I can find someone who can transfer a short recording of her reading from Proust on the old tape that I found to a digital disc that removes the background hiss. Guy Parry phoned and will come round next week to mount mirrors and pictures that have lain around for the last six months. I simply could not make the effort to decide where to put what and still do not know, but they cannot stay on the floor forever.

"In the end I finished some custard and microwaved a packet of chips for dinner.

"I slept badly this night and had a nightmarish dream that Ruth and I were lost in a sort of building complex that was being demolished and could not find the way out. I woke up to find heavy snow falling as forecast. My limbs are even stiffer than usual.

"David and Joyce took me to lunch at the Ashridge Golf Club on Sunday. The clubhouse was near empty because of the snow but the lunch was up to its usual standard except that I had no appetite. Returned to start reading the draft manuscript of Dr. Dalrymple, whom I sometimes refer to as 4D. It is good in parts, but contains quite a few errors.

"Later watched second part of the new nature film on tiger cubs, then yogurt and bed.

"More snow in the morning. I picked up Balbar Singh at station midday and we lunched at the Berkhamsted fish restaurant, which I had in my sights for a couple of years. The fish is good but vegetables poor. We returned to C.V. for a long chat about his studies on simian malaria in man and on Irène's on avian parasites. We watched the orangutan DVD that he greatly enjoyed and tried, unsuccessfully to make him a copy. I took him to the station to catch the 4:00 p.m. train back to London.

"I had just sat down when Mary of the Hospice follow-up service called to see how I was getting on. She seems to like chatting to boost my morale and I do not have the heart to stop her too soon. She obviously means well and it is her job, probably as a volunteer.

"I made another attempt to copy the DVD for Balbar that did not succeed.

"It is Tuesday morning, April 8th. I feel depressed after a restless and painful night. It is frosty outside but bright sunshine. I'll try to rouse myself to send comments to Dr. 4D, and then do some shopping before the fridge gets completely empty. From this morning's email, I see that Dr. 4D is a male, not a female as the name, Dana, led David Warhurst and me to believe.

"The main events of the last two days were hanging pictures and scrolls with Guy. I must say the flat looks much better with things on the walls. I cannot bring myself to throw out the nice walnut-framed chairs I originally got from my first office at CIBA Basle over forty years ago, and buy new ones.

"I received a phone call at teatime from our old friend from Basle days, Paula Bassil. She is selling their home in Australia. Her artist and writer daughter Andrea is there now arranging the matter and working on a new book for her Australian publisher. I had just finished the conversation when Ken Walker arrived with CD containing cleaned-up copy of old tape with Ruth reading from Proust. It's difficult to understand what she says, but the background hiss is gone together with some parts of the speech. However, it is still Ruth. He took the orangutan DVD to see if he can copy it as I was not successful on my PC. I hope he doesn't damage the original. I wish we could locate the missing sixteen-millimeter film that disappeared from the labs at St. Albans.

"Nigel came and we spent an hour chatting about life in Little G. and how to give away my modest fortune. I want to get this cut and dried, as I don't want to leave loose ends should I drop in my tracks at short notice. It is happening to many of my vintage now. The first piece I now look at in the *British Medical Journal* every week is the obituary page. One hundred and nineteen nights survived.

"I spent the afternoon going through box of old photos looking for pictures from China.

"The following evening, a Saturday, Ken arrived with four copies of my orangutan DVD that he kindly copied for me. I invited David and Joyce to have a drink with me in the bar as a change from their always coming here for one. It was crowded and noisy with more old ladies than men, all chatting merrily. One, Felicity, has written a brief account of the former owners and residents of The Mansion. She was most impressed when she showed me an archive photo in her booklet of one-time research workers of Wellcome, George Hitchings and John Vane, both Nobel Prize winners. I told her I was acquainted with them, especially the latter. He was their research director when I was a consultant and strongly supported their development of a new antimalarial, atovaquone. It is currently one of the few that work.

"Next day, Sunday, another bloody Sunday. How I hate the weekends. I phoned Ronnie for a brief chat, but she was waiting for an old Greek friend who is currently staying with her to take her to lunch. I recall she had a Greek boyfriend in 1955 when we were passing by Alexandria. I found myself sleeping on yesterday's newspaper, so I made myself take a walk round the garden before the next lot of showers arrives. Back in the flat, I think of having a couple of boiled eggs for my lunch if I can be bothered.

"Maybe after lunch I will try to assemble a few thoughts about the early artemisinin story of the period around 1980. I'm stimulated by Dana's comment that it must have been quite an exciting time, or words to that effect. On reflection, it was a historical landmark in East-West scientific and political relationships. Boiled eggs and a rehydrated tomato soup make a poor Sunday lunch. It's a deadly, uninspiring, endless Sunday and it is only 4:00 p.m. No email so far today.

"I spent most of the next Monday looking for pictures for Dana. I had problems with the slide scanner but the flatbed scanner worked perfectly. I engaged in a stimulating email dialog morning and afternoon. Dana sounds an interesting man. His son lives near London with a part-British wife and children whom Dana and his wife will visit this summer. Unfortunately, their visit will probably clash with my hip operation.

"David and Joyce arrive late bearing a bottle of excellent Famous Grouse malt whisky that I had never heard of before. David and I drank it happily while Joyce kept us company with my Chilean Leyda Valley red. After all that, I need something other than drinks and nibbles before bed so will have to raid the freezer.

"Mornings are hell. I went to the local post office to send copy of orangutan film to Balbar, then to Great Gaddesden nursery to look for plant to give Rosemary tomorrow. I didn't spot anything but was pleased to see a Peacock butterfly feeding on some flowers there and a robin singing loudly inside the building. Drove back the long way via our old house and had difficulty keeping the tears from my eyes while driving.

"I was invited to have a sherry with Margaret in Number one. We were joined by David, Joyce, and Margaret Twiss from Number three. I could hardly be bothered to make supper.

"I waited on Friday for meat to arrive from Scotland, which it did at midday. It looks nice but after I put it in the freezer, I asked myself why I bothered to get it. Then I remembered it gave me something to feed the odd guest such as sister Ronnie.

"I tried to help David sort out a minor computer email problem and it worked. His daughter Angela's computer refused to either send or accept an email from him because it mentioned the word Viagra that it rejected as spam. Mine does not. I wonder what that signifies.

"Another horrible Saturday morning as I get stiffer day by day. Marika and Jeremy Clark came for coffee about 11:00 a.m. They brought a piece of homemade fig tart, and chocolates made by one of their twin sons, Oliver. He is studying chocolate making. We chatted until 2:30 p.m. Then we ate the tart followed by a packet of soup.

"I just read the first entry in these reflections and am crying. It is Saturday evening.

"David and Joyce, bearing fruit and ice cream came for a chat that cheered me up a bit. After they left I decided to make something to eat and put some microwave rice on. I had a violent reflux pain for some reason and had to wait a couple of hours for it to settle. I read the papers until about 11:00 p.m.

"Over three months gone. It's a routine Sunday morning, heavy mist and dull. It's bed changing day followed by a couple of emails, then more paper reading. I will incorporate David and Joyce's supper contribution into a fruit salad lunch. Such a fascinating life.

"I got up the following Sunday morning with my usual lack of enthusiasm, shaved, bathed, dressed, and broke my sock putter-oner. I don't know how I will be able to dress tomorrow but my priority task is to go out and buy two replacements for this magical tool.

"Where has a whole 19th week gone with nothing to show for it, except I nearly finished preparing documents for my Income Tax return? It is pouring rain and lightning at 11:00 a.m. I'll make a curry lunch rather than eating tonight. By the time my good friends David and Joyce depart, it is often too late to bother about cooking. Last night David was playing bridge so Joyce came and we had a long chat. After she left, I heated a potato in the microwave, for far too short a time again. I ate it reluctantly with a small piece of Gruyere cheese. I watched parts of a Le Carré film that I later recalled seeing ages ago and indulged in a glass of David's malt whisky that he bestowed on me.

"The next Tuesday I phoned Ronnie's German friend and upstairs neighbor, Gerd, to ask about the policy of Gates Foundation for which he works and similar organizations about how they expend their vast donations. I found he agreed with me in principle about need for grass roots approach. He said if I have something to tell people I should write and publish it! I need to decide if I can be bothered.

"I finally took the last volume of collected reprints to Great Missenden for binding. I was greeted by same old dog in its basket by the door, with a very white muzzle now. I parked outside the shop on a double yellow line so I did not dally long. After the simple drive there and back, I felt exhausted for no good reason and was glad to get home in one piece.

"For the last twenty-one weeks I have been living a sort of facade. In recent days, I have immersed myself in a flood of email exchanges with David W. and Dana D. in Washington about the Chinese ideograms for the antimalarial plant, *Artemisia annua*, if that is the correct name. We are now also involved with Elisabeth Hsu, a scholar in Oxford. She has written several papers on the history of artemisinin. A very confusing picture is emerging that we all want to see clarified. In between, David and Joyce maintain their daily support. I forced myself to go to the bar with them in the evening before warming up half the cooked dinner that Joyce sent me. I'll keep the rest for later.

"I am exceptionally stiff today, mainly legs, but also both hands. I'm obliged to take a second dose of paracetamol with codeine, which I am trying not to do. Its constipating effect can cause distress. I must make myself take a turn around the garden while it is still not raining. I tend not to visit the carp pond, as that is where Ruth and I sat together when she was still able to walk that far last year. Even thinking about it brings tears to my eyes.

It's warm but still and cloudy afternoon. I encountered one of the white-haired lady residents and as with everybody here, we greet each other as we meet on the path. She remembered which building I live in and that Ruth was no longer with us and we agreed that one has to keep going—but there are times when I wonder why and if I really want to. I'll make myself a cup of coffee.

"May Bank Holiday and a beautiful warm sunny day. I lunched with David, Joyce, and Bernard who was in good form again after a long period of depression and confusion.

Later in the afternoon, Joyce brought over their friend Carole who used to live in Zambia where her daughter still resides. I'm annoyed with myself because I could not remember the names of the countries bordering Zambia. I printed out a map of Africa from the internet as a reminder. It worries me that I forget so many things these days and hope it is not the onset of mental deterioration.

"Next day another lovely spring morning. Ronnie must be well on her way to Devon by now. I remembered to buy her tomato juice in the C.V. shop as she is temporarily on the wagon due to unstable blood pressure. I'll shop later after my cleaning lady finishes."

Ronnie had a long and tiring journey. When I phoned her at her hotel she sounded exhausted and I had horrid thoughts of her newly emerged hypertension. Let her not try to do too much. She will phone me in the morning.

"As every morning, I pass your two photos, a younger you smiling what Joyce referred to as your 'elfin smile' and the one that Anita Molyneux took two years ago in our old home, a more mature, thoughtful and kind smile that touches my heart every time. 'Hello Sweetheart,' I say, and tears come to my eyes as I hear you say quietly back, 'Hello Love.' Yes, my darling Ruth. I am so lonely, not just for company—that is available here in abundance—but I miss *you*, so deeply, deeply, deeply."

"We have to come to terms with our losses," said one of the kindly, white-haired widows yesterday evening as a group of us sat on the terrace making the best of the newly emerged spring warmth. This is a village of quietly grieving old men and women, all coming to terms with loss and aging. Many have generations of family who visit from time to time, others do not.

"Later this morning Ronnie phoned, feeling better after an early night. She does not think she will make the journey from Switzerland to Devon again and I agree. It is too much of a good thing at her age.

"David came mid-morning with an offer to take me to attend a British Legion luncheon on July 13th at Ashridge College where I would meet old friends from Little G. I accepted in the hope that I will be fit enough by then.

"Drinks on the terrace in the warm evening. I phoned Ronnie who was feeling better again and enjoying revisiting her donkeys.

"Warm and sunny again next morning. Breakfast news is full of cyclone disaster in Burma where the junta idiots block the dispatch of millions of dollars in emergency aid while the estimate of the number of dead already exceeds 100,000. Dictators should all be lined up and shot, slowly.

"I feel lethargic and achy today and accomplished virtually nothing. After a post-lunch snooze, I made myself walk round the garden and try to identify a large tree facing the flat at the far end of the lawn. I worked out it might be a silver maple but Kenny, one of our gardeners who manicures the lawn immaculately, said he thought it was a white oak. In the autumn, I found acorns and acorn cups so Kenny was right. I met a couple of lady residents, one from upstairs and another I see here and there. Holly blue butterflies have appeared already round the Japanese garden where the azaleas, bluebells, and other plants are looking their best. Hope we will have good sun for Ronnie to take some photos next week.

"Already five months gone by.

"Today Sunday May 11 Ronnie will arrive from her donkey holiday in Devon and I will collect her from the bus at Hemel Hempstead if I can find somewhere to park. Otherwise little to recount of the past few days. The email exchange I indulged in for the past weeks with Dana Dalrymple in Washington, David Warhurst, and others concerning artemisinin and the interpretation of ideograms in the old Chinese manuscripts that I photographed in China in 1980, continues to provide an entertaining diversion and ongoing confusion. Luckily, Dana leads the pack and will do any write up of the story in his capacity as an agricultural development specialist for some US government agency.

"Sometimes the hours pass and sometimes they drag. Friday evening played something called 'diminishing whist' in the flat of an ex-Bart's nurse called Rosemarie with her son and two pleasant, elderly widows, Kathleen and Edna; the latter a very Scottish lady from the Aberdeen area. Card evenings are not something I wish to adapt to although it was thoughtful of Rosemarie to invite me. Cards are definitely not my thing apart from playing the occasional game of patience on the computer when I am bored. While I was out Jeff Fryer phoned to see how I was so I phoned him back. He and Mary keep a regular check on me. In a week or two they go to Scotland for a week's holiday that I am sure they both need. Mary is really not fit and I know that life must be something of a struggle for them although they both put a brave face on everything.

"It's another very warm and sunny day. Once my aches and pains settle down a bit I must walk around the gardens. Ruth's crabapple tree is well established and already blooming beautifully, a dark red flower. It is conveniently near a bench at this end of the walking meadow that has a long view over the Berkhamsted valley facing south. The meadow grasses and buttercups in it are looking very fresh now. The Japanese garden is at its best, with colorful azaleas between bluebells and other spring blooms, while some of the early rhododendrons also shine out. The enormous Koi carp are fully awake from their winter vacation and rush to the edge whenever somebody appears, their mouths wide open. The water lily leaves appear and grow visibly by the day. The only things I have not seen at all are tadpoles. I wonder if the frog population was destroyed by the fungus disease that is devastating amphibian populations everywhere. In the pond in our old house, we used to get tadpoles every year, although it was rare to see any mature into frogs.

"This morning my hands are arthritic and this makes me mistype many letters. I seem to get stiffer by the day and wonder how much of this, if any, is psychogenic. I must check again with Lesley Hallan and see whether I can switch to ibuprofen. I am reluctant to take more than a minimum of codeine even though she prescribed these for me. I do not want to add constipation to my woes—I saw how distressing this was for Ruth when she was on opiate painkillers.

"Ronnie came and went. It was a good visit and we enjoyed each other's company, as we never did before. She is amazingly vivacious especially considering that she is ninety-three. I was pleased to share her company with David and Joyce. We had a very agreeable dinner together yesterday at the Marchmont Arms which I had never visited before. The time passed quickly. This afternoon she was to be collected by our newly discovered cousin, Sylvia, who lives in Hampstead Garden suburb, but Sylvia's car developed a fault. I enlisted the help of an old friend, John, who runs a taxi service in Hemel to drive Ronnie to London. John himself, whom I had not seen in well over a year, arrived with his brand new Mercedes and an even bigger belly than usual to collect Ronnie at 4:30 p.m. It was good to see him again as I had not used his taxi service for so long but we greeted each other like long-lost friends which, in a way, we are.

Of course, he had not heard about Ruth.

"Now that Ronnie's visit is at an end the flat seems desperately empty again. I had twice my usual ration of wine, still only two glasses, made myself supper, two more Waitrose pancakes stuffed with sliced sausage. Now I feel extremely depressed and lonely. David and Joyce discreetly stayed away this evening. I am writing now because I think I must write what I feel when I feel it instead of moping. In any case, I am obsessed with not leaving loose ends if I can help it.

"I need to complete several obligations such as, keeping my appointment with my accountant tomorrow to settle my tax affairs, pay John's bill for the taxi when he sends it as I requested, and try to complete the ongoing dialogue with Dana and David W. about Qinghaosu. Then I need to get ready to welcome the Schnurs and Killicks next week and probably get my new hip in early June. Otherwise, it would not be difficult for me to retire quietly and painlessly from the scene. Yesterday, Lindsay sent me an email to tell me that Chris Curtis died. He was the head of entomology at the London School and did superb pioneering work on malaria control by exploiting insecticide-impregnated bed nets. He must have been twenty years younger than me, a very shy, kind man. I presume he died of cancer.

"There are many people whose situation is worse than mine. I must stop feeling sorry for myself—but it would be simple and easy to take the fast route out. It is just that I am so lonely and so much miss my love whom I never did appreciate as I should have. I feel both guilt for that, for the bad times I gave her, and for many other things that even now I do not understand. I live something of a charade. The unknown lady, Mary, who phones me from time to time from the hospice follow-up of the bereaved service, did so only a few nights ago. She probably has an explanation. Joyce, who has a lifetime of experience of helping people, and David, would certainly understand. I have difficulty writing because my eyes fill with tears and the rheumatism in my hands gets worse by the day. I admit that I am secretly afraid of my impending operation, more for the side issues than the operation. That does not worry me much. I have little doubt that I will need to have the other hip replaced before too long, as it is even more painful than the one I am to have replaced. We will see in due course.

"The rest of this evening, I will read the papers and drink a brandy before an early night for a change. Ronnie and I used to talk quite late into the night as we never really knew each other through over eighty years. She is remarkably vivacious and active. We had coffee with my neighbor Margaret one morning. The dear lady is a couple of years younger than Ronnie. Both were drivers during WW II; Margaret with the Red Cross and Ronnie with the Army. They had many experiences in common and got on very well together.

"A cold dull Friday morning made me feel exceptionally stiff. On the email more news from Dana about Chinese ideograms. I was so wrapped up in the subject that I nearly missed the appointment with my accountant Sally. I parked the car and crossed the road when I bumped into David Halloway and Gill, purchasers of Pulridge House East. I had not seen him since we moved.

"Got to my accountant Sally's office on schedule and met her for the first time face to face rather than by phone or email. Found her to be a pleasant, capable young woman who breeds small children and African ridgebacks. The trip was quite exhausting so I drove straight home without doing my shopping. At home, I found a letter from the bank indicating that I had not paid my monthly credit card account. I must have forgotten as I normally pay by internet transfer when the bills arrive. I need to watch this memory problem.

"A miserable cold Saturday morning. Fiddled with email this morning but felt depressed so after lunch I decided to revise my small album of photos of Ruth and insert new ones. I'll have a drink soon. David and Joyce arrived bearing dessert. I had some after a toasted cheese sandwich dinner then watched a documentary on TV.

"Another week passed. Sunday mornings are always bloody.

"Washed clothes, changed bed linen, and put new summer duvet on for the first time even though it is miserably cold these last days and nights. I was obliged to turn the heating on again. Cold mornings give me exceptionally painful limbs and hands. I found I mixed up days for this week's visits between my two diaries, kitchen and study, but found Lee's last email that confirms they are coming tomorrow. Bob and Mireille arrive from Wales on Wednesday so that leaves Tuesday for me to shop. I booked them in downstairs for a fish and chip supper on Friday evening. Now I'll prepare a letter for the Hospice about a donation.

"Had an enjoyable visit yesterday from Lee and Tilley whom I had not seen for years. Lee hoped to come here about a year ago when Ruth was too ill to see any visitors and we had to decline his offer. It seems amazing that I first met Lee in 1966 when we had just gone to Liverpool and he was a student. He retired from his Chair at the Hebrew University in Jerusalem two years ago. He and Tilley are now grandparents by their oldest son and his wife who live in Nottingham. I'm waiting for Bob Killick and Mireille to arrive tomorrow from Wales where they are visiting Bob's brother.

"My video recorder is acting up just when I need it to show them the orangutan DVD so I am expecting a visit from the video technician to fix it. Then I have to shop for my visitors. Technician came, pushed one button that I unknowingly pressed earlier and left with large check in pocket for 'call-out charge.'

"Bob and Mireille arrived from Wales early evening Wednesday and stayed until midday Saturday May 25th. Their very agreeable visit included attending the official opening of the new HQ of the Royal Entomological Society near St. Albans. We were joined for drinks in evening by David and Joyce and for fish and chip supper here on Friday. Bob and Mireille visited the Bakers in Cambridge on Friday, but I was too tired and opted out.

"Saturday morning received a worried email from Ronnie whose blood pressure shot up again. Her GP hinted she may need a scan to help pinpoint the reason for this and she is terrified of the idea since she says she suffers from claustrophobia, so I phoned to reassure her. I spent much of the afternoon making or receiving phone calls to various people. A quiet evening and early night. Saturday nights are not my favorite.

"Next day we had heavy rain as forecast which made me feel extremely rheumatic all over this morning. Decided last night, not for the first time, that my present life is one great charade. I try to be the convivial old man, chatting in friendly fashion with my fellow oldies of Castle Village. Just below the surface, I am simply a sad old man desperately missing Ruth and ready to break into tears at any moment. Accepted invitation to join David and Joyce for sherry chez eux followed by lunch downstairs. Back home to fill in questionnaire for hospital pending my operation in a couple of weeks.

"I get stiffer day by day. I hardly made it to the recycling bins with a bag of newspapers this morning, the last Wednesday of May. I am beginning to dread the next few weeks but simply must put up with it.

"I grimace inwardly whenever a kindly fellow resident says, 'Good morning Wallace (or Peter, or whatever). How are you today?'

"I reply 'Fine thanks. And how are you?' knowing that I feel like shit. Everybody probably feels much as I do, especially if they have no partner.

"Reading most of the day was uninspiring. Threw out a load of newspapers, as I hardly seem to read what I get. I feel like stopping them altogether, but then I would have to buy a book of crosswords to keep my brain from addling. It is strange how some days my mind goes blank and on other days it runs smoothly. I don't think it is necessarily due to the complexity or otherwise of the clues. Sometimes I wonder if I am developing the earliest signs of advancing Alzheimer's as are so many of my contemporaries. I also notice that I make increasing errors in spelling when I type, especially as regards the order in which I type individual letters. Sometimes I get almost a complete word block for ordinary words, then the word I am seeking comes up spontaneously when I stop trying to think what it should be. Perhaps this is simply the aging process rather than something more sinister or perhaps because I am a 'two-finger typist'.

"I am weepy this last morning of May, missing my Ruth and feeling sorry for myself. While about to have a coffee before leaving to visit the chiropodist I got a surprise visit from Tricia Gibson, the vicar of Little Gaddesden. It was very welcome. However, I still felt weepy and I could not avoid it showing. She took it in her capable stride and we chatted about various profound subjects of one sort or another.

"As I returned from what I hope is my final shopping trip to Waitrose after having my feet done, I met Joyce. She insisted on carrying one of my heavy shopping bags upstairs for me. It was very kind of her as she can barely walk herself. I felt a total idiot at my current lack of mobility. After lunch, I phoned the surgery again and heard that the report on my urology examinations just reached there today from the West Herts hospital; a whole month since the last exam—very disgraceful on the part of the NHS. I requested that Dr. Ponsonby from surgery phone me this afternoon to discuss the report. Otherwise, I am not due to see Lesley Hallan until next Wednesday when she comes to C.V. I must ask her about my trigger fingers that get worse by the day. That's all I need now on top of everything else. She did phone. Nothing new from urology but Dr. Ponsonby booked me for more blood checks tomorrow including ESR to see if I have polymyalgia—something else I could well do without.

"David and Joyce called in dessert in hand and I dropped by their apartment before going to bed, birthday present for Joyce in hand.

"Thought much of the night about getting new laptop described in glowing terms by *Guardian* reviewer. Checked it out on PC World this morning after I returned from being bled at surgery. PC World has best offer, but it is not in stores yet. Home delivery will take at least a week, a week too late for me. Perhaps this is telling me I don't really need it. I'll check again after the weekend.

"Bumped into my artist neighbor Dorothea on my way home. She is almost the only person I have spoken to or heard about whose hip replacement was not a success. She did initially seem to do very well. Her situation was complicated when she fractured her femur just before she was due to have her operation. She has lost a lot of weight in recent weeks and looks very sad.

"This evening, a Friday, I am invited to join David and Joyce for a fish supper with their friend from Zambia. It is Joyce's birthday so we will have a drink in their flat before the meal. In the event, we were joined for drinks and supper by Bernard about whom I wrote earlier.

"Tomorrow I am going to look through my few surviving travel notes and try to put them into some sort of order just in case I think seriously of writing an autobiography after all this deliberation. At the end of the day, I still don't think I will do so, but it helps pass time. In a way it is a pity that I destroyed the majority of my travel notes a few years ago but they held too many unhappy memories that were best forgotten as well as a few with more general interest. If I need to, I can try to dredge some memories back from the recesses of my mind as long as they are still recoverable.

"The usual sad start to a Saturday. An unbelievable six months have passed since Ruth and I were parted.

"An email from my nephew John in Melbourne asked how my operation went on May 10th. Perhaps I gave him the wrong date.

"I had pre-op blues all day, Sunday June 1st; could not help it. David and Joyce asked if I would like to lunch with them but did not have the heart to accept. Had a miserable bit of pork from the freezer for lunch with packet of spinach and slept a bit. Jeff phoned to wish me well. He and Mary go to Scotland for a week in a few days' time.

"Watched play on Florence Nightingale and wept again. I am so lonely. All I want is to have my Ruth, to love and be loved by her. Nothing else matters—it is just pretence, putting on a brave face, whatever that means.

"Last evening I read some articles on anesthesia for hip operations and the various risk factors of the operation. The way I feel tonight I would not mind going under and staying there. There is nobody to miss me.

"I spent most of Monday morning assembling bits and pieces of my memoirs into a single file on the PC, and then lost a large part by pressing the wrong button. I asked Norman upstairs how his Wi-Fi works and went to look at his setup. His Norton antivirus tells him he has twenty-seven viruses! He has much less understanding than even I do, so we agreed he would take his computer to the local computer shop for advice.

"After much consideration and learning that Ashlyn's just installed a wireless link, I had a rush of blood to the head and ordered a laptop. Hope it arrives before I go into hospital. That may happen as I just realized I am not going in next Monday, but Tuesday. I must acquire a larger memory. Yes me, not my computer!

"A deadly dull, rainy Tuesday morning. Spent most of afternoon writing financial letters, emails, and other missives. I'm trying to learn how to use laptop with a wireless router in Ashlyn's, if they really have one and it is a suitable model.

"Today is June 4th. Final chat with Dr. Hallan on Wednesday, then interviewed by two nurses from Ashlyn's.

"Friday I decided to have haircut and do minimum shopping before saying au revoir to my car for the next six weeks. I'm becoming more apprehensive by the day and find myself inflicted by multiple minor things, e.g., exacerbation of itchy eczema, outbreak of herpes simplex over sacrum, uncomfortable ingrown toenail in spite of recent chiropodist visit, irritating dry cough, and significantly increased difficulty in walking. Clearly much of this must be psychogenic. The haircut made me look like a condemned prisoner but I could not care less. Ruth would have been very upset.

"No news yet about laptop delivery. I'm beginning to think I was stupid to order it in the first place. Add to list of problems—difficulty in making rational decisions. I phoned Eliane since neither Margrit nor I got through to her phone for a couple of days. I was a bit concerned that she was ill since she told me about having a severe back pain when she last wrote. When I called, she seemed reasonably cheerful so left a message on Margrit's phone to that effect. I think she phoned me back when I was out.

"Fish supper with David, Joyce, and two of their friends after drink at Number four. An agreeable evening but difficult to hear conversation over background noise. Must get my hearing checked one day.

"Slow start to Saturday as usual with increasing concerns about Tuesday. Today of all days I received in the mail a brochure from undertakers about planning for my demise. It seems to be a kind of insurance policy—against terminal poverty, not termination.

"I wrote to Eliane as she wanted the address for Ashlyn's to send me a card. I already had 'Good Wish' cards from David Warhurst and the Clarks. The latter are heading for Penang where Jeremy bought an apartment. Deposited large bag of old newspapers and last two empty wine bottles in recycle bins. I find them more difficult to carry the few yards to the center every time I go. It's about time my hips were fixed.

"Should make myself lunch, but not very enthusiastic about it. I see in reservations list that Margaret opposite in Number one booked herself in and could ask her to join me for Sunday lunch. However, I don't want to keep company with all the dear old ladies every time I need a cooked meal, agreeable as the ladies may be. Sometimes a sandwich solo chez nous and a cup of soup are preferable, especially in my present mood. I will take photos of Ruth to keep me company in the hospital and raise my morale during the coming weeks.

"No personal email today so far and nothing from PC World about the laptop. I finally made lunch of two badly cooked poached eggs, toast, and a packet of soup and listened to classic FM on radio. I wept in my food when they played Richard Strauss's 'Abendrot,' the last of his four final songs for his wife of fifty-four years. Both died before they heard its formal presentation. It is very beautiful and very sad. I found it, with a recording, on Wikipedia and played it again on the PC but with a Russian orchestra and soprano. Not as good as the one on the radio but nonetheless very moving.

"Must fill in a huge questionnaire for Ashlyn's about family background and such. I don't know why they want it but it will pass the time. This Saturday night will conclude 175 days of solitude.

"Sunday morning. For a change, it is a warm early summer's day. Ronnie phoned as I just finished struggling to put on my socks. She still has a problem resolving her hypertension and is not tolerating her medication well. I suggested she ask her GP if a simple diuretic might be adequate, but he should not need me to tell him what to prescribe.

"Margaret Sidford dropped in to ask what she can do for me in my absence and to wish me well. I had to disappoint her on the first score so she kindly invited me again to have lunch with her in the restaurant. It would be ungracious of me to decline even though my instinct was not to accept. I had visions of sitting with a group of garrulous old ladies. I went and we had a pleasant drink in the bar followed by a quiet lunch, just the two of us. After lunch, I invited her to my flat for coffee and a chat. She is a good listener and I talked too much, but she is too polite to tell me so. However, she also has a fund of stories. Like me, she forgets which she has told to whom so the time passed quickly. Before she left, I showed her Ruth's few remaining embroideries and she showed me three delightful and classical wedding photographs, which she had unearthed from a drawer. She was a beautiful young girl who retains her good looks and charm. I advised her to have copies of the photos made for her family. They are beginning to show signs of deterioration and are much too good to risk losing.

"Checked on my email and found I won £10 on the lottery so I reinvested this to cover my forthcoming absence. I have to scrutinize my typing carefully since my progressing trigger fingers seem to throw me out and I make countless typing errors.

"On Monday June 9th I forced myself to put together clothes and other items for the next three weeks; one in hospital and the two in Ashlyn's. It was difficult to concentrate. No sign of my new laptop yet nor any news when I phoned supplier so I am resigned to not getting it in time to be useful.

"Phone calls from Bob, Eva, and email from Vicki. Eva and family lunched with Margrit and Armin near Herisau. David and Joyce invited me for supper for which I am most grateful. Otherwise, I doubt if I would have bothered to eat as David and I both have to get up very early to check into the hospital at 7:15 a.m."

Chapter 23

"In Limbo"—2008

These notes begin with an account of the operation to replace one of my hips and my eventual recovery. I realize in retrospect that my entire existence was in a state of limbo; apologies for the unintended pun. I see a change from much of the preceding account. My notes took on a different tempo; for the most part staccato observations on daily events and impressions. When transcribing the tiny contemporary scrawl from my notebook I notice the tense of the comments oscillates from past to present. Seen objectively this implies similar swings between how I view passing events now, from the historical to a day-to-day, contemporary viewpoint. Perhaps this is all part of the aging process in the human mind. It's rather like the question that old people frequently put to each other, "What day is it?" My state of limbo lasted until August 4th, although my note making style changed little.

The years 2006 and 2007 were ones of great emotional stress as Ruth's illness waxed, waned, and finally terminated in the saddest, most unanticipated fashion we could have imagined. For a number of years following my retirement, and particularly after we decided that I would really give up working, I threshed about mentally. I was looking for a way forward that would gainfully occupy me intellectually. Writing was an obvious possibility, but writing what? Before I gave that question serious attention Ruth became ill. At first it was not grave, but after a promising initial response to six months of treatment, it progressed in a negative direction over the next year.

Over this year and a half, totally unnoticed by me, the stress began to take its toll on my body too. However, this only became evident after Ruth died when I rapidly became incapacitated by hip and leg pains. It was not long before my wise and diligent family physician, Lesley Hallan, sent me for X-rays. Meanwhile I developed a recurrence of problems relating to the inevitable old man's disease, benign prostatic hypertrophy. It was diagnosed several years earlier, but put on hold. Suddenly I was faced with three problems; bad hips, large prostate, and solitude in a large new home. A year after we moved in I still had pictures lining the floor instead of hanging on the walls and numerous possessions unsorted all over the place.

In 2007, when Ruth was admitted as an emergency to the West Herts Hospital, David and Joyce Grigsby, two neighbors in The Mansion, entered my life. They brought to me moral and physical support that was beyond anything I could ever have anticipated or felt I could possibly deserve. Among other old friends from Little Gaddesden, Pat and Ian Catchpole, Vicky Burdess and her family, Pat Crowhurst, and Suzie and Arnab Banerji came to my aid and made it possible for me to survive the weeks before and after I lost Ruth. Her last days passed in the Hospice of St. Francis, an amazing organization. Its existence had only come to my attention when an old friend and colleague, Ralph Muller, died there a few weeks earlier. The loving and sensitive palliative care that Ruth received at the hands of the doctors and nurses at St. Francis was something that I could never have anticipated and for which I remain eternally grateful. The thought of it even now brings tears to my eyes. Their volunteers continue to give me moral support with long telephone chats every few weeks.

On March 5, 2008, I saw Lesley Hallan for a checkup. In the early hours of March 7th I got up to pee and found I filled the toilet with fresh blood. On the 10th, I paid my first visit to Brian Bradnock a Scottish orthopedic surgeon and we made a date for me to have my right hip replaced at a private hospital in Harpenden on June 10th. The delay was deliberate on my part. I was already committed to receiving a number of visits from old friends living overseas during the coming few weeks and from my sister Ronnie, resident in Switzerland. On March 14th, a cystoscopy at the West Herts Hospital showed that I had a massive and very vascular prostate. I was given Fenasteride, an anti-androgenic steroid reputed to shrink that organ and avoid surgery. Ever a realist, between that date and early June I worked with my solicitor and accountant to get my affairs in order.

Lesley Hallan persuaded me that I would need care between being discharged from hospital and returning home. I arranged reluctantly to go from the hospital to Ashlyn's Care Home for two weeks. It is near C.V. Visualizing a dull fortnight, I foolishly arranged to buy a laptop computer to pass the time and maintain my contact with the outside world. The laptop reached me at Ashlyn's, but the ability to use it proved beyond my temporarily addled brain—more of that later.

Operation Day. At 7:00 a.m. on June 10th, David drove me to the hospital in Harpenden to prepare to get a new right hip. At some time in the afternoon, I was transferred to the operating room. After sixty-five years of a sheltered existence following an appendectomy as a medical student, I underwent surgery again. The experience was not a pleasant one, but it opened my eyes to a world outside mine that I had blissfully ignored and from which I was sheltered throughout my entire medical career.

"My memories are partly obscured. At times my short-term memory failed so badly that I often could not remember the name of the person I was talking to. This was partly a result of serious dehydration. That was precipitated by severe diarrhea immediately following the operation, as well as a near total lack of appetite and thirst. These necessitated receiving several liters of intravenous fluids. Attempting to go to the toilet, as I had to do at frequent intervals day and night, was not facilitated by coping simultaneously with an intravenous line, an indwelling urethral catheter leading into a bag, and a newly implanted hip joint as well as an indwelling epidural catheter. I survived a thoroughly miserable, nightmarish few days and nights. It is a relief that my memory was not very acute. My most recent photo of Ruth on the bedside table gave me solace and I talked to her often."

I kept a few notes of my stay in hospital on a small notebook, mainly the names of doctors, nurses and carers who assisted me, which friends visited me and when. My friend David, alone or with Joyce came to see me every day. Pat and Ian came when they could. I'm sure some people called me on my mobile phone, which was in danger of running out of power and money. I recall a bedside phone, but it was too hard to reach. The week from that Tuesday to the next left me with confused memories of events and changes in the ability of my eyes to focus. I found the food unpalatable and the drinks as bad. On the other hand, the majority of the nursing staff were sympathetic and efficient, as were the young house surgeons and physicians who appeared each day, usually to collect blood samples. After my return home, I threw out those notes.

One week later, I was desperate to leave the hospital and transfer to Ashlyn's. David and Joyce managed to maneuver me into the front seat of their car and we headed down the road past C.V. to the care home where we were greeted by an intense smell of 'Parfum d'Appenzell.' This is a jocular term used by Swiss-French when they approach the Appenzell countryside after the lush grass of the alpine slopes has been harvested and the soil replenished with ripe compost from the winter quarters of the cattle. The local farmer was putting heavy manure on the surrounding fields with farmyard slurry. It was not the most agreeable of welcomes, but fortunately much of the odor was kept out when the windows were closed and rain helped diminish the problem after a couple of days. It was replaced, on a lesser scale, by the odor of stale urine from the head of the hard bed. I was warmly greeted by the administrators, Diane and Janice, and the two nursing assistants, Lorraine and Kelly. They came to interview me at home prior to my acceptance to Ashlyn's. I think their main concerns were that I was sufficiently *compos mentis* and could afford their high fees. Two jolly, large and colorful nurses of Caribbean origin, Marianne and Grace, helped settle me in my room, which had a pleasant view out to the front garden full of flowerbeds adjacent to the main entrance.

I came to know most of the nursing and domestic staff who were generally very friendly and helpful. One of those in charge was an excellent and very bright Filipina senior carer, Tess, who worked like a Trojan. She was a trim woman of fifty-seven with glossy black hair and glasses. She was very intelligent and kind with an extraordinary capacity to cope with the demands of the most difficult patients. She maintained good discipline among them even when faced with unreasonable demands that were frequent. Raising her many children and grandchildren must have given her an excellent preparation for the profession of carer. One of her staff was a bright young man with a slight degree of cerebral palsy who was especially helpful and kind, but firm with all the patients. Some were very trying. Another of her delightful and competent staff was Jackie, a smiling young woman with auburn hair fixed in a bun and a beery voice like a character from the soap opera *East Enders*.

I slept miserably that first night fearing developing bedsores and with a massive dressing on my wound. In the morning, I looked out of the window and saw a pleasant view of the walled garden at the front of the building. I was amazed at how my eyesight changed. Without my glasses, everything was amazingly clear but it all blurred when I put them on again. I presume this was an aftereffect of dehydration as the phenomenon slowly reversed itself. From then on I started writing notes again in Ruth's old notebook. I'll include some of them.

"Then, David brought my new laptop, a neat and highly sophisticated machine that runs on its battery. My pre-operative hope was that I would be able to set it up and use it, maybe even with a wireless link to the internet, to pass the time at Ashlyn's. That proved far beyond my resources and my eyesight for several reasons. First, the lettering was very small, and the Word program was a new version that I found confusing. The finger-operated arrow, in lieu of a mouse, confused me. Finally, I would have to install an antivirus program and firewall before attempting to link up to a wireless server. There were two at Ashlyn's. So my new baby remained in limbo, along with me.

"By the Thursday, for the first time in months, I began to feel I was turning the corner for the better. This feeling was reinforced when I received a minor flood of visitors; Tricia our vicar, Pat and Ian, Vicky, all welcome faces. Later I had a phone call from the Hospice, this time from a young-sounding lady named Linda. Mary was not well. They have kept tabs on me since Ruth died as part of their service to support recently bereaved families. It is a strange experience; rather like a confessional where one is encouraged to open one's heart to a stranger, to release hidden and deeply troubling thoughts and sentiments. Self-controlled as I normally am I find it difficult not to break down when I talk to these almost anonymous women about how I am coping with my new life.

"At times, I am tempted to break the thread but have not had the courage to say simply, 'Thank you for the help you have given me, but I do not need it anymore' Mary, who I learn is a grandmother, is well again and phones me about once a month.

"That afternoon I was delighted to receive visits from Pat and Ian, a district nurse, and especially Tricia. It was good to see them. Ian brought me a portable radio but unfortunately, it was not a success.

During the afternoon my American colleague, Dana, (or Dr. 4D as we call him) with whom David Warhurst and I were collaborating was visiting Oxford and phoned me. It was the first time we actually spoke. He sounded exactly as I envisaged him, very lively and humorous. It is a pity we could not meet up on that occasion.

"At last, my memory lapses and visual changes were disappearing. On this Saturday morning I started walking with one stick, my appetite was improving, though the food was marginally better than in the hospital, and I was reading more. At last, I finished '*Digital Fortress*' by Dan Brown and started Khaled Hossein's wonderful story, '*The Kite Runners*'. This is a superbly written book and the style of the writing gave me much to reflect on; it's economical, colorful, and intensely emotional. What a gift. It made me reflect on the art of composition and the parallels between a writer and an artist. The brevity, clarity, and tight word selection of Hossein's phrases seemed to be equivalent to some artists' ability to capture the essence of their subject with a minimum of strokes of the pencil or brush. Our print of Picasso's *Mother And Infant* flashes in my mind's eye. Good writing and art demand spontaneity with an equal dose of sincerity. Nevertheless, the results of both require deep reflection and sometimes much revision.

"David found the chargers for my and Ruth's mobile phones and added a substantial sum to their cash balances so I was no longer dependent on the Ashlyn phone which was frequently occupied. Ronnie told me not long before that she unexpectedly met a younger woman who is a direct cousin of ours on my mother's side. That lady, Sylvia, told her that another member of that part of our family was aged 102. He lives in the same block of apartments that my sister, Pete, and her husband occupied when Ruth and I visited London immediately after our marriage. Sylvia contacted me and arranged to come and see me today. Her arrival coincided with my niece Jennifer's. She and her husband Richard came from their home in Gloucestershire and were joined by David and Joyce. The small room filled to overflowing. Glad as I was to receive their company, I was totally exhausted by the time everybody left. I was not yet fit as my operation wound was not healed and I was sleeping badly. I was extremely stiff. It was, in every sense, the longest day of the year.

"Today, Sunday, I had my first bath in about a fortnight. I was assisted by one of the carers. I found I was totally at ease with the unusual situation of being washed by a young woman. It seemed the most natural thing and I suspect took me back to my infancy for a moment. After breakfast, I returned to 'The Kite Runners' which made me feel weepy. I clearly was not yet psychologically balanced.

"Pat and Ian very generously lent me a portable TV belonging to one of their daughters so I was able to spend much of what would have been a dull, lonely Sunday watching excellent documentary programs. They included interviews with that unique and inspiring man, Nelson Mandela, as well as presentations by Parkinson and Andrew Marr, two of our top broadcasters. Later I located another lounge occupied by one person. Albert, aged ninety, was youthful in his demeanor, with acute hearing and chatty. He informed me that the oldest resident at Ashlyn's was a lady of 104, but she was confined to her room so I never met her. Albert and I nearly had a falling out when I mentioned how much I admired Mandela. He thought I was referring to Mugabe whom we both detest. It took a while before we got that one sorted out and were back on to speaking terms.

"Later that day David Warhurst with his old dog Rhum drove over to see me. Shortly after, we were joined by David and Joyce who had not previously met David. It was always a pleasure to see David W. and chat about old friends, mutual enemies, and science. Moreover, all three of my guests immediately clicked. In due course, they departed, David W. with my best pen that he used to sign a photograph for me.

"I find it strange that at least half the men I met recently, whether old or new acquaintances, are named David and are not even Welsh.

"That evening my right knee became very painful as I discovered when I walked to supper. The 'mad duchess,' as I call one of my table companions, was acting up badly but Tess kept her in check—just. Back in my room, I watched a fascinating TV documentary about the Cornish coast. The news of a train derailment reminded me vividly of my own experience at Wembley Junction on my way home from the London School in December 1984. (See Chapter 16).

"I was up and down much of the night because of the pain in my knee but the morning was beautifully sunny and a good day for Wimbledon. In spite of the bad night and an increasingly sore bottom from spending so much time on my back, I was able to rise and dress more easily and took a pre-breakfast walk to the conservatory outside where the grey squirrels were enlivening the scene.

"I now took my meals in one of the dining rooms where I initially shared a table with an almost silent man. The unfortunate fellow had an acromegalic facies and appalling eating habits. To say the least, he was somewhat disconcerting. I realized this is a feature of whatever malady he suffers so I did my best to ignore it. However, the situation hardly whetted my already abysmal appetite. Fortunately, I soon joined a table with three elderly ladies. The one facing me was white-haired, nearly always smiled, was almost totally deaf, and got around with the aid of a pushchair. She frequently fell down and got bad bruises. On my left was an agreeable, younger widow whom David knows. She retains all her mental faculties except her memory, which she knew was beginning to fail.

"To my right sat a tall, gaunt, grey-haired woman reminiscent of the mad duchess in *Alice In Wonderland*. I kept expecting her to announce, 'Off with her head!' She was as thin as a rake, loved porridge with extra sugar, and hot chocolate. Apart from these, anything else she attempted to eat was thoroughly messed up in her fingers. She seemed to live in a permanent state of perplexity. At an adjacent table sat George, a very large white-haired man with a voracious appetite and a loud falsetto voice that I heard frequently as he occupied a room adjacent to mine. His memory was fading fast but not his sense of humor. He delighted in pulling the legs of the ladies who shared his table. His room neighbor was a genteel man with a super-refined accent reminiscent of the actor Robert Morley. Although he talked rationally, he was unable to remember anything for more than a few minutes and passed his days watching his TV with the sound turned up to maximum volume. Passing me in the passage he would apologize for this but forget about it the next minute. He was, he told me, not antisocial but could not talk at length, which was sadly true.

"Opposite the dining room was a large lounge that reminded me both of the care home where my father Henry spent his last years and Muriel Spark's evocative book, '*Memento Mori*'. Henry used to complain bitterly about the old people, most far younger than him, lined up in chairs round the walls and not one speaking to another. There was a deafening silence in our lounge, disturbed only by a solitary budgerigar in its cage asking vainly for food.

"The day passed fairly quickly as the Wimbledon matches started in the early afternoon. Eva, with her younger daughter Isabel, paid me a quick visit around teatime. They were on their way to take their cat to the vet in Harpenden and Isabel to the orthodontist. Eva, a Swiss-German, has been supportive since Ruth's passing. She helped me communicate with our niece Margrit in Herisau. My attempts to converse in Schweizerdeutsch are a bit primitive. That evening I received another phone call from the support team at the St. Francis hospice who keep tabs on me. This time it was a young woman named Sue. I had the impression that she was well out of her depth talking to an old man like me.

"I had a bad Monday night but filled the waking hours by reflecting again on the exquisite writing of '*The Kite Runners*', so much so that in the morning I phoned David and asked him to bring my new laptop which arrived home in my absence. I wanted to start writing again. During the morning, a district nurse came to change the dressing on my thigh. To my surprise, the nurse was a man who lived almost all his life in a house practically opposite ours in Little G. Yet during nearly thirty years we never knowingly met each other. Since the operation, I was obliged to wear long pressure stockings to minimize the risk of developing deep vein thrombosis and was supposed to wear them for several months. However, I found them to be more and more uncomfortable. I phoned the hospital to ask if I could stop and that was agreed. The relief was immeasurable.

"David brought the laptop later in the morning and we unpacked it without delay. It was smaller than I anticipated, looked very complicated, and proved to be so. After reading the small instruction manual, I was exhausted and took a long post-lunch siesta. After that, I watched the miraculous Nadal playing at Wimbledon. David and Joyce came in again before supper for a brief chat. When they left, I took a short walk in the garden to add to my quota of exercise for the day. Both my operation site and knee were still very painful and I dreaded the coming night. However, I made my mind up I would leave Ashlyn's as originally planned on July 1st.

"I managed to get a better night's sleep with my bottom in the air on top of my duvet. It took the pressure off my increasingly sore sacrum and operation site. The Wednesday morning started well. I was able to put on my socks. Pat and Ian dropped by. Later, a district nurse came to change my dressing. The afternoon was full. I managed to set up my laptop and play a game of solitaire on it before Vicky arrived with another book, 'A Short History Of Tractors In Ukrainian' by Marina Lewycka, a humorous book that received rave reviews. Charles came into the room by chance and Vicky recognized him as one of her former pupils, a bright one. Then David arrived and Ronnie phoned. After tea, I walked round the garden with another resident, a garrulous but bright ex-schoolteacher. No sooner had I returned to my room than Jeff phoned after which I returned to watching Federer in the Wimbledon finals.

"The next day was bath day! Fancy recording that.

"Today, June 26th was George's seventieth birthday; he looks at least eighty. A glass of sherry was offered all round in the lounge to celebrate. It was so foul I could not finish mine. I exchanged a few words with another resident who served in Nigeria in the West African Frontier Force in 1945. However, he is very deaf and the going was hard. Later I continued reading '*The Kite Runners*' about the death of Baba and was overcome with tears; and that after only one sherry. I was delighted to be visited after lunch by Arthur and Geraldine Berry, old friends from Little G. whom I had not seen for a long time. By suppertime I still did not feel very happy. I was becoming nauseated by both the food and the ambiance. I decided to make an effort to go home as soon as possible. My laptop was proving too small for comfort and too difficult to configure; all in all a mistake. I was too mentally and physically disturbed to set it up properly. All I recorded was a heading for a new, late Chapter that I entitled, '*So, from here to eternity? Heaven forbid!*' The title speaks for itself. The thought of another dreary weekend lying ahead of me added to my depression. I unburdened myself to David and Joyce when they came to see me later in the evening."

"After my customary two-hourly nocturnal pee I awoke at 7:00 a.m. feeling extremely gloomy in spite of it being a bright and sunny morning. I managed to wash, shave, and dress but simply could not finish my morning exercises. I felt nauseated with a rapid, weak pulse, so returned to bed. I could not face breakfast in the dining room and asked if my GP could pay me a visit. The district nurse cheered me up a little when, changing my dressing, she told me that my operation wound was healing well. When David called, I was feeling very weepy. I managed to eat a small lunch in bed then decided to make an effort and move to my armchair to await my GP's visit. Elisabeth Ponsonby arrived in mid-afternoon, checked me over and recommended I remain at Ashlyn's longer. She noted that my blood pressure was lower than normal. Before she departed she arranged for me to have a blood sample taken the following Monday.

"David came in the evening by which time I was feeling slightly better but still tired and emotional. I decided to make an effort to go to the dining room for supper, but in slippers and without socks. It was my smiley lady's ninety-third birthday and she was presented with a cake. When her daughter, Jean, came it turned out that she once worked with Wellcome at Berkhamsted Hill and was now the senior secretary to my solicitor. She came with him to visit me in the flat some time earlier. I returned to my room to read after supper but my hands and fingers were tingling and my legs were badly swollen. The swelling was so much that I wondered if I was suffering from an acute vitamin deficiency.

"Another dreadful weekend lay ahead. In spite of sleeping better, I woke asking myself the classical question, 'What day is it today?' After breakfast with the mad duchess and other ladies, I returned to bed for a while but decided to make the effort to get up and walk in the garden. I bumped into the garrulous Marianne but could not face chatting so I returned to my room. I put my feet up and dozed uncomfortably in the armchair. When I woke around midday, I started to read an article in *Saga* magazine about Topol. That was enough to make me cry again. I was getting seriously depressed. I was dwelling on the thought of a bleak future ahead of me and how to avoid it. Then I read a letter in *Saga* about making recordings of peoples' voices. I knew I had one short tape of Ruth reading a piece by Proust but for me her voice was indelibly etched in my memory. Before supper, David and Joyce came bearing fruit and cakes but I had no appetite.

"Later in the evening, I heard a female resident who lived in a room just up the corridor from mine shouting, 'Please let me down. It's so hot here!' This went on for at least fifteen minutes. I rang my bell twice for a carer but nobody came. I wondered if the woman calling was in the dementia unit as the door leading to it was nearly opposite mine. However, when I got up to look, I saw her standing in the entrance to her room still calling loudly for help. There was no way I could intervene so I had to wait until a carer finally arrived.

The incident made me determined to insist on returning home as soon as possible. That night I was unable to go to sleep and my right leg was more restless than ever. I asked for a sedative and was told that none was prescribed for me nor was any available. I settled for a cup of hot milk and watched rubbish on TV until I felt I could try to sleep. In this way, I passed the terrible hour of 11:30 p.m. when Ruth died all those weeks before.

"Here are the gory details that I am including deliberately as a record of the physical and psychological trauma. What somebody goes through after the stress of an operation in old age may seem relatively minor in retrospect. I had a very bad night that included spending half an hour on the toilet trying to pass rock-hard, black stool with little success. My belly, my back, and my limbs were all stiff from the ordeal. In spite of taking paracetamol, I only managed to doze off by about 2:00 p.m. Then I woke up several times with severe pain in my right knee, heel, and back. My sacrum and the right cheek of my backside were so sore that I got up at 6:00 a.m. to sit it out in my uncomfortable armchair. I tried to read the comic book on tractors in Ukraine but could not raise a smile. I felt absolutely bloody and phoned David early asking him to bring me some more soluble paracetamol and Codamyl. He brought that at 9:00 a.m. arriving at the same time as Tess. I broke down and wept. While I was doing so, Ronnie phoned but I could not speak with her. Later David called her back to explain.

"When he left, I tried to do the *Saga* crossword and read a bit more about tractors. This was my first challenge in my new bachelorhood since putting Ruth to rest six months before. I suddenly feared for the future as I saw that I was not managing at all well on either a mental or a physical level. At this moment, I realized how strong a lifeline David and Joyce were throwing me. I never knew such a wonderful couple. Writing that in my notebook made me weep again. I thought of Ruth and missed her more badly than I can ever say. Even transcribing these notes my eyes are flooding with tears again.

"In the late morning, David Warhurst phoned for a chat. He said he would phone me again next week when I am home. I could not remember the name of Rhum, his Scotty dog. Then I watched a program about the animals at Longleat and country life on TV. A little later Geoff Pasvol phoned just as lunch was served. I asked him to call back later. As Charles was bringing me lunch David and Joyce arrived, this time bearing fruit, ice cream, and drugs, including a sedative for the night, and underwear. This coincided with a bowel alarm! I returned the fruit and unneeded drugs. As soon as they left, I headed urgently for the toilet, still with no success. I ate lunch in the hope it would help but could not bring myself to drink the foul tasting tepid water sitting on my table. Now I was worried about the wisdom of taking a sedative in case I had to get up again in the night.

"After lunch, I tried to call Geoff back without success. I did not feel like leaving my room in case I was obliged to talk to anybody and it was too cold anyhow to walk outside. There was little service that day. My bed was unmade although Charles brought me badly needed clean towels. At teatime, Geoff called back. After that, I managed to sleep for a half-hour then reluctantly made the effort to go to the dining room. I still felt bloody awful but decided I would take the sedative that night. I waited for the evening meal and watched a new version of the Pearl Harbor saga, which was astounding from a photographic point of view. During supper, I was able to chat a bit with Jean as the mad duchess had departed to stay with some unfortunate relations. My bowels were a little easier but I still had chronic abdominal pain.

"To my surprise, I slept much better but had wild dreams all night. At 4:00 a.m., I woke to pee but failed to reach the toilet in time and was lucky to be wearing underpants that prevented me from soaking the floor. My knee was still very stiff but otherwise I did not feel too bad.

"When Kelly and Natalie came in to check on me first thing in the morning I asked, 'Is it bath day?' It was not.

"At 8:30 a.m. I tried to phone Ronnie but her line was busy. I think she was talking to David. So far, I seemed to be improving although I still had a left lumbar pain that was probably related to my chronic bad posture in bed and too much sitting. It was a very cool morning. I walked to breakfast and back and was snoozing when Ronnie called so I could tell her that all was well again. I decided to walk down to the laundry to try to find my missing underwear but really to gain some much-needed exercise. By then I made my mind up and told the administrators that I definitely would leave Ashlyn's the next day. On my return to my room, I phoned the hospital to change the appointment I had for Tuesday with a physiotherapist. David arrived bringing a bag for my clothes and told me he would return that evening. When he left, I went to the lounge to participate in the residents' monthly meeting. I made a few comments, 'What about providing cold water in Thermos flasks?' I also paid a few compliments to the staff.

"Around teatime, our old neighbor, Barbara Day, came to see me with Pat Catchpole and we had a long chat about friends and neighbors from Little G. After they left, my GP phoned to say that my urine was normal and I could go home the next day. I was delighted to have her blessing since I already had made the decision to do so.

"Quite unexpectedly, my surgeon Brian Bradnock came to see me early that evening. We had an enjoyable chat for about an hour. I learned of his family life, his invention with an American colleague of a novel instrument called Oscar for removing damaged prostheses, and his special interest in malt whiskies. Later, I tracked a rare specimen named Auchentoshan on the internet and arranged to have a bottle sent to him. We exchanged ideas about writing and books. I told him about the impression made on me by 'The Kite Runners' and the book on tractors. We discussed the rise and fall of the National Health Service from which he recently resigned in protest to take up full-time private surgery. It was a congenial visit. He left after drawing me a map of his home and saying I should come to visit him one day, an invitation that I took, I must admit, with thanks, but a grain of salt.

"David and Joyce returned after supper and confirmed that they would come and collect me to go home the next afternoon. I watched more tennis, feeling relaxed for a change.

"Tuesday July 1 was – Freedom Day. I slept intermittently but without accident, ate too much breakfast, and packed. While I did that, an enormous mattress top was delivered by the social services. I should have been using it at Ashlyn's for the past week, but better late than never. Somehow, I would get it home. I settled my account with Diane and expressed my appreciation for the care I received. I was feeling much better but still wobbly. Chatting with Charles I found that his grandfather was an entomologist named Harley who worked on tsetse flies in West Africa—small world. At last, the district nurse arrived and collected a blood sample. I survived lunch but still felt very lethargic and simply packing my few things exhausted me. It was a beautiful day but I could not raise the energy to walk outside so I watched more tennis.

"David and Joyce collected me at teatime and took me home. I entered my front door with an enormous sigh of relief and had to hold back the tears of pleasure at being back after what seemed a lifetime away. David returned to Ashlyn's to collect the mattress topper that we used to remake the bed. I found to my relief that I had no trouble getting into it. We had a glass of wine together to celebrate before they brought me a delicious light supper of smoked salmon salad and strawberries; a great treat after everything I had eaten the past two weeks. Nurse Melanie came up to welcome me and see how I was getting on. Afterwards Jack Davidson phoned and then everybody's favorite carer, Lily, called to tell me she would be coming round next morning at 7:00 a.m. to help me start the day.

"That night I slept much better on my new mattress but was up at 7:00 a.m. brushing my teeth when Lily arrived to help me with washing and bed making. David came in as I was dressing and again later to make sure all was well and Joyce brought my paper. I had a simple late breakfast, complete with a cold fruit juice for a change, then opened my mail and answered a few urgent letters. My upstairs neighbor Joan dropped by to welcome me, and then Margaret from the flat opposite came to collect my shopping needs. I phoned Jeff to ask for news of his cataract operation, which went well, then made myself lunch, a cheese sandwich, packet soup, and an apple. I was having a post-lunch snooze when Margaret delivered the shopping.

"In the afternoon, I opened my computer to find 312 emails waiting. One told me I won $800,000 in a lottery and another message, £10 in a different lottery. I'm now £10 better off! David and Joyce came in for a drink bearing supper. Afterwards I watched the news briefly then some tennis, did the *Guardian* crossword, and went gratefully to bed.

"Next morning I rose, washed, dressed slowly, and then had breakfast. Later, David took me to the physiotherapy department at Harpenden where Kate Dobson, a gentle-voiced young woman, gave me new exercises to do and arranged for me to start hydrotherapy there on July 8th. I was very tired afterwards. That afternoon I received a phone call from Herbert telling me that his sister Gladys died after a long illness and he was attending her funeral. Shortly after David Evans called to ask if I knew that my old senior technician, Peter Sargeaunt, died. I knew that from an email. Both Gladys and Peter's wife Trixie, who was my secretary at the LSHTM, suffered from Alzheimer's disease, but Trixie still survives. (Alas, no longer.)

"David came for a coffee and Joyce joined us for a drink later. Elisabeth Ponsonby phoned with the news that my hemoglobin had shot down from fourteen to eight grams/liter. No wonder I was feeling so exhausted. Now I had to take a large dose of iron tablets that I did not look forward to ingesting.

"After my usual night, I struggled up and did my exercises. In preparation for my hydrotherapy, Pat and Ian took me to M & S to buy swimming trunks since I no longer had a decent pair. As an encore, I bought a new pair of slacks to replace a pair I believe I gave to the hospice shop by mistake, along with many of Ruth's clothes. While having a coffee there we met Pat's mother whom I had not seen for years. By the time we returned I was exhausted and slept much of the afternoon. During the afternoon, my iron tablets arrived from the pharmacist. Later on I cooked lentils and spinach before David and Joyce arrived for our evening chat and drink. When they left, I read a short while then went back to bed.

"Following another usual night and morning, I fiddled with emails and my new laptop. Ronnie phoned later. After lunch, I discovered how to use what I thought was a Flash Drive, but turned out to be a memory stick for computers, a useful gadget. David and I had a short walk in the garden but even that exhausted me so I watched TV and saw Venus Williams win her fifth final at Wimbledon. David came back later and we had a quick glass together.

"After sleeping late, I struggled through my exercises on the Sunday morning. Thought of joining my neighbor Margaret for lunch in the restaurant but changed my mind and asked to have lunch delivered in the flat, then slept again. Later I cleaned up more emails. I felt rather faint all day, perhaps due to the weather—always a good excuse. Lunch was somehow not agreeable to my palate. Sometime during the day, David and Joyce came bearing sherry. Sylvia phoned, after which I was watching tennis again. Nadal is beating Federer, but rain stopped play. Then Margrit phoned and after that Eva, then Jack. In turn, I phoned Jeff. Later I warmed up some oriental prawns and watched Nadal beat Federer to become the new World Champion.

"Up early on Monday and showered with help from Lily. After breakfast, I wrote to Herbert and Peter Sargeaunt's daughter Janice before tidying up David's photo of the painting of the old Cooper-Wellcome site that was unearthed in the garden house in C.V. Now I can send a copy to someone in the archives section of the Wellcome

Trust. It poured much of the day and I slept again in the afternoon. Joyce kindly brought me lunch, cottage pie, and a sweet. David came later to arrange to take me to Harpenden the next day. Linda phoned me from the hospice as Mary was still not well. I finished the day doing the crossword and reading a little before having another early night.

"Next day David took me to my first hydrotherapy session that I approached with some trepidation. It was quite an agreeable experience directed by a lady named Jill. The exercises emphasized my need to get attention for my left, good, hip before long. I tried to visit Marsh, the butcher in Redbourn, en route but his shop was closed and he may have retired. I was hungry after the session but there is not much food left in the flat, just a sandwich and old rocket. I slept for an hour then started to write my new chapter that I am calling '*In limbo*'. Unfortunately, I was starting to get frequent migraine attacks. However, the excellent cottage pie that Joyce made me yesterday would serve me for tonight's supper. I looked forward to that and a glass of wine that I had later with David and Joyce. After that, it was a short read and bed.

"Usual morning. Did laundry and writing journal. Phoned Wellcome Trust about painting in garden house and arranged a meeting with a Dr. Ross MacFarlane. Wine arrived in afternoon. Snoozed until David and Joyce arrived for a drink. I finally cooked one of my Scottish steaks but it had little taste, no doubt due to my cooking. Read and bed.

"Lily arrived next day, a Thursday and woke me at 6:45 a.m.! Unpacked new wines after breakfast then slept again. Suzie phoned that they would visit on Saturday. Late morning David collected me to shop at Waitrose and I bought a large slice of calf's liver, forgetting that I would have to cook it. Helen called in afternoon to confirm that she will come to the flat to deal with my feet on July 24th. Usual wine with David and Joyce in evening then cooked the liver; not too bad with 'Smash' potato. Made a series of phone calls to Eliane, Eva,

Halloways, and Ian but the Burdesses and Bassils were out.

"Usual Friday morning routine then made 'Thank You' cards, a birthday card for Marija, and ordered malt whisky for Bradnock. Had sandwich, soup, and fruit lunch. I was snoozing when Andrea Bassil called. They sold their house in Australia and she wants to move from Cambridge, but has a problem with Paula. Andrea suggested bringing her here to see me next week, but I discouraged this for the time being. Found an interesting article in the *BMJ* that drew attention to the way in which illness or trauma, physical or psychological, in the frail and elderly can trigger a massive failure of the normal homeostatic mechanisms of multiple organ systems of the body. In a small way, this is obviously what I have been going through following my operation, but luckily, I have overcome most of the problem. Largely only the anemia remains to be treated appropriately and the muscle rehabilitation. Trouble there is that my left, good, hip is starting to give me major concern. It hinders the rehabilitation of the operated, and now pain-free, side. Ended day with fish and chip supper in restaurant downstairs with David and Joyce then read and another early night.

"A beautiful sunny Saturday morning that turned cold. Received 100-page, revised script from Dana that I will study later. I feel very depressed again this morning. Saturdays tend to be bad but consoled myself with thought that Suzie and Arnab were coming in the afternoon. They arrived bearing a large bunch of roses and a wonderful set of CD's by Martha Argerich. David and Joyce came in for usual chat and drink and we discussed the problem of the threat to stop the night nurse-on-call system here in C.V.

"I fussed about what to wear for lunch today at Ashridge College as guest of David and Joyce for British Legion. I met numerous acquaintances from Little G. including Bob and Audrey Cullen. It was a good reception and lunch but found it tiring and was glad to get back to flat. Pat and Ian came over later bringing fruit and flowers, and then Barbara phoned. After evening wine with David and Joyce, I had an early supper of cheese and biscuits, then bed.

"A bright sunny morning to start the week and I was shaved when Lily arrived at 6:45 a.m. Had a long chat with Gerry Burt about the nursing situation. He promised to take the matter up with the Chairman of the CVRA prior to the forthcoming AGM. After lunch, Bernard came in and we talked for the next two hours almost non-stop.

"Off to hydrotherapy with David next day at 9:40 a.m. Coming back I filled his petrol tank and was amazed at how the cost of fuel had risen since I last filled my car about six weeks ago. I just finished sandwich lunch when Bernard phoned and brought over the manuscript of his autobiography together with some photos of his last flight to Prague in a government plane complete with fighter escort on arrival! In the early evening, Linda called again from the hospice. She sounds very much like Lily and is a grandmother, which surprised me. I managed to put my feet up for a short while before David returned and we went down for a drink in the bar. We met several of the village widows; pleasant women whose names I immediately forgot. I heated up a curry for supper. Audrey, Peter Mann's friend, invited me to join her table for Sunday lunch. After supper I read papers then to bed. I seem to watch TV less and less these days.

"It's getting to me! Rose at 6:45 a.m. to shave in preparation for Lily's arrival, and then realize that she comes tomorrow! After breakfast, Kathy from undertakers phoned to say that Ruth's stone was in place but the stonemasons made an error in the engraving. She was going out to have a look and I decided I would look for myself. I wanted to ask David if he could give me a lift but he was out, so decided to take the plunge and drive myself to the church. It was my first attempt to drive since early June. I went out to the car and found that the battery was flat. I phoned Kathy who said they would come and pick me up. The engraver had not painted the outstanding text on the stone, but the background. On returning, I phoned the

RAC. A man arrived shortly after and started the car for me. I had to keep it running for half an hour to charge the battery. Just then David returned and was about to go to the Golf Club. I told him I would try to take the car for a short run and asked if he would tail me in his just to make sure I drove properly. He did and I did. This was a major landmark; driving only thirty-five days after my operation. I was very pleased with myself.

"In the afternoon Barbara Day turned up in her new car; her old one packed up a week or two earlier. After she left, I checked through Dana's new draft of his paper and just finished when David returned for our customary drink. I was cooking supper when Joyce arrived to bring me news of a meeting on nursing that was to take place prior to the AGM. Sadly, she is beginning to have trouble again with her hips, both replaced some years ago. Had an early night in preparation for another early morning.

"The days pass rapidly as I acquire a new routine. I struggle up, wash, shave, and such. Then I exercise, dress, and eat breakfast. I am keeping a separate notebook with a brief diary of daily events, visitors, thoughts, drinks with David and Joyce, journeys with David to hospital for physiotherapy, hydrotherapy, and shopping one day with David to replenish fridge and freezer, and other little items of everyday existence. My leg muscles are slowly building up again. Lily comes twice a week to help me with shower, creaming feet, and legs. She really is a wonderful woman, a young grandmother who has the skill of attending to one's intimate needs with a total absence of self-consciousness on either side. My cleaning lady Chris, is also a welcome visitor, but brought the unhappy news that she is leaving in a few weeks to take on a new job that will be better for her and her family. I will miss her cheerful face and her help and have to get used to a new cleaning lady when she goes.

"Today is the sixty-fifth wedding anniversary of David and Joyce. I ordered a bouquet of flowers to mark the occasion. When David came this morning, I asked him if I could take him or both of them shopping rather than the other way around and he agreed to risk his neck in accepting the offer. I was very pleased to be able to drive. Later Andrea and Paula, then Robert Williams phoned. Afterwards I sorted out emails from Dana.

"I really am beginning to lose it! Last night and this morning, I thought the hot water had failed. I discovered I was turning on the wrong tap.

"This morning Kathy phoned to say that the stonemasons had made good the error on Ruth's stone and took me up there to see for myself. All is now well. After lunch, I relaxed with the accumulated papers and crosswords until Vicki arrived bearing a cake, another book, and good news of their daughter Sophie.

"Joined David, Joyce, their friend Carole, and Bernard who were in for fish supper. Bernard was very talkative but it is such a contrast to the state of depression that he was in only a few weeks ago that nobody complained.

"Usual slow rise and exercises this Saturday then drove to Berkhamsted to get new slacks lengthened after having them shortened too much. Made pasta for lunch with half glass of red wine, but not very enjoyable. Won £6 on Eurolottery so I walked off my euphoria in the garden before the sun went away. Had coffee with Vicki and some of her cake for tea then watched golf before phoning Pat Crowhurst and Jeff.

"Ahead of me, the 218th night.

"Woke up feeling again very gloomy stiff and anxious. After exercising, I deliberately ate a large breakfast of fruit, yogurt, and marmalade. Looked up Bernard on the internet and found some of his wartime record in the Czech contingent of the RAF. I was invited to Audrey's pre-lunch party in the bar with her brother, sister-in-law, David, and Joyce, but it was not a very stimulating occasion because of my frame of mind. Afterwards I read the paper before sleeping yet again but later watched a splendid golfing final at Birkdale.

"Another early Monday morning with Lily then a leisurely day doing crosswords, reading papers, journals, and then emails.

"Mary, my support lady, phoned for a long chat in the evening. She often manages to bring me near to tears, which I fight off. I don't have the heart to tell her I have had enough bereavement support as long as I become depressed from time to time. Elisabeth Ponsonby called to arrange another blood check for me. I finished reading Bernard's remarkable story.

"It is a whole week since David and Joyce's anniversary and little has happened except I am driving again. Today I drove myself for the first time to see the physiotherapist at Harpenden. She told me my operated leg is making good progress. I was very tired when I returned and I know that my good hip is getting worse by the day. Tomorrow I see Brian Bradnock again for a review. I seriously fear that he will recommend having that hip replaced. If so, I will have to discuss my general condition next week with Lesley Hallan. I am frankly very depressed by the prospect and today, like many of the past few days, was thoroughly unproductive in every sense. Of course, I should maintain a positive attitude about the situation since the first operation was very successful. However, I have nobody with whom to share my fears. I do not want to burden my good friends David and Joyce or other friends.

"Each day I keep a diary of the minor incidents that make the days and nights pass. It makes very boring and introverted reading. For example, had a toasted cheese sandwich and soup for lunch, and then snoozed again. In the late afternoon had a drink with David, Joyce, Bernard, and about eight others on the terrace, and then returned Bernard's papers to him with the suggestion that they would contribute a valuable oral history to such archives as those of the RAF and Jewish wartime history of survivors from Eastern Europe.

"I was very apprehensive and nervous all day as I had an appointment with Brian Bradenoch that evening. I occupied the day by drawing up a list of my references to refute the implications by Nick White and all in their 1999 *Lancet* paper. I saw it before but yesterday

Dana copied it to me. It claims that only clinical data are of importance. Not a single mention of experimental studies on drug resistance and its importance or methods of preventing it!

"David drove me to Harpenden in the evening. I did not feel very confident driving in anticipation of hearing I would have to have my left hip replaced. Bradenoch never broached the subject. He made a short check on my mobility, suggested a few new and important exercises to be done daily, dismissed the need to follow up with the physiotherapists, and suggested a further review with X-ray in three months. I was extremely relieved at the short-term prospect but still think I may have to have another operation at some stage as the left hip is very painful and limits my rehabilitation of the operated side. It is doing very well. Finally, to my surprise, he invited me to dinner in two weeks. I accepted gracefully. It seems he has close relations with Elizabeth Ponsonby, who is a neighbor, and was pleased to receive the special malt whisky I sent him—the Auchentoshan 1984.

"I returned to C.V. much relieved and had a beer with David on the terrace. We were joined by Bernard. He looks and sounds more relaxed and almost jolly. I dined later on sausage and mash.

"Rose early on Thursday for Lily, breakfasted, and then took myself shopping. I booked a visit from the computer man from Berkhamsted to help set up my laptop then waited for Helen to come and fix my feet. After lunch, I slept again then listened to speech by Obama who was very impressive.

"In the evening, Bernard entertained David, Joyce, and me at a local Thai restaurant where they ate an enormous meal. David and Bernard accompanied it with large helpings of malt whisky and French red wine. I managed a couple of tempura prawns and part of a mild chicken curry with coconut milk plus a small Singha beer. Even that was too much for me and I was relieved to get home again. Luckily, we went and returned by taxi.

"After usual slow start next morning I drove to surgery to have blood taken, then to Great Missenden to collect my last book of bound reprints from Amanda Slope. On my way back I did a reconnaissance of Bovingdon to locate Brian's house but missed his turn. Made a vegetarian lunch and then slept. Joyce came in for a drink and chat, but David went out to his usual Friday evening meeting. Later I had a fruit supper, did the crossword, read, and bed. I seem to get stuck in the middle of the tractor book.

"Summer arrived last Thursday. Yesterday and today, it is very hot and oppressive which accounts partly for my extreme fatigue. This morning I overslept until 9:00 a.m. slept again after breakfast and again after lunch. Before lunch, I went down to the walking meadow to see Ruth's tree. It is beginning to look healthier. However, I only sat for a few minutes on the bench. I cooked the mussels I had in the freezer and accompanied them with a freshly baked baton and small glass of inferior white wine. I could not keep awake after and am about to go and lie down again; for the first time on our big bed. It was unoccupied since Ruth left us over seven months ago except for a few nights by sister Ronnie. Just as I got up Pat and Ian came in and we went to see Ruth's stone with its engraving. Ian photographed it for me. In the evening David, Joyce, and I had drinks on the terrace after which I cooked pastry and listened to a promenade concert.

"Yet another Saturday night ahead of me.

"It was days before I noticed that from here onwards I was heading my notes with dates in October. Watch it Peters!

"This Sunday morning I woke up with another bad dream feeling very stiff and gloomy. The unaccustomed hot spell seems to be making me depressed. Today the marquee was erected on the lawn just below my windows; very efficiently and very rapidly. Late in the evening nurse Andrea called to see me to express the nursing team's continuing anxiety about their future. I reassured her that not only I, but also other residents were firmly on their side and I would put their case to the AGM.

"Lily arrived at 6:45 a.m. on Monday, followed by my cleaning lady Chris at her usual 10:30 a.m. I worked on notes for my forthcoming intervention at the AGM. Then I arranged for the birthday lunch I will give for Ruth at the King's Head on September 4th. She would have been seventy-nine were she here with us. When I was seventy in 1994, she gave me a total surprise party there and I want her to have one in case she is out there somewhere watching.

"In the evening, there was a convivial welcoming evening for Marquee Week in the Mansion House. I withdrew and went to bed by 9:15 p.m., only to be awakened by a severe lightning storm during the night.

"Usual start to the day except Bernard dropped in early so I took him shopping with me. He had his car and license taken away since his minor accident in C.V. He is furious about this and intends to appeal, which I have no doubt he will.

"I checked in with Lesley Hallan and learned that my hemoglobin is already up from eight to eleven grams/liter. I felt reasonably fit and went to the Castle Village Residents' Association (CVRA) AGM where I made my speech in defense of continuing the current system of nursing cover and derided some of the fatuous arguments put forward by the management for stopping it to save money. I was later thanked by a number of the residents for taking this stand and we were left to await an official response from the management, i.e., the company that owns this and several other retirement villages around the country. After the AGM, I had a pre-lunch sherry with David and Joyce but felt dizzy and tired. I skipped lunch. In mid-afternoon, the computer engineer arrived but I was not capable of taking in what he said so asked him to take my laptop with him to configure it in his workshop. Then I lay down on our big double bed, only the second time it was occupied since last December. I stayed there for the rest of the afternoon. In the evening, I watched a documentary program about Nature in Guyana. For a change, my TV behaved normally, after intermittent spells of terrible reception for the past couple of weeks.

"I woke next morning still exhausted and dizzy and was glad that

Lily came to help me with my shower. After that, I returned to the big bed. When I got up again I phoned the computer shop to ask the engineer to bring my laptop back the following day. Then I returned to bed until about 2:30 p.m. Meanwhile Joyce asked the chef to send some lunch to me. However, I had little appetite and was feeling very low. That evening I wanted to open up the bedroom window but did not as the celebrations were continuing outside. To make matters worse, I had an unpleasant gut but not diarrhea. In the afternoon, Margaret dropped in to see how I was but I was still very dizzy. Later David and Joyce brought me supper but I did not feel like sharing our usual drink or chatting. To pass the evening, I watched TV again. Thank heavens it was still behaving. I went nowhere near my computer all day, not feeling well.

"Somehow, I managed to struggle up on the Friday morning, shave, and dress. David came in early to see how I was but I was still very giddy. I tried to watch TV, but it had another attack of nerves on all stations. The C.V. Marquee Week has been on since Monday. I have been off since midday Wednesday. I was listless all day but decided to fulfill the invitation to have early fish and chip supper with David, Joyce, and Bernard prior to entertainment put on by C.V. singers who have been practicing for weeks. I will see if I can last through and beyond supper. I gave up halfway through the entertainment and retired to bed where I slept badly.

"Determined to get up and shower next morning in spite of a rotten night. I was feeling sad again and losing weight once more so I cancelled my invitation to join Pat Crowhurst and her new husband for midday drinks later in the month. As David was one of the main organizers, I went to the 10:30 a.m. performance of "Desert Island Discs." It was surprisingly good but had to abandon it at the intermission. That evening I was due to join the Mansion table for the gala supper, which I did not welcome one bit. Decided I would have to see how I felt but would certainly not dress up.

"So much for not dressing up. In the end, I decided it had to be all or nothing, so I carried out a dress rehearsal with my old black evening suit not worn for fourteen years. Not surprisingly, I found I had to take in the buttons on the waist. I went down to lobby to find most of the men wearing some sort of evening wear but still felt very uncomfortable. I joined the Mansion table. Luckily we were the first served so I could escape well before the evening was wrapped up without being too conspicuous. I was totally exhausted by all the noise and talking and had to retire early.

"This Sunday I intended to do as little as possible but in the end did my laundry, then went shopping, and made microwave lunch when I got home. That afternoon there was a garden party that included a good jazz group and of course various collections and draws for the benefit of the St. Francis Hospice. However, it was all too much for me and I had to leave after about half an hour. In any case, I could hear everything through the windows of my flat whether I wanted to or not. I was still not feeling well in general and my left hip was playing up increasingly.

"On Monday August 4 I said 'Farewell' to Lily and to Chris both of whom I will miss. Fortunately, Chris managed to get herself replaced by Christina, her old friend who keeps our first floor clean, so that should help. In the afternoon, the computer man brought my laptop back from the computer shop but we could not link it up to any nearby wireless links. I had to contact AOL to send a new wireless server. This entailed hanging on the phone for hours until finally I ordered a new AOL/BT package. That includes a free wireless server and free local phone calls for less than I pay now for my broadband + BT service. I finally finished with the phone just in time to dress for the taxi to take me to dinner at Brian Bradnock's house in Bovingdon.

"As I arrived a little too early Brian took me on a conducted tour of his enormous house and garden. Later his friends Brenda and Peter, Donald and, after dinner, Elisabeth Ponsonby joined us. There ended, at 6.30 pm, my state of being '*In Limbo*' and commenced the next Chapter of my life.

Chapter 24

Escape From Limbo and Back Again
2008

This episode in my life started from 6.30 pm on Monday August 4th 2008.

"By the time his next guests arrived, Brian had walked me the full length of his five-acre garden and back to his outdoor kitchen where a large wood fire was burning. By then I was exhausted but was partially revived by a large Pimms. The evening passed agreeably in the company of his friends, all of whom appeared to enjoy similar affluence and live nearby in what I saw is a very plush neighborhood with large houses, gardens, swimming pools, and the lot. I found myself engaging in conversation that was a sort of game of 'feelers'. I succeeded in not saying too much about myself. With a little help from one of his lady guests our host produced an excellent meal, delicious Aga-made soup, grilled scallops with strips of soft bacon pierced by rosemary spits, a roasted mincemeat hotpot and braised apricots with amarillos, all accompanied by an excellent red wine. Brian is very active in the construction of a superbly stocked and varied garden with a large carp pond and a smaller nature pond, the latter well endowed with wild water plants, duckweed and no doubt large numbers of insects, frogs, newts and others. In addition, there is a large swimming pool near the house. Brian's home and tastes certainly reflect the success of his surgical career which includes both implanting artificial joints, including my right hip, as well inventing a sophisticated instrument for removing them when they need replacing.

"I was worn out by 10:00 p.m. when my taxi arrived to take me home. The driver-owner and I had a friendly discussion about childhood holidays in Broadstairs which I have to admit is rather remote from second homes in the Algarve.

"It's eight weeks since I received my new hip. I woke up to a strong smell of smoke acquired by my clothes when sitting round a wood fire in Brian's garden and felt obliged after showering myself, quite an achievement, to wash shirts and underwear and hang up outer clothes to air. I was joined by David who was interested to hear my account of last evening. Later Joyce joined us for morning coffee after I realized that I forgot to offer any to David and that Joyce might be sitting on her own at home.

"Wrote 'Thank You' letter to Brian after lunch then fiddled for a couple of hours. Still unable to sort out my new BT telephone handset, which is frustrating.

"Monday evening's experience jerked me out of a futile habit I developed. I sort of 'blog' to myself about the minutiae of day-to-day life which is becoming duller and duller. It is far from my idea of trying to put together some of the more interesting events of my past existence; an idea that I have been chewing over for several years, as these notes reveal. My ambition to take a course in 'creative writing' as distinct from 'scientific writing,' was beginning to shape up at about the time I went into hospital. It has plummeted downwards in past weeks as is becoming all too evident.

"In bed on Monday night during a restless spell, I decided the moment had come to change direction back to my original thoughts about writing. However, this time I will not make the mistake of discarding any rough impromptu notes that I have written since early

June. I will write less frequently and probably jump about in a temporal sense from chapter to chapter as memories that seem to be of interest, even autobiographical ones, come to my conscious mind. Reorganizing any writing I achieve and editing it can come much later, if ever. First, I need to seek advice and expert tuition. This year I will be incapable of following a brief weekend residential course, much less a university course residential or otherwise. Perhaps I will be capable of doing that next year. Physically and mentally, I feel remarkably flabby. I am told by friends that after a year of emotional stress and a couple of months of physical problems I can expect no better. I suppose I have no option but to accept this. I just hope these handicaps will pass very soon.

"Shortly before lunch, Bernard came in to tell me that his tirade to our administration about nursing care provoked a rapid response from HQ. He stayed for another hour and a half, giving me an account of much of his later life. This was later in his career than what he described in the interesting and colorful written account I read some time ago. That told of his early life in Czechoslovakia and end-of-war years as an RAF radio operator. To put it mildly, he's quite a character. His account this morning concluded with details of the death of his wife of sixty years from cancer. I did not interrupt him but some paralleled my recent loss of Ruth. It was hard not to shed a tear, which I did not want him to see. He clearly also suffers badly but bravely from his bereavement. The great difference between us is that he has a family living nearby to support him. I confess I was glad when he left. I gratefully accepted his invitation to let him cook a dinner for us when I feel stronger. I have no doubt of his expertise in this field. I admit I find it hard to listen to anybody talk for a long time, interesting or not, and he is certainly a provocative and colorful personality.

"I was just going out to walk round the garden early this afternoon when Margaret from opposite came by to see how I was. We ambled out together with our sticks for a stroll and a chat. At ninety-one or so, she is remarkably lively, although somewhat frail. She has many interesting tales to recount of her life during and soon after WW II when she spent time as a Red Cross driver. I think she or her family lived in a minor castle somewhere in the English countryside, but she told the story to my sister during her visit here in mid-May. I did not give the conversation my full attention. As Ronnie, now ninety-three, was also a driver during that period, they had many similar experiences to exchange. I suspect they were both very lively young women at that time.

"A couple of days later I had a satisfactory visit from Ross Macfarlane, archivist in the Wellcome Trust. As he is dealing with the history of the Cooper-Wellcome takeover period he is seriously interested in acquiring the large painting portraying the old Cooper site on what is now Castle Village—my present home. Neil Castle, who brought the painting to my attention, and Joyce Stones, widow of the late research director of the Wellcome veterinary research center that was established here were delighted. I made it clear that my sole role was to act as the connecting link with the Trust. (See beginning of Chapter 16.)

"The next day the Beijing Olympics and a new war between Georgia and Ossetia opened.

"During the night, I mulled over a potential approach to these memoirs. I considered the possible merits of tackling them topic by topic rather than on a temporal basis, e.g., interest in natural history, aspects of experience in malaria, leishmaniasis, images of Saudi Arabia, university career, and post-retirement research, then of course, Ruth. I have to give it all more thought.

"After buying the new laptop with wireless connectivity I now regret my decision. It has led me to setting up a new system to connect with the internet and modifying my AOL/BT arrangements when the old broadband connection I already have works smoothly. I should have stuck to the old adage, 'If it ain't broke don't fix it.'

"I decided to diverge from my traditional caution and asked

Margaret Sedon, (her name is actually Sidford but this is a typical lapse of memory) to have supper with me downstairs. We were joined by an upstairs neighbor, Margaret Twiss, plus her tripod named Fido, and Olive A. whose husband is temporarily in the hospital. All came to Number two for an agreeable post-dinner coffee and chat.

"On Saturday morning August 9th I signed a document to retire voluntarily from the Medical Register following new government laws about revalidation. There seems no point in continuing on the register since I have not practiced clinical medicine of any kind for years and must be completely out of date anyway. I have been officially a doctor for sixty-one years.

"Yesterday I watched the most spectacular Olympics opening. Today I sat through a few of the preliminary rounds, overshadowed by the fact that my TV has not worked properly for the last couple of weeks. It's probably trouble with the aerial. I must get somebody in to fix it next week.

"It has been a positively foul day, wet and miserable, so I phoned Margrit in Herisau to exchange views on old age. She appreciates having a few words with me. She has turned out, unsophisticated as she is, to be the kindest of Ruth's nieces. Perhaps I will write a few words about them one day, perhaps not.

"To complete the circle I planned to phone Ronnie, then settle down with the newspapers to learn how bad the rest of the world is. I was about to do this when David came in to arrange to visit Audrey this evening to see the first part of a TV documentary about Darwin that we missed a week ago. I chatted with him about the vexed question of what Retirement Villages, the organization behind Castle Village, is planning for the medical cover that we are supposed to receive here. It seems clear that someone in Retirement Villages is trying to make petty economies by reducing or ceasing what some of us consider a critical part of the services provided and that attracted many of the elderly residents to buy property here in the first place.

I raised the question at the recent AGM of the C.V. Residents Association during Marquee Week. I received unsatisfactory responses. We are determined to follow up on everybody's behalf.

"I started the day after Sunday breakfast by phoning Chris Christoffersen who invited me for a Golf Club lunch, and then Ronnie called. Later I phoned the Killicks and rang back to Eliane whose call I missed.

"David Warhurst and Rhum joined me late morning and we lunched downstairs with David and Joyce after having sherry in their flat. I spent an agreeable lunch and post-lunch chatting before David departed at 5:00 p.m. to drive back to Dulwich. I bumped into Barbara E. who invited me to her bar drinks party on September 11th. She does not look well and told me she has cardiac trouble that annoys her, understandably.

"I do not believe I really escaped from limbo yet. Today I set out to shop as my food stocks were running low, but was hindered by severe pain in my left hip. I am seriously thinking of advancing my follow-up consultation with Brian Bradnock but do not want to panic. I anticipate seeing Lesley Hallan two weeks from now. I will talk to her first and ask her advice. I admit the thought of exposing myself to the second operation makes me very anxious in view of the complications I associate with the original operation. However, the current and increasing pain problem on my left side is hindering my rehabilitation and that is undesirable. With nobody but me to push or encourage me, it is easy to let my exercises slip, especially as I am not enthusiastic about physical exercises of the type I should do regularly. At the same time, I do not want to remain partially disabled. I want very much to retain my independence and mobility. The position I am in is all too common. Although many C.V. residents have been through this and emerged far the better at the end, I am sure that a high proportion of them have the moral support of a partner or family, which I have not. I suppose I am basically a coward.

"The next Tuesday was a strange day highlighted by lunch with Bernard's daughter-in-law Pauline and her mother Brenda in Pauline's house in Amersham. They were my opposite neighbors in Liverpool days. It was strange seeing Brenda again. Pauline and her husband, another David, have a big new house and large, not new but very friendly Labrador. Theirs is the largest kitchen cum-dining-room I have seen with abundant stylish fittings in good taste.

"The next day I had coffee with Pat Crowhurst, her new husband Ken, Rosemary, and Rosemary's South African cousin Elizabeth. After lunch David Halloway, purchaser of our former house, came to see me bearing a large fruitcake that Gill made for me. I gave some to David G. when he dropped in for our customary glass. Then I froze two large pieces for later on his advice.

"Although the past couple of days have been eventful, I have not commented on them, which supports the viewpoint that I am slowly emerging from my state of limbo. My diary is full of dates for visits to others or others to me, admittedly only for coffee. I suppose that implies that I am beginning to enlarge my view of the world and interaction with it, not a bad thing.

"When David Halloway was here yesterday, we discussed various matters including the objectives and subjects of writing. In the night, this stimulated me again to reflect on what I would wish to include in anything I wrote for general consumption, as distinct from this introspective diary. I will tackle the matter of my reflections in a piecemeal fashion picking periods and topics at random as they enter my consciousness. Those of interest can be assembled and edited in an orderly fashion later. There is no hurry. This morning I have to decide on the serious matter of do I, or do I not go shopping. It is a very boring, albeit essential task. Meanwhile I will make myself a cup of coffee and start yesterday's crossword.

"That evening I dined with Bernard in his flat. He cooked a very good dinner and told me more about his days as a racehorse owner and restaurateur. I did not have to contribute much to the conversation but still grew tired and was glad to return to The Mansion to which he kindly accompanied me.

"Next day had dental repair work done by Mrs. Kendall.

"The following Sunday Chris Christoffersen entertained me at lunch with him and Grethe at Ashridge golf club. It was the first time I had seen her for nearly a year. She looked and talked much better than I anticipated. On the other hand, Chris has aged greatly since we met at Ruth's memorial service in January. I noticed that his hands were shaky from looking after Grethe who has a modest level of Alzheimer's disease. This must be a great stress for him as he is now ninety-two and has little help at home. Back at their house for coffee it was a pleasure to see their garden full of deer of all colors and ages sitting or grazing peacefully, quite unafraid.

"I went that week to her surgery to talk with Elisabeth Ponsonby about my next move. My blood sample last Friday showed that my hemoglobin has moved little from eleven grams/liter. I must take more iron. We agreed that I should advance my next meeting with Brian and see if he agrees to replacing my left hip fairly soon. I asked Elisabeth to look into the possibility of my convalescing at Gossum's End. I think it would be far preferable to Ashlyn's. There is an acute shortage of such accommodation for post-operative cases in this area as in most of the country.

"Took David on Thursday to the Royal Entomological Society at Chiswell Green where I was greeted like royalty. It seems I may be the Fellow of longest standing, since 1950, although I find this hard to believe. While I looked up some records in the *Zoological Record* with the librarian, Dave Beeson showed David around the new headquarters. These are in a splendid old mansion that the Entomological Society recently bought with some of the proceeds of their sale of forty-one Queen's Gate in South Kensington. David was most impressed. The new premises are splendidly set up now but very isolated. The staff must feel rather lonely at times. It was more crowded when I took Bob and Mireille there for the official opening in May. I managed to locate the record of a new species of biting midge that I sent in 1962 to Tokunaga in Japan. It was one of numerous previously unrecorded or new species that I collected in light traps in Papua New Guinea in the late 1950s. I suspect that Tokunaga described more than one new species in my collection. I will return to the library later in the year and spend a day going through the records carefully. My new species is called *Alluaudomyia petersi* Tokunaga 1963. Work is soon to begin on a large Butterfly World adjacent to the Entomological Society. At the opening of the latter, I met the organizer of the new project, Clive Farrell, who hinted that he could do with some advice from me. I did not take this too seriously as I understand he has already established several of these centers in the UK and I believe overseas.

"Over the past few weeks, I organized a memorial lunch for Ruth that we will hold next Friday, September 4th. It would have been her 79th birthday. Pat and Ian came during the morning to discuss some of the arrangements with me. They brought flowers and many vegetables fresh from their garden. These included a magnificent corn-on-the-cob that alone proved more than adequate for my dinner. When David and Joyce came in for our usual, I passed most of the courgettes and runner beans to them. There were far too many for me to eat, especially as I would have to cook them!

"On Ruth's birthday ten of us, including Tricia Gibson our vicar who blessed Ruth's memorial stone in the churchyard in the rain, joined together at the King's Head for a lunch in her memory.

"I see Brian Bradnock next Wednesday to discuss whether he will operate on my left hip.

"For several weeks, I had been assembling data for *Conversations with myself—the first 84 years* and was just starting on our experiences in Papua, New Guinea. Thanks to the time needed to assemble all this material, I had to change the subheading to *The First 85 Years*. Because of subsequent delays in this work going to press, I later changed the subtitle to *Four Passions: Conversations with myself*. I could no longer forecast if or when it would ever be published.

"Received an email in mid-September from a new editor at Elsevier confirming that the seventh edition of the *Atlas* will be entitled *Peters' Atlas of Tropical Medicine and Parasitology*. With some regret, I had passed this job on to my friend and colleague Geoff Pasvol. He invited Sebastian Lucas to be his co-author. Sebastian is a youngish and very capable tropical pathologist whom I know well. He is now a Professor at King's College Medical School.

"This evening of September 17th my fate was sealed. Brian agreed with me that he should replace my left hip. The new X-ray showed that it looked like a disaster area. The new right hip shone like a beacon buried deep in my femur and articulated flawlessly in my trochanter. It will be the mixture as before, saws and drill into action on October 14th. I still have to try to settle on a post-operative care home for a week or two. Ashlyn's was too depressing for me to return there. Convalescent homes as they used to exist in this country are now very scarce for some reason. Logic says an aging population should cause their number to expand, but the contrary is the case.

"I paid another visit to my chiropodist Helen to take a further dig into my ingrown left big toenail. I was so interested reading the first chapter of a copy of Ronnie's memoirs of a car journey she and her then boyfriend, Sandy, made from Poland to Dover, when they were working with UNRRA just after the end of WW II, that I almost missed my appointment. It was over sixty years ago but she wrote in a relaxed and humorous style. She should have pursued writing as I feel she could have become a first-class author. As it was, it appears that she only preserved half a dozen such vignettes of her early and adventurous life. At least she did preserve them, unlike me. I was stupid and impulsive enough to destroy perhaps twenty years' of contemporary notes that would be invaluable to me today. And for no good reason that I can recall.

"Today, September 18th, would have been Ruth's and my fifty-fifth wedding anniversary. I told nobody, and nobody reminded me. I had an extra glass of whisky before bed.

"Once more, like a prisoner headed for the gallows, I had a haircut to prepare for my coming ordeal.

"Three weeks have passed and I have added virtually nothing new here. This is because I am writing quite extensively. I'm trying to assemble memories of events past and checking for material that I may have forgotten or need to check for accuracy. Meanwhile I received another visit from Bob and Mireille. They spent last weekend here on their way back from an eightieth birthday party for our mutual friend and colleague, Liz Canning. As during their visit at the end of May, Bob and I talked long into the night after Mireille gave up and retired. It was good to chat about old friends and old times but again I was exhausted by the time they left to catch a plane from Luton to Nimes on Monday morning. Once more, I am going in to Harpenden hospital for a hip replacement, the left this time. It has deteriorated rapidly in the past few weeks, so I did not have much problem persuading Brian to move my operation forward a whole month. It happens this coming Tuesday. I just returned from another pre-operation assessment and it already makes me feel tired. I simply cannot wait to get it all behind me.

"For the second day running, we have strong sunshine, a belated Indian summer. Many trees are putting on exceptionally bright autumn colors. Only the chestnuts are sad this year. It seems that huge numbers across the country are infected with one or more diseases that cause the leaves to dry up prematurely. Those trees stand out among other species like sore thumbs. As there are avenues of chestnuts in this area, it would be tragic if we were to lose them.

"I had hoped to take my laptop with me to use if not in the hospital, then in the care home to which I will go from hospital. Fortunately, it is not Ashlyn's that was a sad place in which to convalesce. I was lucky to locate one in Redbourn, halfway between home and the hospital. It looks better and has a room for me. However, there I will not be able to link my laptop to the internet so I will only use it for writing, playing patience, and other tasks. It appears that there may be a fault in the battery since it always seems to need charging even when I have not been using it. I need to get advice as it is not always convenient to plug it into the mains.

"David Warhurst and Rhum are coming to see me Saturday as will our American correspondent Dana Dalrymple whom we have not met face-to-face. He is over here for a conference in York and we planned for he and David to visit Number two when the conference ends. I look forward to it although I really wanted to take everything very easy this week to prepare myself for my second and, I hope, last surgical ordeal. What I should be doing for the next half hour or so is to walk or sit in the garden. Perhaps I will pluck up the courage to do so. I can always go and sit next to Ruth's tree and try to catch up a bit on *New Scientist*.

David and Rhum arrived promptly on Sunday October 12th at 11:30 a.m. followed by Dana at 1:30 p.m. He was just as I anticipated, slightly grey-bearded, bubbling with bonhomie and enthusiasm, a very agreeable companion. I decided to drive them through the country to the Bridgewater Arms for lunch pointing out Pulridge House East en route. However, we could not get near the pub and even had difficulty passing the traffic lined up along the road to get beyond it. We finally decided to lunch at home but called at the pub in Potten End first, only to find that the chef had gone home for the day. So I stuck some rice and curries in the microwave and we had a pleasant lunch with no fuss at 4:30 p.m. By about 6:30 p.m. it was time to disperse. David agreed to drive Dana to his son's home in Bexley where he was to spend the rest of the weekend.

"Today is another bright day of Indian summer. I have been feeling confused since yesterday evening. When David and Joyce dropped by I kept talking as if it today was Monday. I am still confused this morning but I focused on doing the washing, changing the bedding, and other domestic chores instead of moping. Eliane phoned up about 11:00 a.m. For the time being she has more to do than usual; friends' dogs and other pets to be cared for, and sounds quite cheerful. She and Margrit clearly merit a visit from me one day. Perhaps if I am fit enough and feel like making the effort I will go to stay with Ronnie next spring, travel from there to France to stay with Bob and Mireille, and then return via Paris. Bob says that Chabaud has retained his good humor but does not see well now. I suppose we are all changing as we age. Now I must start to focus on preparing for my departure for hospital at 6:00 a.m. on Tuesday, not tomorrow. I took out a special insurance so that David can drive my car. It is more comfortable for me than his, but just hope it will not be needed.

"I took a short stroll as far as the walking meadow and back, and then ate bread, soft cheese, and soup for lunch. I feel seriously sad and lonely again. I listened to music, which made it worse so tried to sleep a while. This is no good. I do not want to return to being 'in limbo.'

"However, that was not to be.

"On October 14th David and Joyce delivered me once more to the hospital at Harpenden into the hands of Brian Bradnock and his anesthetist, Abid Rajah.

"I survived both the hospital and the St. Matthews Care Home for Older People at Redbourn. This was a smaller and somewhat less somber place than Ashlyn's. Nevertheless, many memories of my two weeks there paralleled my earlier experience. One thing remains clearly in my mind. My room was directly opposite the entrance to the first floor dining room and each morning from the relative comfort of my chair, I saw a progression of old ladies making their way to breakfast. They marched at a slow pace, in line, pushing their Zimmer frames before them. To myself I called the procession, 'The charge of the light brigade.' However, I never had the heart to tell them.

"On November 2nd David and Joyce drove me home, safe if not

totally sound. This time I did not feel like describing the gory details of my ordeal. It was enough that I survived it and was home again in my lonely flat. I decided the account of a single experience of a major operation and the events surrounding it were enough for one life story. It would be too much to expect that any reader, generous as he or she might be, would wish the burden of reading the details of the second episode; so that will have to suffice for this chapter.

Chapter 25

A New Start in Life 2008–2009

I awoke just before 4:00 a.m. on Tuesday November 4th for the usual reason, then realized that the news of the American presidential election was about to be announced so turned on to watch BBC 24 news on TV. It was a momentous moment in history. A tall, slender, genial but serious-faced young Afro-American, Barack Obama, was the clear winner. The joy on the faces of the crowds in the streets of Chicago and other cities was something I will never forget. In a few weeks' time when he took office, the world began to change. The USA could start to regain its own and the world's respect that it lost over the past eight years, grave misfortune, and assassins permitting.

The title of this chapter is purely personal. Looking at the world around us carries a negative implication. It seems that apart from the impending inauguration of the new American president, all was doom and gloom. All the premonitory signs over recent months that everybody was about to be hit by major financial turmoil were being realized and formed our everyday news headlines. On top of this mayhem exploded in the Far East with a calamitous terrorist attack on the center of Bombay, cholera was at epidemic proportions in Zimbabwe, and many national economies were nose-diving.

At a personal level, I had indulged being home for the past month. I moved as far as possible at my own slow pace and observed the news out of the corner of my eye. My mind had gradually cleared and my body recovered, although I still walked like a lame duck. My hope was to continue to work on my memoirs and I had attempted to do so. However, my train of thought was disturbed by the desire to keep in touch with the outside world through emails and general information on the internet. Prior to my two operations, I was engaged in a fascinating long-distance collaboration with my American colleague, Dana Dalrymple and with David Warhurst on the Chinese antimalarial artemisinin. The internet opened me up to yet another long-distance project collaborating with another American colleague, Kevin Baird.

I met Kevin a couple of decades ago when he was a member of a US Medical Research Organization team and I advised him on his malaria investigations in Indonesia. He is still investigating the use of antimalarial drugs in the Western Pacific to cure malaria caused by *Plasmodium vivax*. I know about this from my work in TPNG and the personal experience of suffering from a relapse of this parasite after I returned to Europe. Moreover, since over the years, I invested months studying old and new drugs for use against *P vivax* in my rodent surrogate malaria models, I jumped to accept his request to join in his new project. This time another old colleague, Colin Ohrt based in WRAIR, Washington was involved. Once again, I enlisted David W. to join me bringing the benefit of his long experience to bear. We seemed to have an interesting diversion ahead.

That afternoon I went for a follow-up meeting with Brian Bradnock at the hospital in Harpenden. As David and Joyce were on holiday the past ten days with some family members who live in Los Angeles, I had an excuse to drive my own car again, with the blessing of my GP, Lesley Hallan. To my relief but not surprise, Brian closed the book on me and invited me once again for dinner at his house.

I looked on this as confirmation that I was 'out of limbo' and starting a new life.

After my return home, Ken Walker, a resident who was a professional photographer brought me a DVD that he skillfully compiled from part of the black and white video tape made in 1983. It is of the presentation ceremony in the Riyadh Hilton when I received the King Faisal International Prize in Medicine. Since the tape was made in an unusual format, I was not able to watch it for the past twenty-five years and had forgotten its contents. Ken added a few color photos that I had and cut out most of the recording that was irrelevant, poorly recorded, and incomprehensible. He inserted a couple of necessary captions and an appropriate musical background to make a brief, interesting historical document. My first impressions were of how podgy the late King Fahd was and how my girth at that time nearly matched his. What I could not see in the background were the two members of the LSTMH who were in Riyadh at the time of the ceremony and received invitations to attend. One was then Dean, Gordon Smith and the other Patrick Hamilton, a Senior Lecturer in Public Health. Sadly, both died young not many years later. Gordon, who was my age, died of cancer within a few years of retirement. Patrick, who was even younger, died of diabetic hypoglycemia in a hotel room while travelling in the Caribbean.

Our Swiss friend Eva took me to a Memorial Service at the Hospice of St. Francis on the evening of December 2nd. I did not want to risk driving myself there on a frosty night. Apart from the driving itself, I knew it would be an emotional occasion. About twenty people attended the brief and sensitively composed service presided over by the hospice priest known as Liz, a youngish and compassionate woman. She is similar to Tricia Gibson who was so helpful to me that past year. Thirteen days from now would be the first anniversary of Ruth's passing. I unashamedly overflowed with grief throughout the ceremony and was grateful for Eva's quiet support.

Brian's secretary phoned a couple of days later with apologies. He had to postpone next Monday's invitation for dinner. I was relieved since the weather forecast was bad and I did not really feel up to driving there at night just yet. Moreover, I was very fortunate to find myself inundated with invitations here and there. I already had to decline another for Monday. My hosts very kindly agreed to accommodate me the following day and I already had yet another invitation for the evening after that.

I booked myself in for several meals in our restaurant. I could not recall when they were, so I went downstairs to check and learned I was due that evening. Bernard was also booked so I phoned to see if he wanted to share a table. We did and were joined by another couple, Philip and Beryl S. He was the oldest resident at ninety-four and bright as a button. However, his wife was in an early stage of senile dementia, although cheerful. It was the first time I spoke properly to Philip. He was a cultured man, a good but amateur artist, and a linguist with a degree in modern languages.

Back in the flat, I listened to Gergiev conducting Mahler's 6th symphony followed by a very interesting program about Nina Mercouri whom I never previously thought of as anybody other than a pop singer. I was very pleasantly surprised at the depth and scope of her singing as well as her complex personality.

I was busy putting off preparing Christmas cards since every time I decided to start I was diverted to these memoirs. On the morning of December 6th, a Saturday, I was getting started when my nice cleaning lady dropped in unexpectedly to chat with me about her daughter's sad loss of one of her twin baby girls. Fortunately, one baby, although very premature, survived and was in intensive care.

Chris just left when I bumped into my neighbor Margaret from Number one. She said she just saw David and Joyce returning from their American visit. No sooner did I start on my Christmas cards again than I heard a familiar tap on the door. In came my good friends looking none the worse for wear after their overnight flight from Los Angeles. I was delighted to see them again. They returned in the late afternoon for our customary drink and chat before they left for a church supper. What energy!

That year I decided to print a brief newsletter to include in my card. It was based on one of Ruth's hand-embroidered Christmas cards to which I added her handwritten initials and date from 2001. The scene was one of her fantasy winter images with shrubbery, snow, and orange-beaked white birds.

The next Sunday was bad as the following day would be the first anniversary of Ruth's death. Ian and Pat ordered a wreath to be made for me to put by her stone. We cannot bring flowers because, even if they survive the weather, the deer will finish them off overnight. I decided to go with them and perhaps David to the church the next morning to put the wreath in place.

I had prepared a few Christmas presents and cards, but my heart was not in it. I put up not a single decoration. Eva had invited me to lunch with them that day but I declined, as I preferred to be on my own. I had had a mild pain in my abdomen for days like a muscular pain. It might have been caused by sitting hunched over the computer for hours, or from walking in an unnatural way with my new hips. I could not imagine that there was anything more to it.

My email was blocked and I could not get on to the internet. I suspected the local broadband connection was overloaded. It worked satisfactorily early that morning. I knew I had messages I had yet to open from Kevin and David W., which was very frustrating. I would have to be patient and try again later when the red light on the wireless modem went green.

David G. dropped by just then to invite me for a pre-lunch glass of sherry which I declined. He agreed to come with us the next day, which I appreciated, especially as he was with me one year before to say goodbye to Ruth. He and Joyce must have sensed that I was bordering on tears that morning.

Black Monday arrived. David joined me for coffee in case I was feeling low. Then he rejoined me to go to the church where we met Pat and Ian. I was worried about how we would handle the wreath laying but it proved to be a simple matter. In the churchyard a bitter humid wind was blowing. Ian placed the nicely made wreath in front of Ruth's stone and Pat took photos for me. We stood and reflected for a few minutes, saying nothing. I noticed that Ruth has a new neighbor to her right, a woman whose name I did not recognize. From there we drove to the Bridgewater Arms where we sat in front of an agreeably warm fire and had a drink while waiting for lunch. The conversation among the four of us was relaxed. I was glad that David was able to join us as he gets along very well with the Catchpoles and vice versa.

I did not do much in the afternoon apart from sleeping in the armchair. I was awakened by a phone call from Bob Killick. Later I went to bed to be there for the crucial time, just after 9:30 p.m. I thought about Ruth, and then slept only to wake up with a nightmare just before midnight. I was unable to get back to sleep. I got up and read old journals for a couple of hours supported by a large brandy and some dry biscuits after having little supper. I managed to sleep until 6:00 a.m.

While waiting the next morning for a visit from Pat Bleakely for coffee I received a call from a fellow resident named John. He said he would drop in for a chat but I put him off until the following morning. George and Ursula came that afternoon so there went another day.

I could not raise enough energy to do anything important on Christmas Eve. Exactly one year ago, a few friends had joined me to say a final farewell to Ruth at the Amersham crematorium. My instinct was to shut myself away from everybody and everything and hide in my solitary home. For once, I closed the front door as a symbolic exclusion of the outside world. If I could have summoned up the energy, I would have driven to Little G. church to say, "Hello," to Ruth's stone. However, I did not want to bump into anybody while I was doing so. Nor did I want to go into the church with its Christmas decorations. It was too painful and I could readily have wept again as I wrote this. Fortunately, the heating in the flat that was out of action for several days was repaired yesterday. I could at least stay warm.

I finally did not entirely close my front door. David and Joyce correctly took this as a signal that I would welcome their company. As Christmas carols from King's College Cambridge had just started, we sat down and watched on TV as Ruth and I did in past years. The carols were curiously followed by a hilarious old film about making a charity calendar of naked ladies by the members of a country branch of the Women's Institute. So we poured a glass of wine, got plates of nuts, and sat down and watched it together.

Had family lunch on Christmas day, and then listened to a very dull Queen's speech. Later on, I put on a CD of music by Satie and Milhaud, which was more acceptable, but half dozed in my armchair. I finally roused myself to change CDs but lost myself trying to sort out a few items for the *Conversations*.

David and Sam came after snooker ostensibly for Sam to bid me farewell but really to see if I was ready for an evening visit, which I was.

Boxing Day started with no hint of what the day would bring except lunch offered by Norman and Marion upstairs. David, Joyce, Carole, and I were invited together with a frail old lady named Jean. She was stone deaf and constantly complained that her new false teeth hurt her, which I am sure they did. The poor dear was obviously most uncomfortable and opted out of an excellent cold buffet. Norman took her home. The rest of us relaxed and continued to enjoy a very good lunch.

At about teatime we returned to our respective flats. I planned a short nap but this was not to be. There was a tap on the door and Margaret, my old neighbor from opposite came in, accompanied by her son-in-law whom I vaguely recognized. They bore the awful news that her fifty-six year old son had a fatal heart attack that morning. The poor man went downstairs to make a cup of morning tea and never returned.

For the remainder of Boxing Day, a few of us sat with Margaret. In spite of being shattered by the news, she maintained a calmness that was typical of her. We eventually saw her settled for the night, hoping that she would be able to sleep. However, she had my telephone number by her elbow and knew that my flat door would be ajar all night if she needed anything.

On the Sunday morning, I went out about 9:00 a.m. to see how Margaret was faring. Her front door was ajar and she responded immediately when I tapped on it and quietly called her. She was sitting up in bed finishing a cup of tea having just had her breakfast after a sound night's sleep, but her red eyes gave her away. Gradually other neighbors arrived and we all made sure she had sympathetic company for the rest of the day. Tiny as she was at ninety-two years of age Margaret had all her mental faculties about her and was a remarkably resilient character. We and other friends called that day and she astonished us by her ability to rise to the occasion. She was a very sensitive person, poetic in speech and nature, and had written several delightful books of children's poetry.

The end of 2008 passed quickly. I accepted David and Joyce's invitation to join their table for the New Year's Eve buffet dinner but I retired from the fray by 10:30 p.m. I tried to concentrate on writing for the next few days, but constant distractions made it difficult. The weather was foul for days, first very wet and miserable and then cold. On the first Saturday, Jennifer and Richard came to lunch and we spent several hours chatting. By chance, Richard spotted a name he recognized in our *Village Voices*. Gerry Burt joined us later. He lived in Wingrave at the same time as they did and was an old friend. That day was my American cousin Hal's ninety-seventh birthday. Here it was the coldest day for umpteen years at -11 degrees C at Farnborough. Small and large businesses were closing down right, left, and center. In the Middle East, a catastrophic war between intransigent Hamas groups and Israel was killing hundreds of innocent Palestinians in Gaza. For once, the BBC took a very partial view by giving an Israeli dissident almost unlimited time in an interview to put forward the view of a large proportion of the Israeli population who are totally against the war. I hoped it would be repeated by TV stations around the world. Not too many people were saying, "Happy New Year," any more.

On the home front, Margaret was holding up very staunchly to everybody's admiration. My personal progress was being blocked by a recalcitrant ingrown toenail that defied the best efforts of my chiropodist to get it under control. So my 2009 was to start as soon as possible with yet another operation. The first one I had on the same toe was over sixty years earlier when I was a student in Cambridge so I hoped the coming one would see me out.

I recently had received an email from a German colleague whom I had never met although I knew his name. He had just published a paper indicating the likelihood that drug-resistance was beginning to emerge to artemisinin antimalarial combinations in Cambodia. He appears to be one of the few who paid attention to our large number of papers warning of this possibility.

The next fortnight passed rapidly. Balbar Singh brought his wife to meet me and to talk over the outstanding work they have carried out in Sarawak with the simian malaria parasite known as *P. knowlesi*. They have demonstrated quite unequivocally that this parasite, long known to infect macaque monkeys, also frequently produces serious illness and even death in people in parts of Southeast Asia, especially Borneo. Some call it the 'Fifth malaria parasite of Man.' That is a misnomer, as it is primarily a monkey parasite. Janet is a vivacious red-haired Irish woman whom Bal first met when they were working with my former student, Marcel Hommel, at the LSTM. Earlier on, two other visitors had arrived for an all-day discussion of drug-resistant, benign tertian malaria in Southeast Asia, *P vivax*. One was Kevin, the American whom I met many years ago. He is retired from his former post with the US Naval Medical Research Unit in Indonesia and works with a joint Indonesian-Oxford research center in Djakarta where his Indonesian wife is also a medical scientist. We were joined by David W. The ensuing lively discussion went on all day and throughout the pizza lunch that I heated up in the oven. That made three ongoing research projects with which I was involved, the first being with the other American, Dana Dalrymple and David W, about artemisinin. A fourth project was a continuing collaboration with Irène Landau about classifying avian and other malaria parasites. All these projects involved email communication and required a significant amount of literature searching and study via the internet. My ongoing links with Imperial College library and other literature sources were very helpful, indeed essential. I am glad to have brought David into some of this. In fact, his mind is both younger and more agile than mine and his understanding of molecular biology and biochemistry far superior.

Yesterday, January 15th was a sad day for Margaret as her son was cremated. Other neighbors and I managed to spend some time with her in the evening. We admired the way in which she recovered her composure since that morning. It was the only occasion on which I saw her about to shed a tear as her daughter came to take her to the crematorium. She was a great character, both extremely gentle and extremely strong.

Once more I tried to devote time to drawing up my memoirs. The more I wrote the more I recalled. That made it very difficult to draw the line when I had written enough. I passed a few sections to David, Joyce and Ronnie for their frank opinions. I also lent a few snippets to a neighbor named Cecily and to my cousin Sylvia. These two have professional experience in proofreading and editing. I still had no idea what I would be able to do with all this when I had written all I considered worth writing—only my obituary awaited!

Tuesday January 20th would prove, I was sure, to be a momentous day in World history. A man of outstanding intellectual quality and integrity, Barack Hussein Obama, was sworn in as the forty-fourth President of the United States of America and his predecessor was flown out of the White House.

I invited Margaret, Joyce and David to join me in the flat to watch TV proceedings of the moving occasion. Thanks to David's fore-thought, we celebrated the moment with a glass or two of excellent champagne before retiring.

On January 6th, I noted it was the coldest day for umpteen years. On February 2nd, we had the heaviest snow for another umpteen years and much of Britain closed down. However, it was, for me, one to celebrate—I managed to take a few pictures on my new camera, a neat Canon Ixus digital that my friends Jeremy and Marika had helped me buy two weeks before. I was determined to start trying to understand its complexities. That morning I succeeded in photographing the snow-covered garden, transferred the photo to the computer, edited it and emailed it around the world. So far so good.

My hemoglobin went up again, this time to over thirteen grams per deciliter. Both Lesley Hallan and I were pleased but she still quizzed me to ensure that I was eating enough, which I was even if I did not enjoy it. Then she asked me for a favor—would I be prepared to talk with her son who was about to leave school and was interested in taking up medical microbiology. Having just clarified my situation regarding my legal position with the Medical Defense Union as I had voluntarily retired from the Medical Register due to my age and admitted incompetence to practice, I decided that giving advice in this case could be considered a Samaritan act. It did not require my continued status as a legitimate medical practitioner. For that, I have legal protection until doomsday, as I was a member of the Medical Defense Union for over sixty years.

The same morning I told David the news of the condition of our Norwegian friends, the Christoferssens. We were concerned, as David had heard that Grethe was not well and Chris at ninety-one was not much better. A mutual Swedish friend of us all, John Dahl, confirmed this. So David and I had decided to lunch with him on Sunday to cheer him up. Unfortunately, John's wife Margarethe was lingering in hospital waiting to have a broken leg mended. Back in the 1980s, Ruth and I spent every year's end with the four Scandinavians. That continued as late as 2005. We would celebrate Christmas midday dinner with Chris and Grethe at the King's Head in Ivinghoe.

For a couple of weeks in mid-February I waited patiently to attend the foot clinic in Berkhamsted to be assessed about the need for an operation on my painful ingrown toenail. David, who was to take Joyce to town for her morning session at the Citizens' Advice Bureau, offered to take me so I could avoid having to waste time warming up my car. It stood silently outside The Mansion all year round. When we moved here, we had decided not to invest in an expensive garage rental. Imagine my dismay on arising at 7:30 a.m. to prepare for the long-awaited ordeal to find it snowing heavily and relentlessly. It looked bad so that I turned on the news to learn that nearby Hemel Hempstead was one of the worst affected areas in Southern England. Just before 9:00 a.m. I telephoned the foot center expecting nobody would be there. To my surprise, I was greeted by a pleasant young receptionist who relieved my mind by suggesting that it was too hazardous for us to drive into town, advice all three of us welcomed. Unfortunately, the sequel was a further long wait for my bloody toenail.

Thanks to David who drove me to the Hemel Hempstead medical center, I managed to have my toenail assessed, and then had to wait about a month to have a partial nail resection. It would be up to six weeks after that before everything healed again, if things went well.

I did not envisage travelling any distance much before the end of May. So much for a joint birthday party with Jennifer and Ronnie in Switzerland.

After a foul start to the day the sun was shining brightly, but there were still a lot of ice and slush about making walking anywhere other than on a main road or pavement treacherous. In spite of that, I did consider driving into Berkhamsted after lunch—if my car would start.

David, Joyce, and Margaret joined me after supper on an evening in mid-February to watch a DVD of *Slumdog Millionaire*. It was lent to me by Arnab who had a preview copy. It was a fantastic film that we all enjoyed. Margaret contributed a bottle of champagne to accompany the viewing.

At midnight on Sunday March 29th, my sister Ronnie would enter the ninety-fourth year of her life. Forty-eight hours later, I would reach the end of my eighty-fourth year and have to put finis to my memoirs. The sudden realization of how the passage of time had accelerated during the previous year impelled me to decide just when I would have to stop committing this one-sided '*Conversation*' to paper, and then to sit back and to '*Listen*'. I already saw the need to change the timeframe in the title from eighty-four to eighty-five years as days, weeks, and months flew by. I needed to adhere to that decision.

Consequently, I occupied my last few weeks largely with re-reading, correcting, amending, and re-printing what I already had committed to my computer. The question not settled in my mind was; what, if any, illustrations should I incorporate into this work? I decided that it would be permissible to run overtime in order to select and prepare a few pictures that might help a reader to see who, what, and where on earth I had been writing about these past months. But I had yet to make up my mind—first I had to do more *Listening*.

At the end of the day, I still had to decide what I should do with all this. The few friends to whom I had given glimpses of snippets from here and there had all been encouraging—some even went as far as to say that I should try to publish this account. However, they are good friends and unlikely to offer a radically different suggestion. I would probably wake up in the middle of the night, as one often does, with a clear-cut solution in my mind. Thirty-six nights to go!

By the end of the month time was running away with me more and more.

The previous day had been a bad one. It started with the distressing news that my American friend Dana's wife, Helen, whom I never met, died shortly after being diagnosed with brain cancer. He is fortunate in having family members to help him with what was inevitably a distressing loss. In the afternoon of February 26th, I visited my solicitor to discuss further details of my personal affairs, a Living Will, Lasting Power of Attorney, and other death-related paperwork. I wanted to tie up as many loose ends as possible while there was still time, only one month to go. To complete the day my good friend and neighbor, Margaret, fell again and bruised herself severely. So I spent time at her bedside chatting about this and that. The next morning I learned that her daughter arrived later and spent the night with her. I decided to visit Margaret and share a drink with her soon. One of her favorites is Whisky Mac to which she introduced me not long before.

I needed to prepare myself to go to my dental appointment. If it was not my hips, it was my toes, an itching skin, or my eyes, and now my teeth. I wondered what was left. Oh yes, I had to think about having my ears checked. That left only a memory check, if I could remember how to set about that!

On the last day of the month, I realized, after a couple of pre-dinner drinks, that the older we become the less inhibited we are by conventional restrictions on the language we use and other niceties. There are fewer of us—we are the survivors—and if we dress conventionally or casually, speak politely, or use words that we would once have believed were indelicate, we no longer give a damn. The most cultivated amongst us say what we think—and so much the better. If we think it is a bugger to get out of bed in the morning, as most of us do, we do not hesitate to say so. If we disagree with something someone has said, we say so—no offense meant, no offense taken. I find it a healthy and liberating aspect of old age. Let's not pretend we are not old. There was a time when we were extremely young and innocent—let's settle for young—and somebody aged forty was decrepit and unimaginable. Let's forget middle age. At sixty, we began to get concerned about the aging process. By seventy, we stop thinking about it. By eighty plus, we try to put it all into perspective. However, after that, the less we think about it, the less important it seems. Nothing we could or would wish to do is going to change a damned thing. Therefore, we just accept it. After eighty, we dress as we wish, stop thinking about how others dress or speak, and just get on with living life as best we can. What an ideal world! Let's have another drink on that.

One month to go. On the first day of March Arnab and Suzie, bearing roses and cookies, joined me for lunch with David and Joyce. They seemed to get on very well. The two families have much in common as regards their children's education and the interest of the Grigsbys and now Arnab in the film industry. In his shrewd way, Arnab abandoned much of his recent life in finance and is taking an active interest in film production in England. David and Joyce's son, Howard, is a film producer living in Los Angeles, which gave them plenty to discuss. It is fascinating to see the 'hands on' approach Arnab takes with whatever interest he pursues. First, it was ophthalmic surgery, then the medical aspects of insurance, later the complicated world of high finance in the commercial and political worlds and now films.

During the evening, David and Joyce came for a glass and chat. Something interesting always comes up on these welcome occasions. That evening it was advances in dentistry and the applications of electron microscopy, psychic powers, and coincidence.

Nearly a week gone by already and a busy one at that. It started with a session on my feet with Helen, then a letter confirming the date for my toe operation, March 26th. My scanner packed up that evening so I took it to the computer shop in Berkhamsted. They found that the fuse I replaced that morning was a dud, so it is well again. I was sent several invitations including one to photograph the sunset but it didn't materialize. Other invitations were for an excellent concert by a young lady harpist in C.V., supper with Wallace Urry, then a family dinner with Pauline Peters, her father-in-law Bernard, mother Brenda and sister Sarah whom I had not seen for over thirty years. On March 6th I signed papers with Nigel and shopped. I spent the afternoon sending emails and a pdf. In the middle of making the .pdf my scanner failed again. This time I gave the plug a hard bang and it worked once more. I wanted to send the .pdf to Bob Killick. He tells me he, Mireille, and her daughter and granddaughter will come and see me on April 17th and 18th. I managed to book them both guest rooms, which is convenient.

I went to see if there was a sunset that evening, then awaited a visit from David and Joyce. Then I decided to call them to see what view they had from their apartment. The sunset did not materialize nor the space station. We had a drink and chat there instead of at home. After I left David came back to tell me they had spotted my old friend the ISS from their kitchen window. I went back with my camera and took a surprisingly clear photo of that white beacon shining in the western sky above the bungalows. I'll repeat the photo of the ISS as the camera was unsteady. It looked as if it were possible to see some structure, probably the main solar panels. Unfortunately, the sky was too obscure to see it that evening. Another resident in the bar said he and his wife had seen the ISS the previous evening and thought it had the odd structure I noted yesterday, so I may be right.

Cecily returned the manuscripts I lent her with numerous constructive editorial marks, mainly punctuation. I had to reconsider my policy on this when I did my next revision. I was not able to do much then as Marika and Jeremy were coming. Chris came to see me just as I was about to eat my simple lunch. She was anxious to talk about the progress of her surviving granddaughter, Charlotte.

She had just left when Marika and Jeremy arrived bearing biscuits and homemade greetings cards produced by Marika. They were ready to leave when Pat and Ian came in and, shortly after that, David and Joyce. A chat and drink were followed by Pat and Ian's departure and we went to the bar. I needed to speak to tomorrow's luncheon guests and to Cecily about her editing. We agreed that she and I would meet in private session, and then she would read more. I finally returned to Number two just before 10:00 p.m. to find something small for supper.

Sunday 8th March was a busy and agreeable day. I had arranged for David Warhurst to lunch here with me and I invited Peggy and George Dent, Brenda White, and Ken Walker to reciprocate hospitality they had shown me. It was excellent, congenial, and relaxed company. David Prodger and his team served their usual abundant Sunday lunch. Later David W. and I exchanged views on some of the collaborative long-distance, mainly email projects we are involved in with our American colleagues.

Over the past few days, the ISS has been prominent in the early evening sky. I managed to take a couple of photos of it with my new camera. This evening David and Joyce joined me for a glass. Then we went over to their flat to take a few more photos from their bedroom window, this time with a small tripod. One of the first photos gave the impression that the ISS was reflecting light from its solar panels; it appeared as a bright V-shape rather than the usual rough sphere. This may be an artifact caused by a slight movement of the camera. When I transferred the new photos to my computer, the ISS was somewhat clearer than in the original ones and was once more spherical.

Only three weeks were left before I had to close down this record to start serious 'Listening' and revising. It had been helpful to receive feedback from a couple of friends and from Ronnie, to whom I showed snippets of the early drafts. I had not found the time to undertake the self-criticism that is the most important part of these *Conversations*. Meanwhile I staunchly resisted reading any of several novels given to me during the past year, or an account of the history of antimalarial drug development by an American author that I rashly offered to review. I could not resist peeking at the latter, but more than that would have to wait until after April 1st. It would be simple to subconsciously absorb some of the style of another author, especially if the writing is far different from mine and vastly superior.

By chance I just then met my gentle neighbor Margaret and dropped in for a brief chat before we started our lunches, hers 'Meals On Wheels' and mine, Waitrose ex-freezer. The positive nature and resilience of this frail little lady were remarkable. Her life story would fill a book and be far more rewarding to read than mine could possibly be. That day she received some wonderful personal news, something that we all need in these days of doom and gloom. Her face lit up when she revealed it to me in strict confidence. I felt pleased for her and happy that she could confide in me.

After an uninteresting vegetarian lunch cooked in the microwave oven, I finished the weekend papers, tried to do that days' crossword, and walked around the garden to stretch my stiff legs and ventilate my lungs in the chill windy air before settling down again at the computer.

I was feeling listless the next morning and not thinking clearly even after a normal night's sleep. In spite of the day being dry and intermittently sunny, the bitingly chilly wind did not entice me to go out for a walk. I knew I should as my leg muscles were stiff and I found myself swaying from time to time. My efforts at coming to terms with my digital camera settings were not getting far, so I just pushed the button and hoped this sophisticated instrument would know what to do by itself. That usually is the case.

Over the past few weeks I had tried to take stock of myself,

'*Listening*' for the pluses and minuses, looking for loose ends that needed filling before I closed down. I had more or less succeeded in putting my formal affairs in order with Nigel, who added minor codicils to my Will, appointed attorneys in case I lose my marbles and a Living Will in the event I fall hopelessly sick. However, knowing my family's longevity history I was not worried that, barring accidents, these measures would have to be put to use in the near future. I just like to have a certain amount of order in my life and to avoid burdening people more than necessary. It would have been helpful if Ruth and I had produced offspring, but alas, it was not to be. Instead I was, as she would have put it, "Dankbar," to have good friends around me. One day I will, as my long deceased sister-in-law Marianne's even longer deceased husband Robbie used to say, "Lâcher la rampe." We all do, but I am not in a hurry.

So what have I to leave behind me?

A long and largely happy marriage, with an exceptional woman who was far better than I deserved.

An unknown number of people whose quality of life I hope I helped to improve as a physician and others whose lives I may have saved directly or indirectly through some of my research.

A scattering of students around the globe whom I hope I set on a successful path in their lives.

Several very talented younger colleagues whose work in my academic departments may have helped them to establish out-standing careers of their own in the worlds of medicine and science.

Rather a lot of papers and a handful of books mainly on tropical medicine and parasitology.

A new species of malaria parasite, one of *Leishmania*, one parasitic worm, and eighteen new species of mosquitoes. Various colleagues kindly gave my name to another new malaria parasite, to two new biting flies and to three species of butterflies. For what more could one ask?

There was a clear full moon the next night. I was up at about 3:30

a.m. and decided to attempt to take a photo from my window without fussing with a tripod. The result was poor. However, the beauty of using a digital camera is that it doesn't matter how many shots fail. You just remove them from the camera's memory. I am far from knowing how to set up the various control features. Luckily, the automatic settings do it better.

Returning to the lift after collecting my morning paper I found my neighbor half slumped to the floor with a bloody cloth held to her leg. The unfortunate Margaret had damaged herself by either falling or knocking against something in her flat, but she was not sure which. I escorted her to see Nurse Melanie who took charge. Luckily, Margaret's daughter Caroline had arranged to see her that day and arrived shortly after this episode.

A busy Friday 13th March with visits from Vicki and David for coffee in the morning and Margaret Shuffrey looking for Margaret from Number one. The latter did not sustain any serious damage. I hoped she would return home the next day. That evening I was to have another fish and chip dinner with David, Joyce, and Bernard. Meanwhile I decided to relax.

After dinner, David went to a meeting while Joyce and Bernard came up to Number two for coffee. Joyce left quite soon while Bernard chatted about his early life until quite late. He is a tough person, physically as well as mentally. He had to be to survive his adolescent and young adult life in Hitler's Europe. Some of the scars are still there, but he came out on top in spite of everything and had settled down well enough in C.V.

The days were flying past until my story was destined to end.

Our dear friend Margaret was being kept in Watford Hospital three days later. Her daughter Caroline expected her to be discharged on the next day. Caroline and Michael, her husband, had booked Margaret in to Ashlyn's for a short period of respite. Being so frail, she really needed to be looked after full-time for a while. The Mansion House seemed very empty without her.

Spent much of that day reading the book on war and antimalarial drug development, which I was to review. Although it starts rather slowly and a bit naively, the writing improved as it went along. There may be a lesson there somewhere. Although the work has a strong trans-Atlantic bias, I could not complain too much as the author had apologized to me in advance about this and he did include a good quote from my 1970 book.

I almost skipped lunch as young Arun Banerji came to consult me about an essay he was preparing for a competition set by the Medical Research Council. He is a very bright young man and it was enjoyable giving him a sort of tutorial. When he finished at Harrow the next year, he would start in medical school. However, he had not yet decided where he wanted to go. His sister was about to qualify in medicine that year and his older brother in engineering—quite a family.

I managed to complete a stroll round most of the 'walking meadow.' It was the furthest I had been yet. Ruth's young tree was beginning to show new buds; the first ones suffered badly from frost that year.

For the past couple of mid-March days we had pleasant mild weather, which tempted me to go out. With luck, I hoped to be able to take a few pictures that reflected the beginning of spring.

I had more luck than I expected. I came across a large dark ladybird, one that I had never seen before, as well as two freshly emerged comma butterflies. I managed to photograph all of them, plus some spring flowers. A search on the internet suggested that the ladybird might be a variant of a notorious Asian invader that is rapidly spreading from the southeast and threatening the ladybird population of the British Isles. I sent the photo to a specialist for identification and to add to the national records. Within three days I received confirmation that my ladybird was the notorious invader, the Harlequin (*Harmonia axyridis*). It seems to be very common now, especially in the southeast of England.

Saturday March 21st was the first day of spring and the weather was behaving like it. This was nice for Bernard who was throwing a party that evening to celebrate his ninetieth birthday. He had been agonizing over the arrangements for this for weeks. I knew how he must feel. All his family, including his daughter who flew from California for the occasion and his guests were looking forward to it. Now that he had settled in and put a few contretemps behind him, Bernard was becoming increasingly popular with the residents of C.V. He is admired for his resilience since childhood and the success he made of his adventurous life. The other evening he proudly showed David and me a letter he received from an old friend of his, the President of Czechoslovakia, congratulating him on his birthday. That reminds me—I must get a copy of some telegrams that I never saw from Ronnie. They were those our father received for his centenary, one from the present Queen and one from the late Queen Mother.

I was pleased to catch Margaret's daughter Caroline and her husband Michael as they were about to leave for Ashlyn's carrying armfuls of pictures to hang up, plus mail and other items they were taking to make her feel more at home. It seemed that Margaret was recovering well but did not feel at ease in her temporary environment. David and I arranged to visit her the following week if possible prior to my pending toe operation. That would immobilize me for some time.

Luckily I had nearly completed this chapter as the 'Favorites' address section on my computer failed. I would have difficulty finding many of my usual internet addresses. The problem arose for no obvious reason on the Thursday. I spent most of Friday morning trying to resolve it and managed to do so in a mysterious fashion by midday. Then, I lost everything again for an equally mysterious reason by evening. It was extremely frustrating, to say the least. Maybe it was the fault of AOL and not my own stupidity.

Then I had to start preparing for the big party—I must clean my shoes so I can wear them while it is still possible. Meanwhile the weather changed completely. It was again cold, windy, and raining, all phenomena that were forecast to continue throughout the week. So much for my anticipation of going around sockless in open-toed sandals from Thursday on.

Bernard's party was a great success. I had the amusing experience of greeting no less than six Peters at the top table. However, the acoustics in the dining room are such that I was nearly deafened by everybody's need to shout to be heard and the strain of trying to hear what even my immediate neighbors said to me. Luckily, I departed without fuss, among the first guests to take their leave.

Probably because of computer problems, again I felt depressed all next day and was glad when David and Joyce came. No sooner were they settled than Ronnie phoned, so I called her back for a long chat. She seemed to be in good form. I had a phone call from Lee Schnur later. He was over here for a few weeks. He and Tilly hoped to drop in to see me briefly in about a fortnight on their way to the West Country. That would be a pleasant break in what was becoming a bit of a dull life again.

I think my impending trauma and the thought of being partially incapacitated again, were weighing on my mind. Both were impossible to avoid yet hard to accept. I do not like to depend even on willing friends for help, especially for what seem to be trivial problems. Moreover, the desire to offer a level of hospitality to fellow residents at the C.V. bar on my birthday preyed on my mind. I sympathized with Bernard who agonized for weeks over the organization of his big party with over sixty guests plus family.

The last week of March started with another bright spring day with a cold wind and the next day was even colder. I was about to sit down to my routine dull breakfast when Chris came with the latest news of her baby granddaughter who seemed to be making progress. When she left I just finished eating when Christina arrived to tidy up the flat. After another unproductive morning and uninteresting lunch, I fiddled with the computer looking up a few references. Yesterday's intervention does seem to have sped it up. An email told me that my ladybird was added to the national survey database which was something achieved at last. I almost felt like an entomologist again.

I enquired how Margaret was faring in Ashlyn's, but nobody answered the phone. I finally got through and spoke to Jackie. She said Margaret was settling down well but was very tired. I sent her warm greetings from everybody at C.V. and promised to visit her when she was ready to receive callers. When David and I visited Margaret at Ashlyn's a couple of mornings later she was sitting up in bed looking bright-eyed and smiling, with her daughter Caroline by her side. In the evening I passed the good news to the bar residents. They were anxious to know how everybody's favorite was progressing.

That evening I watched another remarkable documentary on the orangutan rehabilitation center with its population of some 600 animals in Indonesia. That was followed by the contrast of an aging Alan Whicker reliving his memorable TV journalist past. I remembered the occasion when Ruth and I met him in an airline lounge accompanied by a glamorous young female assistant. I wasn't allowed to look too closely.

Never a dull moment for my good friend David. He sacrificed himself to drive me next day at crack of dawn, 9:15 a.m. on Thursday 26th March, to my appointment with the surgeon who was to slice my big toe open. I was welcomed by two charming young girls. To my gnarled eye, both looked like teenagers. The youngest and slenderest turned out to be my surgeon. She hardly needed to give me a local anesthetic, but she did and was kind and gentle in doing so. Her equally charming and attractive colleague did the honors with bandaging. I would now have the pleasure of seeing the latter next day, again at the crack of dawn, to have the bandage renewed. All

I had in the way of after effects was cold feet as I could not wear socks for a while. It could have been worse.

I was amused to see in a review of the Whicker program in the *Guardian* that he was a pupil at Haberdashers. I checked whether we were there at the same time. I had no recollection of anybody by that name, but few fellow scholars' names or faces come to mind. By chance, that day Habs was honored by the American preacher, Jesse Jackson, who gave a talk there. Unfortunately, I was otherwise engaged. I do not believe that he was a classmate nor for that matter do I recall that there were any boys originally of African or Asian descent at Habs in my time. Whicker is a year younger than I am so we probably did overlap.

David was dropping in at frequent intervals to see if I had survived the ordeal and Joyce fed me again that evening like the compassionate friend she is. No wonder she and David have such an exceptionally warm family.

The foot was comfortable during the night but I was disturbed by a severe cough. It was so bad at 3:00 a.m. that I got a severe left-sided chest pain. It made me wonder for a moment if I had a cardiac problem. However, I had pneumonia about twenty years ago and remembered how this kind of cough can strain the intercostal muscles and mimic a wide range of sinister problems. I took a couple of paracetamols and managed to sleep again to prepare for an early morning start. By 7:00 a.m. I was up and preparing myself to pay a second visit to the podiatrists courtesy of David.

My toe was doing well. It was redressed by Susie. I now seemed to be developing a noisy upward extension of respiratory infection for good measure! When would all these trivia cease? I was getting worse by the hour so phoned to cancel the visit of Vicki and Soph the following Sunday. It was better not to risk spreading whatever virus I may have had. I would quarantine myself for a couple of days and hope to be better by the end of this chapter. If not, my bar mates would have to have a drink on me in my absence. That would have been a great pity, an anticlimax to the past couple of hundred pages. At least I would have provided tidbits. The last time I had a severe chest infection it was an unusual type of pneumonia. As you will note, I recovered. The way I felt now, I was not too bothered about the outcome. As a 'belt and braces' individual I had everything well under control.

I passed the early evening watching a nostalgic program about the Dave Brubeck quartet that Ruth and I enjoyed so much. It felt like centuries ago. This seemed a very bizarre and somehow tranquil manner to pass the pre-final days of my hitherto crowded existence. My story was nearly ended. Part I was my part. Parts II to IV were our parts. Part V again was to be my part and I dreaded writing it.

On Saturday night 28th March we turned the clocks forward an hour.

That morning I proudly drew the attention of David and Joyce to my shoes. They were on my feet—quite an achievement. Glancing at the *Guardian* illustrated supplement, I found a photograph on the front cover that closely resembled Bob Killick both in looks and pose. I scanned it, removed the name of the actor, and emailed it to him. Touché. Within a couple of hours, I received a rude but friendly acknowledgment in the form of a joke that I will not repeat here.

I had a long chat with Ronnie at midday on Sunday. As usual, her computer was out of action. She was busy preparing for her birthday the following Monday. She had invited about a dozen chums for a meal. She was hosting an old Greek beau who was passing through Geneva. He was really quite a youngster she told me, three years younger than her. He was taking his customary Mediterranean siesta as we spoke. I wondered if Greeks snore. I recall that he appeared on one of these pages some time ago—or was that another Greek beau.

I had an exotic but solitary lunch, a hunk of dry immature Camembert from the fridge, the rest of yesterday's Waitrose coleslaw, better the first time round, and another cup of packet tomato soup.

I finished all but one word of the so-called '*Quick crossword*'. Then I decided to put my head into the garden as the sun was shining and looked welcoming. As soon as I put a foot over the threshold, it started to rain. In the afternoon a friend, Nancy, then in her early 90s, phoned to ask how I was, i.e., when would I go to visit her? I reluctantly told her I would not be circulating for at least six weeks, which did not seem to surprise her.

In the interim, my delightful occasional carer, Lily, was due to call in on Monday to help with my ablutions and change the dressing on my diminished toe.

After all, on March 31st 2009 I too was a survivor. The previous day the monthly issue of our house journal, *Village Voices,* arrived containing a brief contribution entitled by the Editor, David Cawley *The Benefits of Age*. I wrote the piece here on February 23rd. I thought it might stir a resonant chord in the minds of some of my fellow residents.

Truth to tell, I only just made it to these last couple of pages after being laid low for the past week by a combination of a debilitating chest infection and the removal of half a big toenail. It was not a great way to see out my Old Year and welcome in the New. By midday yesterday though, I decided I had enough of feeling sorry for myself. Following the welcome visit of Lily, everybody's favorite carer, I arose from my deathbed, dressed, and knocked back an entire jug of nourishing soup prepared for me by Joyce. This morning I resisted the temptation to go into reverse gear, arose, performed my ablutions, dressed, and descended a bit shakily to collect the morning paper and confirm the cancellation of my seat at today's luncheon club to which I was looking forward. I spent the rest of the morning sorting email. I'll check my post to see who remembered my imminent birthday.

My lunch was delivered to me in the flat unexpectedly as I had opted out. My guardian angels intervened to assure that I did not go hungry. However I needed a couple of hours snooze afterwards to recover before continuing to attempt to master a difficulty with emailing a large picture to the US for Kevin's new review paper on which we were working jointly, i.e., he does the work and I criticize as befits an old man.

My eighty-fifth year was drawing to a close as T.S. Eliot wrote ". . . Not with a bang but a whimper."

On All Fools' Day, here I was just over the fence, me and the new Messiahs, the wise men of the G20. As I was writing these words Barack Obama and Gordon Brown were facing the international press at a pre-summit meeting in London. What impressive men they both are, each in his individual way.

My niece Jennifer and husband Richard arrived bearing gifts for the Birthday Child, i.e., a three-course midday dinner that they cooked in my tiny kitchen. It was excellent and was the first such meal prepared in the home that Ruth and I moved into two years less four days earlier. With help from David and Joyce, I had arranged to hold open house in the bar for all comers in the evening. However, as is the custom here, I did not give advance notice. All the usual habitués, about twenty, turned up and it was a successful, informal, and congenial occasion.

I then signed off. The first stage was passed. I must now do some serious 'listening', study the editorial and other comments my good friends have made on the snippets of '*Conversations*' that they have read, make a serious start on reviewing and amending the lengthy manuscript, think whether to include any illustrations and, if so, which to select.

And so to bed—once more to '*Listen*'.

POSTSCRIPT

I did listen, with both ears and this time, Swiss proverb or not, with both eyes. This is what came into my mind.

Half a thousand nights—What is Love?

Though half a thousand nights have passed,
our love remains.
"Tell me, Old Man, what is love?
You who have lived five and eighty years,
you should know by now."
Perhaps I do.
Love is giving.
Love is giving without knowing why,
without being asked—
at least most of the time.
Love shows itself to you
when the one you give it to
is no longer there to receive it.
Love is what you were bathed in
and didn't know it,
all those five and eighty years.
Love is what brings a tear to your eyes,
when the one you loved
is no longer there to receive it—
and you wish, you so wish,
you had given more.
"Such love is no more for you, my friend.
Dwell on what you had and be glad.
Wipe your eyes, blow your nose
and try to sleep, Old Man."

Bibliography

Burton-Bradley, B.G (ed.) (1990). *A history of medicine in Papua New Guinea. Vignettes of an earlier period.* Australasian Medical Publishing Company Ltd., Kingsgrove.

Greene, G. (1936). *Journey without maps.* Heinemann, London. (Reissued by Vintage Books, London. 2006).

Killick-Kendrick, R. and Peters, W. (1978). *Rodent malaria.* Academic Press, London.

Laufman, H. (2006). *One man's century with pen, brush, fiddle and scalpel.* Victoria, B.C., Trafford Publishing.

MacKinnon, J. (1974). *In search of the Red Ape.* Collins, London.

Molyneux, D.H. and Ashford, R.W. (1983). *The biology of* Trypanosoma *and* Leishmania *parasites of man and domestic animals.* Taylor and Francis, London.

Peissel, M. (1974). *Tiger for breakfast. The Story of Boris of Kathmandu.* Allied Publishers Private Ltd., New Delhi.

Peters, W. (1987). *Chemotherapy and drug resistance in malaria. 2nd.edn. Vols. 1, 2.* Academic Press Ltd., Oxford.

Peters, W. (1992). *A colour atlas of arthropods in clinical medicine.* Wolfe Publishing Ltd., London.

Peters, W. and Killick-Kendrick, R. (eds.) (1987). *The leishmaniases in biology and medicine. Vols. 1, 2.* Academic Press, London.

Peters, W. and Pasvol, G. (2007). *Atlas of Tropical Medicine and Parasitology. 6th edn.* Elsevier Mosby, London.

Power, H.J. (1999). *Tropical Medicine in the twentieth century. A history of the Liverpool School of Tropical Medicine 1898-1990.* Kegan Paul International, London, New York.

Simpson, C. (1955). *Islands of men.* Angus & Roberston, Sydney.

Suyin, Han (1958). *The mountain is young.* Triad Grafton, London.

Webb, J.L.A. Jr. (2009). *Humanity's burden. A global history of malaria.* Cambridge University Press, Cambridge.

Wilkinson, L. and Hardy, A. (2001). Prevention and cure. The London School of Hygiene and Tropical Medicine. A 20th century quest for global public health. Kegan, Paul, London.

About the Author

Draft obituary – the final "*Conversation*" (date of issue to be announced).

Born in London in 1924, Wallace Peters earned his first Medical Degree at St. Bartholomew's Hospital Medical College in 1947. Following training as a Casualty Surgeon, he was conscripted into the Royal Army Medical Corps and posted to West Africa. In 1950, he earned the Diploma of Tropical Medicine and Hygiene in London and was elected a Fellow of the Royal Entomological Society of London.

During the next six years, he practiced tropical medicine in West and East Africa in various organizations. From 1953 to 1955, he conducted field research on malaria in Liberia and Nepal as a World Health Organization (WHO) scientist-entomologist and malariologist. Between assignments, Wallace married Ruth Scheidegger in 1954 in Geneva. From 1956 to 1961, he served as an Assistant Director, Department of Public Health in Papua New Guinea where he established a team to investigate malaria and develop an optimistic plan to control the disease in that region.

Returning to Europe Wallace spent the following five years with CIBA, a Swiss pharmaceutical company, conducting laboratory research on drugs to control malaria and other tropical parasitic diseases. His dominating research theme at CIBA was the need to evolve and deploy combinations of drugs to limit the emergence of drug resistance in human malaria. His position with CIBA gave him opportunities to journey widely throughout the tropics where he gained an invaluable insight into the many problems posed by tropical diseases.

In 1966, Wallace was appointed to the Chair of Medical Parasitology at the Liverpool School of Tropical Medicine. He revitalized the school's program on the chemotherapy of parasitic diseases, especially malaria, which by then was beginning to pose serious resistance to the few available antimalarial drugs. In 1979, he moved to London where he held the Chair of Medical Protozoology at the School of Hygiene and Tropical Medicine until 1989 when he reached the official age of retirement and was made an Emeritus Professor. After this forced retirement, Wallace continued his laboratory research with support first from CAB International Bioscience, then later as an Honorary Research Professor of Imperial College, London.

Between 1947 and 2003 he traveled extensively lecturing and establishing joint research projects in many tropical centers. During one such visit to Brazil, the sight of a mutilating skin disease known as leishmaniasis in Brazilian patients stimulated him to extend his interest to a search for improved treatment of that devastating, but frequently untreatable, condition.

However, Wallace's interests extended well beyond malaria and leishmaniasis. At the international level he served on numerous scientific committees, especially of the World Health Organization. He was a frequent visitor to academic centers in Europe, the Far East, and the United States where he was a consultant to the Walter Reed Army Institute of Research.

In 1975, Wallace was invited to advise the Ministry of Education of the Kingdom of Saudi Arabia on the development of their new medical schools. This led to a request to him to assist the Saudi

Arabian National Council for Science and Technology to help explore the major and increasing problem of leishmaniasis in that country. These fruitful academic and research links continued for the next twenty-two years. Coincidentally, in 1982 the King Faisal Foundation, a philanthropic organization, instituted annual International Prizes for Science and Medicine. He was nominated by London University for and awarded the Prize in Medicine for 1983 for his contributions to research on malaria.

Based on his studies of malaria and mosquitoes in Papua New Guinea, Wallace received an MD degree from the University of London in 1965. Ten years later he was awarded the DSc degree by the same university for his studies on chemotherapy and drug resistance in malaria.

Throughout his career he received numerous accolades including honorary memberships of societies of tropical medicine and parasitology in England, France, Germany, Switzerland, Algeria, and the United States. Other honors included Fellowship of the Royal College of Physicians (London) and Docteur Honoris Causa (University of Paris). Additional awards included the J.H. Choudhury Medal, Calcutta School of Tropical Medicine (1971), Leuckart Medal, German Society of Parasitology (1980), Le Prince Medal, American Society of Tropical Medicine (1994), Prix Emile Brumpt, Société de Pathologie Éxotique (1998), Manson Medal, Royal Society of Tropical Medicine and Hygiene (2004) and Distinguished Parasitologist Award, World Federation of Parasitologists (2010).

Since 1952, Wallace has written or co-authored eight key books on entomology, chemotherapy, tropical medicine, and parasitology. *A Colour Atlas of Tropical Medicine and Parasitology*, first co-authored with H.M. Gilles in 1970, was translated into five languages including Mandarin. The fourth edition was awarded the British Medical Association's First Prize for Medicine in 1996 and the sixth edition (co-authored with G. Pasvol) was awarded First Prize for Public Health in 2007. In the same year the latter work also received an award from the Society of Authors and Royal Society of Medicine for the Best New Edition Authored Book. Over the same period he contributed as sole or collaborating author to forty-three chapters in other books as well as over 340 papers in scientific journals.

Ruth's death from cancer at the end of 2007 left a devastating void from which Wallace slowly emerged with support from his family, and a number of close friends, old and new. Together with the internet, his 'working pizza lunches' for colleagues visiting his apartment became the foci for his continuing intellectual activity.

In his spare time Wallace indulged in photography, entomology and writing.

Lightning Source UK Ltd.
Milton Keynes UK
UKOW03f0900100614

233150UK00001B/229/P

9 781618 970954